新曲綫 | 用心雕刻每一本……
New Curves

http://site.douban.com/110283/
http://weibo.com/nccpub

用心字里行间　雕刻名著经典

商务印书馆(成都)有限责任公司出品

市场营销

第 7 版,双语教学版

〔美〕威廉·普赖德 罗伯特·休斯 杰克·卡普尔 著

孔小磊 译注

商务印书馆
2025年·北京

Marketing, 7th Edition

William M. Pride   Robert J. Hughes   Jack R. Kapoor

Copyright © 2023 Cengage Learning, Inc.

The Commercial Press is authorized by Cengage Learning to publish and distribute exclusively this custom reprint edition. This edition is authorized for sale in the People's Republic of China only (excluding Hong Kong, Macao SAR and Taiwan). Unauthorized export of this edition is a violation of the Copyright Act. No part of this publication may be reproduced or distributed by any means, or stored in a database or retrieval system, without the prior written permission of the publisher.

978-0-357-71794-3

Cengage
200 Pier 4 Boulevard
Boston, MA 02210
USA

此客户定制影印版由圣智学习出版公司授权商务印书馆独家出版发行。此版本仅限在中华人民共和国境内（不包括中国香港、澳门特别行政区及中国台湾）销售。未经授权的本书出口将被视为违反版权法的行为。未经出版者预先书面许可，不得以任何方式复制或发行本书的任何部分。

本书封面贴有Cengage Learning防伪标签，无标签者不得销售。

Contents 目录

Acknowledgments	xiii	致谢	
About the Authors	xiv	作者介绍	

Chapter 1: Exploring the World of Business and Economics — 2
探索商业和经济世界

- **Inside Business:** Tesla Races Ahead of the Competition — 3
  商业透视：特斯拉在竞争中领先
- 1-1 Your Future in the Changing World of Business — 4
  在不断变化的商业世界中展望未来
  - 1-1a Why Study Business? — 5
    为什么学习商学
- **Exploring Careers:** Gen Z Seeks Workplace Diversity — 6
  职业探索：Z世代寻求职场多样性
  - 1-1b Special Note to Business Students — 8
    给商科学生的特别提示
- 1-2 Business: A Definition — 9
  企业的定义
  - 1-2a The Organized Effort of Individuals — 9
    个体有组织的努力
  - 1-2b Satisfying Needs — 10
    满足需求
  - 1-2c Business Profit — 11
    企业利润
- 1-3 Types of Economic Systems — 12
  经济制度的类型
- **Entrepreneurial Success:** The Next Wave of Entrepreneurs Is Here — 14
  创业成功：下一波创业浪潮来了
  - 1-3a Capitalism — 14
    资本主义
  - 1-3b Capitalism in the United States — 15
    美国的资本主义
  - 1-3c Command Economies — 17
    计划经济
- 1-4 Measuring Economic Performance — 18
  衡量经济表现
  - 1-4a The Importance of Productivity in the Global Marketplace — 18
    生产力在全球市场中的重要性
  - 1-4b The Nation's Gross Domestic Product — 19
    国内生产总值
  - 1-4c Other Important Economic Indicators That Measure a Nation's Economy — 20
    衡量一国经济的其他重要经济指标
- 1-5 The Business Cycle — 20
  经济周期
- 1-6 Types of Competition — 22
  竞争的类型
  - 1-6a Perfect Competition — 23
    完全竞争
  - 1-6b Monopolistic Competition — 24
    垄断竞争
  - 1-6c Oligopoly — 25
    寡头垄断
  - 1-6d Monopoly — 25
    垄断
- 1-7 American Business Today — 26
  当代的美国商业
  - 1-7a Early Business Development — 26
    早期的商业发展
  - 1-7b Business Development in the 1900s — 27
    20世纪的商业发展
  - 1-7c A New Century: 2000 and Beyond — 28
    新世纪：2000年及以后
  - 1-7d The Current Business Environment — 28
    当前的商业环境

Technology and Innovation: Today's Biggest Tech Trends	30	技术与创新：当今最大的技术趋势	
1-7e The Challenges Ahead	31	未来面临的挑战	
Summary	32	小　结	
Key Terms	33	关键术语	
Discussion Questions	33	讨论题	
Case 1: The Keys to Zoom's Success	34	案例 1：Zoom 成功的关键	
Building Skills for Career Success	35	为成功的职业生涯培养技能	

Chapter 2: Ethics and Social Responsibility in Business — 36 商业伦理与社会责任

→ *Inside Business:* Marketing Tactics at Purdue Fueled the Opioid Crisis	37	商业透视：美国普渡制药的营销策略加剧了阿片类药物危机	
2-1 Business Ethics Defined	38	商业伦理的定义	
2-2 Ethical Issues in Business	38	商业中的伦理问题	
2-2a Fairness and Honesty	38	公平和诚实	
2-2b Organizational Relationships	39	组织关系	
2-2c Conflicts of Interest	40	利益冲突	
2-2d Communications	41	沟通	
Entrepreneurial Success: Building a Healthy Relationship with Social Media	41	创业成功：与社交媒体建立健康的关系	
2-3 Factors Affecting Ethical Behavior	42	影响伦理行为的因素	
2-3a Individual Factors Affecting Ethics	42	影响伦理的个体因素	
2-3b Social Factors Affecting Ethics	42	影响伦理的社会因素	
2-3c Opportunity as a Factor Affecting Ethics	43	机会是影响伦理的因素	
2-4 Encouraging Ethical Behavior	43	鼓励符合伦理的行为	
2-4a Government's Role in Encouraging Ethics	43	政府在鼓励伦理行为方面的作用	
2-4b Trade Associations' Role in Encouraging Ethics	44	行业协会在鼓励伦理行为方面的作用	
2-4c Individual Companies' Role in Encouraging Ethics	44	公司在鼓励伦理行为方面的作用	
Exploring Careers: The Rise of the Chief Ethics Officer	46	职业探索：首席伦理官的兴起	
2-5 Social Responsibility	47	社会责任	
2-5a The Evolution of Social Responsibility in Business	48	企业社会责任的演变	
2-5b Two Views of Social Responsibility	49	社会责任的两种观点	
2-5c The Pros and Cons of Social Responsibility	50	社会责任的利弊	
2-6 Public Responsibilities of Business	51	企业的公共责任	
2-6a Consumerism	51	消费者权益保护	
Ethics and Social Responsibility: Google Sued for Antitrust Violations	52	商业伦理与社会责任：谷歌被控违反反垄断法	
2-6b Public Health	53	公共健康	
2-7 Responsibilities to Employees	55	对员工的责任	
2-7a Affirmative Action Programs	55	平权行动计划	
2-7b Training Programs for the Hard-Core Unemployed	56	长期失业者培训计划	
2-7c Programs to Reduce Sexual Harassment and Abusive Behavior	57	减少性骚扰和虐待行为的计划	
2-8 Responsibilities to the Environment	58	对环境的责任	

2-8a Environmental Issues	58	环境问题	
2-8b Effects of Environmental Legislation	59	环境立法的影响	
2-8c Business Response to Environmental Concerns	60	企业对环境问题的回应	
Sustaining the Planet: *Is Sustainability Profitable?*	61	**保护地球**：可持续发展有利可图吗	
2-9 Implementing a Program of Social Responsibility	62	实施社会责任计划	
2-9a Commitment of Top Executives	62	高层管理人员的承诺	
2-9b Planning	62	规划	
2-9c Appointment of a Director	62	委任董事	
2-9d The Social Audit	63	社会审计	
Summary	63	小　结	
Key Terms	64	关键术语	
Discussion Questions	64	讨论题	
Case 2: Inside Whole Trade at Whole Foods	65	案例 2：全食超市的全食交易保障	
Building Skills for Career Success	65	为成功的职业生涯培养技能	

Chapter 3: Global Business 67

全球商务

→ **Inside Business:** Starbucks Goes Global for Growth	68	**商业透视**：星巴克走向全球以实现增长	
Entrepreneurial Success: *Alibaba Provides Guidance to Help Entrepreneurs*	69	**创业成功**：阿里巴巴通过提供指导助力企业家	
3-1 The Basis for International Business	69	国际商务基础	
3-1a Absolute and Comparative Advantage	69	绝对优势和比较优势	
3-1b Exporting and Importing	70	进出口	
3-1c Balance of Trade	70	贸易差额	
3-1d The Economic Outlook for Trade	73	国际贸易的经济展望	
Technology and Innovation: *Spotify Makes a Play for Global Dominance*	75	**技术与创新**：Spotify 谋求全球主导地位	
3-2 Methods of Entering International Business	76	进入国际商务的方式	
3-2a Exporting	76	出口	
3-2b Licensing and Franchising	78	许可和特许经营	
3-2c Contract Manufacturing	79	合同制造	
3-2d Joint Ventures and Alliances	79	合资企业和联盟	
3-2e Direct Investment	80	直接投资	
3-2f Multinational Firms	80	跨国公司	
Sustaining the Planet: *IKEA Opens Its First Second-Hand Store*	81	**保护地球**：宜家开设第一家二手店	
3-3 International Business Challenges	81	国际商务挑战	
3-3a Trade Restrictions	81	贸易限制	
3-3b Economic Challenges	84	经济挑战	
Ethics and Social Responsibility: *Opening the Gates to Digital Payments*	85	**商业伦理与社会责任**：打开数字支付的大门	
3-3c Legal and Political Climate	85	法律和政治环境	
3-3d Social and Cultural Barriers	85	社会和文化障碍	
3-4 Facilitators of International Trade	86	国际贸易促进者	

3-4a The General Agreement on Tariffs and Trade and the World Trade Organization	86	关税与贸易总协定和世界贸易组织
3-4b International Trade Agreements and Alliances	86	国际贸易协定和联盟
3-5 Sources of Export Assistance	89	出口援助的来源
3-6 Financing International Business	90	国际商务融资
3-6a The Export-Import Bank of the United States	90	美国进出口银行
3-6b The World Bank	91	世界银行
3-6c The International Monetary Fund	91	国际货币基金组织
Summary	92	小 结
Key Terms	93	关键术语
Discussion Questions	93	讨论题
Case 3: Honda's Strategy Is Electrifying	93	案例 3：本田的战略就是电动化且令人振奋
Building Skills for Career Success	94	为成功的职业生涯培养技能
***Running a Business:** Let's Go Get a Graeter's!*	*96*	经营企业：我们去买个 Graeter's 冰淇淋吧
Building a Business Plan	*97*	制订商业计划

Chapter 4: Building Customer Relationships Through Effective Marketing   101

通过有效的市场营销建立客户关系

→ ***Inside Business:*** Netflix Tops the Competition in Customer Retention	102	商业透视：Netflix 在客户保留率方面领先于竞争对手
4-1 Managing Customer Relationships	103	客户关系管理
Sustaining the Planet: Customer Feedback Pushes Native to Go Plastic-Free	104	保护地球：客户反馈促使 Native 走向无塑料化
4-2 Utility: The Value Added by Marketing	105	效用：通过营销增加价值
4-3 The Marketing Concept	106	营销理念
4-3a Evolution of the Marketing Concept	106	营销理念的演变
4-3b Implementing the Marketing Concept	107	营销理念的实施
4-4 Markets and Their Classification	108	市场及其分类
4-5 Developing Marketing Strategies	108	制定营销策略
4-5a Target Market Selection and Evaluation	108	目标市场的选择和评估
4-5b Creating a Marketing Mix	111	创建营销组合
4-6 Marketing Strategy and the Marketing Environment	113	营销策略与营销环境
4-7 Developing a Marketing Plan	114	制订营销计划
4-8 Market Measurement and Sales Forecasting	115	市场评估和销售预测
4-9 Marketing Information	115	营销信息
4-9a Collecting and Analyzing Marketing Information	115	收集和分析营销信息
Exploring Careers: Trend Alert: Market Research Analysts Are in High Demand	116	职业探索：趋势提醒——市场研究分析师需求量很大
Technology and Innovation: TikTok Uses AI and Big Data to Keep Users Coming Back for More	117	技术与创新：抖音使用人工智能和大数据留住用户
4-9b Marketing Research	118	市场调研
Ethics and Social Responsibility: Marketers Must Embrace Data Ethics	120	商业伦理与社会责任：营销人员必须遵守数据伦理

viii   Marketing

4-10 Types of Buying Behavior	120	购买行为的类型
4-10a Consumer Buying Behavior	120	消费者购买行为
4-10b Business Buying Behavior	122	企业购买行为
Summary	122	小　结
Key Terms	124	关键术语
Discussion Questions	124	讨论题
Case 4: Starbucks Brews Customer Satisfaction	124	案例4：星巴克"酿造"客户满意度
Building Skills for Career Success	125	为成功的职业生涯培养技能

Chapter 5: Creating and Pricing Products That Satisfy Customers　127

创造和定价让顾客满意的产品

→ *Inside Business:* Petco Rebrand Focuses on Pet Health and Wellness	128	商业透视：Petco的品牌重塑专注于宠物健康
5-1 Classification of Products	129	产品分类
5-1a Consumer Product Classifications	129	消费品的分类
5-1b Business Product Classifications	130	工业品的分类
5-2 The Product Life Cycle	131	产品生命周期
5-2a Stages of the Product Life Cycle	131	产品生命周期的各阶段
Sustaining the Planet: Consumers Go Flexitarian with Fake Meat	132	保护地球：消费者选择肉食替代品而成为弹性素食者
5-2b Using the Product Life Cycle	134	产品生命周期的运用
5-3 Product Line and Product Mix	134	产品线和产品组合
5-4 Managing the Product Mix	134	产品组合的管理
5-4a Managing Existing Products	135	现有产品的管理
Exploring Careers: Are You Ready for a Career in Product Management?	136	职业探索：您准备好从事产品管理工作了吗
5-4b Deleting Products	136	淘汰产品
5-4c Developing New Products	137	开发新产品
Technology and Innovation: High-Tech Is High Fashion	139	技术与创新：高科技就是高级时尚
5-4d Why Do Products Fail?	139	为什么产品会失败
5-5 Branding, Packaging, and Labeling	140	品牌、包装和标签
5-5a What Is a Brand?	140	什么是品牌
5-5b Types of Brands	140	品牌的类型
5-5c Benefits of Branding	141	品牌化的好处
5-5d Choosing and Protecting a Brand	142	选择和保护品牌
5-5e Branding Strategies	143	品牌战略
5-5f Brand Extensions	143	品牌延伸
5-5g Packaging	143	包装
5-5h Labeling	145	标签
5-6 Pricing Products	145	产品定价
5-6a The Meaning and Use of Price	145	价格的含义和用途
5-6b Price and Non-Price Competition	146	价格竞争和非价格竞争

Ethics and Social Responsibility: Companies Rebrand to Be More Sensitive	147	商业伦理与社会责任：企业为了对种族和文化更加敏感而重塑品牌
5-6c Buyers' Perceptions of Price	147	购买者对价格的看法
5-7 Pricing Objectives	147	定价目标
5-7a Survival	148	基于生存目标
5-7b Profit Maximization	148	基于利润最大化目标
5-7c Target Return on Investment	148	基于投资回报率目标
5-7d Market-Share Goals	148	基于市场份额目标
5-7e Status-Quo Pricing	148	为了维持现状而定价
5-8 Pricing Methods	149	定价方法
5-8a Cost-Based Pricing	149	成本导向定价
5-8b Demand-Based Pricing	150	需求导向定价
5-8c Competition-Based Pricing	151	竞争导向定价
5-9 Pricing Strategies	151	定价策略
5-9a New-Product Pricing	151	新产品定价
5-9b Differential Pricing	152	差别定价
5-9c Psychological Pricing	153	心理定价
5-9d Product-Line Pricing	154	产品线定价
5-9e Promotional Pricing	154	促销价
5-10 Pricing Business Products	155	工业品定价
5-10a Geographic Pricing	155	地理定价
5-10b Transfer Pricing	155	转让定价
5-10c Discounting	155	折扣
Summary	156	小　结
Key Terms	158	关键术语
Discussion Questions	158	讨论题
Case 5: Shinola Is One to Watch	159	案例 5：值得关注的 Shinola
Building Skills for Career Success	159	为成功的职业生涯培养技能

Chapter 6: Distributing and Promoting Products　161

产品分销和产品促销

→ ***Inside Business:*** Walmart Brings Its Buying Teams Together	162	商业透视：沃尔玛整合了采购团队
6-1 Distribution Channels and Market Coverage	163	分销渠道及市场覆盖
6-1a Commonly Used Distribution Channels	163	常用分销渠道
6-1b Level of Market Coverage	165	市场覆盖水平
6-2 Partnering Through Supply Chain Management	165	通过供应链管理建立伙伴关系
Sustaining the Planet: Millennials Take a Shining to Ethically Sourced Diamonds	166	保护地球：千禧一代青睐符合伦理的钻石
6-3 Marketing Intermediaries: Wholesalers	166	营销中介：批发商
6-3a Wholesalers Provide Services to Retailers and Manufacturers	167	批发商向零售商和制造商提供服务
6-3b Types of Wholesalers	167	批发商的类型
6-4 Marketing Intermediaries: Retailers	168	营销中介：零售商
6-4a Online and Multichannel Retailing	168	线上和多渠道零售

6-4b Types of Retail Stores	*169*	零售店的类型
6-4c Types of Shopping Centers	*171*	购物中心的类型
6-4d Nonstore Retailing	*172*	无店铺零售
6-5 Logistics	174	物流
Technology and Innovation: **Drone Delivery Takes Off**	*174*	**技术与创新**：开启无人机送货时代
6-5a Inventory Management	*175*	库存管理
6-5b Order Processing	*175*	订单处理
6-5c Warehousing	*175*	仓储
6-5d Materials Handling	*176*	物料搬运
6-5e Transportation	*176*	运输
6-6 What Is Integrated Marketing Communications?	177	什么是整合营销传播
6-7 The Promotion Mix: An Overview	178	促销组合：概述
6-8 Advertising	179	广告
6-8a Types of Advertising by Purpose	*179*	按目的划分的广告类型
6-8b Major Steps in Developing an Advertising Campaign	*180*	开展广告活动的主要步骤
6-8c Advertising Agencies	*182*	广告公司
Exploring Careers: **How to Land a Job in an Advertising Agency**	*183*	**职业探索**：如何在广告公司找到工作
6-8d Social and Legal Considerations in Advertising	*183*	广告中的社会和法律因素
6-9 Personal Selling	184	人员推销
6-9a Kinds of Salespersons	*184*	销售人员的种类
6-9b The Personal-Selling Process	*185*	人员推销过程
6-9c Major Sales Management Tasks	*186*	主要的销售管理工作
6-10 Sales Promotion	186	销售促销
6-10a Sales Promotion Objectives	*186*	促销目标
6-10b Sales Promotion Methods	*187*	促销方法
6-10c Selection of Sales Promotion Methods	*188*	促销方式的选择
6-11 Public Relations	188	公共关系
6-11a Types of Public Relations Tools	*188*	公共关系工具的类型
Entrepreneurial Success: **Inside BODEN, an Award-Winning, Latina-Owned PR Company**	*189*	**创业成功**：BODEN 是一家屡获殊荣的拉美裔所有的公关公司
6-11b Uses of Public Relations	*190*	公共关系的运用
Summary	190	小　结
Key Terms	192	关键术语
Discussion Questions	192	讨论题
Case 6: **Casper Thinks Inside the Box**	*192*	**案例 6**：在箱子里思考的 Casper
Building Skills for Career Success	193	为成功的职业生涯培养技能
Running a Business: Graeter's Is "Synonymous with Ice Cream"	*195*	经营企业：Graeter's 是"冰淇淋的代名词"
Building a Business Plan	196	制订商业计划

Chapter 7: Exploring Social Media and e-Business 199

探索社交媒体和电子商业

    → ***Inside Business:*** **Netflix Tops the Competition in Customer Retention** *200*

    商业透视：Netflix 在客户保留率方面领先于竞争对手

English	Page	Chinese
7-1 Why Is Social Media Important?	201	为什么社交媒体很重要
7-1a What Is Social Media and How Popular Is It?	201	什么是社交媒体，它有多受欢迎
7-1b Why Businesses Use Social Media	201	企业为什么要使用社交媒体
7-2 Social Media Tools for Business Use	203	商用社交媒体工具
7-2a Business Use of Blogs	203	博客的商业用途
Exploring Careers: HBO Max Interns Rock TikTok	204	职业探索：HBO Max 实习生玩转抖音
7-2b Photos, Videos, and Podcasts	204	照片、视频和播客
7-2c Social Media Ratings	205	社交媒体评级
7-3 Achieving Business Objectives Through Social Media	206	通过社交媒体实现商业目标
7-3a Social Media Communities	206	社交媒体社区
7-3b Crisis and Reputation Management	207	危机与声誉管理
7-3c Listening to Stakeholders	208	听取利益相关者的意见
Technology and Innovation: VW's April Fools' Day Prank Backfires	208	技术与创新：大众在愚人节的恶作剧适得其反
7-3d Targeting Customers	209	目标客户
7-3e Social Media Marketing for Consumers	209	面向消费者的社交媒体营销
7-3f Social Media Marketing for Other Businesses	210	其他业务的社交媒体营销
7-3g Generating New Product Ideas	211	产生新产品创意
7-3h Recruiting Employees	212	招聘员工
7-4 Developing a Social Media Plan	212	制订社交媒体计划
7-4a Steps to Build a Social Media Plan	212	制订社交媒体计划的步骤
7-4b Measuring and Adapting a Social Media Plan	214	衡量和调整社交媒体计划
7-4c The Cost of Maintaining a Social Media Plan	216	维护社交媒体计划的成本
7-5 Defining e-Business	216	电子商业的定义
7-5a Organizing e-Business Resources	217	组织电子商业资源
7-5b Satisfying Needs Online	217	满足线上需求
Entrepreneurial Success: Why Small Businesses Like Shopify	218	创业成功：为什么小企业喜欢 Shopify
7-5c Creating e-Business Profit	219	创造电子商业利润
7-6 Fundamental Models of e-Business	220	电子商业的基本模式
7-6a Business-to-Business (B2B) Model	220	企业对企业（B2B）模式
7-6b Business-to-Consumer (B2C) Model	221	企业对消费者（B2C）模式
7-7 The Future of the Internet, Social Media, and e-Business	222	互联网、社交媒体和电子商业的未来
7-7a Internet Growth Potential	222	互联网的增长潜力
7-7b Ethical and Legal Concerns	223	伦理和法律问题
Ethics and Social Responsibility: California Ups the Ante on Privacy Protection	224	商业伦理与社会责任：加州加大隐私保护力度
7-7c Future Challenges for Computer Technology, Social Media, and e-Business	225	计算机技术、社交媒体和电子商业的未来挑战
Summary	226	小　结
Key Terms	228	关键术语
Discussion Questions	228	讨论题
Case 7: Target's Big Bet on Digital	228	案例 7：Target 在数字领域的大赌注
Building Skills for Career Success	229	为成功的职业生涯培养技能
Endnotes	231	注释
Glossary	237	术语表

Acknowledgments 致谢

The quality of this book and its supplements program has been helped immensely by the insightful and rich comments of a special set of instructors. Their thoughtful and helpful comments had real impact in shaping the final product. We wish to thank:

Ken Anglin, *Minnesota State University, Mankato*
Ellen A. Benowitz, *Mercer County Community College*
Michael Bento, *Owens Community College*
Laura Bulas, *Central Community College, NE*
Brennan Carr, *Long Beach City College*
Paul Coakley, *The Community College of Baltimore County*
Jean Condon, *Mid-Plains Community College*
Mary Cooke, *Surry Community College*
Dean Danielson, *San Joaquin Delta College*
Gary Donnelly, *Casper College*
Karen Edwards, *Chemeketa Community College*
Donna K. Fisher, *Georgia Southern University*
Mark Fox, *Indiana University South Bend*
Connie Golden, *Lakeland Community College*
Karen Gore, *Ivy Tech Community College—Evansville*
John Guess, *Delgado Community College*
Tom Hendricks, *Oakland Community College*
Robert James, *Macomb Community College*
Eileen Kearney, *Montgomery Community College*
Mary Beth Klinger, *College of Southern Maryland*
Natasha Lindsey, *University of North Alabama*
Emilio Lopez, *Dallas College*
Robert Lupton, *Central Washington University*
John Mago, *Anoka Ramsey Community College*
Pamela G. McElligott, *St. Louis Community College Meramec*

Myke McMullen, *Long Beach City College*
Carol Miller, *Community College of Denver*
Diane Minger, *Dallas College*
Jaideep Motwani, *Grand Valley State*
Mark Nagel, *Normandale Community College*
Dyan Pease, *Sacramento City College*
Jeffrey D. Penley, *Catawba Valley Community College*
Angela J. Rabatin, *Prince George's Community College*
Anthony Racka, *Oakland Community College—Auburn Hills Campus*
Dwight Riley, *Dallas College*
Carol Rowey, *Community College of Rhode Island*
Christy Shell, *Houston Community College*
Cindy Simerly, *Lakeland Community College*
Yolanda I. Smith, *Northern Virginia Community College*
Gail South, *Montgomery College*
Rieann Spence-Gale, *Northern Virginia Comm. College—Alexandria Campus*
Kurt Stanberry, *University of Houston, Downtown*
John Striebich, *Monroe Community College*
Keith Taylor, *Lansing Community College*
Tricia Troyer, *Waubonsee Community College*
Leo Trudel, *University of Maine - Fort Kent*
Anne Williams, *Gateway Community College*
Kevin Wortley, *Dallas College*

We want to thank the following people for their professional and technical assistance: Gwyn Walters, Klarisa Posada, Ashley Nguyen, Kelsey Reddick, Brenda Aram, Theresa Kapoor, David Pierce, Kathryn Thumme, Karen Tucker, Dave Kapoor, Susan Fant, and Jeff Penley.

Many talented professionals at Cengage Learning have contributed to the development of *Foundations of Business, 7e*. We are especially grateful to Erin Joyner, Thais Alencar, Joe Sabatino, Heather Thompson, Clara Kuhlman, Allie Janneck, Stephanie Hall, Megan Guiliani, Angela Sheehan, Sara Greenwood, Hannah May, Amanda Ryan, Tony Winslow, Cara Suriyamongkol, and Nick Perez. Their inspiration, patience, support, and friendship are invaluable.

W. M. P.
R. J. H.
J. R. K.

About the Authors 作者介绍

William M. Pride
Texas A&M University

William M. Pride is Professor of Marketing at Mays Business School, Texas A&M University. He received his PhD from Louisiana State University. He is the author of Cengage Learning's *Marketing*, 20th edition, a market leader. Dr. Pride's research interests are in advertising, promotion, and distribution channels.

Dr. Pride's research articles have appeared in major journals in the fields of advertising and marketing, such as *Journal of Marketing*, *Journal of Marketing Research*, *Journal of the Academy of Marketing Science*, and the *Journal of Advertising*. Dr. Pride is a member of the American Marketing Association, Academy of Marketing Science, Society for Marketing Advances, and the Marketing Management Association. Dr. Pride has taught Principles of Marketing and other marketing courses for more than 45 years at both the undergraduate and graduate levels.

Robert J. Hughes
Dallas College - Richland Campus

Robert J. Hughes (EdD, University of North Texas) specializes in business administration and college instruction. He has taught Introduction to Business for more than 35 years both on campus and online for Richland College—one of seven campuses that are part of the Dallas College System. In addition to *Business* and *Foundations of Business*, published by Cengage Learning, he has authored college textbooks in personal finance and business mathematics; served as a content consultant for two popular national television series, *It's Strictly Business* and *Dollars & Sense: Personal Finance for the 21st Century*; and is the lead author for a business math project utilizing computer-assisted instruction funded by the ALEKS Corporation. He is also active in many academic and professional organizations and has served as a consultant and investment advisor to individuals, businesses, and charitable organizations. Dr. Hughes is the recipient of three different Teaching in Excellence Awards at Richland College. According to Dr. Hughes, after 35 years of teaching Introduction to Business, the course is still exciting: "There's nothing quite like the thrill of seeing students succeed, especially in a course like Introduction to Business, which provides the foundation for not only academic courses, but also life in the real world."

Jack R. Kapoor
College of DuPage

Jack R. Kapoor (EdD, Northern Illinois University) has been a Professor of Business and Economics in the Business and Technology Division at the College of DuPage, where he has taught Introduction to Business, Marketing, Management, Economics, and Personal Finance since 1969. He previously taught at Illinois Institute of Technology's Stuart School of Management, San Francisco State University's School of World Business, and other colleges. Professor Kapoor was awarded the Business and Services Division's Outstanding Professor Award for 1999–2000. He served as an Assistant National Bank Examiner for the U.S. Treasury Department and as an international trade consultant to Bolting Manufacturing Co., Ltd., Mumbai, India.

Dr. Kapoor is known internationally as a coauthor of several textbooks in Business and Personal Finance, including Business MindTap (Cengage Learning), has served as a content consultant for two popular national television series, *Dollars & Sense: Personal Finance for the 21st Century* and *The Business File: An Introduction to Business*, and developed two full-length audio courses in business and personal finance. He has been quoted in many national newspapers and magazines, including *USA Today, U.S. News & World Report*, the *Chicago Sun-Times, Crain's Small Business*, the *Chicago Tribune*, and other publications.

Dr. Kapoor has traveled around the world and has studied business practices in capitalist, socialist, and communist countries.

Marketing

Chapter 1

Exploring the World of Business and Economics
探索商业和经济世界

Why Should You Care?

Studying business will help you choose a career, become a successful employee or manager, start your own business, and become a more informed consumer and better investor.

Learning Objectives

Once you complete this chapter, you will be able to:

1-1 Discuss what you must do to be successful in today's business world.

1-2 Identify the potential risks and rewards of business.

1-3 Describe the two types of economic systems: capitalism and command economy.

1-4 Identify the ways to measure economic performance.

1-5 Examine the different phases in the typical business cycle.

1-6 Outline the four types of competition.

1-7 Summarize the development of American business and the challenges that businesses and society will encounter in the future.

Marketing

Inside Business

商业透视：特斯拉在竞争中领先

Tesla Races Ahead of the Competition

Today Tesla is a household name around the world. Because the company is now the leader in electric vehicles (EVs), it has also become one of the most valuable companies in the world. Although Tesla is relatively young compared to General Motors, Ford, Toyota, and other competitors, the car manufacturer's commitment to innovation and sustainability has propelled it to the front of the pack. Even though Toyota is much larger than Tesla in terms of sales, Tesla's market capitalization has surpassed the Japanese carmaker, demonstrating that investors see a bright future ahead for the electric car company. For any company traded on the stock exchange, market capitalization is calculated by multiplying the current market value for a share of the company's stock by the total number of shares that have been issued. At the time of publication, Tesla was valued at almost $800 billion—not bad for a relative newcomer to the automobile industry.

While Tesla didn't invent the electric car, it set the standard for what an EV should be. The Tesla Roadster was the first highway-legal production vehicle that used lithium-ion batteries, giving it a longer driving range than other EVs on the market. With superior distance and speed and longer battery life, Tesla managed to make its products appealing to a wide range of customers. As Tesla makes record sales and expands globally, it's clear the company's early bet on EVs has paid off.

Tesla's robust supply chain has driven down battery costs, making it even more challenging for other manufacturers to catch up. Even though other automakers including BMW, Ford, General Motors, Mercedes Benz, Nissan, Volkswagen, and some companies you probably don't recognize are investing heavily in EVs, a Tesla automobile is the one that customers want. It's so popular that customers often have to wait for delivery for popular models. While Tesla does face competition from traditional automakers as well as electric car startups, the difference could be that other companies still think of EVs as an afterthought.[1]

Did you know?

Tesla's market capitalization is worth more than Ford and General Motors combined.

Wow! What a challenging world we live in. Just for a moment, think about how the world has changed in the last few years. The United States has experienced a pandemic, non-essential businesses were closed in many states, the unemployment rate increased, and the stock market took a nosedive and then recovered all in a short period of time. Even though the economy has shown signs of improvement, there are still problems and many people worry about the future of the nation and the economy. Simply put, many individuals, business leaders, and politicians worry that the future of the nation's economy could be a bumpy road that leads to another recession.

Regardless of the current state of the economy, keep in mind that our economy continues to adapt and change to meet the challenges of an ever-changing world and to provide opportunities for those who want to achieve success. Our economic system also provides an amazing amount of freedom that allows businesses like Tesla—the company profiled in the Inside Business opening case for this chapter—to adapt to satisfy the needs of customers. To meet increased consumer demands for an electric automobile, the company's managers, engineers, and employees were able to design and build an automobile that consumers really wanted. After initial success, Tesla—a newcomer in the automobile industry—continues to innovate and create new models with self-driving capability. As a result, the company is now profitable and is one of the most valuable companies in the world.

Within certain limits, imposed mainly to ensure public safety, the owners of a business can produce any legal good or service they choose and attempt to sell it at the price they set. This system of business, in which individuals decide what to produce, how to produce it, and at what price to sell it, is called **free enterprise**. Our free-enterprise system ensures, for example, that Amazon.com can sell everything from books, televisions, and toys to computers, cameras, and clothing. Our system gives Amazon's owners and stockholders the right to make a profit from the company's success. It gives Amazon's management the right to compete with bookstore rival Barnes & Noble and retailers Walmart, Best Buy, and Macy's. It also gives you—the consumer—the right to choose.

In this chapter, we look briefly at what business is and how it became that way. First, we discuss what you must do to be successful in the world of business and explore some important reasons for studying business. Second, we define *business,* noting how business organizations satisfy their customers' needs and earn profits. Third, we examine how capitalism and command economies answer four basic economic questions. Next, our focus shifts to how the nations of the world measure economic performance, the phases in a typical business cycle, and the four types of competitive situations. Finally, we look at the events that helped shape today's business system, the current business environment, and the challenges that businesses face.

在不断变化的商业世界中展望未来

1-1 Your Future in the Changing World of Business

Learning Objective
1-1 Discuss what you must do to be successful in today's business world.

The key word in this heading is *changing*. When faced with the COVID-19 pandemic that raced through the world, small business owners, employees, managers, and investors began to ask the question: What effect will non-essential business closures and record high unemployment rates have on the economy? More specifically, many people wanted to know, how does this affect me both now and in the future? Although this is a fair question, it is difficult to answer. For an employee just starting a career or for a college student preparing for a career, the question is even more difficult to answer. Now, as the United States and the world adjust to life after the COVID-19 pandemic and the economy shows signs of recovery, there are opportunities out there for people who are willing to work hard, continue to learn, and possess the ability to adapt to change. Let's begin this course with three basic concepts.

- What do you want?
- Why do you want it?
- Write it down!

Joe Dudley, one of the world's most respected Black business owners, offers the preceding advice to anyone who wants to succeed in business. His advice can help you achieve success. What is so amazing about Dudley's success is that he started a manufacturing business in his own kitchen, with his wife and children serving as the new firm's only employees. He went on to develop his own line of haircare and cosmetic products sold directly to cosmetologists, barbers, beauty schools, and consumers in the United States and in foreign countries. Today, after a lot of hard work and a strong work ethic, Mr. Dudley has built a well-recognized and respected company in the competitive cosmetics industry. He is not only a successful business owner but also a winner of the Horatio Alger Award—an award given to outstanding individuals who have succeeded in the face of adversity.[2]

Although many people would say that Joe Dudley was just lucky or happened to be in the right place at the right time, the truth is that he became a success because he had a dream and worked to turn the dream into a reality. He would be the first to tell you that you have the same opportunities he had. According to Mr. Dudley, "Success is a journey, not just a destination."[3]

Whether you want to obtain part-time employment to pay college and living expenses, begin your career as a full-time employee, or start a business, you must

自由企业
free enterprise the system of business in which individuals are free to decide what to produce, how to produce it, and at what price to sell it

4　　Marketing

bring something to the table that makes you different from the next person. Employers and our economic system are more demanding than ever before. Ask yourself: What can I do that will make employers want to pay me a salary? What skills do I have that employers need? With these two questions in mind, we begin the next section with another basic question: Why study business?

为什么学习商学
1-1a Why Study Business?

The potential benefits of higher education are enormous. To begin with, there are economic benefits. Over their lifetimes, college graduates on average earn much more than high school graduates. Although lifetime earnings are substantially higher for college graduates, so are annual income amounts (refer to Figure 1-1). In addition to higher income, you will find at least four compelling reasons for studying business.

For Help in Choosing a Career What do you want to do with the rest of your life? Like many people, you may find it a difficult question to answer. This business course will introduce you to a wide array of employment opportunities. In private enterprise, these range from small, local businesses owned by one individual to large companies such as American Express and Microsoft owned by thousands of stockholders. There are also employment opportunities with federal, state, county, and local governments and with charitable organizations such as Habitat for Humanity, the Red Cross, and Save the Children. For help in deciding which career might be right for you, read Appendix A "Careers in Business," which appears on the text website.

In addition to career information in Appendix A, a number of websites provide information about career development. To click your career into high gear, you can also use online networking. Websites like Facebook, Twitter, LinkedIn, and other social media sites can help you locate job openings and help prospective employers to find you. To make the most of online networking, begin by identifying and joining sites where you can connect with potential employers, former classmates, and others who may have or may hear of job openings. Next, be sure your online profile, photographs, and posts communicate your abilities and interests. Finally, be ready to respond quickly when you spot a job opening.

One thing to remember as you think about what your ideal career might be is that people often choose a career that is a reflection of what they value and consider most important. What will give one individual personal satisfaction may not satisfy another. For example, one person may dream of a career as a successful corporate executive with a large salary and job security in marketing or technology or financial services. Another person may choose a career that has more modest monetary rewards but that provides the opportunity to help others. What you choose to do with your life will be based on what you feel is most important. And *you* are a very important part of that decision.

▶ **Figure 1-1 Who Makes the Most Money?**

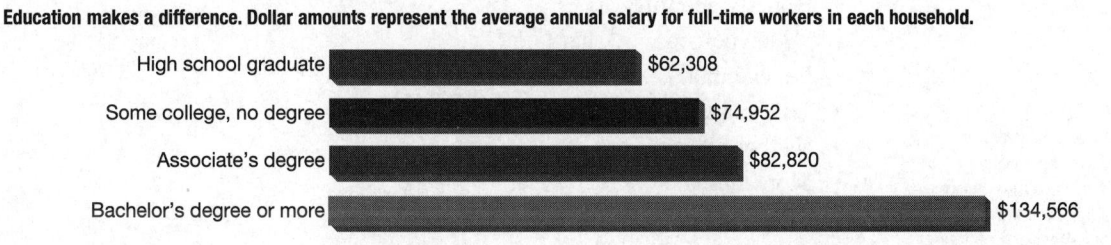

Education makes a difference. Dollar amounts represent the average annual salary for full-time workers in each household.

Education	Average Annual Salary
High school graduate	$62,308
Some college, no degree	$74,952
Associate's degree	$82,820
Bachelor's degree or more	$134,566

Source: "Educational Attainment of Householder—Households with Householder 25 Years Old and Over by Median and Mean Income," The U.S. Census Bureau.

Exploring Careers

职业探索：Z世代寻求职场多样性

Gen Z Seeks Workplace Diversity

When it comes to finding the perfect employer, Generation Z (people born between 1997 and 2012) prioritizes workplace diversity. According to a survey by Tallo, an online platform for students and job seekers, nearly 70 percent say they would be more likely to accept a job offer if the recruiters and materials representing the company were ethnically and racially diverse. In fact, some would even decline a job offer if the firm fell short on these factors. Workplace diversity—the differences among people in a workforce owing to factors such as age, race, ethnicity, gender, sexual orientation, and ability—is a top priority for Gen Z.

Gen Z—the most diverse generation ever—has surpassed Millennials (people born between 1981 and 1996) to become the largest generation. The effects of their entry into the workplace are already felt by companies around the world. Diversity for Gen Z goes beyond race and gender to encompass gender identity and orientation.

Companies that reflect diversity, equity, and inclusion in their branding and marketing materials will be more likely to attract fresh talent. Firms should be prepared to embed these values at the heart of the organization rather than making surface-level claims. With Gen Z on the hunt for organizations that reflect their values and beliefs, the burden is on employers to prioritize diversity issues.

Sources: Based on information in Tamara E. Holmes, "Diverse Workforce a Top Draw for Nearly 7 in 10 Members of Generation Z," *Yahoo Finance*, November 4, 2020; Deloitte, "Understanding Generation Z in the Workplace"; Sheryl Estrada, "Workplace D&I in 2021 Will Keep External Community in Mind," *HR Dive*, January 13, 2021.

To Be a Successful Employee Deciding on the type of career you want is only the first step. To get a job in your chosen field and to be successful at it, you will have to develop a plan, or a road map, that ensures you have the skills and knowledge the job requires. Think about what you'd look for if you were hiring an employee and strive to be that kind of person. You will also be expected to have the ability to work well with many types of people in a culturally diverse workforce. **Cultural** (or **workplace**) **diversity** refers to a system that recognizes and respects the differences among people because of their age, race, ethnicity, gender, sexual orientation, and ability.

This course and the other college courses you take, your instructors, and all of the resources available at your college or university can help you acquire the skills and knowledge you will need for a successful career. But don't underestimate your part in making your dream a reality. In addition to job-related skills and knowledge, employers will also look for the following characteristics when hiring a new employee or promoting an existing employee:

- Honesty and integrity
- Willingness to work hard
- Dependability
- Time management skills
- Self-confidence
- Motivation
- Willingness to learn
- Communication skills
- Professionalism

文化（或职场）多样性
cultural (or **workplace**) **diversity** a system that recognizes and respects the differences among people because of their age, race, ethnicity, gender, sexual orientation, and ability

The road to success can take many different paths! While many people want immediate success, it's important to chart a path that leads to life-long success. It helps to remember what Joe Dudley, the founder of Dudley Beauty Products said: "Success is a journey, not just a destination."

Employers will also be interested in any work experience you may have had in cooperative work/school programs, during summer vacations, or in part-time jobs during the school year. Experience—even part-time work experience—can make a difference when it is time to apply for the job you really want.

Many employees want to become managers because managers often receive higher salaries and can earn promotions within an organization. To be effective, managers must be able to perform four basic management functions: planning, organizing, leading and motivating, and controlling. To successfully perform these management functions, managers must also be able to work effectively with individual employees, other managers within the firm, and people outside the firm. In addition to the four management functions just mentioned, a successful manager will need many of the same characteristics that an employee needs to be successful.

To Start Your Own Business Some people prefer to work for themselves, and they open their own businesses. To be successful, business owners must possess many of the same characteristics that successful employees and managers have, and they must be willing to work hard and put in long hours.

It also helps if a small-business owner has an idea that will provide a product or service that customers want. At the age of 16, Palmer Luckey began building virtual reality headsets in his garage after school and work. While the first prototypes based on his ideas were crude by today's standards, the product showed a great deal of promise. After further development, refinements, and more ideas, the product—now called Oculus—was a success in the marketplace. How successful? Answer: so successful that Facebook paid $2 billion to acquire the company.[4]

Unfortunately, many business firms fail. In fact, only about 50 percent survive the first five years. Typical reasons for business failures include undercapitalization (not enough money), poor business location, poor customer service, unqualified or untrained employees, fraud, lack of a proper business plan, and failure to seek outside professional help. The material in this course will help you to overcome many of these problems.

To Become a Better Informed Consumer and Investor The world of business surrounds us. You cannot buy a home, a new Ford Escape Hybrid from the local Ford dealer, a pair of jeans at Gap Inc., or a hot dog from a street vendor without entering into a business transaction. Because you no doubt will engage

Chapter 1 Exploring the World of Business and Economics

in business transactions almost every day of your life, one very good reason for studying business is to become a more fully informed consumer.

Many people also rely on a basic understanding of business to help them invest for the future. According to Julie Stav, Hispanic stockbroker turned radio and YouTube personality and the author of *Get Your Share: A Guide to Striking It Rich in the Stock Market* and other personal finance help books, it is important to learn the basics about the economy and business, stocks, mutual funds, and other alternatives before investing your money. She also believes that it is never too early to start investing.[5] Although this is an obvious conclusion, just dreaming of being rich does not make it happen. In fact, like many facets of life, it takes planning and determination to establish the type of investment program that will help you accomplish your financial goals.

给商科学生的特别提示
1-1b Special Note to Business Students

It is important to begin reading this text with one thing in mind: *This business course does not have to be difficult.* We have done everything possible to eliminate the problems that you encounter in a typical class. All of the features in each chapter have been evaluated and recommended by instructors with years of teaching experience. In addition, business students—just like you—were asked to critique each chapter component. Based on this feedback, the text includes the following features:

- *Learning objectives* appear at the beginning of each chapter.
- *Inside Business* is a chapter-opening case that highlights how successful, real-world companies do business on a day-to-day basis.
- *Margin notes* are used throughout a chapter to reinforce both learning objectives and key terms.
- *Boxed features* in each chapter highlight how managers, employees, and entrepreneurs can be both ethical and successful. Topics discussed in the boxed features include ethics and social responsibility, suggestions for entrepreneurs, technology and innovation, environmental issues, and exploring different career options.
- *Concept Checks* at the end of each major section within a chapter help you test your understanding of the main issues just discussed.
- *End-of-chapter materials* provide a chapter summary, a list of key terms, discussion questions, and a case about a successful, real-world company.
- The last section of every chapter is entitled *Building Skills for Career Success* and includes exercises devoted to enhancing your social media skills, building team skills, and researching different careers.
- *End-of-part materials* provide a continuing case about Graeter's Ice Cream, a company that operates a chain of retail outlets in the Cincinnati, Ohio, area and sells to Kroger Stores and other retailers and consumers throughout the country. Also, at the end of each major part is an exercise designed to help you develop the components included in a typical business plan.

We've worked hard to make sure this edition reflects what is happening in the world and our nation. We wanted you to know how changes in the economy and world events, and yes, even a pandemic can impact not only business, but also you as a student and a consumer. Just as important, we wanted to create a text and student learning materials that help you be successful.

Because a text should always be evaluated by the students and professors who use it, we would welcome and sincerely appreciate your comments and suggestions. Please feel free to contact us by using one of the following e-mail addresses:

Bill Pride: w-pride@tamu.edu
Bob Hughes: Hughespublishing@outlook.com
Jack Kapoor: kapoorj@att.net

企业的定义

1-2 Business: A Definition

Business is the organized effort of individuals to produce and sell, for a profit, the goods and services that satisfy society's needs. The general term *business* refers to all such efforts within a society (as in "American business"). However, *a business* is a particular organization, such as a Kroger grocery store or a Cracker Barrel Old Country Store. To be successful, a business must perform three activities. It must be organized, it must satisfy needs, and it must earn a profit.

个体有组织的努力
1-2a The Organized Effort of Individuals

For a business to be organized, it must combine four kinds of resources: material, human, financial, and informational. *Material* resources include the raw materials used in manufacturing processes. For example, Mrs. Fields Cookies needs flour, sugar, butter, eggs, and other raw materials to produce the food products it sells worldwide. Material resources can also include buildings and machinery—sometimes referred to as the capital resources needed to produce goods and services. In addition, a company needs human, financial, and informational resources. *Human* resources are the people who furnish their labor to the business in return for wages. The *financial* resource is the money required to pay employees, purchase materials, and generally keep the business operating. *Information* is the resource that tells the managers of the business how effectively the other three resources are being combined and used (refer to Figure 1-2).

Today, businesses are usually organized as one of three specific types. *Service businesses* produce services, such as haircuts, legal advice, or tax preparation. H&R Block provides tax preparation and software and digital products to both businesses and consumers in the United States and around the world. *Manufacturing businesses* process various material resources into tangible goods, such as automobiles and trucks, clothing, or computers. Intel, for example, produces computer chips and other technology components that, in turn, are sold to companies that manufacture computers. Finally, some firms called *marketing intermediaries* buy products from manufacturers and then resell them. Sony Corporation is a manufacturer that produces stereo equipment, televisions, cameras, and other electronic products. These products may be sold to a marketing intermediary—often referred to as a retailer—such as Best Buy or Walmart, which then resells the manufactured goods to consumers in their retail stores.

> **Figure 1-2** Combining Resources

A business must combine all four resources effectively to be successful.

[Diagram: Human resources, Material resources, Informational resources, Financial resources → BUSINESS]

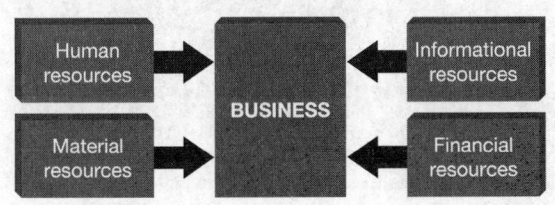

✓ Concept Check

▸ What reasons would you give if you were advising someone to study business?
▸ What factors affect a person's choice of careers?
▸ Once you have a job, what steps can you take to be successful?

Learning Objective
1-2 Identify the potential risks and rewards of business.

商业
business the organized effort of individuals to produce and sell, for a profit, the goods and services that satisfy society's needs

Chapter 1 Exploring the World of Business and Economics

While most people think of retailers as the "store around the corner," today many consumers prefer to shop online. For example, there was a dramatic increase in the number of customers shopping online during the COVID-19 pandemic. While people still needed food, cleaning supplies, toilet paper, and other essential items, they were afraid to venture out to shop at local retailers because of the fear of contracting the virus. As an alternative, they used the internet to order merchandise online and then had their purchases delivered to their home or used "curbside" delivery. As a result, major retailers including Walmart, Amazon, Target, Home Depot, Lowe's, and smaller retailers saw increases in the number of online sales.

To take advantage of the opportunities to sell goods and services online, there are retailers that exist only on the internet and more traditional business firms that sell goods and services in both their brick-and-mortar stores *and* online. For example, Etsy is a highly successful internet retailer. The secret of Etsy's success is that the company provides an online site for buyers looking for unique or custom-made items not found in typical retail stores. Macy's, on the other hand, sells merchandise in both its stores and online. For our purposes, **e-business** can be defined as the organized effort of individuals to produce and sell for a profit, the goods and services that satisfy society's needs *through the facilities available on the internet*. While very similar to the definition of business, an e-business is different because of the last seven words—*through the facilities available on the internet*. e-Business—a topic we will continue to explore throughout this text—has become an accepted method of conducting business and a way for businesses to increase sales and profits and reduce expenses.

满足需求
1-2b Satisfying Needs

The ultimate objective of every firm must be to satisfy the needs of its customers. People generally do not buy goods and services simply to own them; they buy goods and services to use them in order to satisfy their particular needs. In fact, a large number of start-up businesses fail because customers don't need or want what the business is selling. Many experts suggest that talking to customers to determine what needs they have is an essential step that many would-be business owners ignore. In other situations, would-be business owners don't consider if competitors are already meeting the needs of customers in a specific geographic area. Even an

电子商业
e-business the organized effort of individuals to produce and sell for a profit, the goods and services that satisfy society's needs *through the facilities available on the internet*

Oh, thank heaven for 7-Eleven!® This 7-Eleven store in Osaka, Japan, is just one convenience store, but it is part of a company that has over 70,000 stores in 17 different countries. Started in 1927, today 7-Eleven is the largest chain of convenience stores in the world and is built on a basic principle: "Give the customers what they want, when and where they want it."

existing business can fail if it doesn't adapt to changing customer needs and its products or services no longer meet customer needs.

Different people have different needs. Some of us may feel the need for transportation is best satisfied by an air-conditioned BMW with navigation system, turbo V8 engine, stereo system, heated and cooled seats, automatic transmission, power windows, and remote-control side mirrors. Others may believe that a Chevrolet Spark with a four-cylinder engine and manual transmission will do just fine. Both products are available to those who want them, along with a wide variety of other products that satisfy the need for transportation.

When businesses understand their customers' needs and work to satisfy those needs, they are usually successful. Back in 1962, Sam Walton opened his first discount store in Rogers, Arkansas. Although the original store was quite different from the Walmart superstores you see today, the basic ideas of providing customer service and offering goods that satisfied needs at low prices are part of the reason why this firm has grown to become the largest retailer in the world.

企业利润
1-2c Business Profit

A business receives money (sales revenue) from its customers in exchange for goods or services. It must also pay out money to cover the expenses involved in doing business. If the firm's sales revenues are greater than its expenses, it has earned a profit. More specifically, as shown in Figure 1-3, **profit** is what remains after all business expenses have been deducted from sales revenue.

A negative profit, which results when a firm's expenses are greater than its sales revenue, is called a *loss*. A business cannot continue to operate at a loss for an indefinite period of time. Management and employees must find some way to increase sales revenues and reduce expenses to return to profitability. If some specific actions are not taken to eliminate losses, a firm may be forced to close its doors or file for bankruptcy protection. For example, many businesses including JCPenney, Neiman Marcus, J. Crew, and Hertz were forced to file bankruptcy in 2020 because each firm had lower sales revenues and experienced a loss caused by the COVID-19 pandemic. Fortunately, many of the firms that filed for bankruptcy protection were able to reorganize and continue to operate.

Although many people—especially stockholders and business owners—believe that profit is literally the bottom line or most important goal for a business, many stakeholders may be just as concerned about a firm's social responsibility and environmental record. The term **stakeholders** is used to describe all the different people or groups of people who are affected by an organization's policies, decisions, and activities. Many corporations, for example, are careful to point out their efforts to sustain the planet, participate in the green ecological movement, and help people to live better lives in an annual social responsibility report. In its latest report, General Mills describes how it contributed over $93 million in 2019 (the last year that complete statistics are available) to a wide variety of charitable causes, including support for programs that feed the hungry and for nonprofit organizations, schools, and communities in the United States and around the globe.[6]

> **Figure 1-3** The Relationship Between Sales Revenue and Profit

Profit is what remains after all business expenses have been deducted from sales revenue.

Sales revenue
Expenses	Profit

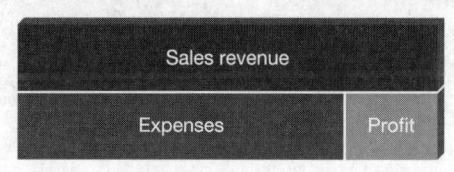

利润
profit what remains after all business expenses have been deducted from sales revenue

利益相关者
stakeholders all the different people or groups of people who are affected by an organization's policies, decisions, and activities

Concept Check

▶ Describe the four resources that must be combined to organize and operate a business.

▶ What is the difference between a manufacturing business, a service business, and a marketing intermediary?

▶ Explain the relationship among profit, business risk, and the satisfaction of customers' needs.

The profit earned by a business becomes the property of its owners. Thus, in one sense, profit is the reward business owners receive for producing goods and services that customers need and want. Profit is also the payment that business owners receive for assuming the considerable risks of business ownership. One of these is the risk of not being paid. Everyone else—employees, suppliers, and lenders—must be paid before the owners.

A second risk that owners must consider is the risk of losing whatever they have invested into the business. A business that cannot earn a profit is very likely to fail, in which case the owners lose whatever money, effort, and time they have invested.

To satisfy society's needs and make a profit, a business must operate within the parameters of a nation's economic system. In the next section, we define economics and describe two different types of economic systems.

经济制度的类型

1-3 Types of Economic Systems

Learning Objective

1-3 Describe the two types of economic systems: capitalism and command economy.

Economics is the study of how wealth is created and distributed. By *wealth,* we mean "anything of value," including the goods and services produced and sold by business. *How wealth is distributed* simply means "who gets what." Experts often use economics to explain the choices we make and how these choices change as we cope with the demands of everyday life. In simple terms, individuals, businesses, governments, and society must make decisions that reflect what is important to each group at a particular time. For example, suppose you want to take a weekend trip to some exotic vacation spot, and you also want to begin an investment program. Because of your financial resources, though, you cannot do both, so you must decide what is most important. Business firms, governments, and to some extent society face the same types of decisions. Each group must deal with scarcity when making important decisions. In this case, *scarcity* means "lack of resources"—money, time, natural resources, and so on—that are needed to satisfy a want or need.

Today, experts often study economic problems from two different perspectives: microeconomics and macroeconomics. **Microeconomics** is the study of the decisions made by individuals and businesses. Microeconomics, for example, examines how the prices of homes affect the number of homes individuals will buy. On the other hand,

经济学
economics the study of how wealth is created and distributed

微观经济学
microeconomics the study of the decisions made by individuals and businesses

Who owns Dairy Queen? There's a chance you've purchased shakes or burgers at DQ, but do you know who owns the restaurant chain? The restaurant chain is part of a multinational corporation—Berkshire Hathaway—a company that owns dozens and dozens of successful companies and was started by Warren Buffett. Today Berkshire Hathaway *and* Dairy Queen meet customer needs, earn profits, and employ thousands of employees because they thrive in a nation with a capitalistic economy.

macroeconomics is the study of the national economy and the global economy. Macroeconomics examines the economic effect of national income, unemployment, inflation, taxes, government spending, interest rates, and similar factors on a nation and society.

The decisions that individuals, business firms, government, and society make, and the way in which people deal with the creation and distribution of wealth determine the kind of economic system, or **economy**, that a nation has.

Over the years, the economic systems of the world have differed in essentially two ways: (1) the ownership of the factors of production and (2) how they answer four basic economic questions that direct a nation's economic activity.

Factors of production are the inputs and resources used to produce goods and services. There are four such factors:

- *Land and natural resources*—elements that can be used in the production process to make appliances, automobiles, and other products. Typical examples include crude oil, forests, minerals, land, water, and even air.
- *Labor*—the time and effort that we use to produce goods and services. It includes human resources—people with skills, knowledge, training, and experiences. Examples include managers and employees.
- *Capital*—facilities, equipment, machines, tools, and man-made items used in the production of goods and services and the operation of businesses. For example, the manufacturing equipment in a Pepperidge Farm production facility or a computer used in the corporate offices of McDonald's are both types of capital. Although most people think of money as capital, it is not one of the basic four factors of production because it is a financial resource used to obtain the factors of production necessary to conceptualize, create, and produce goods and services.
- *Entrepreneurship*—the activity that conceptualizes, creates, and organizes land and natural resources, labor, and capital. It is the willingness to take risks and the knowledge and ability to use the other factors of production efficiently. An **entrepreneur** is a person who risks time, effort, and money to start and operate a business.

A nation's economic system determines how the factors of production are used to meet the needs of society. Today, two different economic systems exist: capitalism

宏观经济学
macroeconomics the study of the national economy and the global economy

经济
economy the way in which people deal with the creation and distribution of wealth

生产要素
factors of production inputs and resources used to produce goods and services

企业家
entrepreneur a person who risks time, effort, and money to start and operate a business

Is this so-much hot air?
No, not really. Fueled by environmental concerns, more and more businesses in industrialized nations are using wind and solar power for their energy needs. Today both wind and solar power are sources of clean and cost-effective energy leading some experts to suggest there's a new natural resource in town.

Chapter 1 Exploring the World of Business and Economics

Entrepreneurial Success

创业成功：下一波创业浪潮来了

The Next Wave of Entrepreneurs Is Here

During the COVID-19 pandemic, the United States experienced the highest unemployment rate since 1929, and that indirectly led to a boom in entrepreneurship. Based on data from the U.S. Census Bureau, new business formations during the pandemic jumped dramatically, reaching a record high.

Since business creation has historically declined during periods of recession, professionals are optimistic about this new wave of entrepreneurship. The sharp increase in applications to form businesses also suggests that the labor market will recover more quickly from the COVID-19 recession than the Great Recession of 2008. After all, new, successful businesses will need to hire employees.

Recessions often give rise to new types of businesses as innovative entrepreneurs capitalize on new opportunities. The Great Recession of 2008, for example, gave birth to the gig economy as unemployed individuals looked for temporary, flexible, or freelance jobs for alternative ways to make money. Apps like Airbnb and Uber became immensely popular. Now, consumer demand suggests several products and services such as home improvement, pet products, home beauty products, gaming, and fitness and health that may offer new business opportunities to meet the needs of customers.

The COVID-19 pandemic disrupted business operations, shifted consumer behavior, and created new opportunities. As a result, entrepreneurs will have to look outside the box to match customer needs with their internal core strengths. As new start-ups emerge, only time will tell which ones will enjoy long-term success.

Sources: Based on information in Michael Sasso and Alexandre Tanzi, "Covid Recession Spawning Entrepreneurs in U.S. Amid Joblessness," *Bloomberg*, October 14, 2020; Adam Singolda, "Op-Ed: Analysis of 8 Billion Page Views Shows Where the Next Hot Start-up Can Thrive," *CNBC*, May 12, 2020; Dr. Anthony M. Criniti, IV, "How to Become a Successful Entrepreneur During the Pandemic," *The Entrepreneur*, July 28, 2020.

---

and command economies. The way each system answers the four basic economic questions listed below determines which type of economy a nation has.

1. *What* goods and services—and how much of each—will be produced?
2. *How* will these goods and services be produced?
3. *For whom* will these goods and services be produced?
4. *Who* owns and who controls the major factors of production?

资本主义

1-3a Capitalism

Capitalism is an economic system in which individuals own and operate the majority of businesses that provide goods and services. Capitalism stems from the theories of the Scottish economist Adam Smith. In his book *Wealth of Nations*, published in 1776, Smith argued that a society's interests are best served when the individuals within that society are allowed to pursue their own self-interest. According to Smith, when individuals act to improve their own fortunes, they indirectly promote the good of their community and the people in that community. Smith went on to call this concept the "invisible hand." The **invisible hand** is a term created by Adam Smith to describe how an individual's own personal gain benefits others and a nation's economy. For example, the only way a small-business owner who produces shoes can increase personal wealth is to sell shoes to customers. To become even more prosperous, the small-business owner must hire workers to produce even more shoes. According to the invisible hand, people in the small-business owner's community not only would have shoes but also would have jobs working for the shoemaker. Thus, the success of people in the community and, to some extent, the nation's economy are tied indirectly to the success of the small-business owner.

资本主义
capitalism an economic system in which individuals own and operate the majority of businesses that provide goods and services

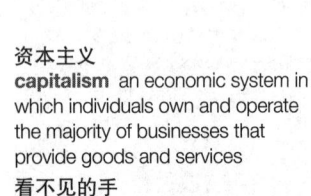

看不见的手
invisible hand a term created by Adam Smith to describe how an individual's personal gain benefits others and a nation's economy

14   Marketing

Adam Smith's capitalism is based on the following fundamental issues—also refer to Figure 1-4.

1. The creation of wealth is the concern of private individuals, not the government.
2. Individuals must own private property and the resources used to create wealth.
3. Economic freedom ensures the existence of competitive markets that allow both sellers and buyers to enter and leave the market as they choose.
4. The role of government should be limited to providing defense against foreign enemies, ensuring internal order, and furnishing public works and education.

One factor that Smith felt was extremely important was the role of government. He believed that government should act only as rule maker and umpire. The French term *laissez-faire* describes Smith's capitalistic system and implies that there should be no government interference in the economy. Loosely translated, this term means "let them do" (as they choose).

Adam Smith's laissez-faire capitalism is also based on the concept of a market economy. A **market economy** (sometimes referred to as a *free-market economy*) is an economic system in which businesses and individuals decide what to produce and buy, and the market determines prices and quantities sold. In today's competitive world, a business like Ford Motor Company must decide *what* type of automobiles it will sell, *how* the automobiles will be produced, and *for whom* the automobiles will be produced. *You,* the consumer, must decide if you will buy a Ford product or an automobile manufactured by another company. Prices are determined by the interaction of consumers and businesses in the marketplace.

美国的资本主义
1-3b Capitalism in the United States

Our economic system is rooted in the laissez-faire capitalism of Adam Smith. However, our real-world economy is not as laissez-faire as Smith would have liked because government participates as more than umpire and rule maker. Our economy is, in fact, a **mixed economy**, one that exhibits elements of both capitalism and socialism.

In a mixed economy, the four basic economic questions discussed at the beginning of this section (*what, how, for whom,* and *who*) are answered through the interaction of households, businesses, and governments. The interactions among these three groups are shown in Figure 1-5.

Households Households, made up of individuals, are the consumers of goods and services as well as owners of some of the factors of production. As *resource owners,* people should be free to determine how their resources are used and also to enjoy the income and wages, rents, interest, and other benefits derived from ownership of their resources. For example, members of households provide businesses with labor. In return, businesses pay wages, which households receive as income.

As *consumers,* household members spend their income to purchase the goods and services produced by business. Today, almost 70 percent of our nation's total production consists of **consumer products**—goods and services purchased by

> **Figure 1-4** Basic Assumptions of Adam Smith's Laissez-Faire Capitalism

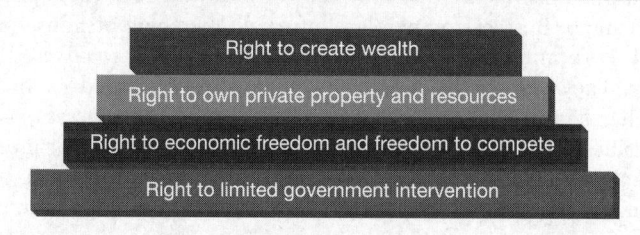

Right to create wealth
Right to own private property and resources
Right to economic freedom and freedom to compete
Right to limited government intervention

市场经济
market economy an economic system in which businesses and individuals decide what to produce and buy, and the market determines prices and quantities sold.

混合经济
mixed economy an economy that exhibits elements of both capitalism and socialism

消费品
consumer products goods and services purchased by individuals for personal consumption

Figure 1-5 The Circular Flow in Our Mixed Economy

Our economic system is guided by the interaction of buyers and sellers, with the role of government being taken into account.

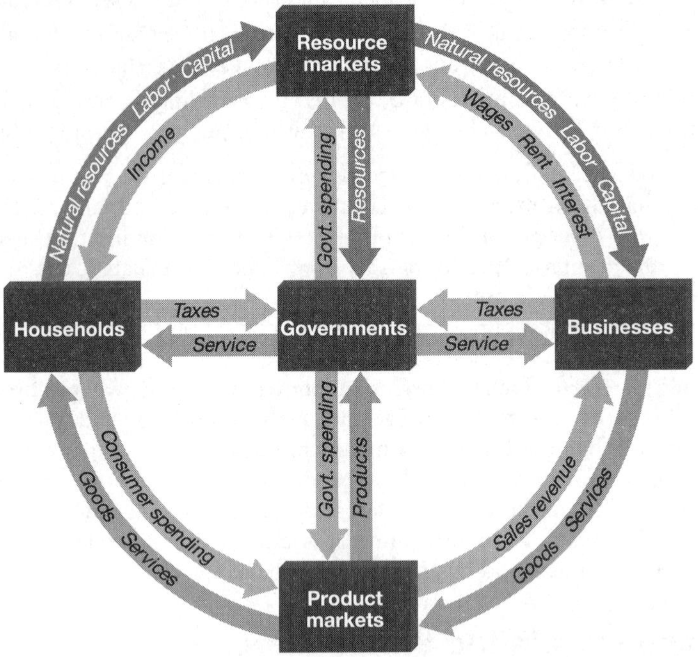

individuals for personal consumption.[7] This means that consumers, as a group, are the biggest customers of American business. Consumer spending is a very important component for the financial health of any nation. Consider what happened in the first six months of 2020 in the United States. When the nation experienced the first cases of the COVID-19 virus, consumer spending began to slow down. Then the situation got even worse when non-essential businesses including restaurants, theaters, and some retailers closed down in March and April in many states. When this happened, many consumers were advised (or told) to stay home, and they began to save money and buy only essential items. The combination of fear of losing their job or reduced hours on the job and not knowing how long the pandemic would last caused a huge drop in consumer spending and an economic downturn. Fortunately, consumer spending and the economy began to turn around in the summer of 2020 as businesses began to reopen, and early research indicated that a vaccine that could protect people from the virus and decrease the number of deaths would be available by the end of the year.

Businesses Like households, businesses are engaged in two different exchanges. They exchange money for resources, labor, and capital and use these resources to produce goods and services. Then they exchange their goods and services for sales revenue. This sales revenue, in turn, is exchanged for additional resources, which are used to produce and sell more goods and services.

When business profits are distributed to business owners, these profits become household income. (Business owners are, after all, members of households.) When the economy is running smoothly, households are willing to invest their money in businesses. They can do so directly by buying stocks issued by businesses, by purchasing shares in mutual funds that purchase stocks in businesses, or by lending money to businesses. They can also invest indirectly by placing their money in bank accounts. Banks and other financial institutions then invest money as part of their normal business operations. Thus, business profits, too, are retained in the business system, and the circular flow in Figure 1-5 is complete. How, then, does government fit in?

Governments The numerous government services are important but they (1) would either not be produced by private business firms or (2) would be produced only for those who could afford them. Typical services include national defense, police, fire protection, education, and construction of roads and highways. To pay for all these services, governments collect a variety of taxes from households (such as personal income taxes and sales taxes) and from businesses (corporate income taxes).

Figure 1-5 shows this exchange of taxes for government services. It also shows government spending of tax dollars for resources and products required to provide these services.

Actually, with government included, our circular flow looks more like a combination of several flows. In reality, it is. The important point is that together the various flows make up a single unit—a complete economic system that provides answers to the basic economic questions. Simply put, the system works.

计划经济
1-3c Command Economies

A **command economy** is an economic system in which the government decides *what* goods and services will be produced, *how* they will be produced, *for whom* available goods and services will be produced, and *who* owns and controls the major factors of production. Today, two types of economic systems—*socialism* and *communism*—serve as examples of command economies.

Socialism In a socialist economy, the key industries are owned and controlled by the government. Land, buildings, and raw materials may also be the property of the state in a socialist economy. Depending on the country, private ownership of smaller businesses is permitted to varying degrees. Usually, people may choose their own occupations, although many work in state-owned industries. Today, China, New Zealand, Canada, Sweden, and Norway are often referred to as socialist nations because they have adopted *some* socialist policies and welfare programs.

What to produce and how to produce it often are determined in accordance with national goals, which are based on projected needs and the availability of resources. The distribution of goods and services—who gets what—is also controlled by the state to the extent that it controls taxes, rents, and wages. Among the professed aims of socialist countries are the equitable distribution of income, the elimination of poverty, and the distribution of social services (such as medical care) to all who need them. The disadvantages of socialism include increased taxation and loss of incentive and motivation for both individuals and business owners.

Communism If Adam Smith was the father of capitalism, Karl Marx was the father of communism. In his writings during the mid-1800s, Marx advocated a classless society whose citizens together owned all economic resources. All workers would then contribute to this *communist* society according to their ability and would receive benefits according to their need.

Since the breakup of the Soviet Union and economic reforms in China and most of the Eastern European countries, the best remaining example of communism is DPRK. Today, the basic four economic questions (what, how, for whom, and who) are answered through centralized government plans. Emphasis is placed on the production of goods and services the government needs rather than on the needs of consumers, so there are frequent shortages of consumer goods.

> ### ✓ Concept Check
> ▶ What are the four basic economic questions? How are they answered in a capitalist economy?
> ▶ Describe the four basic assumptions required for a laissez-faire capitalist economy.
> ▶ Why is the American economy called a mixed economy?
> ▶ How does capitalism differ from socialism and communism?

计划经济
command economy an economic system in which the government decides *what* goods and services will be produced, *how* they will be produced, *for whom* available goods and services will be produced, and *who* owns and controls the major factors of production

Chapter 1 Exploring the World of Business and Economics

衡量经济表现

1-4 Measuring Economic Performance

Learning Objective

1-4 Identify the ways to measure economic performance.

Consider for just a moment the following questions:

- Are U.S. workers as productive as workers in other countries?
- Is the gross domestic product for the United States increasing or decreasing?
- How does inflation affect the prices that consumers pay for products and services?

Information needed to answer these questions is easily obtainable from many sources. More important, the answers to these and other questions can be used to gauge the economic health of the nation.

生产力在全球市场中的重要性

1-4a The Importance of Productivity in the Global Marketplace

One way to measure a nation's economic performance is to assess its productivity. While there are other definitions of productivity, for our purposes, **productivity** is the average level of output per worker per hour. An increase in productivity results in economic growth because a larger number of goods and services are produced by a given labor force. To see how productivity affects you and the economy, consider the following three questions:

Question: *How does an increase in productivity affect the economy?*

Answer: Because of increased productivity, it takes fewer workers to produce more goods and services. As a result, employers can reduce costs, earn more profits, and may sell their products or services for less. Finally, productivity growth helps American business to compete more effectively with other nations in a global, competitive world.

Question: *Is an increase in productivity always good?*

Answer: Fewer workers producing more goods and services can lead to lower salary expenses for employers and higher unemployment rates for workers. In this case, increased productivity is good for employers but not good for unemployed workers.

生产力 / 生产率
productivity the average level of output per worker per hour

How do you improve productivity? Most experts agree the most important factors needed to improve worker productivity are workers who feel appreciated and valued for the contributions they make to the organization, and being part of an inclusive team. In fact, sharing ideas and different opinions and being part of "the team" are often the foundation for improving a company's productivity.

18 Marketing

Question: *How does a nation improve productivity?*

Answer: Reducing costs and enabling employees to work more efficiently are at the core of all attempts to improve productivity. Increased productivity is one of the key factors that account for an increase in a nation's gross domestic product.

国内生产总值

1-4b The Nation's Gross Domestic Product

In addition to productivity, a measure called *gross domestic product* can be used to measure the economic well-being of a nation. **Gross domestic product (GDP)** is the total dollar value of all goods and services produced by all people within the boundaries of a country during a specified time period—usually a one-year period. For example, the values of automobiles produced by employees in an American-owned General Motors plant and a Japanese-owned Toyota plant *in the United States* are both included in the GDP for the United States. The U.S. GDP was $20.9 trillion in 2020.[8] (*Note:* At the time of publication, 2020 was the last year for which statistics were available.)

The GDP figure facilitates comparisons between the United States and other countries because it is the standard used in international guidelines for economic accounting. It is also possible to compare the GDP for one nation over several different time periods. This comparison—often called the GDP growth rate—allows observers to determine the extent to which a nation is experiencing economic growth on an annual or quarterly basis. For example, government economic experts project the U.S. GDP will grow approximately 2 percent each year from 2019 to 2029.[9]

To make accurate comparisons of the GDP for different years, we must adjust the dollar amounts for inflation. **Inflation** is a general rise in the level of prices. (The opposite of inflation is deflation.) **Deflation** is a general decrease in the level of prices. By using inflation-adjusted figures, we are able to measure the *real* GDP for a nation. In effect, it is now possible to compare the goods and services produced by a nation in constant dollars—dollars that will purchase the same amount of goods and services. Figure 1-6 depicts the GDP of the United States in current dollars

Figure 1-6 GDP in Current Dollars and in Inflation-Adjusted Dollars

The change in GDP and real GDP for the United States from one year to another year can be used to measure economic growth.

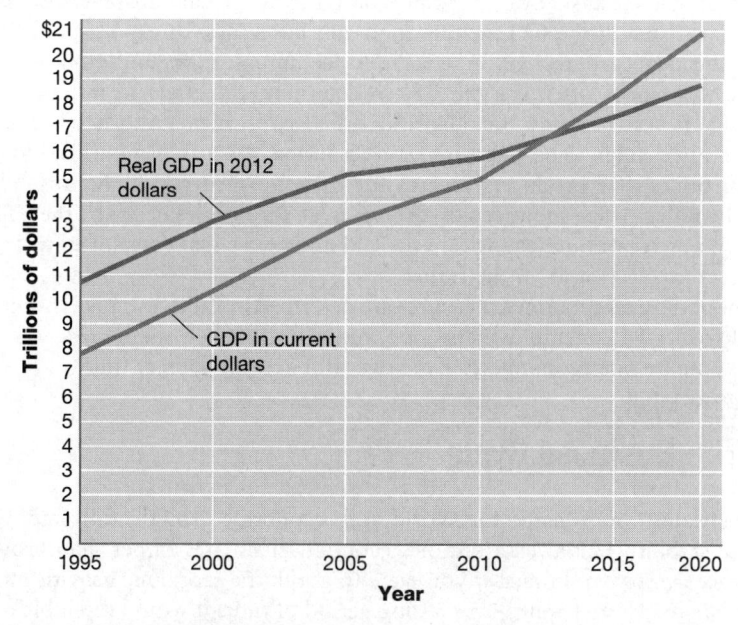

Source: U.S. Bureau of Economic Analysis website at www.bea.gov (accessed January 28, 2021).

国内生产总值
gross domestic product (GDP) the total dollar value of all goods and services produced by all people within the boundaries of a country during a specified time period—usually a one-year period

通货膨胀
inflation a general rise in the level of prices

通货紧缩
deflation a general decrease in the level of prices

Chapter 1 Exploring the World of Business and Economics

Table 1-1 Common Measures Used to Evaluate a Nation's Economic Health

Economic Measure	Description
1. Balance of trade	The difference between the value of a nation's exports and a nation's imports over a specific period of time.
2. Consumer confidence index	A measure of how optimistic or pessimistic consumers are about the nation's economy. This measure is usually reported on a monthly basis.
3. Corporate profits	The total amount of profits made by corporations over selected time periods.
4. Inflation rate	An economic statistic that tracks the increase in prices of goods and services over a period of time. This measure is usually reported monthly and calculated on an annual basis.
5. National income	The total income earned by various components of the economy, including employees, interest and rental income, profits from businesses, and other types of income.
6. New housing starts	The total number of new homes started during a specific time period.
7. Prime interest rate	The lowest interest rate that banks charge their most credit-worthy customers.

✓ Concept Check

- How does an increase in productivity affect business?
- What is the difference between the gross domestic product and the real gross domestic product? Why are these economic measures significant?
- How does inflation affect the prices you pay for goods and services?
- How is the producer price index related to the consumer price index?

失业率
unemployment rate the percentage of a nation's labor force unemployed at any time

消费者价格指数
consumer price index (CPI) a monthly index that measures the changes in prices of a fixed basket of goods purchased by a typical consumer in an urban area

生产者价格指数
producer price index (PPI) a monthly index that measures prices that producers receive for their finished goods

Learning Objective
1-5 Examine the different phases in the typical business cycle.

and the real GDP in inflation-adjusted dollars. Note that between 1995 and 2020, America's real GDP grew from almost $10.7 trillion to $18.8 trillion.[10]

衡量一国经济的其他重要经济指标
1-4c Other Important Economic Indicators That Measure a Nation's Economy

In addition to productivity, GDP, and real GDP, other economic measures exist that can be used to evaluate a nation's economy. One very important statistic is the unemployment rate. The **unemployment rate** is the percentage of a nation's labor force unemployed at any time. Although the unemployment rate for the United States is typically about 4 to 6 percent, it peaked during the COVID-19 pandemic when the unemployment rate reached almost 15 percent when non-essential businesses were closed in many states. By the end of 2020, the unemployment rate had dropped to just over 6 percent. This is an important statistic—especially if you are unemployed.

The **consumer price index (CPI)** is a monthly index that measures the changes in prices of a fixed basket of goods purchased by a typical consumer in an urban area. Goods listed in the CPI include food and beverages, transportation, housing, clothing, medical care, recreation, education, communication, and other goods and services. Economists often use the CPI to determine the effect of inflation on not only the nation's economy but also individual consumers. Another index is the producer price index. The **producer price index (PPI)** is a monthly index that measures prices that producers receive for their finished goods. Because changes in the PPI reflect price increases or decreases at the wholesale level, the PPI is an accurate predictor of both changes in the CPI and prices that consumers will pay for many everyday necessities in the future.

Some additional economic measures are described in Table 1-1. Like the measures for GDP, real GDP, unemployment rate, and price indexes, these measures can be used to compare one economic statistic over different periods of time.

经济周期
1-5 The Business Cycle

All industrialized nations of the world seek economic growth, full employment, and price stability. However, a nation's economy fluctuates rather than grows at a steady pace every year. In fact, if you were to graph the economic growth rate for a country like the United States over a long period of time, it would resemble a roller-coaster ride with peaks (high points) and troughs (low points). These fluctuations

Business Cycle

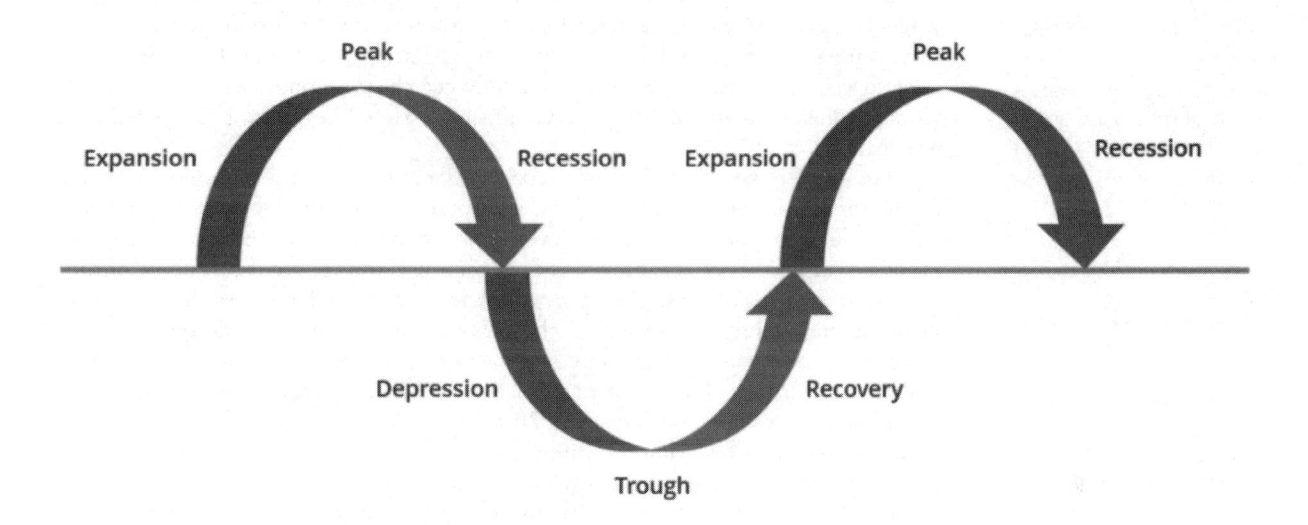

```
Expansion    Peak    Recession    Expansion    Peak    Recession
                Depression    Recovery
                         Trough
```

are generally referred to as the **business cycle**, that is, the recurrence of periods of growth and recession in a nation's economic activity.

At the time of publication, the U.S. economy is showing signs of improvement after the effects of a global pandemic. Key economic indicators including the gross domestic product, the stock market, and consumer spending have improved, and the unemployment rate has decreased. And yet, there are concerns about the size of the national debt—a topic described later in this section. There are also concerns about the effect of possible changes by the Biden administration and how those changes could affect individuals, businesses, and the nation's economy. In addition, many experts worry about the economies of foreign nations around the globe and social unrest throughout the world.

The changes that result from either economic growth or an economic downturn affect the demand for products and services that consumers are willing to buy and, as a result, the amount of products and services produced by business firms. Generally, the business cycle consists of four phases: the peak (sometimes called prosperity), recession, the trough, and recovery (sometimes called expansion).

During the *peak period* (prosperity), the economy is at its highest point and unemployment is low. Total income is relatively high. As long as the economic outlook remains prosperous, consumers are willing to buy products and services. In fact, businesses often expand and offer new products and services during the peak period to take advantage of consumers' increased buying power.

Generally, economists define a **recession** as two or more consecutive three-month periods of decline in a country's GDP. Although the recession of 2020 lasted only a few months before the economy began to recover, most recessions are longer. For example, the Great Recession of 2008 lasted 18 months. During a recession, it is typical for the unemployment rate to increase and consumer buying power to

经济周期
business cycle the recurrence of periods of growth and recession in a nation's economic activity
经济衰退
recession two or more consecutive three-month periods of decline in a country's GDP

Chapter 1 Exploring the World of Business and Economics

Concept Check

- What are the four phases in the typical business cycle?
- At the time you are studying the material in this chapter, which phase of the business cycle do you think the U.S. economy is in? Justify your answer.
- How can the Federal Reserve and government use monetary policy and fiscal policy to reduce the effects of an economic crisis?

经济萧条
depression a severe recession that lasts longer than a typical recession and has a larger decline in business activity when compared to a recession

货币政策
monetary policies Federal Reserve's actions to promote maximum employment, stabilize prices, and increase or decrease interest rates.

财政政策
fiscal policy government influence on the amount of savings and expenditures; accomplished by altering the tax structure and by changing the levels of government spending

联邦赤字
federal deficit a shortfall created when the federal government spends more in a fiscal year than it receives

国债
national debt the total of all federal deficits

Learning Objective

1-6 Outline the four types of competition.

竞争
competition rivalry among businesses for sales to potential customers

decline. As buying power declines, consumers tend to purchase essential items and are reluctant to purchase frivolous or non-essential items. In response to a recession, many businesses focus on producing the products and services that provide the most value to their customers. Companies and government at all levels often postpone or go slow on major projects during a recession.

Economists define a **depression** as a severe recession that lasts longer than a typical recession and has a larger decline in business activity when compared to a recession. A depression is characterized by extremely high unemployment rates, low wages, reduced purchasing power, lack of confidence in the economy, a decline in stock values, and a general decrease in business activity. While the United States has experienced many recessions, there have only been a few economic depressions. The worst depression, often called "the Great Depression," began in 1929 lasted over ten years.

The third phase of the business cycle is the *trough*. The trough of a recession or depression is the turning point when a nation's production and employment bottom out and reach their lowest levels. Some experts believe that effective use of monetary and fiscal policies can speed up recovery and reduce the amount of time the economy is in recession. **Monetary policies** are the Federal Reserve's actions to promote maximum employment, stabilize prices, and increase or decrease interest rates. Through **fiscal policy**, the government can influence the amount of savings and expenditures by altering the tax structure and changing the levels of government spending. For example, during the 2020 pandemic crisis both the Federal Reserve's monetary policies (lower interest rates) and the government's fiscal policies (stimulus packages) were used to stabilize the economy.

One of the concerns about the government's recent stimulus programs is the national debt. Although the federal government collects almost $4 trillion in annual revenues, the government usually spends more than it receives, resulting in a **federal deficit**. For example, the government had a federal deficit for each year between 2002 and 2020. The total of all federal deficits is called the **national debt**. Today, the U.S. national debt is over $27 trillion or approximately $83,000 for every man, woman, and child in the United States.[11]

Recovery (or *expansion*) is the movement of the economy from the trough, when a nation's production and employment bottom out and reach their lowest levels, to the next peak in a business cycle. For example, the recession that began in December 2008 lasted 18 months while the recovery that followed the 2008 recession lasted 128 months until February 2020.[12] During the recovery stage of a business cycle, high unemployment rates decline, income increases, and both the ability and the willingness to buy rise for consumers, businesses, and governments.

竞争的类型
1-6 Types of Competition

Our capitalist system ensures that individuals and businesses make the decisions about what to produce, how to produce it, and what price to charge for the product. Mattel, Inc., for example, can introduce new versions of its famous Barbie doll, license the Barbie name, change the doll's price and method of distribution, and attempt to produce and market Barbie in other countries or over the internet at www.mattel.com. Our system also allows customers the right to choose between Mattel's products and those produced by competitors.

As a consumer, you get to choose which products or services you want to buy. Competition like that between Mattel and other toy manufacturers is a necessary and extremely important by-product of capitalism. Business **competition** is essentially a rivalry among businesses for sales to potential customers. In a capitalistic economy, competition also ensures that a firm will survive only if it serves its customers well by providing products and services that meet needs. Economists recognize

Marketing

four different degrees of competition ranging from ideal, complete competition to no competition at all. These are perfect competition, monopolistic competition, oligopoly, and monopoly. For a quick overview of the different types of competition, including numbers of firms and examples for each type, look at Table 1-2.

完全竞争

1-6a Perfect Competition

Perfect (or **pure**) **competition** is the market situation in which there are many buyers and sellers of a product, and no single buyer or seller is powerful enough to affect the price of that product. As pointed out in Table 1-2, real-world examples of perfect competition are corn, wheat, peanuts, and many agricultural products. For perfect competition to exist, there are five very important concepts.

- We are discussing the market for a single product, such as bushels of wheat.
- There are no restrictions on firms entering the industry.
- All sellers offer essentially the same product for sale.
- All buyers and sellers know everything there is to know about the market (including, in our example, the prices that all sellers are asking for their wheat).
- The overall market is not affected by the actions of any one buyer or seller.

When perfect competition exists, every seller should ask the same price that every other seller is asking. Why? Because if one seller wanted 50 cents more for their products than all the others, that seller would not be able to sell a single product. Buyers could—and would—do better by purchasing the same products from the competition. On the other hand, a firm willing to sell below the going price would sell all its products quickly. However, that seller would lose sales revenue (and profit) because buyers are willing to pay more.

In perfect competition, the price of each product is determined by the actions of all buyers and all sellers together through the forces of supply and demand.

The Basics of Supply and Demand The **supply** of a particular product is the quantity of the product that producers are willing to sell at each of various prices. Producers are rational people, so we would expect them to offer more of a product for sale at higher prices and to offer less of the product at lower prices, as illustrated by the supply curve in Figure 1-7.

The **demand** for a particular product is the quantity that buyers are willing to purchase at each of various prices. Buyers, too, are usually rational, so we would expect them—as a group—to buy more of a product when its price is low and to buy less of the product when its price is high, as depicted by the demand curve in Figure 1-7.

The Equilibrium, or Market, Price There is always one certain price at which the demand for a product is equal to the quantity of that product produced. Suppose

Table 1-2 Four Different Types of Competition
The number of firms determines the degree of competition within an industry.

Type of Competition	Number of Business Firms or Suppliers	Real-World Examples
1. Perfect	Many	Corn, wheat, peanuts, many agricultural products
2. Monopolistic	Many	Clothing, shoes
3. Oligopoly	Few	Automobiles, airlines
4. Monopoly	One	Many local public utilities, software protected by copyright

完全竞争
perfect (or **pure**) **competition** the market situation in which there are many buyers and sellers of a product, and no single buyer or seller is powerful enough to affect the price of that product

供给
supply the quantity of a product that producers are willing to sell at each of various prices

需求
demand the quantity of a product that buyers are willing to purchase at each of various prices

Figure 1-7 Supply Curve and Demand Curve

The interaction of a supply curve and a demand curve is called the equilibrium or market price. This interaction indicates a single price and quantity at which suppliers will sell products and buyers will purchase them.

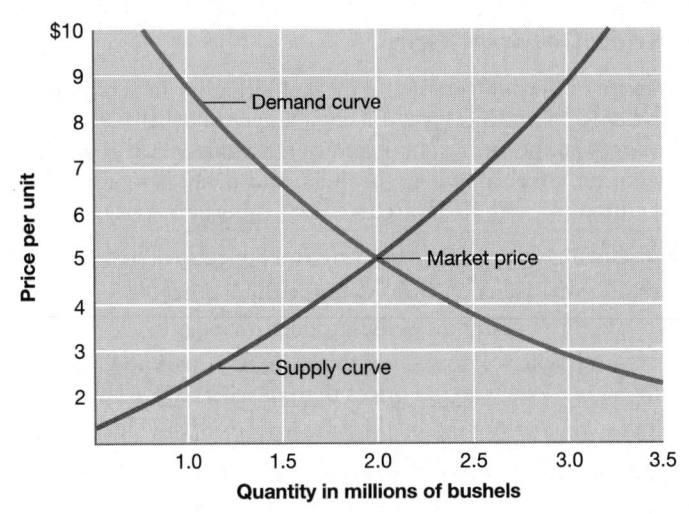

that producers are willing to *supply* two million bushels of wheat at a price of $5 per bushel and that buyers are willing to *purchase* two million bushels at a price of $5 per bushel. As shown in Figure 1-7, supply and demand are in balance, or in equilibrium, at the price of $5. Economists call this price the *market price*. The **market price** of any product is the price at which the quantity demanded is exactly equal to the quantity supplied.

In theory and in the real world, market prices are affected by anything that affects supply and demand. The *demand* for wheat, for example, might change if researchers suddenly discovered that it offered a previously unknown health benefit. Then buyers would demand more wheat at every price. Or the *supply* of wheat might change if new technology permitted the production of greater quantities of wheat from the same amount of acreage. Other changes that can affect the market price of wheat are shifts in buyer tastes, the development of new products, fluctuations in income owing to inflation or recession, or even changes in the weather that affect the production of wheat.

Perfect competition is quite rare in today's world. Many real markets, however, are examples of monopolistic competition.

垄断竞争
1-6b Monopolistic Competition

Monopolistic competition is a market situation in which there are many buyers along with a relatively large number of sellers. Real-world examples of products sold in a monopolistically competitive market include clothing, shoes, soaps, furniture, and many consumer items. The various products available in this type of competitive market are similar in nature, and they are all intended to satisfy the same basic need. However, each seller attempts to make its product different from the others by providing unique product features, an attention-getting brand name, unique packaging, or services such as free delivery or a lifetime warranty.

Product differentiation is the process of developing and promoting differences between a company's products and all competitive products. It is a fact of life for the producers of many consumer goods, from soaps to clothing to furniture to shoes. A furniture manufacturer such as Bush Industries sees what looks like a mob of competitors, all trying to chip away at its share of the ready-to-assemble furniture

市场价格
market price the price at which the quantity demanded is exactly equal to the quantity supplied

垄断竞争
monopolistic competition a market situation in which there are many buyers along with a relatively large number of sellers who differentiate their products from the products of competitors

产品差异化
product differentiation the process of developing and promoting differences between a company's products and all competitive products

How does competition affect a retailer like Macy's? For Macy's, competition is a way of life. Executives know they must compete with Dillard's, Target, Walmart, Amazon, and other retailers—all businesses that sell clothing and many other products. Each retailer uses product differentiation to differentiate its merchandise from competitors on the basis of price, quality, brand names, customer service, and other factors that can entice a customer to shop at one store instead of a competitor.

market. By differentiating each of its products from all similar products produced by competitors, Bush Industries obtains some limited control over the market price of its product.

寡头垄断
1-6c Oligopoly

An **oligopoly** is a market (or industry) situation in which there are few sellers. Generally, these sellers are quite large, and sizable investments are required to enter into their market. Examples of oligopolies are the automobile, airline, car rental, cereal, and farm implement industries.

Because there are few sellers in an oligopoly, the market actions of each seller can have a strong effect on competitors' sales and prices. For instance, when General Motors began offering cash incentives to encourage consumers to purchase new Chevrolet and GMC trucks at the beginning of 2021, Ford, Nissan, and Toyota began offering similar incentives and for the same reasons—to attract new-car buyers and to retain their market share. In the absence of much price competition, product differentiation becomes the major competitive weapon; this is very evident in the advertising of the major automobile manufacturers.

垄断
1-6d Monopoly

A **monopoly** is a market (or industry) with only one seller, and customers can only buy the product or service from that seller. In a monopoly, there is no close substitute for the product or service. Because only one business is the seller of a product or service, it would seem that it has complete control over price. However, no business can set its price at some astronomical amount just because there is no competition; the business would soon find that it has no customers or sales revenue either. Instead, the business in a monopoly position must consider the demand for its product and set the price at the most profitable level.

寡头垄断
oligopoly a market (or industry) in which there are few sellers

垄断
monopoly a market (or industry) with only one seller, and customers can only buy the product or service from that seller

Chapter 1   Exploring the World of Business and Economics

> **Concept Check**
> - Is competition good for business? Is it good for consumers?
> - Explain how the equilibrium or market price of a product is determined.
> - Compare the four forms of competition.

Classic examples of monopolies in the United States are public utilities, including companies that provide local gas, water, sewer services, or electricity. Each utility firm operates in a *natural monopoly*, an industry that requires huge start-up costs that act as a deterrent for potential competitors. Natural monopolies are permitted to exist, but they operate under the scrutiny and control of various state and federal agencies. Although many public utilities are still classified as natural monopolies, there is increased competition in many areas of the country. For example, consumers now have a choice when selecting a company that provides electrical service to both homes and businesses in many areas of the country.

A legal monopoly—sometimes referred to as a *limited monopoly* or *statutory monopoly*—is created when a government entity issues a license, franchise, copyright, patent, or trademark. Because Microsoft owns the trademarks on its popular logos, it can control how both trademarks and logos are used by other businesses or individuals. Except for natural monopolies and legal monopolies, federal antitrust laws discourage or prohibit both monopolies and attempts to form monopolies in order to ensure that competitive markets exist and customers have a choice for products or services they need or want to purchase.

当代的美国商业

1-7 American Business Today

> **Learning Objective**
> 1-7 Summarize the development of American business and the challenges that businesses and society will encounter in the future.

Although our economic system is far from perfect, it provides Americans with a high standard of living compared with people in other countries throughout the world. **Standard of living** is a loose, subjective measure of how well off an individual or a society is, mainly in terms of want satisfaction through goods and services. Also, our economic system offers solutions to many of the problems that plague society and provides opportunities for people who are willing to work and to continue learning.

To understand the current business environment and the challenges ahead, it helps understand how business developed.

早期的商业发展

1-7a Early Business Development

Our American business system has its roots in the knowledge, skills, and values that the earliest settlers brought to this country. The first settlers in the United States were concerned mainly with providing themselves with basic necessities—food, clothing, and shelter. Almost all families lived on farms, and the entire family worked at the business of surviving. They used their surplus of agricultural products for trading, mainly by barter, among themselves and with the English trading ships that called at the colonies. As this trade increased, small businesses began to appear. Some settlers were able to use their skills and their excess time to work under the domestic system of production. The **domestic system** was a method of manufacturing in which an entrepreneur distributed raw materials to various homes, where families would process them into finished goods. The entrepreneur then offered the goods for sale.

Then, in 1793, a young English apprentice mechanic named Samuel Slater opened a textile mill in Pawtucket, Rhode Island, to spin raw cotton into thread. Slater's textile mill was America's first use of the **factory system** of manufacturing, in which all the materials, machinery, and workers required to manufacture a product are assembled in one place. The Industrial Revolution in America was born.

A manufacturing technique called *specialization* was used to improve productivity. **Specialization** is the separation of a manufacturing process into distinct tasks and the assignment of different tasks to different individuals.

Entrepreneurs continued to invent new machinery during the 1800s. Often, historians call this time period the golden age of invention and innovation. At the same time, new means of transportation greatly expanded the domestic markets for American products. Certainly, many basic characteristics of our modern business system took form during this time period.

生活水平
standard of living a loose, subjective measure of how well off an individual or a society is, mainly in terms of want satisfaction through goods and services

家庭生产制度
domestic system a method of manufacturing in which an entrepreneur distributed raw materials to various homes, where families would process them into finished goods to be offered for sale by the entrepreneur

工厂制度
factory system a system of manufacturing in which all the materials, machinery, and workers required to manufacture a product are assembled in one place

专业化
specialization the separation of a manufacturing process into distinct tasks and the assignment of different tasks to different individuals

26   Marketing

20世纪的商业发展

1-7b Business Development in the 1900s

Industrial growth and prosperity continued well into the 20th century. Henry Ford's moving automotive assembly line, which brought the work to the worker, refined the concept of specialization and helped spur on the mass production of consumer goods. Fundamental changes occurred in business ownership and management as well. No longer were the largest businesses owned by one individual; instead, more companies were owned by stockholders who were willing to invest in—but not to operate—a business.

To understand the major events that shaped the United States during the 20th century, it helps to remember that the economy was compared to a roller-coaster ride earlier in this chapter—periods of economic growth followed by periods of economic slowdown. The following are major events that shaped the nation's economy during the period from 1910 to 2000:

- The 1929 stock market crash and the Great Depression
- Federal government involvement in business in order to stimulate the economy, reduce unemployment, and ease the problems during the Great Depression
- World War I, World War II, the Korean War, and the Vietnam War
- Rapid economic growth and higher standard of living during the 1950s and 1960s
- The social responsibility movement during the 1960s
- A shortage of crude oil and higher prices for most goods in the mid-1970s
- High inflation, high interest rates, and reduced business profits during the last part of the 1970s and early 1980s
- Sustained economic growth in the 1990s

Unfortunately, by the last part of the 1990s, an increasing number of business failures, higher interest rates, and concerns about the financial markets and the economy were signs that larger economic problems were on the way.

Think for a moment what Henry Ford would think about today's automated factories. It's fair to assume he would be amazed at how manufacturing has developed in just over 100 years. While today's factories are definitely more advanced, don't underestimate the significance of Ford's assembly line back in 1913. Simply put, it not only changed the way automobiles like the one in this photo were manufactured, but it also led to changes in the way just about everything else was manufactured.

Chapter 1   Exploring the World of Business and Economics

新世纪：2000 年及以后
1-7c A New Century: 2000 and Beyond

According to many economic experts, the first part of the 21st century might be characterized as the best of times and the worst of times rolled into one package. On the plus side, technology became available at an affordable price. Both individuals and businesses could now access information with the click of a button. They also could buy and sell merchandise online as e-commerce became a new type of retailing.

In addition to information technology, the growth of service businesses also changed the way American firms do business in the 21st century. Because service businesses employ over 80 percent of the nation's workforce, we now have a service economy.[13] A **service economy** is an economy in which more effort is devoted to the production of services than to the production of goods. Typical service businesses include restaurants, dry cleaners, real estate, movie theaters, repair companies, and other services.

On the negative side, it is hard to watch television, surf the Web, listen to the radio, or read the newspaper without hearing news about the economy, social and political unrest in the world, and lingering health and economic problems caused by the COVID-19 pandemic. Because many economic indicators suggest that either current or future problems could affect the nation's economy, there is still a certain amount of pessimism surrounding the nation's economy and the global economy. In addition, there are other concerns including social unrest; political uncertainty on the national, state, and local levels; global terrorism; and the threat of wars around the globe.

当前的商业环境
1-7d The Current Business Environment

Before reading on, answer the following question:

In today's competitive business world, which of the following environments affects business?

a. The competitive environment
b. The global environment
c. The technological environment
d. The economic environment
e. All of the above

Correct Answer: e. All the environments listed in the above question affect business today.

The Competitive Environment As noted earlier in this chapter, competition is a basic component of capitalism. Every day, business owners must figure out what makes their businesses successful and how the goods and services they provide are different from the competition. Often, the answer is contained in the basic definition of business provided on page 9. Just for a moment, review the definition:

Business is the organized effort of individuals to produce and sell, for a profit, the goods and services that satisfy society's needs.

In the definition of business, note the phrase *satisfy society's needs*. These three words say a lot about how well a successful firm competes with competitors. If you meet customer needs, then you have a better chance at success.

The Global Environment Related to the competitive environment is the global environment. Not only do American businesses have to compete with other American businesses, but they also must compete with businesses from all over the globe.

服务经济
service economy an economy in which more effort is devoted to the production of services than to the production of goods

Technology, technology, and more technology! What would happen if you didn't have your cell phone or if you couldn't use a computer for the next 24 hours? For many people, it would be catastrophic. For businesses, it would be just as bad. Many businesses rely on technology to operate. Without technology to process customer payments, track inventory, maintain accounting records, and other critical business activities, it would be impossible to function. For many businesses, it could mean they might have to "close the doors" until their technology was restored.

Firms in other countries including China, Japan, India, Germany, Vietnam, and most of the remaining European and Asian countries around the world also compete with U.S. firms. There was once a time when the label "Made in the United States" gave U.S. businesses an inside edge both at home and in the global marketplace. Today, because business firms in other countries manufacture and sell goods, the global marketplace has never been more competitive.

While many foreign firms are attempting to sell goods and services to U.S. customers, U.S. firms are also increasing both sales and profits by selling goods and services to customers in other countries. In fact, there are many "potential" customers in developing nations that will buy goods and services manufactured by U.S. firms. For example, Procter & Gamble sells laundry detergent, soap, health and grooming products, and baby products in Asia, Europe, India, the Middle East, Africa, Latin America, and North America. And Procter & Gamble is not alone. Unilever, DuPont, Johnson & Johnson, General Motors, and many more U.S. companies are also selling goods and services to customers in countries all over the globe.

The Technological Environment The technological environment for U.S. businesses has never been more challenging. Changes in communication with customers, manufacturing equipment, and distribution of products are all examples of how technology has changed everyday business practices. For example, many businesses are now using social media to provide customers with information about products and services. For our purposes **social media** is defined as online interaction that allows people and businesses to communicate and share ideas, personal information, and information about products or services. Because of rapid developments in social media and the increased importance of technology and information, businesses will need to spend additional money to keep abreast of an ever-changing technological environment and even more money to train employees to use the new technology.

New and creative ways to use technology are also changing the way that products are now manufactured and distributed to customers. Today, many manufacturers are using sophisticated automated equipment to improve employee productivity,

社交媒体
social media the online interaction that allows people and businesses to communicate and share ideas, personal information, and information about products or services

Technology and Innovation

技术与创新：当今最大的技术趋势

Today's Biggest Tech Trends

The technological environment is ever-changing, and it's critical for businesses to keep pace or risk being left behind. The biggest trends in today's tech world include artificial intelligence, blockchain technology, and extended reality.

Artificial intelligence (AI) involves computers performing tasks that traditionally require human intelligence. Since programming an AI-based system is cost-prohibitive for most organizations, many professionals will interact with the technology through available platforms, such as e-mail marketing software. Additionally, automation in manufacturing and supply chains is greatly improving with the use of AI and robotics. With the number of AI providers growing, adoption of the technology will continue to increase for years to come.

Blockchain, a secure digital ledger, has many applications, from supply chain management to cryptocurrency. The hype around blockchain has been around for years, but now there is an emerging shared belief that blockchain technology will become a top strategic priority for many businesses and organizations. Popular uses for the technology include recording transactions, data validation, data access, data sharing, and identity protection.

Extended reality (XR) encompasses technologies that create an immersive or all-in experience, namely virtual reality (VR) and augmented reality (AR). Many consumers have interacted with VR and AR in the form of video games and smartphone features such as VR headsets or social media apps, but XR has even more unlocked potential. Businesses that get a better handle on XR will discover new methods of customer engagement.

AI, blockchain, and XR are just a few of the technologies shaking up the world of business. Keeping up with key trends and investing in new technologies that add value to the business will help organizations stay ahead of the curve. Knowledge and experience about emerging technologies will also help workers and job seekers advance their careers.

Sources: Based on information in Deloitte, "C-Suite Briefing: 5 Blockchain Trends for 2020," March 2020; Bernard Marr, "The 7 Biggest Technology Trends in 2020 Everyone Must Get Ready for Now," *Forbes*, September 30, 2019; Anis Uzzaman, "Top Business and Technology Trends in 2021," *Inc.*, December 15, 2020.

---

increase product quality, and lower expenses. Technology has also changed the way customers purchase products and the way those products are delivered. For example, if you purchase merchandise on Amazon's e-commerce website, you don't necessarily wait days to receive your merchandise. Depending on your location and if the merchandise is available, your purchase could be delivered the same day. While this type of technology-driven delivery system is expensive, it is one reason why Amazon has grown to be one of the largest retailers in the world.

The Economic Environment The economic environment must always be considered when making business decisions. This fact is especially important when the nation's economy takes a nosedive or an individual firm's sales revenues and profits are declining. Consider what happened when non-essential businesses were ordered to close in many states because of the COVID-19 pandemic. Both small and large non-essential businesses had no sales revenues and had to use cash reserves to pay expenses. In many cases employees were placed on leave or lost their jobs. As businesses began to reopen, customers began to buy products and services, and businesses brought back furloughed employees or hired new employees.

In addition to economic pressures, today's socially responsible managers and business owners must be concerned about the concept of sustainability. According to the U.S. Environmental Protection Agency, **sustainability** is the ability to create and maintain conditions under which present and future generations can

可持续性
sustainability the ability to create and maintain conditions under which present and future generations can exist in productive harmony, and permit fulfilling the social, economic, and other requirements of future and present generations

30 Marketing

exist in productive harmony, and permit fulfilling the social, economic, and other requirements of future and present generations.[14] Although the word *green* used to mean a color in a box of crayons, today green means a new way of doing business. As a result, a combination of forces, including economic factors, growth in population, increased energy use, and concerns for the environment, is changing the way individuals live and businesses operate.

When you look back at the original question we asked at the beginning of this section, clearly, each different type of environment—competitive, global, technological, and economic—affects the way a business does *business*. As a result, there are always opportunities for improvement and challenges that must be considered.

未来面临的挑战
1-7e The Challenges Ahead

There it is—the American business system in brief.

When it works well, it provides a standard of living that few countries can match and many opportunities for personal advancement for those willing to work hard and continue to learn. However, like every other system devised by humans, it is not perfect. Our capitalist economic system may give us prosperity, but it also gave us the Great Depression of the 1930s, the economic problems of the 1970s and the early 1980s, and a volatile stock market, high unemployment, and business failures caused by the COVID-19 pandemic.

Obviously, the system can be improved. Certainly, there are plenty of people who are willing to tell us exactly what they think the American economy needs. However, these people often provide us only with conflicting opinions. Who is right and who is wrong? Even the experts cannot agree.

The experts do agree, however, that several key issues will challenge our economic system (and our nation) over the next decade. Some of the questions to be resolved include:

- How can we deal with social unrest, discrimination, and inequality in society?
- How can we create a more stable economy and create new, quality jobs for the unemployed?
- How can we reduce the number of low-income workers and increase the number of middle- and higher-income workers?
- How can we use research and technology to make American workers more productive and American firms more competitive in the global marketplace?
- How can we preserve the benefits of competition and small business in our American economic system?
- How do we reduce the national debt and stimulate business growth?
- How can we conserve natural resources and sustain our environment?
- How can we meet the needs of low-income families, single parents, older Americans, and the less fortunate who need healthcare and social programs to exist?

The answers to these questions are anything but simple. While there have been (and always will be) challenges for a nation like the United States, Americans have always been able to solve many of their problems through ingenuity and creativity. Now, as we continue the journey through the 21st century, we need that same ingenuity and creativity not only to solve our current problems but also to compete in the global marketplace and build a nation and economy for future generations.

The American business system is not perfect by any means, but it does work reasonably well. We discuss some of its problems in Chapter 2 as we examine the topics of social responsibility and business ethics.

✓ Concept Check

▶ How does your standard of living affect the products or services you buy?

▶ What is the difference between the domestic system and the factory system?

▶ Choose one of the environments that affect business or society and explain how it affects a small electronics manufacturer located in Portland, Oregon.

▶ What do you consider the most important challenge that will face people in the United States in the years ahead?

Summary 小 结

1-1 Discuss what you must do to be successful in today's business world.

When faced with the COVID-19 pandemic that raced through the world, small business owners, employees, managers, investors, and a large number of people began to ask the question: What effect will non-essential business closures and record high unemployment rates have on the economy? More specifically, many people asked, how does this affect me both now and in the future? Although this is a fair question, it is difficult to answer. Certainly, for a college student taking business courses or an employee just starting a career, the question is even more difficult to answer. And yet there are still opportunities out there for people who are willing to work hard, continue to learn, and possess the ability to adapt to change. By studying business, you can become a better employee or manager or you may decide to start your own business. You can also become a better consumer and investor.

1-2 Identify the potential risks and rewards of business.

Business is the organized effort of individuals to produce and sell, for a profit, the goods and services that satisfy society's needs. Four kinds of resources— material, human, financial, and informational—must be combined to start and operate a business. The three general types of businesses are service businesses, manufacturers, and marketing intermediaries. Today, marketing intermediaries sell goods and services in brick-and-mortar stores, online, or both. Profit is what remains after all business expenses are deducted from sales revenue. It is the payment that owners receive for assuming the risks of business—primarily the risks of not receiving payment and of losing whatever has been invested in the firm. Although many people believe that profit is literally the bottom line or most important goal for a business, the ultimate objective of a successful business is to satisfy the needs of its customers. In addition to profit, many corporations are careful to point out their efforts to sustain the planet, participate in the green ecological movement, and help people to live better lives.

1-3 Describe the two types of economic systems: capitalism and command economy.

Economics is the study of how wealth is created and distributed. An economic system must answer four questions: *What* goods and services will be produced? *How* will they be produced? *For whom* will they be produced? And *Who* owns and who controls the major factors of production? The factors of production are land and natural resources, labor, capital, and entrepreneurship. Capitalism (on which our economic system is based) is an economic system in which individuals own and operate the majority of businesses that provide goods and services. Capitalism stems from the theories of Adam Smith. Smith's pure laissez-faire capitalism is an economic system based on the assumptions described in Figure 1-4.

Our economic system today is a mixed economy and exhibits elements of both capitalism and socialism. In the circular flow that characterizes our business system (refer to Figure 1-5), households and businesses exchange resources, labor, and capital for goods and services, using money as the medium of exchange. In a similar manner, the government collects taxes from businesses and households and purchases products and resources with which to provide services.

In a command economy, government, rather than individuals, owns many of the factors of production and provides the answers to the three other economic questions. Socialist and communist economies are—at least in theory— command economies.

1-4 Identify the ways to measure economic performance.

One way to evaluate the performance of an economic system is to assess changes in productivity, which is the average level of output per worker per hour. Gross domestic product (GDP) can also be used to measure a nation's economic health and is the total dollar value of all goods and services produced by all people within the boundaries of a country during a one-year period. It is also possible to adjust GDP for inflation and thus to measure real GDP. Other economic indicators include a nation's balance of trade, consumer confidence index, consumer price index (CPI), corporate profits, inflation rate, national income, new housing starts, prime interest rate, producer price index (PPI), and unemployment rate.

1-5 Examine the different phases in the typical business cycle.

A nation's economy fluctuates rather than grows at a steady pace every year. These fluctuations are generally referred to as the business cycle. Generally, the business cycle consists of four states: the peak (sometimes called prosperity), recession, the trough, and recovery (sometimes called expansion). Some experts believe that effective use of monetary policy (the Federal Reserve's decisions to promote maximum employment, stabilize prices, and increase or decrease interest rates) and fiscal policy (the government's influence on the amount of savings and expenditures) can speed up recovery.

A federal deficit occurs when the government spends more than it receives in taxes and other revenues. At the time of publication, the national debt is over $27 trillion or approximately $83,000 for every man, woman, and child in the United States.

1-6 Outline the four types of competition.

Competition is essentially a rivalry among businesses for sales to potential customers. In a capitalist economy, competition works to ensure the efficient and effective operation of business. Competition also ensures that a firm will survive only if it serves its customers well by providing goods and services that meet their needs. Economists recognize four degrees of competition. Ranging from most to least competitive, the four degrees are perfect competition, monopolistic competition, oligopoly, and monopoly. The factors of supply and demand generally influence the price that customers pay producers for goods and services.

1-7 Summarize the development of American business and the challenges that businesses and society will encounter in the future.

To understand the major events that shaped the United States, it helps to remember that the economy was compared to a roller-coaster ride earlier in this chapter—periods of economic growth followed by periods of economic slowdown. Events and a changing business environment including the Great Depression, government involvement in business, wars, rapid economic growth, the social responsibility movement, a shortage of crude oil, high inflation, high interest rates, reduced business profits, increased use of technology, and social media all have shaped business and the economy.

Now more than ever before, the way a business operates is affected by the competitive environment, global environment, technological environment, and economic environment. As a result, business has a number of opportunities for improvement and challenges for the future.

Key Terms   关键术语

You should now be able to define and give an example relevant to each of the following terms:

- free enterprise
- cultural (or workplace) diversity
- business
- e-business
- profit
- stakeholders
- economics
- microeconomics
- macroeconomics
- economy
- factors of production
- entrepreneur
- capitalism
- invisible hand
- market economy
- mixed economy
- consumer products
- command economy
- productivity
- gross domestic product (GDP)
- inflation
- deflation
- unemployment rate
- consumer price index (CPI)
- producer price index (PPI)
- business cycle
- recession
- depression
- monetary policies
- fiscal policy
- federal deficit
- national debt
- competition
- perfect (or pure) competition
- supply
- demand
- market price
- monopolistic competition
- product differentiation
- oligopoly
- monopoly
- standard of living
- domestic system
- factory system
- specialization
- service economy
- social media
- sustainability

Discussion Questions   讨论题

1. What factors caused American business to develop into a mixed economic system rather than some other type of economic system?

2. Does an individual consumer really have a voice in answering the four basic economic questions described on page 14?

3. Is gross domestic product a reliable indicator of a nation's economic health? What might be a better indicator?

4. Discuss this statement: "Business competition encourages improved product quality and increased customer satisfaction."

5. Is government participation in our business system good or bad? What factors can be used to explain your position.

6. Choose one of the challenges listed on page 31 and describe possible ways in which business and society could help to solve or eliminate the problem in the future.

Case 1

案例 1：Zoom 成功的关键

The Keys to Zoom's Success

Zoom—a video conference technology company based in San Jose, California—not only broke into a highly competitive industry, but it also became an industry leader. Zoom's success can be attributed to good leadership, a growing market, a customer orientation, accessibility, and the ability to secure funding.

Eric Yuan is the CEO and founder of Zoom. He got the idea for the company when he was in college in the 1980s and regularly took a 10-hour train ride to visit his then-girlfriend. He knew there had to be an easier way to see her. At the time, video communication was a distant dream as widespread consumer internet use was still years away. After relocating from China to the United States in 1997, Yuan landed a software developer job at Webex, an online communications company, in the midst of the so-called dot-com boom. The dot-com era was marked by a period of rapid growth in internet use. While excessive investor speculation of internet firms caused a stock market bubble that would eventually burst, Webex remained strong. When Cisco acquired Webex in 2007 for $3.2 billion, Yuan became the vice president of engineering, overseeing more than 800 employees. Yuan, however, wasn't happy with the company's online service, which often cut in and out and lacked various modern features. His calls to update the platform were ignored, so he left in 2011 to build a cloud-based video-conferencing tool of the future that prioritized customers and their needs.

Zoom, founded in 2011, entered the video communications market at a time when consumer and business demand for video conference products was increasing. It was around the same time that Apple introduced FaceTime and Skype was acquired by Microsoft for $8.5 billion. Almost a decade later when the COVID-19 pandemic struck, the demand for Zoom's products accelerated as the need to communicate from a distance became more prevalent than ever.

Yuan decided that his company's vision would be "video is the new voice" and its goal would be to deliver happiness. It's this customer orientation that has contributed to Zoom's success. From Yuan's experience at his previous company, he knew consistent and quality video connections should be a priority. To add to that, Zoom offers 24/7 customer service, which Yuan would often take part in during Zoom's early years. Yuan would reach out to any individual who canceled their service. This focus on customer service is a large reason behind Zoom's high customer satisfaction ratings.

Another key element in Zoom's success is accessibility. When it launched, Zoom had several competitive advantages. For instance, its software identified the user's device, eliminating the need for multiple versions of the software. Additionally, it had high security protections in place that kept bugs out. But perhaps most important to the customer, Zoom was able to operate on slow internet connections. From the start, Zoom was easy to use, and this holds true today. Case in point, when someone is invited to a Zoom meeting, they need only to click a link to attend. Even if users choose to register for a basic account, it's free to host up to 100 participants with an unlimited number of meetings. Premium features are available on Pro, Business, and Enterprise accounts at competitive rates. This is known as a "freemium" pricing model. By offering free entry-level access, Zoom has opened up its platform to the masses and lowered barriers to product trial.

Many start-ups struggle to find financing. Initial funding for Zoom came from Webex executives who knew Yuan and believed in his ability to build a quality product. Though Zoom didn't see profits for many years, investors kept investing because of the platform's promising future. When Zoom made its initial public offering (IPO) on the Nasdaq stock market, it was already growing and profitable, a rarity for tech companies. With an IPO price of $36 per share, Zoom was valued at $9.2 billion. Now, the video communications company is valued at close to $100 billion.

Yuan's ability to identify a growing market and create a superior product that was easy to use led to Zoom's present-day success. The COVID-19 pandemic only accelerated Zoom's path to the front of the pack. As people worked from home, students attended school online, and friends gathered for virtual happy hours, Zoom emerged as the go-to service. Looking to the future, Zoom is focusing on new products and winning over large clients. Maintaining its customer orientation and continuing to innovate will better prepare Zoom for future growth opportunities and challenges.[15]

Questions

1. What entrepreneurial traits did Eric Yuan—the founder of Zoom—have that enabled him to turn an idea into a very successful company in a very competitive market?
2. One of the benchmarks of a successful business is satisfying the needs of its customers. How is Zoom meeting the needs of its customers?
3. One reason Zoom has been successful is that it is easy to use. What other factors have made Zoom a popular choice for video conferencing?

Building Skills for Career Success　为成功的职业生涯培养技能

1. Social Media Exercise

Today, many companies use Facebook, Twitter, Instagram, and other social media sites in addition to their corporate website. Think of three of your favorite car companies and conduct a quick search using a search engine like Google or Yahoo! Then answer the following:

1. Name the social networks for each company.
2. Compare each of their Facebook pages. How many "likes" does each company have? Are there multiple pages for the company? How much interaction (or engagement) is on each Facebook page?
3. What business goals do you think each company is trying to reach through their Facebook presence?

2. Building Team Skills

Over the past few years, employees have been expected to function as productive team members instead of working alone. People often believe that they can work effectively in teams, but many people find working with a group to be a challenge.

College classes that function as teams are more interesting and more fun to attend, and students generally learn more about the topics in the course. One way to begin creating a team is to learn something about each student in the class. This helps team members to feel comfortable with each other and fosters a sense of trust.

Assignment

1. Find a partner, preferably someone you do not know.
2. Each partner has two to three minutes to answer the following questions:
   a. What is your name, and where do you work?
   b. What interesting or unusual thing have you done in your life? (Do not talk about work or college; rather, focus on such things as hobbies, travel, family, and sports.)
   c. Why are you taking this course, and what do you expect to learn? (Satisfying a degree requirement is not an acceptable answer.)
3. Introduce your partner to the class. Use one to two minutes, depending on the size of the class.

3. Researching Different Careers

In this chapter, *entrepreneurship* is defined as the willingness to take risks and the knowledge and ability to use the other factors of production efficiently. An *entrepreneur* is a person who risks time, effort, and money to start and operate a business. Some people believe that these terms apply only to small businesses. However, employees with entrepreneurial attitudes are often viewed as more valuable and can advance more rapidly in large companies.

Assignment

1. Use the internet or go to the local library and research how large firms, especially large corporations, are rewarding employees who have entrepreneurial skills.
2. Find answers to the following questions:
   a. Why is an entrepreneurial attitude important in large corporations today?
   b. What makes an entrepreneurial employee different from other employees?
   c. How are these employees being rewarded, and are the rewards worth the effort?
3. Write a two-page report that summarizes your findings.

Chapter 2

Ethics and Social Responsibility in Business
商业伦理与社会责任

Why Should You Care?

Business ethics and social responsibility issues have become extremely relevant in today's business world. Business schools teach business ethics to prepare managers to be more responsible. Corporations are developing ethics and social responsibility programs to help meet these needs in the workplace.

Learning Objectives

Once you complete this chapter, you will be able to:

2-1 Define *business ethics*.

2-2 Identify the types of ethical concerns that arise in the business world.

2-3 Discuss the factors that affect the level of ethical behavior in organizations.

2-4 Explain how organizations can encourage ethical decision making in business.

2-5 Describe how our current views on the social responsibility of business have evolved.

2-6 List the responsibilities businesses have to the public, especially with regard to consumer rights and public health.

2-7 Analyze how present employment practices are being used to counteract past abuses.

2-8 Describe the major environmental issues and businesses' response to them.

2-9 Identify the steps a business must take to implement a program of social responsibility.

36

Marketing

Inside Business
商业透视：美国普渡制药的营销策略加剧了阿片类药物危机

Marketing Tactics at Purdue Fueled the Opioid Crisis

The opioid crisis has killed more than 450,000 people in the United States since 1999 largely due to illegal and misleading marketing. Purdue Pharma LP, a privately held pharmaceutical company, reached an $8.34 billion settlement for its marketing and distribution of OxyContin, an addictive painkiller, after years of state and federal investigations. Purdue is not the only company implicated in the crisis. Manufacturer Johnson & Johnson and distributors McKesson, Cardinal Health, and AmerisourceBergen have also faced legal action.

Ethical misconduct at Purdue included illegal kickbacks, funding pain treatment groups, misrepresentations made to the Drug Enforcement Administration (DEA), and marketing messages that minimized the addictive nature of OxyContin. The drugmaker used marketing data to target physicians who were the highest opioid prescribers as well as physicians in states with lighter prescription regulations. After compiling detailed prescriber profiles, Purdue would attempt to influence the physicians' prescribing patterns. In two instances, Purdue paid doctors to influence them to write more opioid prescriptions. Additionally, the company made false claims about the safety of the product.

Purdue's unethical and illegal actions had a direct impact on society, fueling the opioid crisis and a culture of corruption throughout its supply chain. Purdue has since made changes in leadership, operations, governance, and oversight to keep the company in compliance with the law. Purdue's owners, the Sackler family, created an image of philanthropy and avoided being publicly tied to the opioid crisis. Now, many prominent institutions will no longer accept donations from the family. However, neither the Sackler family nor top Purdue executives will face prison time as a result of the settlement.[1]

Did you know?
Purdue Pharma's corporate values are integrity, courage, innovation, and collaboration.

Obviously, organizations want to be seen as responsible corporate citizens and recognize the need to harmonize their operations with environmental demands and other social concerns. However, as shown in the opening vignette, not all firms have adopted a mindset that includes social responsibility and ethics in their strategies, decisions, and activities. Some managers still regard such business programs as a poor investment, in which the cost is not worth the return. Other managers—indeed, most managers—view the cost of these programs as a necessary business expense, similar to wages or rent.

Most managers today are finding ways to balance an agenda of socially responsible activities with the drive to generate profits. This also happens to be a good way for organizations to demonstrate their values and to attract like-minded employees, customers, and shareholders. In a highly competitive global business environment, an increasing number of companies are seeking to set themselves apart by developing a reputation for ethical and socially responsible behavior.

We begin this chapter by defining *business ethics* and examining ethical issues. Next, we look at the standards of behavior in organizations and how ethical behavior can be encouraged. We then turn to the topic of social responsibility. We explore the evolution of the idea of social responsibility, compare and contrast two present-day models of social responsibility, and present arguments for and against increasing the social responsibility of business. We then explore business responsibilities toward the public. Next, we discuss how social responsibility in business has affected employment practices and environmental concerns. Finally, we consider the commitment and planning that go into a firm's program of social responsibility.

Learning Objective
2-1 Define *business ethics*.

Concept Check
▶ What is meant by business ethics?
▶ How do business ethics differ from personal ethics?

Learning Objective
2-2 Identify the types of ethical concerns that arise in the business world.

伦理
ethics the study of right and wrong and of the morality of the choices individuals make

商业伦理
business ethics the application of moral standards to business situations

商业伦理的定义
2-1 Business Ethics Defined

Ethics is the study of right and wrong and of the morality of the choices individuals make. An ethical decision or action is one that is "right" according to some standard of behavior. When there is strong consensus regarding a particular unethical action, society may demand laws to prohibit it. **Business ethics** is the application of moral standards to business situations. Recent court cases involving unethical behavior have helped make business ethics a matter of public concern. In one such case, concert promoter Billy McFarland was convicted of fraud, sentenced to six years in prison, and ordered to pay millions in restitution for bilking concert goers and investors of the Fyre Festival. Concert goers, who had paid as much as $100,000 to attend, were led to expect to hobnob with celebrities and models while enjoying lavish accommodations and popular bands, but found nothing of the kind when they arrived. McFarland also faces numerous lawsuits related to the ill-fated festival, and several celebrities who endorsed it on social media were fined.[2] While all unethical business actions do not result in fines and jail time, they do harm others by eroding trust in business decisions and decision makers. Regardless of their legality, all business decisions can be judged as right or wrong.

商业中的伦理问题
2-2 Ethical Issues in Business

Ethical issues often arise out of a business's relationships with investors, customers, employees, creditors, suppliers, or competitors. Each of these stakeholder groups has specific concerns and usually exerts pressure on the organization's managers. Investors, for example, want management to make sensible financial decisions that will boost sales, profits, and returns on their investments. Customers expect a firm's products to be safe, reliable, and reasonably priced. Employees demand to be treated fairly in hiring, promotion, and compensation decisions. Creditors require accounts to be paid on time and the accounting information furnished by the firm to be accurate. Competitors expect the firm's competitive practices to be fair and honest. Chick-fil-A, for example, sued 17 chicken suppliers, including Tyson Foods, Perdue Farms, and Pilgrim's Pride, accusing them of price-fixing—colluding to keep the prices it pays for poultry artificially high. The fast-food restaurant chain contends that the suppliers engaged in anticompetitive behavior by conspiring to share confidential bidding and pricing information in order to sustain higher chicken prices, resulting in consumers paying more for inferior chicken. A court will have to resolve the dispute.[3]

Businesspeople face ethical issues every day, and some of these issues can be difficult to assess. Although some types of issues arise infrequently, others occur regularly. Let's take a closer look at several ethical issues.

公平和诚实
2-2a Fairness and Honesty

Fairness and honesty in business are two important ethical concerns. Besides obeying all laws and regulations, businesspeople are expected to refrain from knowingly deceiving, misrepresenting, or intimidating others. The consequences of failing to do so can be expensive. For example, NeuroMetrix, Inc., paid more than $4 million to settle Federal Trade Commission (FTC) charges that it deceptively promoted its Quell electrical nerve stimulation device. The commission claimed the company misled customers when it falsely touted the device as "clinically proven" and "Food and Drug Administration (FDA) cleared" for treating pain, when it was neither. In addition to the fine, the company and its marketers were ordered not to make any further false or misleading claims about the product.[4]

38 Marketing

If consumers feel they have been deceived or that companies have been unfair, they will take their business elsewhere and may even ask regulators to intervene. For instance, the Securities and Exchange Commission (SEC) charged the stock-trading app Robinhood with giving customers misleading information about the actual costs of trading with the app and failing to obtain the best reasonably available terms to execute their orders. The SEC blamed the app for depriving customers of $34 million in total. Robinhood paid $65 million to settle the case and updated its procedures to ensure that it executes the best trades possible for its users.[5]

组织关系
2-2b Organizational Relationships

Businesspeople may be tempted to place their personal welfare above the welfare of others or the welfare of the organization. As an example, Kristin M. Lapree was convicted of misappropriating more than $700,000 of funds while she worked as the business manager of Wisconsin-based Rettler Corporation. She was sentenced to six years in prison and ordered to pay restitution.[6] Aside from the legality of such actions, they may threaten the livelihood of employees and the business itself and harm relations with customers, suppliers, and others.

Relationships among co-workers often create ethical problems. Unethical behavior in these areas includes taking credit for others' ideas or work, not meeting one's commitments in a mutual agreement, and pressuring others to behave unethically. Managers and executives have even more power to pressure others due to their ability to provide rewards and sanctions. Consider Wells Fargo, which suffered incalculable damage to its reputation after investigators revealed that managers had pressured employees to achieve unrealistic sales quotas, which led many bank employees to open fake accounts for customers without their knowledge. The company ultimately paid billions of dollars to settle criminal and civil charges; several of its executives also face charges as a result of the scandal.[7] The Global Business Ethics Survey reported that 22 percent of workers around the world say

Ethics violations Ethics violations can be more than humiliating. Ethics violators sometimes go to prison, pay large fines, lose their jobs, lose their families, and pay expensive legal fees.

Chapter 2   Ethics and Social Responsibility in Business

they feel pressured to compromise their organization's ethics guidelines and policies, or to break the law; in North America, that value is 31 percent.[8]

One issue related to fairness and honesty is **plagiarism**—knowingly taking someone else's words, ideas, or other original material without acknowledging the source. When exposed, the consequences of plagiarism can be grave. For example, the U.S. Army War College rescinded the master's degree that it had awarded U.S. Senator John Walsh after an academic review by the college determined that Walsh had copied significant parts of his final paper from other sources. Walsh withdrew from his reelection campaign soon after the scandal.[9]

When misconduct occurs in business, investors also suffer. Investors and owners must be able to trust that companies are acting in their best interests and reporting their activities truthfully. They have the right to expect that all actions by a firm contribute toward a return on their investment. Two issues that raise flags for investors are executive compensation packages that are out of line with performance and the conflict of interest that may occur when a chief executive officer also sits on the board of directors—the group that oversees the CEO. In recent years, investors have protested high executive compensation, particularly when those executives do not generate strong profits for the owners. Shareholders have voted against executive compensation packages at a number of companies, including Electronic Arts, Ameriprise, Disney, and more.[10] Activist investors have also protested companies whose CEOs also sit on the board of directors, which can result in a conflict of interest when the CEO's performance is under review.

利益冲突
2-2c Conflicts of Interest

A **conflict of interest** results when businesspeople take advantage of a situation for their own personal interest rather than for the employer's interest. Examples of situations involving conflicts of interest generally involve an employee who has divided loyalties, such as a manager who is dating a subordinate, an employee with a close relative who works for a competitor, a purchasing manager who chooses to do business with another firm in which he is an investor, or a firm that advises clients without informing them that it has a relationship with some of the products it recommends. Even the appearance of a conflict of interest can jeopardize a businessperson's credibility. As an example, Louis DeJoy came under fire for failing to divest his ownership shares of XPO Logistics—where he previously served as CEO and chairman—when he was appointed Postmaster General by then President Donald Trump. His continued equity stake in XPO, a transportation and logistics firm that has million-dollar contracts with the U.S. Postal Service, created a conflict of interest for him when making shipping decisions for the federal agency. After the backlash, DeJoy agreed to sell his XPO stock.[11] In such cases, consumers and taxpayers have the right to know whether the head of a major government agency may be favoring certain contractors over others in order to benefit financially.

Conflicts of interest may occur when payments and gifts make their way into business deals. Although bribes—gifts, favors, or payments offered with the intent of influencing an outcome—are often part of business negotiations overseas, it is illegal for American businesspersons and companies to use bribes in the United States or abroad. Defending against bribery charges can be costly and affect future business negotiations. A wise rule to remember is that anything given to a person that might unfairly influence that person's business decision is a bribe, and all bribes are unethical.

剽窃
plagiarism knowingly taking someone else's words, ideas, or other original material without acknowledging the source

利益冲突
conflict of interest when businesspeople take advantage of a situation for their own personal interest rather than for the employer's interest

At Procter & Gamble (P&G), all employees are obligated to act solely in the best interests of the company. P&G defines a conflict of interest as when an employee has a personal relationship or financial or other interest that could interfere with this obligation, or when employees use their position with the company for personal gain. The company requires employees to disclose all potential conflicts of interest and to take prompt actions to eliminate a conflict when the company asks them to do so. Generally, P&G prohibits employees from receiving gifts, entertainment, or other gratuities from people with whom the company does business because doing so could imply an obligation on the part of the company and potentially pose a conflict of interest.[12]

沟通
2-2d Communications

Business communications, especially advertising, can present ethical questions. False and misleading advertising is illegal and unethical, and it can infuriate customers. For example, angry consumers filed suit against the Folger Coffee Company, arguing that 30.5 ounce canisters of Folgers ground coffee claim to contain enough to make 240 servings, but actually hold just 173 servings when prepared according to the instructions on the canister. Disgruntled consumers have filed similar lawsuits against other coffee makers.[13] In another example, the Federal Trade Commission fined Williams-Sonoma $1 million and ordered the retailer to stop claiming that some products sold in Williams-Sonoma and Pottery Barn stores are "Made in USA," when they contained significant imported components.[14] Sponsors of advertisements aimed at children must be especially careful to avoid misleading messages. Advertisers of health-related products also must take precautions to guard against deception when using such descriptive terms as *low fat, fat free,* and *light.* In fact, the Federal Trade Commission has issued guidelines on the use of these labels.

✓ Concept Check

▶ What are the different types of ethical concerns that may arise in the business world?

▶ Explain and give an example of how advertising can present ethical questions.

Entrepreneurial Success

创业成功：与社交媒体建立健康的关系

Building a Healthy Relationship with Social Media

Social media has long been criticized for its negative impact on society. For example, algorithms are often designed to manipulate users to stay on social networks as long as possible. It has also had immeasurable implications for data privacy. But despite these downfalls, social media still holds value for entrepreneurs as a source of inspiration, tools, insights, and community. With just a few simple changes, entrepreneurs can build a healthier relationship with social media.

For startups, establishing a brand on social media is critical, and an opportunity exists for creative, thoughtful engagement. However, it's important to be in control of your tech environment. Many apps allow users to reduce their screen time. A tool called Mailbrew rounds up social feeds and email newsletters into a single daily digest, and an app called Freedom blocks distracting apps on desktop and mobile devices to help users be more productive. Utilizing such resources can help you become the master of your devices.

Entrepreneurs can also set a positive example for their team members by promoting work-life balance and setting clear parameters for "on" and "off" times. Many entrepreneurs work around the clock, so it can be challenging to step away from the laptop and call it a day. But, by protecting off hours, entrepreneurs can cultivate a more productive work environment. In the end, unplugging can be positive for mental health and help people replenish their energy.

It's up to the next generation of business owners to disrupt the social media cycle. Rather than calling it quits, entrepreneurs can redefine their connection with their devices and build a healthier relationship with social media.

Sources: Based on information in Aytekin Tank, "How Entrepreneurs Can Harness The Power of Social Media for Good," *Entrepreneur*, October 22, 2020; Adi Robertson, "Telling People to Delete Facebook Won't Fix the Internet," *The Verge*, September 4, 2020.

Chapter 2 Ethics and Social Responsibility in Business

2-3 Factors Affecting Ethical Behavior

Learning Objective
2-3 Discuss the factors that affect the level of ethical behavior in organizations.

Is it possible for an individual with strong moral values to make ethically questionable decisions in a business setting? What factors affect a person's inclination to make either ethical or unethical decisions in a business organization? Although the answers to these questions are not entirely clear, three general sets of factors do appear to influence the standards of behavior in an organization.[15] As shown in Figure 2-1, these include individual factors, social factors, and opportunities.

2-3a Individual Factors Affecting Ethics

Several factors influence an individual's ethical choices and behavior in an organization, including personal knowledge, values, and goals. How much an individual knows about an issue is one factor. A decision maker with a greater amount of knowledge regarding a situation may take steps to avoid ethical problems, whereas a less-informed person may unknowingly make choices that could lead to ethical problems. Individuals' moral values and central, value-related attitudes also clearly influence their business behavior and choices. Most organizations do not try to change an employee's personal ethics but instead strive to hire people with good character and values that complement their own. The actions of specific individuals in scandal-plagued companies, such as Wells Fargo, Volkswagen, Theranos, Turing Pharmaceuticals, and Enron, often raise questions about individuals' personal character and integrity. Finally, most people join organizations to accomplish personal goals. The types of personal goals an individual aspires to and how they choose to pursue them have a significant impact on that individual's behavior in an organization.

2-3b Social Factors Affecting Ethics

Many social factors can affect ethical behavior within a firm, including cultural norms, actions and decisions of co-workers, values and attitudes of "significant others," and the use of the internet. A person's behavior in the workplace, to some degree, is determined by cultural norms, and these social factors vary from one culture to another. For example, in some countries it is acceptable and ethical for customs agents to receive gratuities for performing ordinary, legal tasks that are a part of their jobs, whereas in other countries these practices would be viewed as unethical and perhaps illegal. The actions and decisions of co-workers may also shape a person's sense of business ethics. For example, if your co-workers peruse YouTube and Instagram on company time and at company expense, you might come to view that behavior as acceptable and ethical because everyone does it. The moral values and attitudes of "significant others"—spouses, friends, and relatives,

> **Figure 2-1** Factors That Affect the Level of Ethical Behavior in an Organization

LEVEL OF ETHICAL BEHAVIOR
- Individual factors
- Social factors
- Opportunity

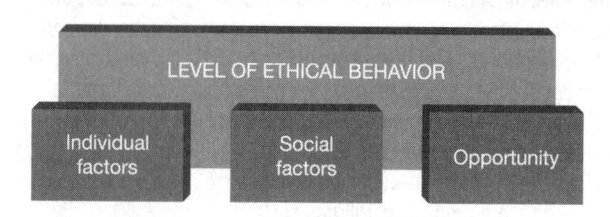

Source: Based on O. C. Ferrell and Larry Gresham, "A Contingency Framework for Understanding Ethical Decision Making in Marketing," *Journal of Marketing* (Summer 1985), 89.

for instance—also can affect an employee's perception of what is ethical and unethical behavior in the workplace.

The internet also presents challenges for firms whose employees enjoy easy access through convenient high-speed connections at work. An employee's behavior online can be viewed as offensive to co-workers and possibly lead to lawsuits against the firm if employees engage in unethical behavior on controversial websites not related to their job. Moreover, if an employee posts controversial content on social media using their employer's email, Instagram, or Twitter account, that content may run counter to the company's core values and reflect negatively on the company. Interestingly, one recent survey of employees found that most workers assume that their use of technology at work will be monitored. A large majority of employees approved of most monitoring methods such as monitoring faxes and email, tracking Web use, and even recording telephone calls.

机会是影响伦理的因素
2-3c Opportunity as a Factor Affecting Ethics

Several factors related to opportunity affect ethics in an organization. *Opportunity* refers to the amount of freedom an organization affords an employee to behave unethically if he or she makes that choice. If the employee is rewarded in some way for an unethical choice—receiving praise or a bonus, for example—or fails to suffer any kind of consequence, he or she is more likely to make that same choice in the future. In some organizations, certain company policies and procedures reduce the opportunity to be unethical. For example, at some fast-food restaurants, one employee takes your order and receives your payment, and another fills the order. This procedure reduces the opportunity to be unethical because the person handling the money is not dispensing the product, and the person giving out the product is not handling the money.

The existence of codes of ethics and other policies on ethics, as well as the importance management places on these policies are other elements of opportunity (codes of ethics are discussed in more detail in the next section). The degree of enforcement of company policies, procedures, and ethical codes is a major force affecting opportunity. When employees see that violations are dealt with consistently and firmly, they are less likely to act unethically knowing that doing so will bring repercussions.

Now that we have considered some of the factors believed to influence the level of ethical behavior in the workplace, let us explore what can be done to encourage ethical behavior and to discourage unethical behavior.

鼓励符合伦理的行为
2-4 Encouraging Ethical Behavior

Most authorities agree that there is room for improvement in business ethics. A more problematic question is: Can business be made more ethical in the real world? The majority opinion on this issue suggests that government, trade associations, and individual firms indeed can promote acceptable levels of ethical behavior.

政府在鼓励伦理行为方面的作用
2-4a Government's Role in Encouraging Ethics

The government can encourage ethical behavior in business by enacting more stringent regulations and laws. One example is the landmark **Sarbanes-Oxley Act of 2002**, which provides sweeping legal protection for those who report corporate misconduct. Among other things, the law deals with corporate responsibility,

> **Concept Check**
> - Describe several individual factors that influence the level of ethical behavior in an organization.
> - Explain several social factors that affect ethics in an organization.
> - How does opportunity influence the level of ethical behavior in the workplace?

Learning Objective
2-4 Explain how organizations can encourage ethical decision making in business.

2002 年萨班斯－奥克斯利法案
Sarbanes-Oxley Act of 2002 provides sweeping legal protection for employees who report corporate misconduct

Chapter 2 Ethics and Social Responsibility in Business

Sarbanes-Oxley Act The Sarbanes-Oxley Act of 2002 includes tough provisions to deter and punish corporate and accounting fraud and corruption. The legislation passed with unanimous support.

conflicts of interest, and corporate accountability. However, rules require enforcement, and the unethical businessperson frequently seems to "slip something by" without getting caught. Increased regulation may help, but it cannot solve the entire ethics problem.

行业协会在鼓励伦理行为方面的作用
2-4b Trade Associations' Role in Encouraging Ethics

Trade associations can and often do provide ethical guidelines for their members. These organizations, which operate within particular industries, are in an excellent position to exert pressure on members to stop engaging in questionable business practices that may harm all firms in the industry. For example, a pharmaceutical trade group adopted a new set of guidelines intended to end the extravagant dinners and expensive gifts sales representatives often give to physicians to persuade them to prescribe a particular medicine. However, enforcement and authority vary from association to association. Because trade associations exist for the benefit of their members, harsh measures may be self-defeating. Trade associations must also ensure that their codes do not contain provisions that may run afoul of antitrust laws.

公司在鼓励伦理行为方面的作用
2-4c Individual Companies' Role in Encouraging Ethics

Enforced codes of ethics are perhaps the most effective way to encourage ethical behavior within organizations. A **code of ethics** is a written guide to acceptable and ethical behavior as defined by an organization; it outlines uniform policies, standards, and punishments for violations. Because a code of ethics informs employees what is expected of them and what will happen if they violate the rules, it can go a long way toward encouraging ethical behavior. However, codes cannot possibly cover every situation. Companies also must create an environment in which employees recognize the importance of complying with the written code. Managers must provide direction by fostering communication, actively modeling and encouraging ethical decision making, and training employees to make ethical decisions. However, codes that are not enforced are likely to be viewed as lip service by employees and other stakeholders. Figure 2-2 offers snippets of some of the guiding principles behind well-known companies' codes of ethics.

伦理准则
code of ethics a guide to acceptable and ethical behavior as defined by the organization

44 Marketing

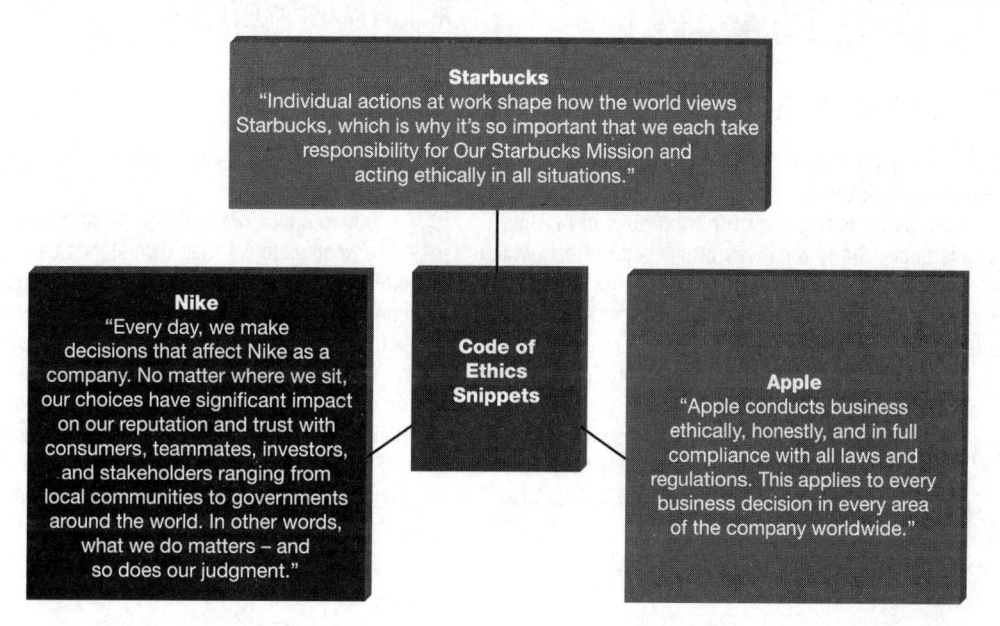

Figure 2-2 Defining Acceptable Behavior at Starbucks, Nike, and Apple

Code of Ethics Snippets

Starbucks
"Individual actions at work shape how the world views Starbucks, which is why it's so important that we each take responsibility for Our Starbucks Mission and acting ethically in all situations."

Nike
"Every day, we make decisions that affect Nike as a company. No matter where we sit, our choices have significant impact on our reputation and trust with consumers, teammates, investors, and stakeholders ranging from local communities to governments around the world. In other words, what we do matters – and so does our judgment."

Apple
"Apple conducts business ethically, honestly, and in full compliance with all laws and regulations. This applies to every business decision in every area of the company worldwide."

Sources: Starbucks, "Business Ethics and Compliance: Standards of Business Conduct"; Nike, "Inside the Lines: The NIKE Code of Ethics"; Apple, "Business Conduct: The Way We Do Business Worldwide".

Beginning in the 1980s, an increasing number of organizations created and implemented ethics codes. Today, about 95 percent of *Fortune* 1000 firms have a formal code of ethics or conduct. For example, the ethics code of Starbucks defines the firm's mission and values and includes provisions relating to policies and procedures; laws and regulations; relationships with customers, suppliers, competitors, and the community; conflicts of interest; handling of proprietary information; and more. Starbucks' code also details how employees can express concerns or find guidance in ambiguous situations and even provides a graphical decision-making framework that employees can apply to difficult decisions.[16]

In the wake of a number of corporate scandals and the Sarbanes-Oxley Act, many large companies now have created a new executive position, the chief ethics (or compliance) officer. Assigning an ethics officer who guides ethical conduct provides employees someone to consult if they are not sure of the right thing to do. An ethics officer meets with employees and top management to provide ethical advice, establishes and maintains an anonymous confidential service to answer questions about ethical issues, and takes action on ethics code violations.

Sometimes even employees who want to act ethically may find it difficult to do so. Unethical practices can become ingrained in an organization. Employees with high personal ethics may then take a controversial step called *whistle-blowing*. **Whistle-blowing** is informing the press or government officials about unethical practices within an organization. Consider Teresa Ross, who brought a lawsuit against Group Health Cooperative (GHC, now Kaiser Foundation Health Plan's Washington subsidiary) under the False Claims Act, which permits whistle-blowers to sue companies they believe have defrauded the government. Ross, who worked as Director of Risk Adjustment Services for the healthcare firm, believed that GHC was defrauding Medicare by inflating or altering patients' diagnoses in order to receive

举报
whistle-blowing informing the press or government officials about unethical practices within one's organization

Chapter 2 Ethics and Social Responsibility in Business

Exploring Careers

职业探索：首席伦理官的兴起

The Rise of the Chief Ethics Officer

With artificial intelligence (AI) applications spreading throughout the business world, executives now rank ethics issues as one of the top risks of AI. Bias, for instance, can find its way into AI algorithms, which can lead to discrimination. This mounting concern has contributed to the rise of the chief ethics officer. Ethics officers are executives who provide oversight to guide the organization through legal and ethical standards.

Though the role does not have a set job description like other C-suite roles, some companies are looking to the chief ethics officer to ensure AI algorithms are fair and unbiased. AI has been integrated into a variety of functions, from recruiting and contact tracing to facial recognition and email marketing. Candidates for the chief ethics officer role may have a background in business law and human resources, though some tech departments are hiring dedicated AI ethics officers.

Due to a lack of regulation for AI development, it's up to companies to set their own standards and policies. The ethics officer can assess risks, create a code of ethics, conduct internal training programs, ensure compliance with regulations, monitor ongoing ethical conduct, and act on violations of the company's ethics code. In addition to AI, other tech issues to consider are privacy, data collection, and security. The chief ethics officer can play a critical part in eliminating bias, guarding against unintended consequences, and holding individuals and organizations accountable.

Sources: Based on information in "Rise of the Chief Ethics Officer," *Forbes*, March 27, 2019; Geoff Nudelman, "20 Minutes With: Hypergiant Industries' Chief Ethics Officer Will Griffin on Diversity and Ethics in Technology," *Barron's*, September 7, 2020; Merve Hickok, "What Does an AI Ethicist Do? A Guide for the Why, the What, and the How," *Medium*, April 27, 2020.

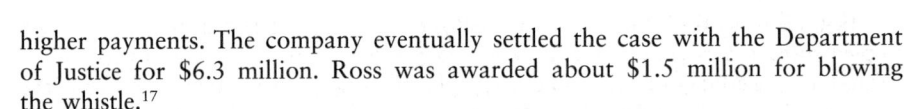

---

higher payments. The company eventually settled the case with the Department of Justice for $6.3 million. Ross was awarded about $1.5 million for blowing the whistle.[17]

Whistle-blowing, however, can have serious repercussions for employees: Those who "blow the whistle" may face retaliation and sometimes even lose their jobs. The Sarbanes-Oxley Act of 2002 protects whistle-blowers who report corporate misconduct. Any executive who retaliates against a whistle-blower can be held criminally liable and imprisoned for up to ten years. Federal employees who report misconduct are likewise protected by the Whistleblower Protection Act of 1989.

When companies set up anonymous hotlines to advise employees who are unsure how to handle ethically questionable situations, employees actually may be more likely to engage in whistle-blowing. When firms instead create an environment that educates employees and nurtures ethical behavior, fewer ethical problems arise. Ultimately, the need for whistle-blowing is greatly reduced.

It is difficult for an organization to develop ethics codes, programs, and procedures to deal with all relationships and every situation. Michael Josephson, an expert on workplace ethics, says, "The objective of such programs is to establish a business culture in which it's easier to do the right thing than the wrong thing, and where concerned co-workers and vigilant supervisors repress illegal or improper conduct that can potentially endanger or embarrass the company."[18] When no company policies or procedures exist or apply, a quick test to determine if a behavior is ethical is to see if others—co-workers, customers, and suppliers—approve of it. Ethical decisions will always withstand scrutiny. Openness and communication about choices will often build trust and strengthen business relationships. Table 2-1 provides some general guidelines for making ethical decisions.

✓ Concept Check

- How can the government encourage the ethical behavior of organizations?
- What is the role of trade associations in encouraging ethics?
- What is whistle-blowing? Who protects the whistle-blowers?

Table 2-1 Guidelines for Making Ethical Decisions

1. Listen and learn	Recognize the problem or decision-making opportunity that confronts your company, team, or unit. Don't argue, criticize, or defend yourself—keep listening and reviewing until you are sure that you understand others.
2. Identify the ethical issues	Examine how co-workers and consumers are affected by the situation or decision at hand. Examine how you feel about the situation, and attempt to understand the viewpoint of those involved in the decision or in the consequences of the decision.
3. Create and analyze options	Try to put aside strong feelings such as anger or a desire for power and prestige and come up with as many alternatives as possible before developing an analysis. Ask everyone involved for ideas about which options offer the best long-term results for you and the company. Then decide which option will increase your self-respect even if, in the long run, things don't work out the way you hope they will.
4. Identify the best option from your point of view	Consider it and test it against some established criteria, such as respect, understanding, caring, fairness, honesty, and openness.
5. Explain your decision and resolve any differences that arise	This may require neutral arbitration from a trusted manager or taking "time out" to reconsider, consult, or exchange written proposals before a decision is reached.

Source: Based on information in Tom Rusk with D. Patrick Miller, "Doing the Right Thing," *Sky* (Delta Airlines), August 1993, 18–22.

社会责任

2-5 Social Responsibility

Social responsibility is the recognition that business activities have an impact on society and the consideration of that impact in business decision making. Alphabet and its subsidiary Google, for example, have pledged to donate $14.5 million to support initiatives to combat racial injustice, inequity, and violence, including grants to the Center for Policing Equity and Equal Justice Initiative.[19] Obviously, social responsibility costs money. It is perhaps not so obvious—except in isolated cases—that social responsibility is also good business. Many companies contribute resources, knowledge, and products as well as money to help neighbors and others during times of crisis. For example, Procter & Gamble's orange Loads of Hope trucks are a welcome sight during disaster relief efforts. Residents in disaster areas can drop off loads of dirty laundry at the mobile laundromats, and volunteers use Tide products and high-efficiency machines to wash, dry, and even fold their clothes. Thus far, the program has helped nearly 48,000 families and brought a sense of normalcy and hope back to survivors so that they can focus on more pressing matters.[20] Efforts like these bring positive associations for brands that can help them stand out in a competitive market. Customers eventually find out which firms act responsibly and which do not. Just as easily as they can purchase a product made by a company that is socially responsible, they can choose against buying from the firm that is not.

Even small businesses can develop social responsibility programs. For example, P. Terry's, which operates 19 fast-food hamburger stands in Central Texas, donates 100 percent of its profits from one day each quarter to a local charity. The company, which has donated more than $1 million to local nonprofits, lets customers know about upcoming charity days through its social media accounts.[21] In general, people are more likely to want to work for and buy from such organizations.

Learning Objective

2-5 Describe how our current views on the social responsibility of business have evolved.

社会责任
social responsibility the recognition that business activities have an impact on society and the consideration of that impact in business decision making

Social responsibility is good business. Natural disasters create opportunities for companies to engage in socially responsible behavior. Procter & Gamble's Loads of Hope program takes in disaster survivors' dirty laundry and returns it to them clean and folded, allowing them to deal with more important problems.

Chapter 2 Ethics and Social Responsibility in Business

Table 2-2 10 Best Corporate Citizens

1. Owens Corning
2. Citi
3. General Mills
4. Cisco
5. HP
6. Intel
7. Ecolab
8. General Motors
9. Hess
10. Accenture

Source: "100 Best Corporate Citizens of 2020," *3BL Media*.

Increasingly, companies large and small are striving to be good corporate citizens. **Corporate citizenship** is adopting a strategic approach to fulfilling economic, ethical, environmental, and social responsibilities. This requires balancing the needs, desires, and demands of a diverse group of stakeholders including investors, employees, customers, regulators, competitors, neighborhoods and communities, and social activists. Consider Chris Kempczinski, president and CEO of McDonald's, who views the company's role in society as going beyond feeding Big Macs to customers: "What we realized is that for 65 years, McDonald's purpose has been to both feed and foster communities. To our franchisees, suppliers and employees, the words 'billions served' aren't just about the burgers and fries we serve, but the tens of thousands of communities around the world that we serve." One way the company does that is through its longtime sponsorship of Ronald McDonald House Charities, which helps support the families of sick and injured children during treatment.[22] Table 2-2 lists the best corporate citizens as evaluated by 3BL Media.

企业社会责任的演变
2-5a The Evolution of Social Responsibility in Business

Business is far from perfect in many respects, but its record of social responsibility today is much better than that in past decades. In fact, present demands for social responsibility have their roots in outraged reactions to the abusive business practices of the early 1900s.

During the first quarter of the 20th century, businesses were free to operate pretty much as they chose. Government protection of workers and consumers was minimal. As a result, people either accepted what business had to offer or they did without. Working conditions often were deplorable by today's standards. The average workweek in most industries exceeded 60 hours, no minimum-wage law existed, and employee benefits were almost nonexistent. Workplaces were crowded and unsafe, and industrial accidents were the rule rather than the exception. To improve working conditions, employees organized and joined labor unions. During the early 1900s, however, businesses—with the help of government—were able to use court orders, brute force, and even the few existing antitrust laws to defeat union attempts to improve working conditions.

During this period, consumers generally were subject to the doctrine of **caveat emptor**, a Latin phrase meaning "let the buyer beware." In other words, "what you see is what you get," and if it is not what you expected, too bad. Although victims of unscrupulous business practices could take legal action, going to court was very expensive, and consumers rarely won their cases. Moreover, no consumer groups or government agencies existed to publicize their consumers' grievances or to hold sellers accountable for their actions.

Before the 1930s, most people believed that competition and the action of the marketplace would, in time, correct abuses. Government, therefore, became involved in day-to-day business activities only in cases of obvious abuse of the free-market system. Six of the most important business-related federal laws passed between 1887 and 1914 are described in Table 2-3. As you can see, these laws were aimed more at encouraging competition than at correcting abuses, although two of them did deal with the purity of food and drug products.

The collapse of the stock market on October 29, 1929, triggered the Great Depression. Factory production fell by almost half, and up to 25 percent of the nation's workforce was unemployed. Public pressure soon mounted for the government to "do something" about the economy and about worsening social conditions. Soon after Franklin D. Roosevelt became president in 1933, he instituted programs to restore the economy and improve social conditions. The government passed laws to correct what many viewed as the monopolistic abuses of big business, and provided various social services for individuals. These massive federal programs became the foundation for increased government involvement in the dealings between business and society.

企业公民
corporate citizenship adopting a strategic approach to fulfilling economic, ethical, environmental, and social responsibilities

买者自慎
caveat emptor a Latin phrase meaning "let the buyer beware"

Marketing

Table 2-3 Early Government Regulations That Affected American Business

Government Regulation	Major Provisions
Interstate Commerce Act (1887)	First federal act to regulate business practices; provided regulation of railroads and shipping rates
Sherman Antitrust Act (1890)	Prevented monopolies or mergers where competition was endangered
Pure Food and Drug Act (1906)	Established limited supervision of interstate sales of food and drugs
Meat Inspection Act (1906)	Provided for limited supervision of interstate sales of meat and meat products
Federal Trade Commission Act (1914)	Created the Federal Trade Commission to investigate illegal trade practices
Clayton Antitrust Act (1914)	Eliminated many forms of price discrimination that gave large businesses a competitive advantage over smaller firms

As government involvement has increased, so has everyone's awareness of the social responsibility of business. Today's business owners are concerned about the return on their investment, but at the same time most of them demand ethical behavior from employees. In addition, employees demand better working conditions, and consumers want safe, reliable products. Various advocacy groups echo these concerns and also call for careful consideration of the Earth's delicate ecological balance. Therefore, managers must operate in a complex business environment—one in which they are just as responsible for their managerial actions as for their actions as individual citizens. Interestingly, today's high-tech and internet-based firms fare relatively well when it comes to environmental issues, worker conditions, animal testing, and charitable donations.

社会责任的两种观点
2-5b Two Views of Social Responsibility

Government regulation and public awareness are *external* forces that have increased the social responsibility of business. However, business decisions are made within the firm—there, social responsibility begins with the attitude of management. Two contrasting philosophies, or models, define the range of management attitudes toward social responsibility.

According to the traditional concept of business, a firm exists to produce quality goods and services, earn a reasonable profit, and provide jobs. In line with this concept, the **economic model of social responsibility** holds that society will benefit most when business is left alone to produce and market profitable products that society needs. The economic model has its origins in the 18th century, when businesses were owned primarily by entrepreneurs or owner-managers. Competition was vigorous among small firms, and short-run profits and survival were the primary concerns. To the manager who adopts this traditional attitude, social responsibility is someone else's job. After all, stockholders invest in a corporation to earn a return on their investment, not because the firm is socially responsible, and the firm is legally obligated to act in the economic interest of its stockholders. Moreover, profitable firms pay federal, state, and local taxes that are used to meet the needs of society. Thus, managers who concentrate on profit believe that they fulfill their social responsibility indirectly through the taxes paid by their firms. As a result, social responsibility becomes the problem of the government, various environmental groups, charitable foundations, and similar organizations.

In contrast, some managers believe that they have a responsibility not only to stockholders but also to customers, employees, suppliers, and the general public. This broader view is referred to as the **socioeconomic model of social responsibility**, which places emphasis not only on profits but also on the impact of business decisions on society.

社会责任的经济模式
economic model of social responsibility the view that society will benefit most when business is left alone to produce and market profitable products that society needs

社会责任的社会经济模式
socioeconomic model of social responsibility the concept that business should emphasize not only profits but also the impact of its decisions on society

Chapter 2 Ethics and Social Responsibility in Business

Recently, increasing numbers of managers and firms have adopted the socioeconomic model, and they have done so for at least three reasons. First, business is dominated by the corporate form of ownership, and the corporation is a creation of society. If a corporation does not perform as a good citizen, society can and will demand changes. Second, many firms have begun to take pride in their social responsibility records, among them Starbucks, HP, Colgate-Palmolive, and Coca-Cola. Of course, many other corporations are much more socially responsible today than they were ten years ago. Third, many businesspeople believe that it is in their best interest to take the initiative in this area. The alternative may be legal action brought against the firm by some special-interest group; in such a situation, the firm may lose control of its activities.

社会责任的利弊
2-5c The Pros and Cons of Social Responsibility

Business owners, managers, customers, and government officials have debated the pros and cons of the economic and socioeconomic models for years. Each side seems to have four major arguments to reinforce its viewpoint.

Proponents of the socioeconomic model maintain that a business must do more than simply seek profits. To support their position, they offer the following arguments:

1. Because business is a part of our society, it cannot ignore social issues.
2. Business has the technical, financial, and managerial resources needed to tackle today's complex social issues.
3. By helping resolve social issues, business can create a more stable environment for long-term profitability.
4. Socially responsible decision making by firms can prevent increased government intervention, which would force businesses to do what they fail to do voluntarily.

These arguments are based on the assumption that a business has a responsibility not only to its stockholders but also to its customers, employees, suppliers, and the general public.

Opponents of the socioeconomic model argue that business should do what it does best: earn a profit by manufacturing and marketing products that people want. Those who support this position argue as follows:

1. Business managers are responsible primarily to stockholders, so management must be concerned with providing a return on owners' investments.
2. Corporate time, money, and talent should be used to maximize profits, not to solve society's problems.
3. Social problems affect society in general, so individual businesses should not be expected to solve these problems.
4. Social issues are the responsibility of government officials who are elected for that purpose and who are accountable to the voters for their decisions.

These arguments obviously are based on the assumption that the primary objective of business is to earn profits and that government and social institutions should deal with social problems.

Today, few firms are either purely economic or purely socioeconomic in outlook; most have chosen some middle ground between the two extremes. However, our society generally seems to want—and even to expect—some degree of social responsibility from business. Thus, within this middle ground, businesses are leaning toward the socioeconomic view. In the next several sections, we look at some results of this movement in four specific areas: the public, employment practices, the environment, and implementation of social responsibility programs.

> ✓ **Concept Check**
>
> ▶ What is social responsibility? How can business be socially responsible?
>
> ▶ Outline the historical evolution of business social responsibility.
>
> ▶ Explain two views on the social responsibility of business.
>
> ▶ What are the arguments for and against increased social responsibility?

企业的公共责任
2-6 Public Responsibilities of Business

In recent years, more businesses have adopted the idea that they have basic responsibilities to the public, particularly to consumers and public health.

消费者权益保护
2-6a Consumerism

Consumerism consists of all activities undertaken to protect the rights of consumers. The fundamental issues pursued by the consumer movement fall into three categories: environmental protection, product performance and safety, and information disclosure. Although consumerism has been with us to some extent since the early 19th century, the consumer movement became stronger in the 1960s. It was then that President John F. Kennedy declared that the consumer was entitled to a new "Bill of Rights."

The Basic Rights of Consumers President Kennedy's Consumer Bill of Rights asserted that consumers have a right to safety, to be informed, to choose, and to be heard. Two additional rights added since 1975 are the right to consumer education and the right to courteous service. These six rights are the basis of much of the consumer-oriented legislation passed during the last 55 years. These rights also provide an effective outline of the objectives and accomplishments of the consumer movement.

The consumers' right to safety means that the products they purchase must be safe for their intended use, must include thorough and explicit directions for proper use, and must be tested by the manufacturer to ensure product quality and reliability. Federal agencies, such as the Food and Drug Administration and the Consumer Product Safety Commission, have the power to force businesses that make or sell defective products to take corrective actions such as offering refunds, recalling defective products, issuing public warnings, and reimbursing consumers—all of which can be expensive. Moreover, consumers and the government have been winning an increasing number of product-liability lawsuits against sellers of defective products. The amount of the awards in these suits has been increasing steadily. For example, a Florida man won $41.1 million when he sued R.J. Reynolds Tobacco Company and Phillip Morris USA, claiming that for decades they had concealed the hazards of smoking, which led him to develop severe COPD.[23] Yet another major reason for improving product safety is consumers' demand for safe products. People simply will stop buying a product they believe is unsafe or unreliable.

The right to be informed means that consumers must have access to complete information about a product before they buy it. Detailed information about ingredients and nutrition must be provided on food containers, information about fabrics and laundering methods must be attached to clothing, and lenders must disclose the true cost of borrowing the money they make available to customers who purchase merchandise on credit. In addition, manufacturers must inform consumers about the potential dangers of using their products. Manufacturers that fail to provide such information can be held responsible for personal injuries suffered because of their products. For example, Maytag provides customers with a lengthy booklet that describes how they should use their new washing

> **Learning Objective**
> **2-6** List the responsibilities businesses have to the public, especially with regard to consumer rights and public health.

消费者权益保护
consumerism all activities undertaken to protect the rights of consumers

The right to safety The Consumer Bill of Rights asserts buyers' basic rights. The right to safety means that products must be safe for their intended use and tested by the producer to ensure product quality and safety.

Chapter 2 Ethics and Social Responsibility in Business

machines. Sometimes such warnings seem excessive, but they are necessary if user injuries (and resulting lawsuits) are to be avoided.

The right to choose means that consumers must have a choice of products, offered by different manufacturers and sellers, to satisfy a particular need. The government has done its part by encouraging competition through antitrust legislation. The greater the competition, the greater is the choice available to consumers. Competition and the resulting freedom of choice provide additional benefits for customers by reducing prices. For example, when personal computers were introduced, they cost more than $5,000. Thanks to intense competition and technological advancements, personal computers today can be purchased for less than $500.

The right to be heard means that someone will listen and take appropriate action when customers complain. In fact, management began to listen to consumers after World War II, when competition between businesses that manufactured and sold consumer goods increased. One way that firms gained a competitive edge was to listen to consumers and provide the products they said they wanted and needed. Today, businesses are listening even more attentively, and many larger firms have consumer relations departments that can be contacted easily via email and social media. Other groups listen, too. Most large cities and some states have consumer affairs offices to act on citizens' complaints.

In 1975, President Gerald Ford added to the Consumer Bill of Rights *the right to consumer education,* which entitles people to be fully informed about their rights as consumers. In 1994, President Bill Clinton added a sixth right, *the right to service,* which entitles consumers to convenience, courtesy, and responsiveness from manufacturers and sellers of consumer products.

Ethics and Social Responsibility

商业伦理与社会责任：谷歌被控违反反垄断法

Google Sued for Antitrust Violations

Google, the world's largest search engine and one of the largest companies in the United States, faces a series of lawsuits centered around anticompetitive behavior. The Department of Justice and 11 state attorneys general filed a lawsuit against the company to prevent it from using anticompetitive practices to maintain its monopolies in the search and search advertising markets. Anticompetitive behavior negatively affects both consumers and competitors. Among other things, stifling competition inhibits innovation and reduces the options available to consumers.

Complaints against the tech giant include entering into exclusionary agreements that prohibit preinstallation of competing search services and using monopoly profits to pay for preferential treatment for its products. Google has responded to the lawsuit, saying it believes there is nothing wrong with its business agreements. A separate case from more than 30 states alleges Google uses its general search monopoly to discriminate against vertical search companies like Yelp and Kayak. A third lawsuit from a smaller group of states alleges Google uses its position in the advertising marketplace to create unfair conditions for advertisers and publishers, taking in a higher percentage of online ad spending.

Though on a surface level it may seem Google is being targeted for being successful, the accusations made against the company are serious. The distinction between competitive behavior and anticompetitive behavior is that being competitive relates to efforts taken to become the best while being anticompetitive relates to suppressing the competition. Antitrust laws are intended to promote competition and protect consumers. Lawsuits such as the ones Google faces stand to reshape the tech industry.

Sources: Based on information in Department of Justice, "Justice Department Sues Monopolist Google For Violating Antitrust Laws," October 20, 2020; Gilad Edelman, "Google's Antitrust Cases: A Guide for the Perplexed," *Wired*, December 18, 2020; Federal Trade Commission, "Guide to Antitrust Laws".

Major Consumerism Forces The major forces in consumerism are individual consumer advocates and organizations, consumer education programs, and consumer laws. Consumer advocates take it upon themselves to protect the rights of consumers. They band together into consumer organizations, either independently or under government sponsorship. They write letters and advocate for stricter legislation concerning practices that may harm consumers. In Europe, for example, some consumer groups have complained to regulators that Amazon's Prime membership service is difficult to cancel, manipulating users into sticking with a plan they no longer want. Public Citizen, a consumer group in the United States, has made a similar complaint to the Federal Trade Commission.[24] Some consumer advocates and organizations encourage consumers to boycott products and businesses to which they have objections.

Educating consumers to make wiser purchasing decisions is perhaps one of the most far-reaching aspects of consumerism. Increasingly, consumer education is becoming a part of high school and college curricula and adult education programs. These programs cover many topics—for instance, what major factors should be considered when buying specific products, such as insurance, real estate, automobiles, appliances and furniture, clothes, and food; the provisions of certain consumer-protection laws; and the sources of information that can help individuals become knowledgeable consumers.

Major advances in consumerism have come through federal legislation. Some laws enacted in the last 60 years to protect your rights as a consumer are listed and described in Table 2-4.

Most businesspeople now realize that they ignore consumer issues only at their own peril. Managers know that improper handling of consumer complaints can result in lost sales, bad publicity, and lawsuits.

公共健康
2-6b Public Health

Many people believe that businesses have a basic responsibility to contribute to the general well-being of the public, starting with ensuring that their products do not harm anyone. Beyond this basic responsibility, however, there is disagreement as to how far businesses' responsibility to public health should extend, especially about issues such as obesity, smoking, heart disease, alcohol use, and even smartphone use while driving. These issues are not black and white, but exploring them can help us find balance among the desires and demands of various stakeholders.

Obesity has become a major public health topic in recent years, with more than one-third of adult Americans being categorized as obese. Other countries are experiencing similar trends. People who are obese or significantly overweight face higher rates of diabetes, strokes, heart disease, and some types of cancer, and the swelling numbers of these illnesses place a great burden on the healthcare system, the costs of which are borne by society. Public health advocates have called for companies—particularly those that market sugary drinks and fast food—to modify their products or at least their advertising in an effort to reduce the consumption of these products, which have been shown to contribute to rising rates of obesity. Perhaps as a result, some producers of these products have suffered losses and are responding with new ideas and products. Coca-Cola, for example, discontinued hundreds of brands, including some with higher levels of sugar, such as Odwalla. In recent years, the beverage giant has introduced or acquired new beverage brands such as Fairlife milk, Simply juices, and Topo Chico mineral waters that have less sugar and/or provide health benefits.[25] Other companies, including Panera and Starbucks, are posting the calories in their offerings right on their menus and apps to help people make better choices.

Another major public health topic facing business relates to smoking and tobacco products. The relationship between smoking—even secondhand smoke—and cancer has been well documented, but some consumers still demand to buy cigarettes and tobacco

Table 2-4 Major Federal Legislation Protecting Consumers Since 1960

Legislation	Major Provisions
Federal Hazardous Substances Labeling Act (1960)	Required warning labels on household chemicals if they were highly toxic
Kefauver-Harris Drug Amendments (1962)	Established testing practices for drugs and required manufacturers to label drugs with generic names in addition to trade names
Cigarette Labeling Act (1965)	Required manufacturers to place standard warning labels on all cigarette packages and advertising
Fair Packaging and Labeling Act (1966)	Called for all products sold across state lines to be labeled with net weight, ingredients, and manufacturer's name and address
Motor Vehicle Safety Act (1966)	Established standards for safer cars
Truth in Lending Act (1968)	Required lenders and credit merchants to disclose the full cost of finance charges in both dollars and annual percentage rates
Credit Card Liability Act (1970)	Limited credit card holder's liability to $50 per card and stopped credit card companies from issuing unsolicited cards Required credit bureaus to provide credit reports to consumers regarding their own credit files; also provided for correction of incorrect information
Consumer Product Safety Commission Act (1972)	Established an abbreviated procedure for registering certain generic drugs
Fair Credit Billing Act (1974)	Amended the Truth in Lending Act to enable consumers to challenge billing errors
Equal Credit Opportunity Act (1974)	Provided equal credit opportunities for all individuals regardless of sex or marital status Provided for minimum disclosure standards for written consumer-product warranties for products that cost more than $15
Amendments to the Equal Credit Opportunity Act (1976, 1994)	Prevented discrimination based on race, creed, color, religion, age, and income when granting credit
Fair Debt Collection Practices Act (1977)	Outlawed abusive collection practices by third parties
Nutrition Labeling and Education Act (1990)	Required the Food and Drug Administration to review current food labeling and packaging focusing on nutrition label content, label format, ingredient labeling, food descriptors and standards, and health messages
Telephone Consumer Protection Act (1991)	Prohibited the use of automated dialing and prerecorded voice calling equipment to make calls or deliver messages
Consumer Credit Reporting Reform Act (1997)	Placed more responsibility for accurate credit data on credit issuers; required creditors to verify that disputed data are accurate and to notify a consumer before reinstating the data
Children's Online Privacy Protection Act (2000)	Placed parents in control over what information is collected online from their children younger than 13 years; required commercial website operators to maintain the confidentiality, security, and integrity of personal information collected from children
Do Not Call Implementation Act (2003)	Directed the FCC and the FTC to coordinate so that their rules are consistent regarding telemarketing call practices including the Do Not Call Registry and other lists, as well as call abandonment
Credit Card Accountability, Responsibility, and Disclosure Act (2009)	Provided the most sweeping changes in credit card protections since the Truth in Lending Act of 1968
Dodd-Frank Wall Street Reform and Consumer Protection Act of 2010	Promoted the financial stability of the United States by improving accountability and responsibility in the financial system; established a new Consumer Financial Protection Agency to regulate home mortgages, car loans, and credit cards; became Public Law on July 21, 2010

products. While most people agree that businesses should not knowingly sell products that harm customers, what should they do when consumers continue to demand those products? CVS Health earned significant publicity several years ago when it announced that it would stop selling cigarettes in its stores, even though it lost $2 billion in revenue from doing so.[26] In recent years, the rise of vaping has further compounded the issue. Marketers of e-cigarettes and vaping products insist that their products are safer than cigarettes and even tout them as a method to stop smoking. Health advocates, however, say they are still harmful, and worry that the vapors—which often come in flavors such as bubblegum and pina colada—may be especially attractive to minors. Some cities have banned e-cigarettes along with conventional ones, and federal regulators are studying the devices to determine whether further regulation is needed.

One growing concern is the use of smartphones and smartphone apps while driving. Should cell phone service providers take steps to prevent customers from texting and using apps that distract from driving or merely advise them to refrain from these activities? AT&T launched its "It Can Wait" promotion campaign to ask customers to avoid texting while driving, and more than 38 million users pledged not to. The cell phone service provider asked customers to use the hashtag #X to alert their friends and followers that they are about to be unreachable on social media because they are driving.[27] There are other issues businesses face with regard to public health, including labeling products that contain genetically modified organisms (GMOs), making questionable claims about the health benefits of supplements and ingredients, where and how to provide affordable housing for the homeless, and many more.

✓ Concept Check

▸ Describe the six basic rights of consumers.

▸ What are the major forces in consumerism today?

▸ What are some of the federal laws enacted in the last 60 years to protect your rights as a consumer?

▸ What are some of the issues businesses must consider with regard to public health?

对员工的责任
2-7 Responsibilities to Employees

Everyone should have the opportunity to land a job for which they are qualified and to be rewarded on the basis of ability and performance. This is a fundamental issue for Americans, and it also makes good business sense. Yet, over the years, this opportunity has been denied to members of various racial, religious, political, national, and other underrepresented groups, and members of these groups are often singled out for unfavorable treatment in the workplace.

The federal government responded to the outcry of minority groups during the 1960s and 1970s by passing a number of laws forbidding discrimination in the workplace. Yet, more than 50 years after passage of the Civil Rights Act of 1964, abuses still exist. An example is the disparity in income levels for Whites, Blacks, Hispanics, and Asians, as illustrated in Figure 2-3. Lower incomes and higher unemployment rates also characterize Native Americans, people with disabilities, and women. Responsible managers have instituted a number of programs to counteract the results of discrimination.

Learning Objective

2-7 Analyze how present employment practices are being used to counteract past abuses.

平权行动计划
2-7a Affirmative Action Programs

An **affirmative action program** is a plan designed to increase the number of employees from underrepresented groups at all levels within an organization. Employers with federal contracts of more than $50,000 per year must have written affirmative action plans. The objective of such programs is to ensure that members of underrepresented groups are represented within the organization in approximately the same proportion as in the surrounding community. If 25 percent of the electricians in a geographic area in which a company is located are Black, then approximately 25 percent of the electricians it employs also should be Black. Affirmative action plans encompass all areas of human resources management: recruiting, hiring, training, promotion, and pay.

Unfortunately, affirmative action programs have been plagued by two problems. The first involves quotas. In the beginning, many firms pledged to recruit and hire a

平权行动计划
affirmative action program a plan designed to increase the number of employees from underrepresented groups at all levels within an organization

Figure 2-3 Comparative Income Levels

Real Median Household Income by Race and Hispanic Origin: 1967 to 2019

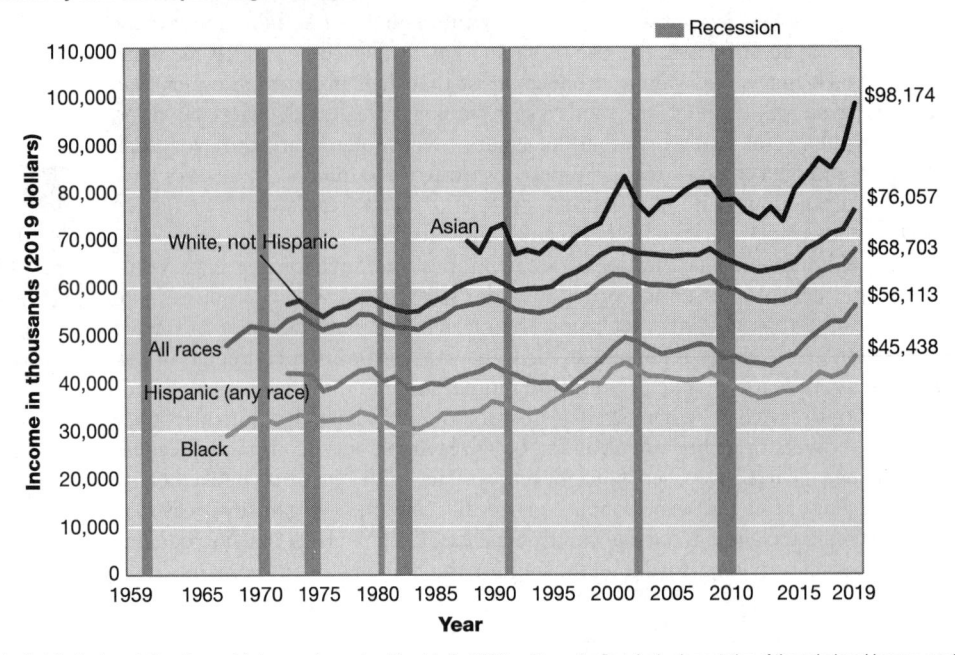

[Chart showing real median household income from 1959 to 2019 with recession bars. 2019 values: Asian $98,174; White, not Hispanic $76,057; All races $68,703; Hispanic (any race) $56,113; Black $45,438. Y-axis: Income in thousands (2019 dollars), 0 to 110,000.]

Note: The data for 2017 and beyond reflect the implementation of an updated processing system. The data for 2013 and beyond reflect the implementation of the redesigned income questions. The data points are placed at the midpoints of the respective years. Median household income data are not available prior to 1967.

Source: U.S. Census Bureau, Current Population Survey, 1968 to 2020 Annual Social and Economic Supplements.

certain number of people from underrepresented groups by a specific date. To achieve this goal, they were forced to consider only applicants from underrepresented groups for job openings; if they hired nonminority workers, they would be defeating their own purpose. However, the courts have ruled that such quotas are unconstitutional even though their purpose is commendable. They are, in fact, a form of discrimination called *reverse discrimination.*

The second problem is that although most such programs have been reasonably successful, not all businesspeople are in favor of affirmative action programs. Managers not committed to these programs can "play the game" and still discriminate against workers. To help solve this problem, Congress created (and later strengthened) the **Equal Employment Opportunity Commission (EEOC)**, a government agency with the power to investigate complaints of employment discrimination and sue firms that practice it.

平等就业机会委员会
Equal Employment Opportunity Commission (EEOC) a government agency with the power to investigate complaints of employment discrimination and the power to sue firms that practice it

The threat of legal action has persuaded some corporations to amend their hiring and promotional policies, but the discrepancy between men's and women's salaries still exists, as illustrated in Figure 2-4. For more than 60 years, women have consistently earned only about 80 cents for each dollar earned by men.

长期失业者培训计划
2-7b Training Programs for the Hard-Core Unemployed

For some firms, social responsibility extends far beyond placing a help-wanted advertisement in the local newspaper. These firms have assumed the task of helping

Workplace diversity A company with a diverse workforce benefits in a number of ways.

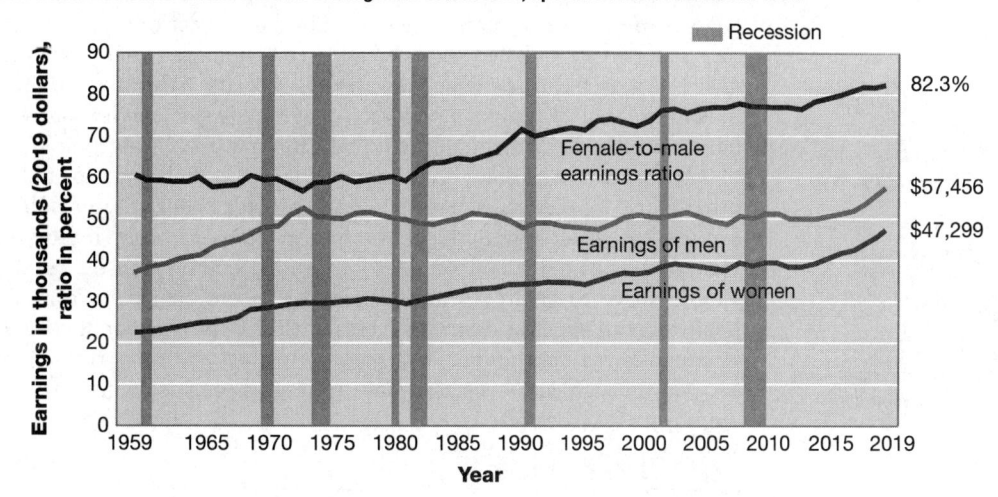

Figure 2-4 Relative Earning of Male and Female Workers

The ratio of women's to men's annual full-time earnings was 80% in 2019, up from 74% first reached in 1996.

Note: The data for 2017 and beyond reflect the implementation of the redesigned income questions. The data for 2013 and beyond reflect the implementation of the redesigned income questions. The data points are placed at the midpoints of the respective years. Data on earnings of full-time, year-round workers are not readily available before 1960. Data are for people aged 14 and older for years prior to 1980.

Source: U.S. Census Bureau, Current Population Survey, 1961 to 2020 Annual Social and Economic Supplements.

---

the **hard-core unemployed**, workers with little education or vocational training and a long history of unemployment. These individuals may not have gained employable skills and education due to disabilities, systemic racism, economic factors, or personal issues. For example, Midas Hospitality, a hotel development and management firm, teamed up with the Boone Center, Inc., a vocational training facility for adults with intellectual and developmental disabilities, to create a program to prepare students for hotel housekeeping jobs in the St. Louis area.[28] In the past, such workers often were turned down routinely by personnel managers, even for the most menial jobs.

减少性骚扰和虐待行为的计划

2-7c Programs to Reduce Sexual Harassment and Abusive Behavior

Another hot button issue in the workplace is addressing sexual harassment, bullying, and other abusive behaviors. The Workplace Bullying Institute (WBI) defines bullying in the workplace as repeated work sabotage; verbal abuse; and/or abusive conduct that is threatening, humiliating, or intimidating. The stress of bullying can result in physical and mental health issues that can ultimately cost employers many hours of lost worker productivity as well as lower morale and higher turnover. The WBI has found that 19 percent of respondents to a survey have suffered abusive conduct at work; 19 percent say they have witnessed it in the workplace.[29] Other researchers have found much higher rates of bullying. Moreover, research by the WBI suggests that half of victims do not report their bullying out of fear of further harassment because their bully is in a position of power.[30] Even football players can be subject to bullying in the workplace: Former Miami Dolphins tackle Jonathan Martin left the team because he felt he could not continue to do his job in the face of repeated bullying from other teammates.[31]

When bullying takes on sexual overtones, it becomes sexual harassment, which the U.S. Equal Employment Opportunity Commission defines as unwelcome sexual advances, requests for sexual favors, and other verbal or physical harassment of a physical nature. Unlike bullying, sexual harassment is illegal.[32] It can also result in poor morale, high turnover, and expensive lawsuits. For example, two women filed

长期失业者
hard-core unemployed workers with little education or vocational training and a long history of unemployment

Chapter 2 Ethics and Social Responsibility in Business

a $500 million class-action lawsuit against McDonald's, claiming that the sexual harassment they endured at corporate-owned restaurants in Florida created a "hostile work environment" for all women working in those stores. In addition to those charges, the women claimed the company did not act to stop the harassment when they reported it, and that they endured retaliation after their complaints.[33] With the #MeToo movement heightening awareness of sexual harassment in the workplace, it's no surprise that employers paid a record $68 million to survivors of workplace sexual harassment in 2019 through the Equal Employment Opportunity Commission.[34]

To create a workplace environment that stifles bullying, sexual harassment, and other abusive conduct, managers need to provide programs, much like the ones that are used to foster more ethical conduct in the workplace. In addition to creating formal policies that define and prohibit unacceptable abusive conduct, companies should strive to create an antibullying organizational culture by modeling good behavior and sending a strong message that improper conduct will be punished. Companies may even want to go a step further and offer training and additional services through employee assistance programs such as counseling to ensure that all employees feel supported.[35]

> **Concept Check**
> - What is an affirmative action program? What is its purpose?
> - Why did Congress create (and later strengthen) the Equal Employment Opportunity Commission?
> - How can businesses reduce sexual harassment and abusive behavior at the workplace?

对环境的责任

2-8 Responsibilities to the Environment

> **Learning Objective**
> **2-8** Describe the major environmental issues and businesses' response to them.

According to a report published by the U.S. Sentencing Commission, the most common federal offense committed by organizations is not fraud or money laundering but environmental crime. Environmental offenses made up nearly a third of all crimes committed by organizations, followed by fraud at 21 percent and food/drug crimes at 12.2 percent. Seventy percent of the environmental crimes were water-related, 16.7 percent affected wildlife, 8.3 percent involved hazardous materials, and 5 percent were air-related.[36]

A growing social consciousness by the public and some business managers, fostered by government legislation, has led to major efforts to reduce environmental pollution, conserve natural resources, and reverse some of the worst damage caused by past negligence in this area.

环境问题

2-8a Environmental Issues

A significant environmental issue is the amount of waste produced by businesses and society. For example, by some estimates, the United States throws out one-third of all the food produced, and grocery stores are responsible for as much as 10 percent of that. One reason for the large amount of grocery waste is consumer expectations: Consumers bypass fruits and vegetables that do not appear to be perfect, so supermarkets discard any produce that doesn't meet that expectation, even when that produce is otherwise safe and healthy.[37] The disposal problem has grown over the past few years because modern technology has continued to produce increasing amounts of chemical and radioactive waste. U.S. manufacturers produce an estimated 40 to 60 million tons of contaminated oil, solvents, acids, and sludge each year. Service businesses, utility companies, hospitals, and other industries also dump vast amounts of wastes into the environment. While companies today strive to reduce waste from operations as much as possible, much still winds up in landfills. A shortage of landfills, owing to stricter regulations, makes garbage disposal a serious problem in some areas. Incinerators help to solve the landfill-shortage problem, but they bring with them their own problems. They reduce the amount of garbage and also leave tons of ash to be buried—ash that often has a higher concentration of toxicity than the original garbage. Increasingly, plastic waste winds up in the ocean, where it accumulates into huge "garbage patches" or breaks down into microplastics that harm marine life.

Another major environmental issue is **pollution**, the contamination of water, air, or land through the actions of people in an industrialized society. Pollution harms water and air quality, threatens human and animal health, degrades habitats, and contributes to climate change. Among the serious threats to people posed by pollutants are respiratory irritation, asthma, cancer, kidney and liver damage, anemia, and heart failure. Businesspeople harm the environment when they unwittingly—or knowingly—dump hazardous chemicals and waste in unapproved ways. For example, Bernhard Schulte Shipmanagement was fined $1.75 million for improperly discharging a ship's bilge waste water into Hawaiian waters and failing to log the discharge as required by law. The Singapore-based company must also implement an environmental compliance plan for all of its vessels operating in U.S. waters.[38] For decades, environmentalists have been warning us about the dangers of industrial pollution. Unfortunately, business and government leaders either ignored the problem or were not concerned about it until pollution became a threat to life and health in America.

环境立法的影响
2-8b Effects of Environmental Legislation

As in other areas of concern to our society, legislation and regulations play a crucial role in pollution control. The laws outlined in Table 2-5 reflect the scope of current environmental legislation: laws to promote clean air, clean water, and even quiet work and living environments. Of major importance was the creation of the Environmental Protection Agency (EPA), the federal agency charged with enforcing laws designed to protect the environment.

污染
pollution the contamination of water, air, or land through the actions of people in an industrialized society

Table 2-5 Summary of Major Environmental Laws

Legislation	Major Provisions
National Environmental Policy Act (1970)	Established the Environmental Protection Agency (EPA) to enforce federal laws that involve the environment
Clean Air Act Amendment (1970)	Provided stringent automotive, aircraft, and factory emission standards
Water Quality Improvement Act (1970)	Strengthened existing water pollution regulations and provided for large monetary fines against violators
Resource Recovery Act (1970)	Enlarged the solid-waste disposal program and provided for enforcement by the EPA
Water Pollution Control Act Amendment (1972)	Established standards for cleaning navigable streams and lakes and eliminating all harmful waste disposal by 1985
Noise Control Act (1972)	Established standards for major sources of noise and required the EPA to advise the Federal Aviation Administration on standards for airplanes
Clean Air Act Amendment (1977)	Established new deadlines for cleaning up polluted areas; also required review of existing air quality standards
Resource Conservation and Recovery Act (1984)	Amended the original 1976 act and required federal regulation of potentially dangerous solid-waste disposal
Clean Air Act Amendment (1987)	Established a national air quality standard for ozone
Oil Pollution Act (1990)	Expanded the nation's oil spill prevention and response activities; also established the Oil Spill Liability Trust Fund
Clean Air Act Amendments (1990)	Required that motor vehicles be equipped with onboard systems to control about 90% of refueling vapors
Food Quality Protection Act (1996)	Amended the Federal Insecticide, Fungicide and Rodenticide Act and the Federal Food Drug and Cosmetic Act; the requirements included a new safety standard—reasonable certainty of no harm—that must be applied to all pesticides used on foods
American Recovery and Reinvestment Act (2009)	Provided $7.22 billion to the EPA to protect and promote "green" jobs and a healthier environment

Pollution Oil spills can have long-lasting effects on our wildlife and other natural resources. As our population and businesses expand, the need to reduce pollution at its source becomes more important.

When they are aware of a pollution problem, many firms are proactive in addressing it rather than wait to be cited by the EPA. Other owners and managers, however, take the position that environmental standards are too strict. (Loosely translated, this means that compliance with present standards is too expensive.) Consequently, it often has been necessary for the EPA to take legal action to force firms to install antipollution equipment and to clean up waste storage areas. Americold Logistics, for example, was fined $41,500 for illegally leaking pollutants into a creek and violating its Washington state industrial stormwater permit, among other EPA charges. The company, which promptly acknowledged and acted to resolve the issues, agreed to develop and implement plans to reduce pollutants leaving its food warehouse facility.[39]

Experience has shown that the combination of environmental legislation, voluntary compliance, and EPA action can succeed in restoring the environment and keeping it clean. However, much still remains to be done.

企业对环境问题的回应
2-8c Business Response to Environmental Concerns

One of the most effective ways that companies can reduce their impact on the environment is to reduce waste from operations and other activities. Identifying and eliminating inefficiencies in production and operations is where most firms begin that process. Finding alternative uses for waste is another. For example, leftover food from supermarkets and restaurants is often donated to local food banks or sold to farmers who feed it to livestock. Most companies strive to recycle as much as possible. **Recycling** involves converting used materials into new products or components for new products in order to prevent their unnecessary disposal. Companies can recycle waste paper, glass, rubber, metals, some plastic packaging, and other materials so that they or their components can be reprocessed into new products and kept out of landfills. As an example, Madewell gives customers $20 toward a new pair of Madewell jeans when they bring in worn-out or out-of-style jeans of any brand. The clothing company donates the used denim to the Cotton's Blue Jeans Go Green program, which turns it into insulation for homes, preventing 529 tons of waste from going into a landfill thus far.[40]

Another way businesses strive to be more environmentally conscious is through the use of "greener" forms of power to counter their use of huge quantities of energy during operations and other activities. Companies can audit their operations to identify places where more efficient and environmentally friendly products can be used to save energy, such as using LED light bulbs—which reduce heat as well as power use—and even natural sunlight to light workplaces. Many companies are turning to alternative forms of power generation,

回收利用
recycling converting used materials into new products or components for new products in order to prevent their unnecessary disposal

Reducing dependence on fossil fuels Today's businesses (and consumers) are more open to alternative sources of energy because they are concerned about the negative impact of conventional energy sources.

Sustaining the Planet

保护地球：可持续发展有利可图吗

Is Sustainability Profitable?

Sustainability has taken the spotlight as environmental consciousness grows among consumers, business professionals, and investors. Though sustainability was once an afterthought for many organizations, more than ever shoppers are looking for products and brands that align with their values. Long story short: sustainability leads to profitability.

In the not-too-distant past, it was difficult to convince investors that sustainability and profitability were linked. Now, with many companies aligning executive bonuses with sustainability targets, there's a growing consensus that environmental, social, and governance practices are strategic priorities. This shift has caused businesses to evaluate their supply chains, from materials to transportation, to find opportunities to limit their environmental impact. Environmental goals often include water reduction, zero waste to landfill, and lowering carbon energy use. Additionally, companies can focus on making products more durable, reusable, repairable, and recyclable.

Investors, who now see that the future is green, often have specific environmental expectations and put pressure on companies to evolve. Many organizations have reaped the benefits of leading with sustainability. According to *The Wall Street Journal*, the most sustainably managed companies in the world include Sony (hardware), Philips (medical equipment), Cisco Systems (hardware), Merck (biotechnology and pharmaceuticals), and Iberdrola (electric utilities and power generators). These organizations have all prioritized environmental concerns while maintaining high profits, showing that sustainability can play a critical role in an organization's future success.

Sources: Based on information in Dieter Holger and Olivia Bugault, "CEOs Increasingly See Sustainability as Path to Profitability," *The Wall Street Journal*, October 12, 2020; Fabiana Negrin Ochoa, Dieter Holger, Maitane Sardon, and Catherine Lindsay, "The 100 Most Sustainably Managed Companies in the World," *The Wall Street Journal*, October 13, 2020.

---

including solar and wind power which do not rely on diminishing sources of fossil fuels. New Belgium Brewing in Fort Collins, Colorado, became the first company to be 100 percent powered by the wind, but many other companies have followed suit. A number of Fortune 500 businesses, including Google, Apple, Starbucks, Cisco, and Bank of America, get 100 percent of their electricity from renewable energy sources such as wind and solar.[41]

Recognizing public demand for greater environmental responsibility, more and more firms are adopting environmentally friendly practices and products that are less harmful to the environment. **Green marketing** is the process of creating, making, delivering, and promoting products that are environmentally safe. It may include making modifications to products, manufacturing processes, packaging, and/or promotion activities to make or deliver products that are better for the environment. Chipotle Mexican Grill, for example, built its reputation as a green marketer by abiding by its "Cultivate a Better World" mission, which requires using real ingredients that "are responsibly sourced and classically cooked with people, animals and the environment in mind." To live by that mission, the company strives to use only natural animal products (treated humanely and fed a vegetarian diet that does not include growth hormones or antibiotics), organic ingredients, and where possible, local sources. It also educates consumers and other stakeholders about its efforts through a Real Foodprint tracker on its app as well as a regularly released Sustainability Report that details its sustainability goals and progress in reaching them. It is significant that Chipotle has not yet achieved all its sustainability goals, but its mission guides the firm in all decision making and activities.[42]

Recognizing that consumers increasingly prefer to purchase from businesses that make recycling, green energy, and sustainability a strategic priority, companies are increasingly touting their green efforts. However, green marketers must take care to ensure that their claims are backed by evidence that shows a significant

绿色营销
green marketing the process of creating, making, delivering, and promoting products that are environmentally safe

> ✓ **Concept Check**
>
> ▶ What are the major environmental issues facing society today?
>
> ▶ Summarize major provisions of federal environmental laws enacted since 1970.
>
> ▶ What is businesses' response to environmental concerns?

environmental benefit and does not mislead consumers or they may run afoul of the Federal Trade Commission.[43] Companies that take their green marketing efforts too far, without relevance or support for their environmental claims risk being labeled guilty of *green washing*.

As we have seen, more businesses are trying harder to make their activities and products sustainable going forward, but what about cleaning up past environmental messes—oil spills, improperly stored industrial wastes, polluting emissions, and more—that harm the environment today? Many business leaders offer one answer: Use tax money to clean up the environment and to keep it clean. They reason that business is not the only source of pollution, so business should not be forced to absorb the entire cost of the cleanup. Environmentalists disagree. They believe that the cost of proper treatment and disposal of industrial wastes is an expense of doing business. In either case, consumers ultimately will bear a large part of the cost—either as taxes or in the form of higher prices for goods and services.

实施社会责任计划

2-9 Implementing a Program of Social Responsibility

> **Learning Objective**
>
> **2-9** Identify the steps a business must take to implement a program of social responsibility

A firm's decision to be socially responsible is a step in the right direction—but only the first step. The business then must develop and implement a program to reach this goal. The program will be affected by the firm's size, financial resources, past record in the area of social responsibility, and competition. Above all, however, the program must have the firm's total commitment or it will fail.

An effective program for ethics and social responsibility requires time, money, and organization. In most cases, developing and implementing such a program will require four steps: securing the commitment of top executives, planning, appointing a director, and preparing a social audit.

高层管理人员的承诺

2-9a Commitment of Top Executives

Without the support of top executives, any program will soon falter and become ineffective. At CitiGroup, the board of directors maintains the Ethics, Conduct, and Culture Committee, which oversees the financial conglomerate's ethics and compliance program.[44] As evidence of their commitment to social responsibility, top managers should develop a policy statement that outlines key areas of concern. Such statements set a tone of positive support and later will serve as a guide for other employees as they become involved in the program.

规划

2-9b Planning

Next, a committee of managers should be appointed to plan the program. Whatever form their plan takes, it should deal with each of the issues described in the top managers' policy statement. If necessary, outside consultants can be hired to help develop the plan.

委任董事

2-9c Appointment of a Director

After the social responsibility plan is established, a top-level executive should be appointed to implement the organization's plan. This individual should be charged with recommending specific policies and helping individual departments to understand and live up to the social responsibilities the firm has assumed. Depending on the size of the firm, the director may require a staff to handle the program on a day-to-day basis. For example, at Cisco, Tae Yoo, Senior Vice President of Corporate Affairs, administers the technology giant's corporate social responsibility program, including applying its resources to facilitate problem solving that has positive impacts on people, society, and the Earth.[45]

社会审计
2-9d The Social Audit

At specified intervals, the program director should prepare a social audit for the firm. A **social audit** is a comprehensive report of what an organization has done and is doing with regard to social issues that affect it. This document provides the information the firm needs to evaluate and revise its social responsibility program. Typical subject areas include human resources, community involvement, the quality and safety of products, business practices, and efforts to reduce pollution and improve the environment. The information included in a social audit should be as accurate and as quantitative as possible, and the audit should reveal both positive and negative aspects of the program. Caesars Entertainment, which operates casinos, evaluates its corporate citizenship efforts annually and then issues a report describing its performance for a variety of stakeholders including employees, investors, and the media. Caesars' Corporate Citizenship Report details its performance in meeting goals in the areas of responsible gaming, employee development, environmental stewardship, and community investment.[46]

Today, many companies listen to concerned individuals within and outside the company. For example, the Citi Ethics Line listens to and acts on concerns expressed by employees and others about possible violations of company policies, laws, or regulations, such as improper or unethical business practices, as well as health, safety, and environmental issues. Employees are encouraged to communicate their concerns, as well as ask questions about ethical issues. The Ethics Line is available to all Citi employees, as well as concerned individuals outside the company.

社会审计
social audit a comprehensive report of what an organization has done and is doing with regard to social issues that affect it

✓ Concept Check

- What steps must a business take to implement a program of social responsibility?
- What is the social audit? Who should prepare a social audit for the firm?

Summary   小 结

2-1 Define *business ethics*.

Ethics is the study of right and wrong and of the morality of choices. Business ethics is the application of moral standards to business situations.

2-2 Identify the types of ethical concerns that arise in the business world.

Ethical issues arise often in business situations out of relationships with investors, customers, employees, creditors, or competitors. Businesspeople should make every effort to be fair, to consider the welfare of customers and others within the firm, to avoid conflicts of interest, and to communicate honestly.

2-3 Discuss the factors that affect the level of ethical behavior in organizations.

Individual, social, and opportunity factors all affect the level of ethical behavior in an organization. Individual factors include knowledge level, moral values and attitudes, and personal goals. Social factors include cultural norms and the actions and values of co-workers and significant others. Opportunity factors refer to the amount of leeway that exists in an organization for employees to behave unethically if they choose to do so.

2-4 Explain how organizations can encourage ethical decision making in business.

Governments, trade associations, and individual firms can establish regulations and guidelines for defining ethical behavior. Governments can pass stricter regulations and laws. Trade associations provide ethical guidelines for their members. Companies provide and enforce codes of ethics—written guides to acceptable and ethical behavior as defined by an organization—and create an atmosphere in which ethical behavior is encouraged. An ethical employee working in an unethical environment may resort to whistle-blowing to bring a questionable practice to light.

2-5 Describe how our current views on the social responsibility of business have evolved.

In a socially responsible business, management realizes that its activities have an impact on society and considers that impact in the decision-making process. Before the 1930s, workers, consumers, and government had very little influence on business activities; as a result, business leaders gave little thought to social responsibility. All this changed with the Great Depression. Government regulations, employee demands, and consumer awareness combined to create a demand that businesses act in socially responsible ways.

The basic premise of the economic model of social responsibility is that society benefits most when business is left alone to produce profitable goods and services. According to the socioeconomic model, business has as much responsibility to society as it has to its owners. Most managers adopt a viewpoint somewhere between these two extremes.

2-6 List the responsibilities businesses have to the public, especially with regard to consumer rights and public health.

Consumerism consists of all activities undertaken to protect the rights of consumers. Although concerns over consumer rights have been around to some extent since the early 19th century, the movement became more powerful in the 1960s when President John F. Kennedy initiated the Consumer Bill of Rights. The six basic rights of consumers include the right to safety, the right to be informed, the right to choose, the right to be heard, and the rights to consumer education and courteous service. Today, many people believe that businesses have a basic responsibility to contribute to the general wellbeing of the public. Other issues businesses face relate to public health, including addressing products that contribute to obesity and cancer.

2-7 Analyze how present employment practices are being used to counteract past abuses.

Legislation and public demand have prompted some businesses to correct past abuses in employment practices—mainly with regard to minority groups. Affirmative action and training of the hard-core unemployed are two types of programs that have been used successfully. Another issue in the workplace is addressing sexual harassment and other abusive behaviors, such as bullying and verbal abuse.

2-8 Describe the major environmental issues and businesses' response to them.

A growing social consciousness, fostered by government legislation, has led to major efforts to reduce waste and pollution, conserve natural resources, and reverse some of the worst damage caused by past negligence in this area. Current environmental laws, enforced by the Environmental Protection Agency, promote clean air, clean water, and even quiet work and living environments. However, much still remains to be done. Many companies are looking for ways to reduce their environmental footprint, such as improving operations to reduce waste, recycling, using alternative forms of energy, including solar and wind power, and engaging in green marketing—the process of creating, making, delivering, and promoting products that are environmentally safe.

2-9 Identify the steps a business must take to implement a program of social responsibility.

A program to implement social responsibility in a business begins with total commitment by top management. The program should be planned carefully, and a capable director should be appointed to implement it. Social audits should be prepared periodically as a means of evaluating and revising the program.

Key Terms 关键术语

You should now be able to define and give an example relevant to each of the following terms:

- ethics
- business ethics
- plagiarism
- conflict of interest
- Sarbanes-Oxley Act of 2002
- code of ethics
- whistle-blowing
- social responsibility
- corporate citizenship
- caveat emptor
- economic model of social responsibility
- socioeconomic model of social responsibility
- consumerism
- affirmative action program
- Equal Employment Opportunity Commission (EEOC)
- hard-core unemployed
- pollution
- recycling
- green marketing
- social audit

Discussion Questions 讨论题

1. When a company acts in an ethically questionable manner, what types of problems are caused for the organization and its customers?
2. What factors affect ethical behavior and choices? How can businesses use this knowledge to further ethical behavior in their organizations?
3. How can employees take an ethical stand regarding a business decision when their superior already has taken a different position?
4. How can businesses encourage employees to make ethical choices?
5. Overall, would it be more profitable for a business to follow the economic model or the socioeconomic model of social responsibility?
6. Why should business take on the task of training the hard-core unemployed?
7. To what extent should the blame for vehicular air pollution be shared by manufacturers, consumers, and government?
8. Why is there so much government regulation involving social responsibility issues? Should there be less?

Case 2   案例 2：全食超市的全食交易保障

Inside Whole Trade at Whole Foods

Whole Foods Market, a natural supermarket chain, was founded in Austin, Texas, in 1980. At the time, the market for natural, unprocessed foods was small, but the company soon expanded to new cities as demand grew. Now, the grocer can be found in 500 locations across North America and the United Kingdom. Since the beginning, responsible sourcing has been a core component of Whole Foods' business. This stakeholder orientation focuses on the needs of its customers, its employees, its communities, and people at every level of its supply chain.

The Whole Trade Guarantee is Whole Foods' ethical trading program. It supports ethical trade, proper working conditions, and environmental protection in the production of the products it sells. Products with this label meet rigorous quality standards and come from certified farms that have a history of positive impacts on their employees, supply chain partners, communities, and the environment. Through the program, Whole Foods provides funds to the farms they work with to support various community initiatives such as community centers, medical services, and dental care. Programs such as Whole Trade support Whole Foods' mission to nourish both people and the planet.

Whole Foods has often been called "Whole Paycheck" because of the more expensive price tags on its products. However, Whole Foods believes that, as a responsible buyer, it has a duty to monitor its impact on the environment and individuals throughout the supply chain. Pressure from retailers to lower costs can lead to farm owners exploiting workers to deliver products cheaply. One of Whole Foods' goals is to provide its shoppers with affordable, sustainable food that also supports farmers and farmworkers.

Beyond creating win–win partnerships with its suppliers, Whole Foods ultimately views customers as its most important stakeholder. To differentiate itself from its competitors, Whole Foods emphasizes the quality of its products over price. The company has a variety of quality standards to ensure its customers get the best, including standards for its meat, eggs, seafood, supplements, beauty products, and household cleaners. In addition, Whole Foods bans more than 100 ingredients such as high-fructose corn syrup.

Employees at Whole Foods are another top priority. Full-time team members are offered comprehensive health insurance. The company also provides its team members with career and learning development, volunteer programs through the Whole Planet Foundation, and team member assistance plans. In addition to competitive pay, the company also offers 401(k) plans and health savings accounts, discounts, and paid time off.

All of these efforts combined help Whole Foods earn profits, which in turn creates value for its shareholders. Profits are essential for any business to survive, and Whole Foods believes it has a responsibility to its parent company, Amazon, to use its capital in the best way possible to achieve the best results possible. Not everyone was pleased when Amazon acquired Whole Foods in 2017 for $13.4 billion. Many employees noticed a change in working conditions such as heavier workloads and budget cuts. Amazon also sought to make Whole Foods' products more affordable by purchasing a greater number of products from national food distributors rather than local farms. Prices have since returned to pre-Amazon levels but other initiatives—such as discounts for Amazon Prime members—remain to provide customers with more value.

Whole Food's strong relationships with its supply chain partners are fostered by its Whole Trade program. This is a core strength that can be leveraged by both Whole Foods and Amazon to stand out. Though many criticized Amazon's acquisition of Whole Foods due to their cultural differences, Amazon's deep pockets and robust supply chain knowledge will surely benefit Whole Foods in the long run. By committing to ethical and sustainable trading practices, Whole Foods sets itself apart from traditional supermarkets.[47]

Questions

1. Why do you think Whole Foods wants to support the farmers and farmworkers in its supply chain?
2. Why are customers willing to pay a premium for goods at Whole Foods?
3. How does Whole Foods meet the needs of its customers?

Building Skills for Career Success   为成功的职业生涯培养技能

1. Social Media Exercise

Lego has been making children's toys since the 1930s and its iconic plastic building blocks since 1958. Company executives, wanting their products to have a lasting legacy, have launched several initiatives to leave the world a better place.

Visit Lego's website to learn more about these initiatives and search for Lego on YouTube.

1. What responsibilities do you think Lego has to its customers—the children as well as their parents?

2. Are these initiatives consistent with the firm's mission and values? Why or why not?
3. Search YouTube and then describe how Lego's sustainability efforts compare with those of rivals like Mattel and Hasbro.

2. Building Team Skills

A firm's code of ethics outlines the kinds of behaviors expected within the organization and serves as a guideline for encouraging ethical behavior in the workplace. It reflects the rights of the firm's workers, shareholders, and consumers.

Assignment

1. Working in a team of four, find a code of ethics for a business firm. Start the search by asking firms in your community for a copy of their codes, by visiting the library, or by searching and downloading information from the internet.
2. Analyze the code of ethics you have chosen, and answer the following questions:
   a. What does the company's code of ethics say about the rights of its workers, shareholders, consumers, and suppliers? How does the code reflect the company's attitude toward competitors?
   b. How does this code of ethics resemble the information discussed in this chapter? How does it differ?
   c. As an employee of this company, how would you personally interpret the code of ethics? How might the code influence your behavior within the workplace? Give several examples.

3. Researching Different Careers

Business ethics has been at the heart of many discussions over the years and continues to trouble employees and shareholders. Stories about dishonesty and wrongful behavior in the workplace appear on a regular basis in newspapers and on the national news.

Assignment

Prepare a written report on the following:

1. Why can it be so difficult for people to do what is right?
2. What is your personal code of ethics? Prepare a code outlining what you believe is morally right. The document should include guidelines for your personal behavior.
3. How will your code of ethics affect your decisions about:
   a. The types of questions you should ask in a job interview?
   b. Selecting a company in which to work?

Chapter

3

Global Business
全球商务

Learning Objectives

Once you complete this chapter, you will be able to:

3-1 Explain the economic bases for and importance of international business.

3-2 Explore the methods by which a firm can organize for and enter into international markets.

3-3 Discuss the challenges businesses face when entering international markets, especially the restrictions nations place on international trade.

3-4 Identify the facilitators of international trade, including international trade agreements and international economic organizations working to foster trade.

3-5 Describe sources of export assistance.

3-6 Identify institutions that can help businesses and nations finance international business.

Why Should You Care?

Free trade—are you for or against it? Most economists support free-trade policies, but public support can be lukewarm, and certain groups are adamantly opposed, contending that "trade harms large segments of U.S. workers," "degrades the environment," and "exploits the poor."

Inside Business

商业透视：星巴克走向全球以实现增长

Starbucks Goes Global for Growth

Starbucks, the world's largest coffeehouse chain, has more stores internationally than it does in the United States as a result of putting global expansion at the center of its growth strategy. Domestically, Starbucks has slowed new store openings and closed locations deemed redundant in dense metro areas in order to put the company in a more profitable position. While Starbucks tackles changing consumer behavior in the United States, other countries present valuable growth opportunities.

An aggressive push into China, Starbucks' fastest-growing market, has been successful for the company. According to Starbucks China CEO and chairperson Belinda Wong, at one point in time, Starbucks opened a new store in China every 15 hours. The company announced plans to invest $150 million in a roasting plant in China, deepening its commitment to building the Starbucks brand throughout Asia. The company's only other non-U.S. roasting facility is in Amsterdam to support Europe.

To penetrate China's coffee market, the coffeehouse chain focused on rolling out innovation even faster than in the United States. For example, to appeal to local tastes, the menu in China includes a variety of tea-based beverages as well as exclusive drink categories. Additionally, Starbucks rolled out delivery in Beijing and Shanghai and 11 other cities in China before it expanded delivery in the United States. The Asia-Pacific market accounts for approximately half of Starbucks' global new store growth.[1]

Did you know?
Starbucks has 32,000 stores across more than 80 markets.

Like Starbucks, many companies, large and small, do business around the world. Did you know that only 31 percent of the Coca-Cola Company's sales come from North America? Asia-Pacific and Latin American markets generate 14 percent and 11 percent, respectively, of the revenues of the beverage giant.[2] Even small businesses can find great success in global markets. One such company is Combustion Associates of Corona, California, a small business founded by husband-and-wife immigrants from Bangladesh. The company designs, manufactures, and exports large power generators to developing countries.[3] Whether they buy or sell products across national borders, these companies are all contributing to the volume of international trade that is fueling the global economy.

Theoretically, international trade is every bit as logical and worthwhile as interstate trade between, say, California and Washington. Yet, nations tend to restrict the import of certain goods for a variety of reasons. For example, the United States restricted the import of Mexican fresh tomatoes because they were undercutting price levels of domestic fresh tomatoes. Despite such restrictions, international trade has increased almost steadily since World War II. Many of the industrialized nations have signed trade agreements intended to reduce problems in international business and to help less-developed nations participate in world trade. Individual firms around the world have seized the opportunity to compete in foreign markets by exporting products and increasing foreign production, as well as by other means.

In this chapter, we describe international trade in terms of modern specialization, whereby each country trades the surplus goods and services it produces most efficiently for products its citizens and organizations need. We also consider the importance and extent of international trade with the U.S. economy. Next, we explore several methods of entering international markets. We then examine the challenges business organizations face when engaging in trade across borders and identify organizations working to

Entrepreneurial Success

创业成功：阿里巴巴通过提供指导助力企业家

Alibaba Provides Guidance to Help Entrepreneurs

Alibaba, one of the world's largest e-commerce companies, invests in Hong Kong and Taiwan-based entrepreneurs through its not-for-profit arm, the Alibaba Entrepreneurs Fund. In addition to investment capital, Alibaba provides guidance to help individuals scale their businesses, making use of Alibaba's tools and resources. The e-commerce giant aims to build Hong Kong's start-up ecosystem by fueling entrepreneurship and innovation.

According to a survey conducted by Alibaba and KPMG, corporate executives benefit from collaborating with start-ups because it helps keep them up to date on the latest innovations. Entrepreneurs develop new ideas, find solutions that address society's needs, diversify the economy, and create upward mobility. Lynk, one of the businesses Alibaba has invested in, is the first-ever Software-as-a-Service platform built on an expert network. The service allows businesses to easily connect with a diverse set of 840,000 advisors rather than hiring experts in-house. The company has raised more than $30 million in capital.

By supporting the entrepreneurial landscape in China, Alibaba's marketplace and other platforms will benefit. The Alibaba Entrepreneurs Fund follows a venture capitalist model, except profits from the company's venture investments are returned to the fund for reinvestment, ensuring capital is always available. Independent professionals with start-up experience evaluate and select the entrepreneurs that will receive funding and strategic guidance from Alibaba's network of business leaders. The not-for-profit looks for innovative start-ups in the big data, cleantech, e-commerce, fintech, and logistics sectors, among others. Alibaba then leverages its resources to help the entrepreneurs grow their businesses.

Sources: Based on information in "Alibaba Hong Kong Entrepreneurs Fund Launches JUMPSTARTER 2021 Global Pitch Competition," *Business Wire*, July 28, 2020; Alibaba Entrepreneurs Fund, "Transforming Hong Kong Through Entrepreneurship"; Catherine Shu, "Lynk, a 'Knowledge -as-a-Service' Platform with More Than 840,000 Experts, Raises $24 Million," *TechCrunch*, January 27, 2021.

---

facilitate global trade. We also outline the various sources of export assistance available from the federal government. Finally, we identify some of the institutions that provide the complex financing necessary for modern international trade.

国际商务基础
3-1 The Basis for International Business

International business encompasses all business activities that involve exchanges across national boundaries. Thus, a firm is engaged in international business when it buys some portion of its input from, or sells some portion of its output to, an organization located in a foreign country. (A small retail store may sell goods produced in some other country. However, because it purchases these goods from American distributors, it is not engaged in international trade.)

绝对优势和比较优势
3-1a Absolute and Comparative Advantage

Some countries are better equipped than others to produce particular goods or services. The reason may be a country's natural resources, its labor supply, or even customs or a historical accident. In such cases, it would be advantageous for a country to specialize in the production of such products so that it can produce them most efficiently. The country could use what it needed of these products and then trade the surplus for products it could not produce efficiently on its own. Saudi Arabia thus has specialized in the production of crude oil and petroleum products; South Africa, in diamonds; and Australia, in wool. Each of these countries is said to have an absolute advantage with regard to a particular product. An **absolute advantage** is the ability to produce a specific product more efficiently than any other nation.

> **Learning Objective**
> **3-1** Explain the economic bases for and importance of international business.

> 国际商务
> **international business** all business activities that involve exchanges across national boundaries
>
> 绝对优势
> **absolute advantage** the ability to produce a specific product more efficiently than any other nation

Chapter 3 Global Business 69

A U.S. absolute advantage. The United States has long specialized in the production of wheat. Because of its specific geography and climate, the United States enjoys an absolute advantage—the ability to produce wheat more efficiently than countries in other parts of the world.

One country may have an absolute advantage with regard to several products, whereas another country may have no absolute advantage at all. Yet it is still worthwhile for these two countries to specialize and trade with each other. To see why this is so, imagine that you are the president of a successful manufacturing firm and that you can accurately type 90 words per minute. Your assistant can type 80 words per minute but would run the business poorly. Thus, you have an absolute advantage over your assistant in both typing and managing. However, you cannot afford to type your own letters because your time is better spent in managing the business. That is, you have a comparative advantage in managing. A **comparative advantage** is the ability to produce a specific product more efficiently than any other product. Your assistant, on the other hand, has a comparative advantage in clerical duties because he or she can do that better than managing the business. Thus, you spend your time managing, and you leave the document preparation to your assistant. Overall, the business is run as efficiently as possible because you are each working in accordance with your own comparative advantage.

The same is true for nations. Goods and services are produced more efficiently when each country specializes in the products for which it has a comparative advantage. Moreover, by definition, every country has a comparative advantage in some product. The United States has many comparative advantages—in research and development, high-technology industries, and identifying new markets, for instance.

进出口
3-1b Exporting and Importing

Suppose that the United States specializes in producing corn. It then will produce a surplus of corn, but perhaps it will have a shortage of wine. France, on the other hand, specializes in producing wine but experiences a shortage of corn. To satisfy both needs—for corn and for wine—the two countries should trade with each other. The United States should export corn and import wine. France should export wine and import corn.

Exporting is selling and shipping raw materials or products to other nations. The Boeing Company, for example, exports its airplanes to a number of countries for use by their airlines. On a smaller scale, the Liriope Factory, a small Louisiana nursery, has expanded the customer base for its ground cover plants by exporting to European markets.[4] Figure 3-1 shows selected top merchandise-exporting states in the United States.

Importing is purchasing raw materials or products in other nations and bringing them into one's own country. Thus, buyers for Macy's department stores may purchase rugs in India or raincoats in England and have them shipped back to the United States for resale.

贸易差额
3-1c Balance of Trade

Importing and exporting are the principal activities in international trade. They give rise to an important concept called the *balance of trade*. A nation's **balance of trade** is the total value of its exports minus the total value of its imports over

比较优势
comparative advantage the ability to produce a specific product more efficiently than any other product

出口
exporting selling and shipping raw materials or products to other nations

进口
importing purchasing raw materials or products in other nations and bringing them into one's own country

贸易差额
balance of trade the total value of a nation's exports minus the total value of its imports over a specified period of time

70 Marketing

Figure 3-1 Selected Top Exporting States

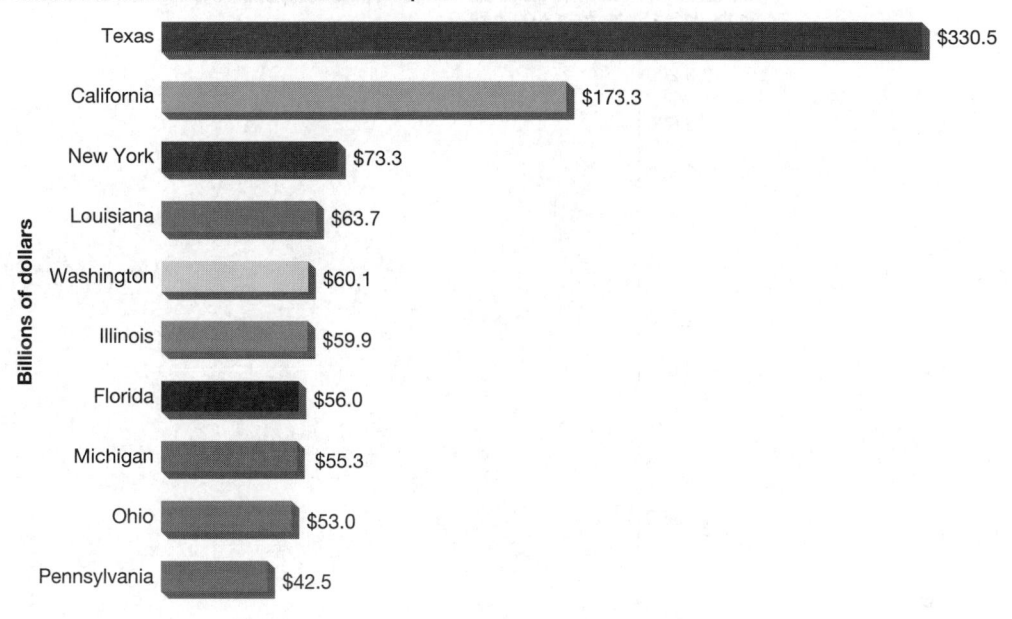

Texas and California account for about one-third of all U.S. exports.

State	Billions of dollars
Texas	$330.5
California	$173.3
New York	$73.3
Louisiana	$63.7
Washington	$60.1
Illinois	$59.9
Florida	$56.0
Michigan	$55.3
Ohio	$53.0
Pennsylvania	$42.5

Source: Daniel Workman, "America's Top 20 Export States," *World's Top Exports*, March 2020.

a specified period of time. If a country imports more than it exports, its balance of trade is negative and is said to be *unfavorable*. On the other hand, when a country exports more than it imports, it is said to have a *favorable* balance of trade.

In 2020, the United States imported $2,810.6 billion worth of goods and services and exported $2,131.9 billion worth. It thus had a trade deficit of $678.7 billion.[5] A **trade deficit** is a negative balance of trade (refer to Figure 3-2). However, the United States has consistently enjoyed a large and rapidly growing surplus in services, such as computer and banking services. For example, in 2020, the United States imported $460.1 billion worth of services and exported $697.1 billion worth, thus creating a favorable balance of $237 billion.[6]

贸易逆差
trade deficit a negative balance of trade

U.S. exports. U.S. aircraft and spacecraft products represent the third largest U.S. exports.

Chapter 3   Global Business

Figure 3-2 U.S. International Trade in Goods and Services

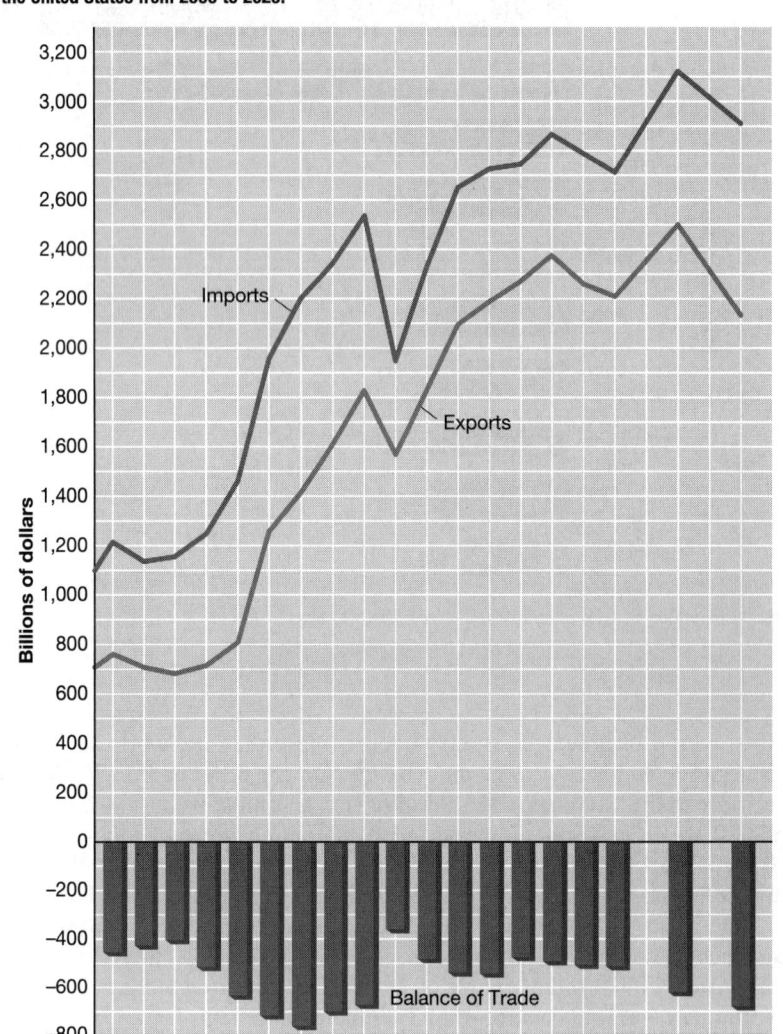

If a country imports more goods than it exports, the balance of trade is negative, as it was in the United States from 2000 to 2020.

Sources: U.S. Department of Commerce, International Trade Administration; U.S. Bureau of Economic Analysis, "U.S. International Trade in Goods and Services, December 2020," February 5, 2021; U.S. Bureau of Economic Analysis, "U.S. International Trade in Goods and Services, December 2018," March 6, 2019.

Question: *Are trade deficits bad?*

Answer: It's complicated. A negative balance of trade is often viewed as unfavorable because the country must export money to pay for its excess imports. However, trade deficits also mean that consumers at home have the benefit of a wider variety of products at competitive prices. Consider the iPhone, which is manufactured in China. If it were to be made in the United States, it likely would retail for $2,000, but lower supply and labor costs overseas mean that Apple can sell most models for less than $1,000, or twice as many.[7] These lower prices also help stifle the threat of inflation. In the long run, though, trade deficits give rise to sending more jobs overseas where costs are often significantly lower, thereby resulting in less job creation at home. This is indeed what is happening in the United States.

A nation's **balance of payments** is the total flow of money into a country minus the total flow of money out of that country over a specified period of time. Balance of payments, therefore, is a much broader concept than balance of trade. It includes imports and exports, of course. However, it also includes investments, money spent by foreign tourists, payments by foreign governments, aid to foreign governments, and all other receipts and payments. A continual deficit in a nation's balance of payments (a negative balance) can cause other nations to lose confidence in that nation's economy. Alternatively, a persistent surplus may indicate that the country encourages exports but limits imports by imposing trade restrictions.

国际贸易的经济展望

3-1d The Economic Outlook for Trade

International trade is a major growth vehicle for the United States. More than 40 million full- and part-time jobs, or about one out of every five jobs in the United States, depend on international trade. The percentage of American jobs tied to global trade has doubled since 1992, growing from 10.4 percent to 20.2 percent.[8] In 2018, for the first time, the U.S. exports exceeded $2.5 trillion, up from $25 billion in 1960.[9] Many other countries have experienced similar growth. This dramatic increase in trade volume over the past 60 years has been one of the most important factors in the rise of living standards around the world. During this time, exports have become increasingly important to the U.S. economy. Exports as a percentage of U.S. GDP have increased steadily since 1970, except during recessions. Table 3-1 shows U.S. exports and imports for selected world areas in 2020, and Table 3-2 shows the value of U.S. merchandise exports to, and imports from, each of the nation's eight major trading partners. Note that Canada and Mexico are our best partners for our exports; China and Mexico, for imports.

Although the worldwide recessions of 1991, 2001–2002, and 2008–2009 slowed the rate of growth, and the global COVID-19 pandemic economic crisis caused the sharpest decline in more than 75 years, globalization is a reality of our time. In the United States, international trade now accounts for over one-fourth of gross domestic product (GDP). As trade barriers decrease, new competitors enter the global marketplace, creating more choices for consumers and new opportunities for job seekers. Looking ahead, the International Monetary Fund (IMF), an international bank with 190 member nations, expected global growth to continue, albeit more slowly as world economies recover from the pandemic and social unrest. The IMF

Table 3-1 U.S. Exports and Imports of Goods for Selected World Areas in 2020 in Billions of Dollars

Selected World Area*	Exports	Imports
North America	$468	$596
Europe	$332	$577
Euro Area	$213	$368
European Union	$232	$415
Pacific Rim	$376	$825
South/Central America	$130	$91
Africa	$22	$24
OPEC	$35	$19
Other Countries	$74	$209

*Countries may be included in more than one area grouping.

Source: U.S. Department of Commerce, Bureau of Economic Analysis, "Monthly U.S International Trade in Goods, December 2020".

国际收支

balance of payments the total flow of money into a country minus the total flow of money out of that country over a specified period of time

Table 3-2 Top Trading Partners: Value of U.S. Merchandise Exports and Imports of Goods, 2020

Rank	Country	Exports ($ billions)	Imports ($ billions)	Total Trade ($ billions)	Percent of Total Trade
1	China	124.6	435.4	560.1	14.9
2	Mexico	212.7	325.4	538.1	14.3
3	Canada	255.4	270.4	525.8	14.0
4	Japan	64.1	119.5	183.6	4.9
5	Germany	57.8	115.1	172.9	4.6
6	Korea, South	51.2	76.0	127.2	3.4
7	United Kingdom	59.0	50.2	109.2	2.9
8	Switzerland	18.0	74.8	92.8	2.5

Source: U.S. Department of Commerce, Census Bureau, "Top Trading Partners".

expected the world economic growth to be 5.5 percent and 4.2 percent in 2021 and 2022, respectively,[10] although the lingering economic effects of the COVID-19 pandemic may reduce that. Let's take a quick look at trade with some major nations and regions.

Canada and Western Europe Due in part to sharing a border and language, the economic relationship between the United States and Canada is one of the most efficient, most integrated, and most dynamic in the world. Together, the two nations generated 703.8 billion in bilateral trade in 2019—almost $2 billion a day, or $23,000 every second.[11] The nearly 450 million residents of the European Union make its member countries attractive trading partners, generating an estimated trade in goods of more than $658 billion in 2020.[12] Most other advanced economies, including Norway, Sweden, Switzerland, and the United Kingdom, are also major importers to and buyers of exports from the United States. Thanks in part to stability, similar per capita incomes, and growing economies, these relationships are likely to endure.

Mexico and Latin America Mexico, another leading trading partner, represents a tremendous opportunity for businesses looking for new markets. Latin America is home to 10 Free Trade Area countries and more than 650 million consumers. In addition to Mexico, these countries include Chile, Colombia, Peru, and the six countries of the Dominican Republic-Central America FTA or "CAFTA-DR" (Costa Rica, The Dominican Republic, El Salvador, Guatemala, Honduras, and Nicaragua). U.S. trade in goods with Central and South American nations added up to $221 billion a year in 2020[13] and is expected to grow as trade barriers among the nations ease.

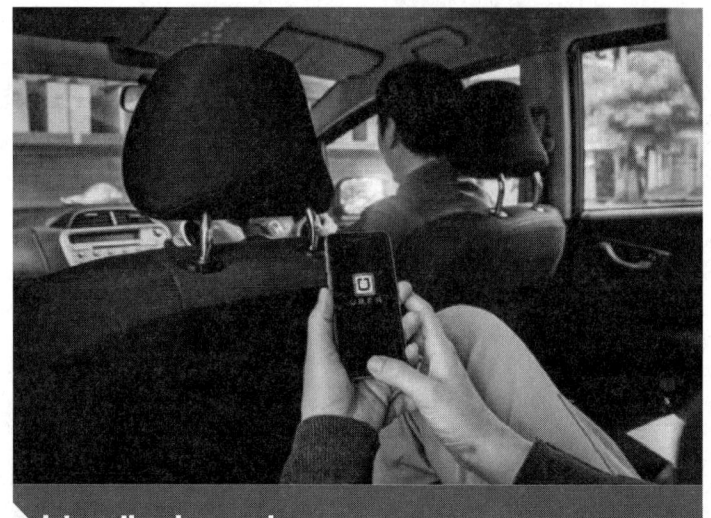

International expansion. Uber continues its globalization efforts by offering its services in more than 10,000 cities worldwide.

Technology and Innovation

技术与创新：Spotify 谋求全球主导地位

Spotify Makes a Play for Global Dominance

Spotify, a Swedish digital music, podcast, and video streaming service, has more than 354 million users in 93 markets. Although the company controls about one-third of the global music-streaming market, it faces steep competition for consumer dollars against Pandora, Apple Music, YouTube Music, Tidal, and Amazon Music, among others. To grow its market share, Spotify is eyeing global expansion.

Spotify sees international growth as an opportunity to stay ahead of the streaming competition. Russia, one of Spotify's latest markets, is the fastest-growing market for music. In addition, Spotify expanded to Albania, Belarus, Bosnia and Herzegovina, Croatia, Kazakhstan, Kosovo, Moldavia, Montenegro, North Macedonia, Serbia, Slovenia, and Ukraine. In each market, Spotify works with local distributors and establishes local partnerships to offer a local experience on a global platform.

Spotify follows a freemium pricing strategy, meaning it offers free entry-level access, hoping to convert free users into premium subscribers. Its premium service eliminates advertisements and allows users to download music, skip an unlimited number of songs, and access Spotify's full library of music. This pricing strategy is not unique, however, as many of its competitors, including Pandora and Amazon Music, also offer free versions of their platforms.

To increase revenue, leadership at Spotify says it will increase subscription prices in mature markets where it offers more value than it did previously. The company has been busy developing and releasing original and exclusive content in 16 markets to differentiate the platform from competitors. Spotify's goal is to solidify its dominance in the audio streaming market while increasing earnings from active subscribers.

Sources: Based on information in Spotify, "Company Info"; David Trainer, "It Sounds Like Spotify Is In Trouble," *Forbes*, October 13, 2020; Kenneth Li, Supantha Mukherjee, "Spotify Expands to Russia and 12 Other Countries," *Reuters*, July 14, 2020; Sarah Perez, "Spotify CEO Says Company Will 'Further Expand Price Increases'," *TechCrunch*, October 29, 2020.

Asia Japan is the world's third largest economy and the United States' fourth largest trading partner. China's emergence as a global economic power has been among the most dramatic economic developments of recent decades. Indeed, China has grown to be the world's second largest economy, and the United States shares more than half a trillion dollars in annual bilateral trade. Also, as the emerging middle class in India, buys U.S. products, it means jobs and income for the U.S. middle class. With a market of over 1.35 billion of the world's consumers and per capita incomes expected to grow, India's vast market promises U.S. companies continued demand for goods and services.

Africa Sub-Saharan Africa is home to 1.1 billion people in 46 countries with immense natural resources that offer great trade potential. U.S. trade to and from Africa has tripled over the past decade, and U.S. exports of goods to this region now exceed $22 billion.[14] Although some of these nations have experienced conflict and stagnating economies, Ghana, Rwanda, Ethiopia, and others have experienced dramatic economic growth in recent years. Companies are increasingly looking for opportunities in these growing economies, whose residents are younger than average and have growing disposable incomes.

Middle East/North Africa Some of the countries of the Middle East and North Africa (MENA)—particularly Egypt and Saudi Arabia—have become important trading partners to the United States. Although political instability in the region has been a challenge to developing long-term relationships, the vast natural resources and growing per capita incomes make the region desirable to companies.

> ✓ **Concept Check**
> ▸ Why do firms engage in international trade?
> ▸ What is the difference between an absolute advantage and a comparative advantage?
> ▸ What is the difference between balance of trade and balance of payments?
> ▸ Which nations are the principal trading partners of the United States?

Chapter 3 Global Business

进入国际商务的方式
3-2 Methods of Entering International Business

Learning Objective

3-2 Explore the methods by which a firm can organize for and enter into international markets.

A firm that has decided to enter international markets can do so in several ways. These different approaches require varying degrees of involvement, investment, and risk. Typically, a firm begins its international operations at the simplest level. Then, depending on its goals, it may progress to higher levels of involvement. Table 3-3 describes the steps in entering international markets.

出口
3-2a Exporting

Exporting can be a relatively low-risk method of expanding operations by entering foreign markets. As an example, the Canadian firm LED Roadway Lighting Ltd. manufactures energy-efficient road lighting products that can help cities and utilities meet their goals to cut costs and reduce their climate footprint. To expand its business beyond Canada, the company began exporting its products to customers

Table 3-3 Steps in Entering International Markets

Step	Activity	Marketing Tasks
1	Identify exportable products	Identify key selling features Identify needs that they satisfy Identify the selling constraints that are imposed
2	Identify key foreign markets for the products	Determine who the customers are Pinpoint what and when they will buy Do market research Establish priority, or "target," countries
3	Analyze how to sell in each priority market (methods will be affected by product characteristics and unique features of country/market)	Locate available government and private-sector resources Determine service and backup sales requirements
4	Set export prices and payment terms, methods, and techniques	Establish methods of export pricing Establish sales terms, quotations, invoices, and conditions of sale Determine methods of international payments, secured and unsecured
5	Estimate resource requirements and returns	Estimate financial requirements Estimate human resources requirements (full- or part-time export department or operation) Estimate plant production capacity Determine necessary product adaptations
6	Establish overseas distribution network	Determine distribution agreement and other key marketing decisions (price, repair policies, returns, territory, performance, and termination). Know your customer (use U.S. Department of Commerce international marketing services)
7	Determine shipping, traffic, and documentation procedures and requirements	Determine methods of shipment (air or ocean freight, truck, rail) Finalize containerization Obtain validated export license Follow export-administration documentation procedures
8	Promote, sell, and be paid	Use international media, communications, advertising, trade shows, and exhibitions Determine the need for overseas travel (when, where, and how often?) Initiate customer follow-up procedures
9	Continuously analyze current marketing, economic, and political situations	Recognize changing factors influencing marketing strategies Constantly reevaluate

Source: U.S. Department of Commerce, International Trade Administration, Washington, DC.

in Caribbean nations, where high power rates allow customers to quickly realize savings from using LED lighting products. LED Roadway Lighting continues to look for new export opportunities such as the United Kingdom.[15] Exporting opens up several levels of involvement to exporting firms.

At the most basic level, the exporting firm may sell its products outright to an *export-import merchant,* which is a type of wholesaler specializing in international trade. This merchant assumes all the risks of product ownership, distribution, and sale. It may even purchase the goods in the producer's home country and assume responsibility for exporting the goods. An important and practical issue for domestic firms dealing with foreign customers is securing payment. Figure 3-3 depicts a simplified version of the process. This is a two-sided issue that reflects the mutual concern rightly felt by both parties to the trade deal: The exporter would like to be paid before shipping the merchandise, whereas the importer obviously would prefer to know that it has received the shipment before releasing any funds. Neither side wants to take the risk of fulfilling its part of the deal only to discover later that the other side has not. The result would lead to legal costs and complex, lengthy dealings that would waste everyone's resources. This mutual level of mistrust, in fact, makes good business sense and has been around since the beginning of trade centuries ago. The solution then was the same as it still is today—for both parties to use a mutually trusted go-between who can ensure that the payment is held until the merchandise is in fact delivered according to the terms of the trade contract. The go-between representatives employed by the importer and exporter are still, as they were in the past, the local domestic banks involved in international business.

Alternatively, the exporting firm may ship its products to an *export-import agent,* which arranges the sale of the products to foreign intermediaries for a commission or fee. The agent is an independent firm—like other agents—that sells and may perform other marketing functions for the exporter. The exporter, however, retains title to the products during shipment and until they are sold.

An exporting firm also may establish its own *sales offices,* or *branches,* in foreign countries. These installations are international extensions of the firm's distribution system. They represent a deeper involvement in international business than the other exporting techniques we have discussed—and thus they carry a greater risk. The exporting firm maintains control over sales, and it gains both experience in and knowledge of foreign markets. Eventually, the firm also may develop its own sales force to operate in conjunction with foreign sales offices.

Figure 3-3 Exporting to International Markets

After signing contracts, the importer will ask its local bank to issue a *letter of credit* for the funds needed to pay for the merchandise. The transporter of the merchandise provides the exporter evidence of the shipment via a *bill of lading.* The exporter signs over title to the merchandise and issues a *draft* from its bank, which orders the importer's bank to pay for the merchandise.

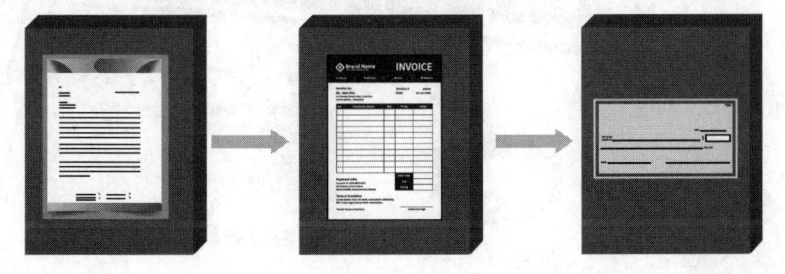

Another option is via a **trading company**, which provides a link between buyers and sellers in different countries. A trading company, as its name implies, is not involved in manufacturing or owning assets related to manufacturing. It buys products in one country at the lowest price consistent with quality and sells to buyers in another country. An important function of trading companies is taking title to products and performing all the activities necessary to move the products from the domestic country to a foreign country. For example, large grain-trading companies operating out of home offices both in the United States and overseas control a major portion of the world's trade in basic food commodities. These trading companies sell homogeneous agricultural commodities that can be stored and moved rapidly in response to market conditions.

In the early 1990s, many developing nations had major restrictions on converting domestic currency into foreign currency. Therefore, companies that wanted to export had to resort to barter agreements with importers. **Countertrade** is essentially an international barter transaction in which goods and services are exchanged for different goods and services. As an example, Iran has purchased rice and other imports from India with payment in crude oil.[16] Countertrade is still used today, particularly for trade with countries that have difficult relations with the home nation.

许可和特许经营
3-2b Licensing and Franchising

Licensing and franchising represent slightly more complex arrangements for international trade. **Licensing** is a contractual agreement in which one firm permits another to produce and market its product and to use its brand name in return for a royalty or other compensation. For example, Yoplait yogurt is a French yogurt licensed for production in the United States. The Yoplait brand maintains an appealing French image, and in return, the U.S. producer pays the French firm a percentage of its income from sales of the product.

Licensing is especially advantageous for small manufacturers wanting to launch a well-known domestic brand internationally. For example, Swedish-owned Electrolux licenses many of its products to firms in India, China, and many other countries. Licensing thus provides a simple method for expanding into a foreign market with virtually no investment. On the other hand, if the licensee does not maintain the licensor's product standards, the product's reputation may be damaged.

贸易公司
trading company provides a link between buyers and sellers in different countries

对等贸易
countertrade an international barter transaction

许可
licensing a contractual agreement in which one firm permits another to produce and market its product and to use its brand name in return for a royalty or other compensation

Another possible disadvantage is that a licensing arrangement may not provide the original producer with any foreign marketing experience.

Franchising is similar to licensing in that it is a contractual arrangement for an individual or organization to operate facilities, typically stores, on behalf of another. A franchisor allows a franchisee to use the franchisor's brand name and methods of doing business in its own stores in exchange for fees and royalties. This arrangement can enable a popular brand to expand into overseas markets with relatively little investment. Consider that consumers around the world can get donuts, muffins, bagels, and coffee at 3,200 Dunkin' restaurants in 36 countries, in addition to 8,500 restaurants in the United States.[17]

合同制造
3-2c Contract Manufacturing

Companies that want a little more control over their products and are willing to take on a greater degree of risk may engage in contract manufacturing. **Contract manufacturing** occurs when one firm employs another business—often in another country—to manufacture its products or product components to the domestic firm's specifications. The resulting product typically carries the domestic firm's name. In fact, many U.S. companies use contract manufacturing to take advantage of lower labor costs in other countries, which can help lower the prices of their products to consumers. Contract manufacturing is used far more often than you might guess, and it is common in the electronics, automotive, and fashion industries, among others. Consider Swedish fast-fashion retailer H&M, which contracts with hundreds of different companies in 40 countries to produce its trendy clothing. Recently, the firm has begun identifying the company, country, and even factory producing each item of clothing for interested consumers and stakeholders.[18]

Indeed, **outsourcing**, the contracting of manufacturing and/or other activities to overseas companies that specialize in those activities and can offer them at a lower cost, has become very common in recent years. Many companies have achieved significant cost savings from outsourcing manufacturing to countries such as India, Bangladesh, Vietnam, and the Philippines, where labor costs and taxes are significantly lower than in the United States. In most cases, these savings are passed on to shareholders and to consumers in the form of lower prices. However, outsourcing is controversial because it has resulted in the loss of American manufacturing jobs and higher unemployment in manufacturing sectors.

合资企业和联盟
3-2d Joint Ventures and Alliances

A *joint venture* is a partnership formed to achieve a specific goal or to operate for a specific period of time. A joint venture with an established firm in a foreign country provides immediate market knowledge and access, reduced risk, and control over product attributes. However, joint-venture agreements established across national borders can become extremely complex. As a result, joint-venture agreements generally require a very high level of commitment from all the parties involved. A joint venture may be used to produce and market an existing product in a foreign nation or to develop an entirely new product. For example, New York-based Pfizer, one of the world's leading pharmaceutical companies, entered into a joint venture with BioNTech, a German biotechnology company, to create and distribute a vaccine for the COVID-19 virus.[19]

A **strategic alliance**, a more recent form of international business structure, is a partnership formed to create competitive advantage on a worldwide basis. Strategic alliances are very similar to joint ventures. The number of

合同制造
contract manufacturing an arrangement in which one firm contracts with another business, often in another country, to manufacture products or product components to its specifications

外包
outsourcing an arrangement in which one firm contracts manufacturing or other activities to a firm in another country that specializes in those activities and can offer them at a lower cost than domestic firms

战略联盟
strategic alliance a partnership formed to create competitive advantage on a worldwide basis

Joint venture. Large pipelines can involve multiple countries. They can be organized based on the use of joint ventures.

Chapter 3　Global Business

strategic alliances is growing at an estimated rate of about 20 percent per year. In fact, in the automobile and computer industries, strategic alliances are becoming the predominant means of competing. International competition is so fierce and the costs of competing on a global basis are so high that few firms have all the resources needed to do it alone. Thus, individual firms that lack the internal resources essential for international success may seek to collaborate with other companies. An example of such an alliance is the agreement between Honda and General Motors to collaborate to make electric vehicles using technologies from both firms.[20]

直接投资
3-2e Direct Investment

At a still deeper level of involvement in international business, a firm may invest directly in its own facilities, that is, its own production and marketing facilities in one or more foreign nations. This *direct investment* provides complete control over operations, but it carries a greater risk than the joint venture. The firm is really establishing a subsidiary in a foreign country. Most firms do so only after they have engaged in simpler levels of international trade and acquired some knowledge of the host country's markets.

Direct investment may take either of two forms. In the first, the company builds or purchases manufacturing and other facilities in a foreign country. It uses these facilities to produce its own established products and to market them in that country and perhaps in neighboring countries. Firms such as General Motors, Dow Chemical, and Colgate-Palmolive are multinational companies with worldwide manufacturing facilities.

A second form of direct investment in international business is the purchase of an existing firm in a foreign country under an arrangement that allows it to operate independently of the parent company. When Sony Corporation (a Japanese firm) decided to enter the motion picture business in the United States, it chose to purchase Columbia Pictures Entertainment, Inc., rather than start a new motion picture studio from scratch.

跨国公司
3-2f Multinational Firms

A **multinational corporation** is a firm that operates on a worldwide scale without ties to any specific nation or region. The multinational firm represents the highest level of involvement in international business. It is equally "at home" in most countries of the world. In fact, as far as the operations of the multinational enterprise are concerned, national boundaries exist only on maps. It is, however, organized under the laws of its home country. Table 3-4 shows the ten largest foreign and U.S. public multinational companies; the ranking is based on a composite score reflecting each company's best three out of four rankings for sales, profits, assets, and market value.

> ✓ **Concept Check**
>
> ▸ List the most common methods of entering international business.
>
> ▸ Two methods of engaging in international business may be categorized as either direct or indirect. How would you classify each of the methods described in this chapter? Why?
>
> ▸ In what ways is a multinational corporation different from a large corporation that does business in several countries?

跨国公司
multinational corporation a firm that operates on a worldwide scale without ties to any specific nation or region

▸ **Table 3-4** The Ten Largest Foreign and U.S. Multinational Corporations

Rank	Company	Business	Country	Revenue ($ millions)
1	Walmart	General Merchandise	United States	523,964
2	Sinopec	Energy	China	407,009
3	State Grid	Power Grids	China	383,906
4	China National Petroleum	Energy	China	379,130
5	Royal Dutch Shell	Energy	Netherlands	352,106
6	Saudi Aramco	Petroleum	Saudi Arabia	329,784
7	Volkswagen	Automobiles	Germany	282,760
8	BP	Energy	United Kingdom	282,616
9	Amazon	Internet and Retail	United States	280,522
10	Toyota	Automobiles	Japan	275,288

Source: "Global 500," *Fortune*.

Sustaining the Planet

保护地球：宜家开设第一家二手店

IKEA Opens Its First Second-Hand Store

IKEA, a ready-to-assemble furniture retailer, has a reputation for sustainability. The company's goal is to become 100 percent circular. The term *circular economy* refers to an economic system that eliminates waste and keeps products in use. For IKEA, this translates to creating products with renewable or recycled materials, helping customers extend the life of their products, and developing circular capabilities in its supply chain. One way IKEA is achieving this is through its secondhand store concept.

IKEA opened its first secondhand store in Sweden, its home country. Consumers donate their furniture at municipal recycling centers. The furniture is repaired or repurposed in IKEA's repair shop and then sold below the item's initial price. IKEA's goal is to be circular by 2030. By then, the company also aims to reduce more greenhouse gas emissions than emitted by its value chain. Helping customers get more use out of their products is key to achieving both goals.

The store is located in ReTuna Shopping Centre, a mall where all products sold are either reused or recycled. IKEA hopes to learn more about secondhand retail, including how to attract shoppers and what causes customers to donate products. To incentivize individuals to return old IKEA furniture, the company offered local customers vouchers. If IKEA's secondhand store is successful, it will roll out the concept in additional markets.

Sources: Based on information in Anna Ringstrom, "IKEA Opens Pilot Second-Hand Store in Sweden," *World Economic Forum*, October 30, 2020; IKEA, "Why the Future of Furniture Is Circular".

国际商务挑战

3-3 International Business Challenges

Specialization and international trade can result in the efficient production of want-satisfying goods and services on a worldwide basis. As we have noted, international business generally is increasing. Yet the nations of the world continue to erect barriers to free trade. They do so for reasons ranging from internal political and economic pressures to simple mistrust of other nations. In this section, we examine the types of trade restrictions that nations may apply, the arguments for and against trade restrictions, and additional challenges to international trade.

Learning Objective

3-3 Discuss the challenges businesses face when entering international markets, especially the restrictions nations place on international trade.

贸易限制

3-3a Trade Restrictions

Nations generally are eager to export their products. They want to provide markets for their industries and to develop a favorable balance of trade. Hence, most trade restrictions are applied to imports from other nations.

Tariffs Perhaps the most commonly applied trade restriction is the tariff, also known as a customs or import duty. A **tariff** is a tax levied on a particular foreign product entering a country. For example, the United States imposed a 2.2 percent import duty on fresh Chilean tomatoes, an 8.7 percent duty if tomatoes are dried and packaged, and nearly 12 percent if tomatoes are made into ketchup or salsa. Two types of tariffs are revenue tariffs and protective tariffs; both have the effect of raising the price of the product in the importing nations, but for different reasons. *Revenue tariffs* are imposed solely to generate income for the government. *Protective tariffs,* on the other hand, are imposed to protect a domestic industry from competition by keeping the price of competing imports level with or higher than the price of similar domestic products. Because fewer units of the product will be sold at the increased price, fewer units will be imported. The French and Japanese agricultural sectors would both shrink drastically if their nations abolished the protective tariffs that

关税

tariff a tax levied on a particular foreign product entering a country

Chapter 3 Global Business 81

keep the price of imported farm products high. In recent years, the United States has imposed significantly greater tariffs on imports of products from around the world, ranging from Scotch whiskey to Chinese electronics, ostensibly to protect domestic industries from foreign competition. However, when countries alter their trade policies to include more tariffs, other countries are likely to respond in kind, which can lead to a *trade war* that oftentimes harms producers in all involved countries.

Some countries rationalize their protectionist policies as a way of offsetting an international trade practice called *dumping*. **Dumping** is the exportation of large quantities of a product at a price lower than that of the same product in the home market. Thus, dumping drives down the price of the domestic item. Recently, the Foil Trade Enforcement Working Group of the Aluminum Association, which represents U.S. aluminum manufacturers, claimed that low-priced aluminum foil from Armenia, Brazil, Oman, Russia, and Turkey was being sold in the United States at less than fair value prices. The producers contend that the dumped foil is harming the domestic industry, and they therefore asked to obtain an antidumping duty through the government to offset the advantage of the foreign product.[21]

Nontariff Barriers A **nontariff barrier** is a nontax measure imposed by a government to favor domestic over foreign suppliers. Nontariff barriers create obstacles to the marketing of foreign goods in a country and increase costs for exporters. The following are a few examples of government-imposed nontariff barriers:

- An **import quota** is a limit on the amount of a particular good that may be imported into a country during a given period of time. The limit may be set in terms of either quantity (so many pounds of beef) or value (so many dollars' worth of shoes). Quotas also may be set on individual products imported from specific countries. Once an import quota has been reached, imports are halted until the specified time has elapsed.
- An **embargo** is a complete halt to trading with a particular nation or of a particular product. The embargo is used most often as a political weapon. At present, the United States has import embargoes against Iran and DPRK—both the result of extremely poor political relations.
- An **exchange control** is a restriction on the amount of a particular foreign currency that can be purchased or sold. By limiting the amount of foreign currency importers can obtain, a government limits the amount of goods importers can purchase with that currency. This has the effect of limiting imports from the country whose foreign exchange is being controlled.
- A nation can increase or decrease the value of its money relative to the currency of other nations. **Currency devaluation** is the reduction of the value of a nation's currency relative to the currencies of other countries.

Devaluation increases the cost of foreign goods, whereas it decreases the cost of domestic goods to foreign firms. For example, suppose that the British pound is worth $2. In this case, an American-made $2,000 computer can be purchased for £1,000. However, if the United Kingdom devalues the pound so that it is worth only $1, that same computer will cost £2,000. The increased cost, in pounds, will reduce the import of American computers—and all foreign goods—into England. On the other hand, before devaluation, a £500 set of English bone china will cost an American $1,000. After the devaluation, the set of china will cost only $500. The decreased cost will make the china—and all English goods—much more attractive to U.S. purchasers.

Bureaucratic red tape is more subtle than the other forms of nontariff barriers. Yet it can be the most frustrating trade barrier of all. A few examples are the restrictive application of standards and complex requirements related to product testing, labeling, and certification.

倾销
dumping exportation of large quantities of a product at a price lower than that of the same product in the home market

非关税壁垒
nontariff barrier a nontax measure imposed by a government to favor domestic over foreign suppliers

进口配额
import quota a limit on the amount of a particular good that may be imported into a country during a given period of time

禁运
embargo a complete halt to trading with a particular nation or of a particular product

外汇管制
exchange control a restriction on the amount of a particular foreign currency that can be purchased or sold

货币贬值
currency devaluation the reduction of the value of a nation's currency relative to the currencies of other countries

Reasons for and against Trade Restrictions Various reasons are given for trade restrictions either on the import of specific products or on trade with particular countries. We have noted that political considerations usually are involved in trade embargoes. Other frequently cited reasons for restricting trade include the following:

- *To equalize a nation's balance of payments.* This may be considered necessary to restore confidence in the country's monetary system and in its ability to repay its debts.
- *To protect new or weak industries.* A new, or infant, industry may not be strong enough to withstand foreign competition. Temporary trade restrictions may be used to give it a chance to grow and become self-sufficient. Of course, once an industry is protected from foreign competition, it may not want to give up the protections, and these "temporary" trade restrictions may become permanent.
- *To protect national security.* Restrictions in this category generally apply to technological products that must be kept out of the hands of potential enemies. For example, strategic and defense-related goods cannot be exported to unfriendly nations.
- *To protect the health of citizens.* Products may be embargoed because they are dangerous or unhealthy (e.g., farm products contaminated with insecticides).
- *To retaliate for another nation's trade restrictions.* A country whose exports are taxed by another country may respond by imposing tariffs on imports from that country.
- *To protect domestic jobs.* By restricting imports, a nation can protect jobs in domestic industries. However, while protectionist policies can have positive effects in the short run, they can be harmful in the long term.

Trade restrictions have immediate and long-term economic consequences—both within the restricting nation and in world trade patterns. These include the following:

- *Higher prices for consumers.* Higher prices may result from the imposition of tariffs or the elimination of foreign competition, as described earlier. For example, imposing quota restrictions and import protections adds $25 billion annually to U.S. consumers' apparel costs by directly increasing costs for imported apparel.
- *Restriction of consumers' choices.* Again, this is a direct result of the elimination of some foreign products from the marketplace and of the artificially high prices that importers must charge for products that are still imported.
- *Misallocation of international resources.* The protection of weak industries results in the inefficient use of limited resources. The economies of both the restricting nation and other nations eventually suffer because of this waste.
- *Loss of jobs.* The restriction of imports by one nation must lead to cutbacks—and the loss of jobs—in the export-oriented industries of other nations. Furthermore, trade protection has a significant effect on the composition of employment. U.S. trade restrictions—whether on textiles, apparel, steel, or automobiles—benefit only a few industries while harming many others. The gains in employment

accrue to the protected industries and their primary suppliers, and the losses are spread across all other industries. A few states gain employment, but many other states lose employment.

Consider that former President Donald Trump's protectionist policies—intended to slash the nation's trade deficit with China and stem job losses in American manufacturing—ultimately did neither. Instead, Trump's trade policy, which relied heavily on tariffs, resulted in a trade war with China which ultimately raised the prices of important Chinese imports while reducing American exports to China, at a cost of American jobs in affected industries. While jobs did grow in a few industries, so did the trade deficit with China.[22]

经济挑战

3-3b Economic Challenges

Businesspeople desiring to engage in international trade must also recognize that there are likely to be differences in countries' standards of living, individual income and buying power, national resources, and infrastructure. Among the world's nations, the United States has the highest GDP, which we defined in Chapter 1 as the value of all products produced by all people within a nation in a specified time period. While GDP can provide an estimate of the size of a national economy, businesspeople are often more interested in per capita GDP (a nation's GDP divided by its population) as this gives more insight into a nation's standard of living and market potential. Consider that the GDP per capita of the United States is $63,051, yet a number of countries have higher rates of GDP per capita, including Switzerland, Norway, and Luxembourg.[23] Businesspeople can also find tremendous opportunities in countries with far less incomes. The countries of Brazil, Russia, India, China, and South Africa (BRICS) have in recent years experienced rapid economic expansion and growing middle classes, making them very attractive markets for companies looking to develop their brands.

Another economic challenge is that in most cases nations use different currencies. The value of the American dollar, European euro, and the Japanese yen has a significant impact on product prices in most countries. Many countries allow the value of their currencies to float, or fluctuate according to supply and demand on the foreign exchange market. In recent times, the value of the U.S. dollar has been strong relative to other currencies. This means that U.S. exports cost more when purchased using euros in Europe or renminbi in China. Because the value of a nation's currency can change from day to day, the change in value can also affect how much profit (or loss) a firm may realize on an international transaction.

Another factor that can affect the attractiveness of and opportunities within another country is its level of *infrastructure*—the transportation, energy transmission, communication networks, and other systems that facilitate the functions of civilization. Developing countries may have less reliable infrastructure systems, which may create challenges when introducing certain types of products. On the other hand, a lack of communications and utility infrastructure in some countries spurred entrepreneurs to invest in wireless and alternative energy technologies and solutions at a faster rate than in the United States. As an example, in many developing countries, a significant percentage of the population lacks reliable access to banking services. Safaricom, a large Kenyan telecom provider, partnered with banks, nonprofit organizations, and microcredit organizations to launch M-Pesa, a payment platform. M-Pesa functions as a digital wallet allowing users to send and receive payments via an app and to save and withdraw funds from Safaricom retail stores throughout Kenya. As M-Pesa grew and competing apps from other telecoms proliferated, these services have boosted the percentage of Kenyans using financial services from 26 percent to 75 percent in just a decade.[24]

Ethics and Social Responsibility

商业伦理与社会责任：打开数字支付的大门

Opening the Gates to Digital Payments

It may be surprising to learn that digital payment services have been established in developing countries for more than a decade. M-Pesa, a mobile phone-based money transfer and financing service, serves millions in Kenya who previously were limited to cash and informal networks, lifting nearly 200,000 individuals out of poverty. Now, a coalition of nonprofits and tech companies, including the Bill and Melinda Gates Foundation and Google, want to build on the digital payment revolution M-Pesa started.

The coalition, called Mojaloop Foundation, will facilitate the development of real-time digital payment systems through an open-source platform. Open-source software includes the source code so developers can alter and distribute it. One major goal is to digitally connect the fragmented financial service offerings currently available such as M-Pesa. M-Pesa and its imitators are mostly privately owned and operated, often resulting in high transaction fees between systems. Mojaloop Foundation aims to reduce friction.

Bridging the gap between these banking and payment systems could add value to each service rather than pitting them against each other as competitors. Another of Mojaloop's goals is to boost the global economy. Studies show that when affordable digital finance tools are available in developing nations, economies grow by 6 percent. But providing the software is only one piece of the puzzle. Mojaloop will also connect experts with countries to tackle problems and influence government policies.

Sources: Based on information in David Z. Morris, "Google and Gates Foundation to Help Spread Digital Payments in Developing Countries," *Fortune*, May 6, 2020; Mojaloop Foundation, "Mission".

法律和政治环境
3-3c Legal and Political Climate

Beyond infrastructure and economic issues, the laws, regulatory agencies, political systems, and special-interest groups within a country all have a great impact on international business. In the United States, as in many countries, the political, legal, and regulatory forces of the environment are closely interconnected. Even when different countries seem similar, differences in legal, political, or regulatory conditions in their home countries can shape trade. We have already mentioned some of the challenges that businesses may face when they engage in international trade: trade restrictions such as tariffs and import quotas often are the result of the political will within the country.

Additionally, rules that Americans take for granted may differ in other nations. Privacy rules in Europe, for example, are considerably stricter than within the United States, as are rules related to advertising to children. On the other hand, U.S. law prohibits direct involvement in payoffs and bribes by American businesspersons and companies. The Foreign Corrupt Practices Act (FCPA) of 1977 also makes it illegal for U.S. firms to attempt to make large payments or bribes to influence policy decisions of foreign governments. These laws can make it challenging for U.S. companies to compete with foreign firms that do engage in these practices.

社会和文化障碍
3-3d Social and Cultural Barriers

One of the most significant barriers to international trade relates to social and cultural issues. Differences due to religious institutions, values, customs, social systems, and language can affect communications, negotiations, and perceptions of products and companies. Obviously, language can be problematic when translating advertising and other communications into other languages. On more than one occasion, such efforts led to comical yet potentially disastrous situations. For example, KFC's long-running slogan "Finger lickin' good" was translated in China as "Eat your fingers off," while Schweppes'

Concept Check

- List and briefly describe the principal restrictions that may be applied to a nation's imports.
- What reasons are generally given for imposing trade restrictions?
- What are some economic challenges that businesspeople need to consider in international trade?
- How can the political and legal climate of a nation affect trade?
- Describe some social and cultural factors that can influence product acceptance in another country.

Learning Objective

3-4 Identify the facilitators of international trade, including international trade agreements and international economic organizations working to foster trade.

关税与贸易总协定（关贸总协定）
General Agreement on Tariffs and Trade (GATT) an international organization of nations dedicated to reducing or eliminating tariffs and other barriers to world trade

世界贸易组织
World Trade Organization (WTO) powerful successor to GATT that facilitates world trade among member nations by mediating disputes and fostering efforts to reduce trade barriers

经济共同体
economic community an organization of nations formed to promote the free movement of resources and products among its members and to create common economic policies

---

carbonated water was translated in Italy as "toilet water."[25] Even when language is shared, words may still mean different things. Consider that "football" is a leading sport outside the United States—but the term refers to what Americans call soccer.

Cultural barriers can impede acceptance of products in foreign countries. For example, illustrations of feet are regarded as offensive in Thailand. Even so simple a thing as the color of a product or its package can present a problem. In Japan, black and white are the colors of mourning, so they should not be used in packaging. In Brazil, purple is the color of death. And in Egypt, green is never used on a package because it is the national color. Many retailers on the internet have yet to come to grips with the task of designing an online shopping site that is attractive and functional for all global customers. When customers are unfamiliar with particular products from another country, their general perceptions of the country itself affect their attitude toward the product and help to determine whether they will buy it.

国际贸易促进者
3-4 Facilitators of International Trade

Although the previous pages may make international trade seem daunting, there are many organizations and agreements that facilitate trade across national borders, including the World Trade Organization (WTO) and numerous free trade agreements.

关税与贸易总协定和世界贸易组织
3-4a The General Agreement on Tariffs and Trade and the World Trade Organization

At the end of World War II, the United States and 22 other nations organized the body that came to be known as GATT. The **General Agreement on Tariffs and Trade (GATT)** was an international organization of 164 nations dedicated to reducing or eliminating tariffs and other barriers to world trade. Headquartered in Geneva, Switzerland, GATT provided a forum for tariff negotiations and a means for settling international trade disputes and problems. It also conferred "most-favored-nation status (MFN)," meaning that each GATT member nation was to be treated equally by all contracting nations. Therefore, MFN ensured that any tariff reductions or other trade concessions were extended automatically to all GATT members.

From 1947 to 1994, the body sponsored eight rounds of negotiations to reduce trade restrictions. Three were especially constructive. The *Kennedy Round,* which began in 1964, was successful in reducing tariffs and other barriers to trade in industrial and agricultural products by an average of more than 35 percent. The *Tokyo Round,* which was completed in 1979, negotiated phased tariff cuts of 30 to 35 percent and removed or eased nontariff barriers such as import quotas, unrealistic quality standards for imports, and unnecessary red tape in customs procedures. In 1986, the *Uruguay Round* was able to lower tariffs by greater than one-third, reform trade in agricultural goods, write new rules of trade for intellectual property and services, and strengthen the dispute-settlement process. Arguably the most significant result of the Uruguay Round was the creation of the World Trade Organization (WTO) on January 1, 1995. The **World Trade Organization (WTO)** is an international forum that facilitates world trade among member nations by mediating disputes and fostering continued efforts to reduce trade barriers. Membership in the WTO obliges 164 member nations to observe GATT rules.

国际贸易协定和联盟
3-4b International Trade Agreements and Alliances

The primary objective of the WTO is to remove barriers to trade on a worldwide basis. On a smaller scale, an **economic community** is an organization of nations formed to promote the free movement of resources and products among its members and to create common economic policies. A number of economic communities now exist.

Marketing

The United States-Mexico-Canada Agreement (USMCA) The *United States-Mexico-Canada Agreement (USMCA)* joined the United States with its first- and second-largest export trading partners, Canada and Mexico, in 2020. USMCA replaced an earlier accord, the *North American Free Trade Agreement (NAFTA)*, which went into effect in 1994. NAFTA gradually eliminated tariffs on goods produced and traded among the three nations and created a free trade area of more than 503 million people. After 25 years, NAFTA succeeded in its core goals of expanding trade and investment between the United States, Canada, and Mexico. For example, from 1993 to 2017, trade among the NAFTA nations increased nearly fourfold to $1.3 trillion, significantly more than U.S. trade with other countries.[26] Companies in all three nations experienced growth in exports, while consumers gained better prices and selection.

USMCA. The United States-Mexico-Canada Agreement has unlocked opportunities for millions of Americans by supporting Made-in-America jobs and exports. Many American small business exporters' first customers are in Canada or Mexico.

However, NAFTA critics maintained that it resulted in the loss of American jobs to Mexico, harmed workers by eroding labor standards, undermined national sovereignty, and did nothing to help the environment. Moreover, the original accord was unable to address technological changes that had occurred since its implementation, particularly with regard to intellectual property rights. Some critics felt that Mexico and Canada got more out of the deal than the United States. In 2018, the three nations began renegotiating the agreement that ultimately became the United States-Mexico-Canada Agreement.

USMCA retains a number of NAFTA's provisions but updates it in significant ways:

- The agreement will be formally reviewed at least every six years to ensure that it remains beneficial to all three nations.
- It has significant dispute resolution systems, which the prior agreement lacked.
- It strengthens labor laws and provides for greater enforcement of them, creating a more equitable situation for U.S. workers.
- It includes provisions related to digital technology and intellectual property.
- It includes funds to address environmental issues stemming from trade between the three nations.[27]

The European Union Operating as a single market with 27 countries, the European Union (EU), also known as the European Economic Community and the Common Market, was formed in 1957 by six countries—France, the Federal Republic of Germany, Italy, Belgium, the Netherlands, and Luxembourg. Its objective was freely conducted commerce among these nations and others that might later join. Many more nations have joined the EU since then. The citizens of the United Kingdom voted in 2016 to exit the European Union; however, "Brexit" did not actually go into effect until January 2020. The EU, with a population of 450 million, is now an economic force to be recognized by even the most advanced economies such as of the United States and Japan.

Since 2002, 19 member nations of the EU have been participating in a common currency, the euro, which facilitates trade by removing the need to convert different currencies used in transactions across borders. The euro, used by over 341 million Europeans, is the single currency of the European Monetary Union nations. However, the remaining eight EU members still maintain their own currencies.

The Dominican Republic-Central America Free Trade Agreement (CAFTA-DR) The Central American Free Trade Agreement (CAFTA) was created in 2003 by the United States and four Central American countries—El Salvador, Guatemala, Honduras, and Nicaragua. The CAFTA became CAFTA-DR when the Dominican Republic joined the group in 2007. Costa Rica joined CAFTA-DR as the sixth member in 2009. CAFTA-DR creates the third-largest U.S. export market in Latin America, behind only Mexico and Brazil.

The Association of Southeast Asian Nations (ASEAN) The Association of Southeast Asian Nations, with headquarters in Jakarta, Indonesia, was established in 1967 to promote political, economic, and social cooperation among its seven member countries: Indonesia, Malaysia, the Philippines, Singapore, Thailand, Brunei, and Vietnam. With three new members, Cambodia, Laos, and Myanmar, this region of more than 667 million people, and GDP of $3.3 trillion, is already our fifth-largest trading partner.

The Commonwealth of Independent States The Commonwealth of Independent States was established in December 1991 as a free trade association of 11 republics of the former Soviet Union. Today, its members include Armenia, Azerbaijan, Belarus, Kazakhstan, Kyrgyzstan, Moldova, Russia, Tajikistan, and Uzbekistan. Ukraine and Georgia no longer participate.

Comprehensive and Progressive Agreement for Trans-Pacific Partnership (CPTPP) In 2011, the leaders of twelve countries—Australia, Brunei Darussalam, Canada, Chile, Japan, Malaysia, Mexico, New Zealand, Peru, Singapore, Vietnam, and the United States—agreed to form the Trans-Pacific Partnership, which would have been the world's largest free trade agreement. However, the United States withdrew from the agreement in 2017, and the remaining members renegotiated the treaty, which then became known as the *Comprehensive and Progressive Agreement for Trans-Pacific Partnership*. This partnership will boost the economies of the member countries, lower barriers to trade and investment, increase exports, and create more jobs. There is speculation that the United States may rejoin the free trade agreement after the election of President Joseph R. Biden.

The Common Market of the Southern Cone (MERCOSUR) Headquartered in Montevideo, Uruguay, the *Common Market of the Southern Cone (MERCOSUR)* was established in 1991 under the Treaty of Asuncion to unite Argentina, Brazil, Paraguay, and Uruguay as a free-trade alliance; Venezuela became a member later. In more recent times, Colombia, Ecuador, Peru, Bolivia, Chile, Guyana, and Surinam have enrolled as associate members.

✓ **Concept Check**
- Define and describe the major objectives of the World Trade Organization (WTO) and the international economic communities.
- What is the U.S.-Mexico-Canada Agreement (USMCA)? What is its importance for the United States, Canada, and Mexico?

出口援助的来源

3-5 Sources of Export Assistance

There are a number of federal and state agencies that can assist U.S. firms interested in developing export-promotion programs. The services and programs of these agencies can help American firms to compete in foreign markets and create new jobs in the United States. As an example, the state of Texas, one of the leading exporting states, offers several programs, resources, and even grants for small and medium-sized Texas companies looking to export their products. The state's Export Assistance Program can also facilitate the participation of delegations of small businesses in export-oriented trade shows and missions around the world.[28] Table 3-5 provides an overview of selected U.S. government export assistance programs.

These and other sources of export information enhance the business opportunities of U.S. firms seeking to enter expanding foreign markets. Another vital energy factor is financing.

Learning Objective
3-5 Describe sources of export assistance.

✓ **Concept Check**
- List some key sources of export assistance. How can these sources be useful to small business firms?

▶ **Table 3-5** U.S. Government Export Assistance Programs

International Trade Administration	Promotes trade and investment and enforces U.S. trade laws and agreements
U.S. Commercial Service	Part of the International Trade Administration; offers assistance and information to exporters through its domestic and overseas commercial offices
Advocacy Center	Part of the International Trade Administration; assists U.S. firms competing for major projects with foreign governments
Small Business Administration U.S. Export Assistance Centers	Provide assistance in export marketing and trade finance
Small Business Administration, Office of International Trade	Publishes many helpful guides to assist small and medium-sized companies

国际商务融资
3-6 Financing International Business

Learning Objective

3-6 Identify institutions that can help businesses and nations finance international business.

International trade compounds the concerns of financial managers. Currency exchange rates, tariffs and foreign exchange controls, and the tax structures of host nations all affect international operations and the flow of cash. In addition, financial managers must be concerned both with the financing of their international operations and with the means available to their customers to finance purchases.

Fortunately, along with business in general, a number of large banks have become international in scope. Many banks have established branches in major cities around the world. Citi, for example, provides banking and finance services to both consumer and business customers in offices in 96 countries.[29] Thus, like firms in other industries, they can provide services to their customers where and when they are needed. In addition, financial assistance is available from U.S. government and international sources.

One such source is the U.S. Small Business Administration, which provides up to $5 million in short-term loans to U.S. small business exporters. The agency also provides up to $500,000 in export development financing to buy, produce goods, or provide services for exports to small businesses that have exporting potential but need funds to cover the initial costs of entering an export market. Several of today's international financial organizations were founded many years ago to facilitate free trade and the exchange of currencies among nations. Some, such as the Inter-American Development Bank, are supported internationally and focus on developing countries. Others, such as the Export-Import Bank, are operated by one country but provide international financing.

美国进出口银行
3-6a The Export-Import Bank of the United States

The **Export-Import Bank of the United States**, created in 1934, is an independent agency of the U.S. government whose function is to assist in financing the exports of American firms. *Ex-Im Bank,* as it is commonly called, extends and guarantees credit to overseas buyers of American goods and services and guarantees short-term financing for exports. It also cooperates with commercial banks in helping American exporters to offer credit to their overseas customers. In the last decade, Ex-Im Bank

美国进出口银行
Export-Import Bank of the United States an independent agency of the U.S. government whose function is to assist in financing the exports of American firms

Mission possible. The Export-Import Bank of the United States (Ex-Im Bank), with 87 years of experience, is the official export credit agency of the United States. Ex-Im Bank's mission is to assist in financing the export of U.S. goods and services to international markets. Its goal is to end extreme poverty by 2030, promote shared prosperity, and support the global sustainable development agenda.

has supported more than 1.44 million jobs in the United States. In 2019, nearly 90 percent of the Bank's transactions—nearly 2,100—directly supported American small businesses.[30]

世界银行
3-6b The World Bank

A **multilateral development bank (MDB)** is an internationally supported bank that provides loans to developing countries to help them grow. The most familiar is the **World Bank**, a cooperative of 189 member countries, which operates worldwide. Established in 1944 and headquartered in Washington, DC, the bank provides low-interest loans, interest-free credits, and grants to developing countries. The loans and grants help these countries to:

- supply safe drinking water
- build schools and train teachers
- increase agricultural productivity
- expand citizens' access to markets, jobs, and housing
- improve healthcare and access to water and sanitation
- manage forests and other natural resources
- build and maintain roads, railways, and ports, and
- reduce air pollution and protect the environment.[31]

In addition to the World Bank, four other MDBs operate primarily in Central and South America, Asia, Africa, and Eastern and Central Europe. All are supported by the industrialized nations, including the United States.

The Inter-American Development Bank The *Inter-American Development Bank (IDB),* the oldest and largest regional bank, was created in 1959 by 19 Latin American countries and the United States. The bank, which is headquartered in Washington, DC, makes loans and provides technical advice and assistance to countries. Today, the IDB is owned by 48 member nations.

The Asian Development Bank With 68 member nations, the *Asian Development Bank (ADB),* created in 1966 and headquartered in the Philippines, promotes economic and social progress in Asian and Pacific regions. The U.S. government is the second-largest contributor to the ADB's capital, after Japan.

The African Development Bank The African Development Bank (AFDB), also known as *Banque Africaines de Development,* was established in 1964 with headquarters in Abidjan, Ivory Coast. Its members include 54 African and 27 non-African countries from the Americas, Europe, and Asia. The AFDB's goal is to foster the economic and social development of its African members. The bank pursues this goal through loans, research, technical assistance, and the development of trade programs.

European Bank for Reconstruction and Development Established in 1991 to encourage reconstruction and development in Eastern and Central European countries, the London-based *European Bank for Reconstruction and Development* is owned by 69 countries and two intergovernmental institutions (the European Union and the European Investment Bank). Its loans are geared toward developing market-oriented economies and promoting private enterprise.

国际货币基金组织
3-6c The International Monetary Fund

The **International Monetary Fund (IMF)** is an international bank with 190 member nations that makes short-term loans to developing countries experiencing balance-of-payment deficits. This financing is contributed by member nations, and it must be

多边开发银行
multilateral development bank (MDB) an internationally supported bank that provides loans to developing countries to help them grow

世界银行
World Bank a cooperative banking institution with 189 member countries

国际货币基金组织
International Monetary Fund (IMF) an international bank that makes short-term loans to developing countries experiencing balance-of-payment deficits

> **✓ Concept Check**
>
> ▶ What is the Export Import Bank of the United States? How does it assist U.S. exporters?
>
> ▶ What is a multilateral development bank (MDB)? Who supports these banks?
>
> ▶ What is the International Monetary Fund? What types of loans does the IMF provide?

repaid with interest. Loans are provided primarily to fund international trade. Created in 1945 and headquartered in Washington, DC, the bank's main goals are to:

- promote international monetary cooperation
- facilitate the expansion and balanced growth of international trade
- promote exchange rate stability
- assist in establishing a multilateral system of payments, and
- make resources available to members experiencing balance-of-payment difficulties.

Summary 小 结

3-1 Explain the economic bases for and importance of international business.

International business encompasses all business activities that involve exchanges across national boundaries. International trade is based on specialization, whereby each country produces the goods and services that it can produce more efficiently than any other goods and services. A nation is said to have an absolute or comparative advantage relative to these goods. International trade develops when each nation trades its surplus products for those in short supply.

International trade involves selling and shipping raw materials or products to other nations (exporting) and/or purchasing raw materials or products in other nations and bringing them into one's own country (importing). A nation's balance of trade is the difference between the value of its exports and the value of its imports. Its balance of payments is the difference between the flow of money into and out of the nation. Generally, a negative balance of trade is considered unfavorable. The United States has largely positive and growing trade relationships with most countries around the world.

3-2 Explore the methods by which a firm can organize for and enter into international markets.

A firm can enter international markets in several ways that require varying degrees of involvement, investment, and risk. It may export its products and sell them through foreign intermediaries or its own sales organization abroad, or it may sell its exports outright to an export-import merchant. It may license or franchise a foreign firm to produce and market its products. It may outsource or contract an overseas firm to manufacture its products, or it may enter into a joint venture or strategic alliance with a foreign firm. It may establish its own foreign subsidiaries, or it may develop into a multinational corporation.

Generally, each of these methods represents an increasingly deeper level of involvement in international business, with exporting being the simplest and the development of a multinational corporation the most involved.

3-3 Discuss the challenges businesses face when entering international markets, especially the restrictions nations place on international trade.

Despite the benefits of world trade, nations tend to use tariffs and nontariff barriers (import quotas, embargoes, and other restrictions) to limit trade. Tariffs—taxes levied on products entering a country—may be imposed to generate revenue or to protect domestic industries from foreign competition. These restrictions typically are justified as being needed to protect a nation's economy, industries, citizens, or security. They can result in the loss of jobs, higher prices, fewer choices in the marketplace, and the misallocation of resources. Businesspeople must recognize that there are differences in countries' standards of living, individual income and buying power, national resources, and infrastructure. The laws, regulatory agencies, political systems, and special-interest groups within a country all have a great impact on international business. Differences due to religious institutions, values, customs, social systems, and language can affect communications, negotiations, and perceptions of products and companies.

3-4 Identify the facilitators of international trade, including international trade agreements and international economic organizations working to foster trade.

The General Agreement on Tariffs and Trade (GATT) was formed to dismantle trade barriers and provide an environment in which international business can grow. Today, the World Trade Organization (WTO) and various economic communities carry on this mission. Among the most significant of these world economic communities are the European Union, the United States-Mexico-Canada Agreement, the Dominican Republic-Central America Free Trade Agreement, the Association of Southeast Asian Nations, the Commonwealth of Independent States, Comprehensive and Progressive Agreement for Trans-Pacific Partnership, and the Common Market of the Southern Cone.

3-5 Describe sources of export assistance.

Many government and international agencies provide export assistance to U.S. and foreign firms. Some of the most important sources of export assistance include the International Trade Administration, the Small Business Administration, and other governmental and international agencies.

3-6 Identify institutions that can help businesses and nations finance international business.

The financing of international trade is more complex than that of domestic trade. Institutions such as the Ex-Im Bank and the International Monetary Fund have been established to provide financing and ultimately to increase world trade for American and international firms.

Key Terms 关键术语

You should now be able to define and give an example relevant to each of the following terms:

- international business
- absolute advantage
- comparative advantage
- exporting
- importing
- balance of trade
- trade deficit
- balance of payments
- trading company
- countertrade
- licensing
- contract manufacturing
- outsourcing
- strategic alliance
- multinational corporation
- tariff
- dumping
- nontariff barrier
- import quota
- embargo
- exchange control
- currency devaluation
- General Agreement on Tariffs and Trade (GATT)
- World Trade Organization (WTO)
- economic community
- Export-Import Bank of the United States
- multilateral development bank (MDB)
- World Bank
- International Monetary Fund (IMF)

Discussion Questions 讨论题

1. When should a firm consider expanding from strictly domestic trade to international trade? When should it consider becoming further involved in international trade? What factors might affect the firm's decisions in each case?
2. Some politicians think tariffs will reduce their countries' trade deficits. Are they correct?
3. What effects might the devaluation of a nation's currency have on its business firms, its consumers, and the debts it owes to other nations?
4. Should imports to the United States be curtailed, by 20 percent or so, to eliminate our trade deficit? What might happen if this were done?
5. When the U.S. dollar is strong relative to other nations' currencies, what is the effect on imports and exports?
6. How can another country's cultural and political climate influence a firm's efforts to export there?
7. The United States restricts imports but, at the same time, supports the WTO and international banks whose objective is to enhance world trade. As a member of Congress, how would you justify this contradiction to your constituents?
8. How can a firm obtain the expertise needed to produce and market its products in another part of the world, for example, the EU?

Case 3 案例3：本田的战略就是电动化且令人振奋

Honda's Strategy Is Electrifying

Honda Motor Company, a Japan-based multinational motorcycle manufacturer, was founded by Soichiro Honda in 1937. Honda, a Japanese engineer and innovator, built Honda Motor Company from the ground up. The automotive manufacturer, which started with 12 employees retrofitting bicycles with engines, has grown to more than 218,000 employees producing 19 million motorcycles, nearly 5 million automobiles, and more than 5 million power products every year. Today, Honda continues to innovate as the automotive market accelerates its transition to electric and hybrid technology.

Soichiro Honda always had an interest in vehicles. He founded Tokai Seiki (Eastern Sea Precision Machine Company) to make piston rings. Though he won a contract with Toyota, he lost the contract when it became evident that quality was lacking. He visited Toyota factories across Japan to learn more about quality control and perfect his product. Eventually, he created acceptable pistons using an automated process that could employ unskilled war-time laborers. At the start of World War II, Tokai Seiki was placed under the control of the Ministry of Commerce and Industry, and Honda was demoted at his own company. After the war, Honda sold what remained of Tokai Seiki to Toyota and used the profits to open the Honda Technical Research Institute.

With just a dozen employees in 1946, the company built and sold motorized bicycles using the former Imperial Army's generator engines. Demand was high, and the Honda Technical Research Institute soon ran out of stock. The company set out to make its own engine. Honda liquidated his business and used the money to incorporate Honda Motor Company. Its first complete motorcycle, the Honda 1949 D-Type, was just the start. The company grew to become the largest manufacturer of motorcycles by 1964.

In 1959, Honda Motor Company expanded into North America, opening its first overseas subsidiary in Los Angeles. Around this time, Honda opened Honda R&D Co., Ltd. to independently focus on research and development. Over the next several decades, Honda Motor Company continued to expand its product lines as well as operations and exports, opening its first overseas production facility in Belgium and becoming the first Japanese car manufacturer to open a production facility in the United States. Honda is now a household name with a reputation for producing quality cars and motorcycles.

Though Honda Motor Company is the world's largest manufacturer of internal combustion engines, it has had its sights set on new mobility for decades. In 2002, the company offered customers in the United States and Japan the Honda FCX, a fuel-cell powered car. Regulatory change and shifting consumer behavior in Europe have accelerated Honda's long-term electrification plans for the region, a strategy the company calls "Electric Vision." These changes have pushed Honda to introduce electrified powertrains for all of its European mainstream models several years ahead of schedule. Additionally, the company's advanced two-motor hybrid technology seen in the Honda Jazz hatchback and CR-V Hybrid has been met with acclaim across Europe. In a traditional hybrid model, an electric motor assists the car's engine, but in the Jazz hybrid electric vehicle, an electric engine assists the motor.

In the United States, on the other hand, Honda has a long road ahead to an electric future. Honda phased out the Clarity EV, its only all-electric car in the U.S. market at the time, leaving its fuel-cell and plug-in hybrid models. Buyers were unimpressed with its 89-mile driving range. In contrast, both the Chevy Bolt EV and Tesla Model 3 travel around 240 miles. To focus on the next generation of products, Honda partnered with rival General Motors (GM) to create two new all-electric vehicles using GM's proprietary Ultium battery and hands-free driver-assist technology wrapped in Honda's design. Strategic alliances such as this allow companies to pool resources, combine scale and manufacturing efficiencies, and create a competitive advantage.

By 2030, the majority of Honda's cars will be electric, zero-emission vehicles. Though there is still much progress to be made in the United States, Honda is quickly bringing its Electric Vision strategy to life in Europe. Additionally, Honda stands to greatly benefit from its strategic partnership with GM. Honda Motor Company's long history and its reputation for quality show that Honda is a company that knows how to innovate and adapt.[32]

Questions

1. How did Honda Motor Company build its reputation for producing quality cars and motorcycles?
2. What are the advantages of Honda's strategic alliance with GM?
3. How is Honda adapting to regulatory change and shifting consumer behavior in Europe?

Building Skills for Career Success 为成功的职业生涯培养技能

1. Social Media Exercise

Although Nike was founded in the Pacific Northwest and still has its corporate headquarters near Beaverton, Oregon, the company has become a multinational enterprise. The firm employs more than 75,000 people across six continents and is now a global marketer of footwear, apparel, and athletic equipment.

Because it operates in more than 170 countries around the globe and manufactures products in more than 500 factories in 39 different countries, sustainability is a big initiative for Nike. Today, Nike uses the YouTube social media site to share its sustainability message with consumers, employees, investors, politicians, and other interested stakeholders. To learn about the company's efforts to sustain the planet, follow these steps:

- Go to YouTube website.
- Enter the words "Nike" and "Sustainability" in the search window and click the search button.

1. View at least three different YouTube videos about Nike's sustainability efforts.
2. Based on the information in the videos you watched, do you believe that Nike is a good corporate citizen because of its efforts to sustain the planet? Why or why not?
3. Prepare a one- to two-page report that describes how Nike is taking steps to reduce waste, improve the environment, and reduce its carbon footprint while manufacturing products around the globe.

2. Building Team Skills

The United States-Mexico-Canada Agreement (USMCA), which replaced the North American Free Trade Agreement (NAFTA), went into effect in 2020. It has made a difference in trade among the countries and has affected the lives of many people.

Assignment

1. Working in teams and using the resources of your library, investigate USMCA. Answer the following questions:
   a. What are USMCA's objectives?
   b. What are its benefits?
   c. What impact have NAFTA and USMCA had on trade, jobs, and travel?
   d. Some Americans were opposed to the implementation of NAFTA. What were their objections? Were any of these objections justified?
   e. Have NAFTA and USMCA influenced your life? How?
2. Summarize your answers in a written report. Your team also should be prepared to give a class presentation.

3. Researching Different Careers

Today, firms around the world need employees with special skills. In some countries, such employees are not always available, and firms then must search abroad for qualified applicants. One way they can do this is through global workforce databases. As business and trade operations continue to grow globally, you may one day find yourself working in a foreign country, perhaps for an American company doing business there or for a foreign company. In what foreign country would you like to work? What problems might you face?

Assignment

1. Choose a country in which you might like to work.
2. Research the country. The CIA's World Fact Book and the International Trade Administration are good places to start. Find answers to the following questions:
   a. What language is spoken in this country? Are you proficient in it? What would you need to do if you are not proficient?
   b. What are the economic, social, and legal systems like in this nation?
   c. What is its history?
   d. What are its culture and social traditions like? How might they affect your work or your living arrangements?
3. Describe what you have found out about this country in a written report. Include an assessment of whether you would want to work there and the problems you might face if you did.

Running a Business 经营企业

我们去买个 Graeter's 冰淇淋吧
Let's Go Get a Graeter's!

Only a tiny fraction of family-owned businesses are still growing four generations and more than 150 years after their founding, but happily for lovers of premium-quality ice cream, Graeter's is one of them.

Now a nearly $125 million firm with national distribution, Graeter's was founded in Cincinnati in 1870 by Louis Charles Graeter and his wife, Regina Graeter. The young couple made ice cream and chocolate candies in the back room of their shop, sold them in the front room, and lived upstairs. Ice cream was a special treat in this era before refrigeration, and the Graeters started from scratch every day to make theirs from the freshest, finest ingredients. Even after freezers were invented, the Graeters continued to make ice cream in small batches to preserve the quality, texture, and rich flavor.

After her husband's death, Regina's entrepreneurial leadership became the driving force behind Graeter's expansion from 1920 until well into the 1950s. At a time when few women owned or operated a business, Regina opened 20 new Graeter's stores in the Cincinnati area and added manufacturing capacity to support this ambitious—and successful—growth strategy. Her sons and grandchildren followed her into the business and continued to open ice-cream shops all around Ohio and beyond. Today, three of Regina's great-grandsons run Graeter's with the same attention to quality that made the firm famous. In her honor, the street in front of the company's ultramodern Cincinnati factory is named Regina Graeter Way.

The Scoop on Graeter's Success

Graeter's fourth-generation owners are Richard Graeter II (CEO), Robert (Bob) Graeter (vice president of operations), and Chip Graeter (vice president of retail operations). They grew up in the business, learning through hands-on experience how to do everything from packing a pint of ice cream to locking up the store at night. They also absorbed the family's dedication to product quality, a key reason for the company's enduring success. "Our family has always been contented to make a little less profit in order to ensure our long-term survival," explains the CEO.

Throughout its history, Graeter's has used a unique, time-consuming manufacturing process to produce its signature ice creams in small batches. "Our competition is making thousands and thousands of gallons a day," says Chip Graeter. "We are making hundreds of gallons a day at the most. All of our ice cream is packed by hand, so it's a very laborious process." Graeter's "French pot" manufacturing method ensures that very little air gets into the product. As a result, the company's ice cream is dense and creamy, not light and fluffy—so dense, in fact, that each pint weighs nearly a pound.

Another success factor is the use of simple, fresh ingredients like high-grade chocolate, choice seasonal fruits, and farm-fresh cream. Graeter's imports some ingredients, such as vanilla from Madagascar, and buys other ingredients from U.S. producers known for their quality. "We use a really great grade of chocolate," says Bob Graeter. "We don't cut corners on that . . . Specially selected great black raspberries, strawberries, blueberries, and cherries go into our ice cream because we feel that we want to provide flavor not from artificial or unnatural ingredients but from really quality, ripe, rich fruits." Instead of tiny chocolate chips, Graeter's products contain giant chunks formed when liquid chocolate is poured into the ice-cream base just before the mixture is frozen and packed into pints.

Maintaining the Core of Success

Graeter's "fanatical devotion to product quality" and its time-tested recipes have not changed over the years. The current generation of owners is maintaining this core of the company's success while mixing in a generous dash of innovation. "If you just preserve the core," Bob Graeter says, "ultimately you stagnate. And if you are constantly stimulating progress and looking for new ideas, well, then you risk losing what was important. . . . Part of your secret to long-term success is knowing what your core is and holding to that. Once you know what you're really all about and what is most important to you, you can change everything else."

One of those "important" things is giving back to the community and its families via local charities and other initiatives. "Community involvement is just part of being a good corporate citizen," observes Richard Graeter. When Graeter's celebrated a recent new store opening, for example, it made a cash donation to the neighborhood public library. It is also a major sponsor of The Cure Starts Now Foundation, a research foundation seeking a cure for pediatric brain cancer. In line with its focus on natural goodness, Graeter's has been doing its part to preserve the environment by recycling and by boosting production efficiency to conserve water, energy, and other resources.

Graeter's Looks to the Future

Even though Graeter's recipes reflect its 19th-century heritage, the company is clearly a 21st-century operation. It has more than 200,000 Facebook "likes," connects with brand fans on Twitter and Instagram, and invites customers to subscribe to its email newsletter. The company sells its products online, shipping orders via United Parcel Service to ice-cream lovers across the continental United States. Its newly opened production facility uses state-of-the-art refrigeration, storage, and sanitation—yet the ice cream is still mixed by hand rather than by automated equipment. With an eye toward future growth, Graeter's is refining its information system to provide managers with all the details they need to make timely decisions in today's fast-paced business environment.

Graeter's competition ranges from small, local businesses to international giants such as Unilever, which owns Ben & Jerry's, and Froneri, which owns Haagen-Dazs. Throughout the economic ups and downs of recent years, Graeter's has continued to expand, and its ice creams are now distributed through 4,000 stores in 46 states. Oprah Winfrey and other celebrities have praised its products in public. But the owners are just as proud of their hometown success. "Graeter's in Cincinnati is synonymous with ice cream," says Bob Graeter. "People will say, 'Let's go get a Graeter's.'"[34]

Questions

1. How have Graeter's owners used the four factors of production to build the business over time?
2. Which of Graeter's stakeholders are most affected by the family's decision to take a long-term view of the business rather than aiming for short-term profit? Explain your answer.
3. Knowing that Graeter's competes with multinational corporations as well as small businesses, would you recommend that Graeter's expand by licensing its brand to a company in another country? Why or why not?

Building a Business Plan

制订商业计划

A *business plan* is a carefully constructed guide for a person starting a business. The purpose of a well-prepared business plan is to show how practical and attainable the entrepreneur's goals are. It also serves as a concise document that potential investors can examine to see if they would like to invest or assist in financing a new venture. A business plan should include the following 12 components:

- Introduction
- Executive summary
- Benefits to the community
- Company and industry
- Management team
- Manufacturing and operations plan
- Labor force
- Marketing plan
- Financial plan
- Exit strategy
- Critical risks and assumptions
- Appendix

The goal of these exercises in this textbook is to help you work through the preceding components to create your own business plan. In the exercise for this part, you will make decisions and complete the research that will help you develop the intro-duction for your business plan and the benefits to the com-munity that your business will provide. In the exercises for Parts 2 through 6, you will add more components to your plan and eventually build a plan that actually could be used to start a business. The flowchart shown in Figure 3-4 gives an overview of the steps you will be taking to prepare your business plan.

The First Step: Choosing Your Business

One of the first steps for starting your own business is to decide what type of business you want to start. Take some time to think about this decision. Before proceeding, answer the following questions:

- Why did you choose this type of business?
- Why do you think this business will be successful?
- Would you enjoy owning and operating this type of business?

Warning: Do not rush this step. This step often requires much thought, but it is well worth the time and effort. As an added bonus, you are more likely to develop a quality business plan if you really want to open this type of business.

Now that you have decided on a specific type of business, it is time to begin the planning process. The goal for this part is to complete the introduction and benefits-to-the-community components of your business plan.

Chapter 3 Global Business

Figure 3-4 Business Plan

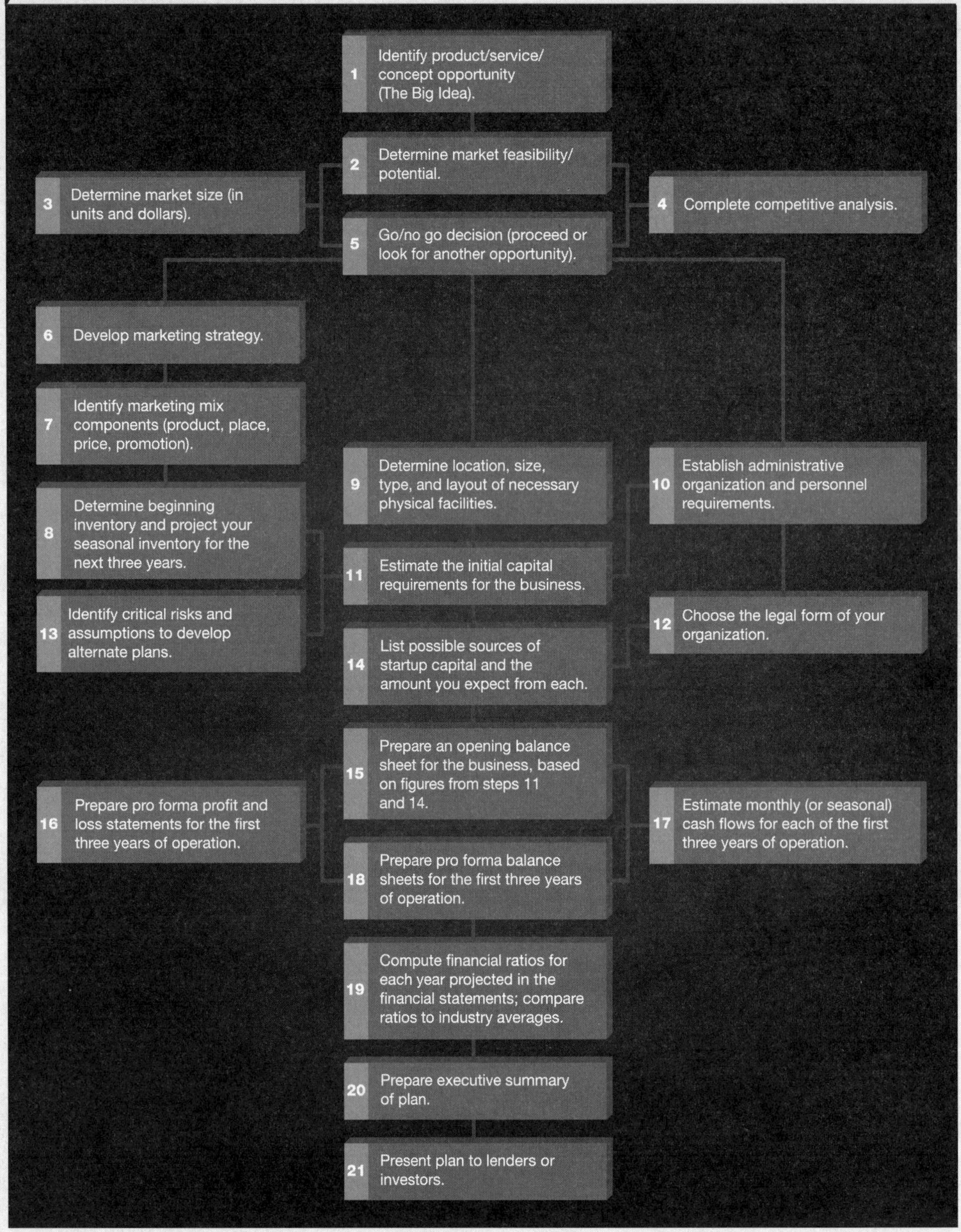

1. Identify product/service/concept opportunity (The Big Idea).
2. Determine market feasibility/potential.
3. Determine market size (in units and dollars).
4. Complete competitive analysis.
5. Go/no go decision (proceed or look for another opportunity).
6. Develop marketing strategy.
7. Identify marketing mix components (product, place, price, promotion).
8. Determine beginning inventory and project your seasonal inventory for the next three years.
9. Determine location, size, type, and layout of necessary physical facilities.
10. Establish administrative organization and personnel requirements.
11. Estimate the initial capital requirements for the business.
12. Choose the legal form of your organization.
13. Identify critical risks and assumptions to develop alternate plans.
14. List possible sources of startup capital and the amount you expect from each.
15. Prepare an opening balance sheet for the business, based on figures from steps 11 and 14.
16. Prepare pro forma profit and loss statements for the first three years of operation.
17. Estimate monthly (or seasonal) cash flows for each of the first three years of operation.
18. Prepare pro forma balance sheets for the first three years of operation.
19. Compute financial ratios for each year projected in the financial statements; compare ratios to industry averages.
20. Prepare executive summary of plan.
21. Present plan to lenders or investors.

Source: Hatten, Timothy, *Small Business Management*, Fifth Edition. Copyright 2012 Cengage Learning.

Before you begin, it is important to note that the business plan is not a document that is written and then set aside. It is a living document that an entrepreneur should refer to continuously in order to ensure that plans are being carried through appropriately. As entrepreneurs begin to execute the plan, they should monitor the business environment continuously and make changes to the plan to address any challenges or opportunities that were not foreseen originally.

Throughout this course, you will, of course, be building your knowledge about business. Therefore, it will be appropriate for you to continually revisit parts of the plan that you have already written in order to refine them based on your more comprehensive knowledge. You will find that writing your plan is not a simple matter of starting at the beginning and moving chronologically through to the end. Instead, you probably will find yourself jumping around the various components, making refinements as you go. In fact, the second component—the executive summary—should be written last, but because of its comprehensive nature and its importance to potential investors, it appears after the introduction in the final business plan. By the end of this course, you should be able to put the finishing touches on your plan, making sure that all the parts create a comprehensive and sound whole so that you can present it for evaluation.

The Introduction Component

1.1. Start with the cover page. Provide the business name, street address, telephone number, Web address (if any), name(s) of owner(s) of the business, and the date the plan is issued.

1.2. Next, provide background information on the company and include the general nature of the business: retailing, manufacturing, or service; what your product or service is; what is unique about it; and why you believe that your business will be successful.

1.3. Then include a summary statement of the business's financial needs, if any. You probably will need to revise your financial needs summary after you complete a detailed financial plan.

1.4. Finally, include a statement of confidentiality to keep important information away from potential competitors.

The Benefits-to-the-Community Component

In this section, describe the potential benefits to the community that your business could provide. Chapter 2 in your textbook, "Ethics and Social Responsibility in Business," can help you in answering some of these questions. At the very least, address the following issues:

1.5. Describe the number of skilled and nonskilled jobs the business will create, and indicate how purchases of supplies and other materials can help local businesses.

1.6. Next, describe how providing needed goods or services will improve the community and its standard of living.

1.7. Finally, state how your business can offer attractive wages; develop new technical, management, or leadership skills; and provide other types of individual growth.

Review of Business Plan Activities

Read over the information that you have gathered. Because the Building a Business Plan exercises at the end of Parts 2 through 6 are built on the work you do in Part 1, make sure that any weaknesses or problem areas are resolved before continuing. Finally, write a brief statement that summarizes all the information for this part of the business plan.

Chapter 4

Building Customer Relationships Through Effective Marketing

通过有效的市场营销建立客户关系

Learning Objectives

Once you complete this chapter, you will be able to:

4-1 Describe the meaning of *marketing* and the importance of managing customer relationships.

4-2 Explain how marketing adds value by creating several forms of utility.

4-3 Discuss the development of the marketing concept and how it is implemented.

4-4 Define what markets are and classify them.

4-5 Describe the two major components of a marketing strategy—target market and marketing mix.

4-6 Explain how the marketing environment affects strategic market planning.

4-7 Examine the major components of a marketing plan.

4-8 Describe how market measurement and sales forecasting are used.

4-9 Explain how marketers collect and analyze information useful for marketing decision making.

4-10 Identify the major steps in the consumer buying decision process and the sets of factors that may influence this process.

Why Should You Care?

Marketers are concerned about building long-term customer relationships. To develop competitive product offerings, business people must identify acceptable target customer groups and understand their behaviors.

Inside Business

商业透视：Netflix 在客户保留率方面领先于竞争对手

Netflix Tops the Competition in Customer Retention

Netflix, the world's largest subscription-based streaming service, is deep in the trenches of the streaming war. Competitors such as Amazon Prime Video, Hulu, Disney+, HBO Max, Peacock, and Apple TV+ crowd the market, and Netflix's first-mover advantage is quickly fading. Netflix must continue to adapt and innovate to stay ahead.

One data point, however, suggests that Netflix has a strong hold on its top spot: churn rate. *Churn rate* refers to the percentage of subscribers who do not renew their subscriptions during a given time frame. As competition heats up, one would expect Netflix's churn rate to suffer, but so far that hasn't been the case. The company's churn is between 2 and 3 percent, which is below all of its rivals. Subscription services HBO and Showtime often see their churn rates spike following a popular series finale, underscoring one of Netflix's key strengths: its extensive content library. The data indicate that customers see value in Netflix beyond a single television show.

Netflix further adds value to its product through personalization, an area where other streaming services lag behind. By investing in exclusive shows and movies, as well as page personalization, search algorithms, and personalized messaging and marketing, Netflix satisfies its customers' needs for content and a quality browsing experience. The homepage not only recommends content a subscriber is likely to enjoy, but it also goes as far as to personalize the artwork for each show and movie to an image the individual is more likely to select. The company uses machine learning, text analytics, and collaborative filtering to power its search function. All of these elements contribute to Netflix's high customer retention and demonstrate that the company has a firm grasp on the marketing concept.[1]

Did You Know?

Netflix has more than 200 million subscribers.

市场营销

marketing the activity, set of institutions, and processes for creating, communicating, delivering, and exchanging offerings that have value for customers, clients, partners, and society at large

价值

value a customer's estimation of the worth of a product based on a comparison of its costs and benefits, including quality, relative to other products

Like Netflix, organizations use marketing activities to inform customers about their range of products and how these products can satisfy customer demand and create value. Understanding customers' needs and wants are crucial to providing the products that satisfy them. Although marketing encompasses a diverse set of decisions and activities, it always begins and ends with the customer. The American Marketing Association defines **marketing** as the "activity, set of institutions, and processes for creating, communicating, delivering, and exchanging offerings that have value for customers, clients, partners, and society at large."[2] **Value** is a customer's estimation of the worth of a product based on a comparison of its costs and benefits, including quality, relative to other products. For some people, value means the lowest price, but for others it might mean products that cost more but last a long time. The marketing process involves eight major functions and numerous related activities, all of which are essential to the marketing process (refer to Table 4-1).

In this chapter, we examine how marketing activities add value to products. We begin by exploring how organizations seek to maintain positive relationships with customers through marketing activities and develop products that create utility. We trace the evolution of the marketing concept and describe how organizations practice it. Next, we shift our focus to classifying markets and developing marketing strategy by targeting an appropriate marketing mix at a target market. We also examine the uncontrollable factors in the marketing environment and the major components of a marketing plan. Then we consider tools for strategic market planning, including market measurement, sales forecasts, marketing analytics, and marketing research. Finally, we look at the forces that influence consumer and organizational buying behavior.

Table 4-1 Eight Major Marketing Functions

Exchange functions: All companies—manufacturers, wholesalers, and retailers—buy and sell to market their merchandise.

1. **Buying** includes obtaining raw materials to make products, knowing how much merchandise to keep on hand, and selecting suppliers.
2. **Selling** creates possession utility by transferring the title of a product from seller to customer.

Physical distribution functions: These functions involve the flow of goods from producers to customers.

3. **Transporting** involves selecting a mode of transport that provides an acceptable delivery schedule at an acceptable price.
4. **Storing** goods is often necessary to sell them at the optimal selling time.

Facilitating functions: These functions help the other functions to take place.

5. **Financing** helps at all stages of marketing. To buy raw materials, manufacturers often borrow from banks or receive credit from suppliers. Wholesalers may be financed by manufacturers, and retailers may receive financing from the wholesaler or manufacturer. Finally, retailers often provide financing to customers.
6. **Standardizing** sets uniform specifications for products or services. Grading classifies products by size and quality, usually through a sorting process. Together, standardizing and grading facilitate production, transportation, storage, and selling.
7. **Risk taking**—even though competent management and insurance can minimize risks—is a constant reality of marketing because of such losses as bad-debt expense, obsolescence of products, theft by employees, and product-liability lawsuits.
8. **Gathering** market information is necessary for making all marketing decisions.

客户关系管理

4-1 Managing Customer Relationships

Without relationships with customers, businesses would not be successful. Therefore, maintaining positive relationships with customers is an important goal for marketers. The term **relationship marketing** refers to marketing decisions and activities focused on achieving long-term, satisfying relationships with customers. Relationship marketing deepens and reinforces the buyer's trust in the company, which, as the customer's loyalty grows, increases a company's understanding of the customer's needs and desires. Successful marketers respond to customers' needs and strive to increase value to buyers continually over time. Eventually, this interaction becomes a solid relationship that fosters cooperation and mutual trust. The internet has expanded and improved relationship marketing options for many firms by making targeted communication faster, cheaper, and easier. Digital technologies allow firms to connect to consumers and interact with them in real time. This not only improves the speed at which firms can innovate, but also makes consumers feel more satisfied because they feel the firm is listening to them.

To build long-term customer relationships, marketers rely on marketing research and information technology. **Customer relationship management (CRM)** focuses on using information about customers to create marketing strategies that develop and sustain desirable customer relationships. By increasing customer value over time, organizations try to retain and increase long-term profitability through customer loyalty. Because CRM is such an important part of creating and building customer loyalty, many companies have developed high-tech tools aimed at helping them to identify their more profitable customers and to manage relations with them over the long term. Starbucks, for example, rewards regular customers through an app that records their purchase history and offers them free food or drink on their birthday or after accruing points.

Learning Objective

4-1 Describe the meaning of *marketing* and the importance of managing customer relationships.

关系营销
relationship marketing establishing long-term, mutually satisfying buyer–seller relationships

客户关系管理
customer relationship management (CRM) using information about customers to create marketing strategies that develop and sustain desirable customer relationships

Developing long-term customer relationships. Many companies spend a considerable amount of money on marketing programs to develop and maintain long-term relationships with their customers—especially the valuable ones. Often it's more profitable to retain these customers by offering them big rewards than to attract new customers who may never develop the same loyalty.

The data accumulated from the app, along with store sales data and information about weather, holidays, and special events helps Starbucks understand customers' ordering habits so that it can personalize their experience and make astute recommendations according to time of day and weather—even if they normally frequent a different store. With nearly 20 million users, the Starbucks app helps the company build long-term relationships.[3] The accessibility of technology has contributed to a more even playing field for firms of all sizes.

Managing customer relationships requires identifying patterns of buying behavior and using this information to focus on the most promising and profitable customers. Companies must be sensitive to customers' requirements and desires and establish communication to build customers' trust and loyalty. In some instances, it may be more profitable for a company to focus on satisfying a valuable existing customer than to attempt to attract a new one who may never develop the same level of loyalty. This involves determining how much customers will spend over their lifetime. The **customer lifetime value (CLV)** is a measure

Sustaining the Planet

保护地球：客户反馈促使 Native 走向无塑料化

Customer Feedback Pushes Native to Go Plastic-Free

Native, a personal care company, understands the importance of developing long-term, satisfying relationships with its customers. The direct-to-consumer company, best known for its cult-favorite aluminum-free deodorant, enjoys a dedicated and loyal fan base. When its customers asked Native to reconsider its plastic packaging, the company listened and then introduced paper-based applicators for its all-natural products.

With an influx of customer requests for sustainable packaging, Native gathered and analyzed the feedback from a variety of sources including social media, customer service phone calls, and surveys. This marketing research revealed that customer communication related to environmentally conscious packaging had increased by more than 900 percent. After developing a prototype for the new packaging, Native sold 200 units, collected feedback, and analyzed the data. Based on input from the early adopters, Native made final tweaks before initiating a full rollout. The product innovation team is now considering ways to switch to 100 percent plastic-free packaging across its entire product mix.

Native has long relied on brand advocates to spread the word about the company's products. For example, Native leverages the 15,000 five-star reviews it has collected from customers to promote its deodorant, body wash, bar soap, and toothpaste. In the company's early years, Native knew it was onto something special when its repeat purchase rate reached 50 percent. By engaging with these loyal customers, Native can better understand their wants and needs, build a sense of trust, and deepen relationships.

Sources: Based on information in Kathryn Lundstrom, "Customer Feedback Inspired Native's New Plastic-Free Paper Packaging for Its Deodorant," *AdWeek*, July 20, 2020; Eric Bandholz, "Native Deodorant Founder on Scaling to $100 Million in 2 Years," *Practical Ecommerce*, October 9, 2020; Madge Maril, "Native's Cult-Favorite Deodorant Now Comes In Plastic-Free Packaging," *The Zoe Report*, June 24, 2020.

of a customer's worth (sales minus costs) to a business during one's lifetime.[4] CLV also includes the intangible benefits of retaining lifetime-value customers, such as their ability to provide feedback to a company and refer new customers of similar value, and these are important considerations as well. The amount of money a company is willing to spend to retain such customers is also a factor. In general, when marketers focus on customers chosen for their lifetime value, they earn higher profits in future periods than when they focus on customers selected for other reasons.[5] It is a fairly straightforward task to calculate CLV. In fact, businesses can utilize reliable free online tools to calculate CLV. Because the loss of a potential lifetime customer can result in lower profits, managing customer relationships has become a major focus of marketers.

> ✓ **Concept Check**
> - Why is managing customer relationships important?
> - How can technology help to build long-term customer relationships?
> - What are the benefits of retaining customers?

效用：通过营销增加价值

4-2 Utility: The Value Added by Marketing

Utility is the ability of a good or service to satisfy a human need. The latest Xbox, Nike Air Jordan athletic shoes, or Mercedes Benz luxury car all satisfy human needs. Thus, each possesses utility. There are four kinds of utility (refer to Figure 4-1).

Form utility is created by converting production inputs into finished products. Marketing efforts may influence form utility indirectly because the data gathered as part of marketing research are frequently used to determine the size, shape, and features of a product.

The three kinds of utility that are created directly by marketing are place, time, and possession utility. **Place utility** is created by making a product available at a location where customers wish to purchase it. A pair of shoes is given place utility when it is shipped from a factory to a department store or made available for sale at Zappos.com.

Time utility is created by making a product available when customers wish to purchase it. For example, Halloween costumes may be manufactured in April but not displayed until September, when consumers start buying them. By storing the costumes until there is a demand, the manufacturer or retailer provides time utility.

Possession utility is created by transferring title (or ownership) of a product to a buyer. For a product as simple as a pair of shoes, ownership usually is transferred by means of a sales slip or receipt. For such products as automobiles and homes, the transfer of title is a more complex process. Along with the title to products, the seller transfers the right to use that product.

> **Learning Objective**
> 4-2 Explain how marketing adds value by creating several forms of utility.

> 客户终身价值
> **customer lifetime value (CLV)** a measure of a customer's worth (sales minus costs) to a business over one's lifetime
>
> 效用
> **utility** the ability of a good or service to satisfy a human need
>
> 形式效用
> **form utility** utility created by converting production inputs into finished products
>
> 地点效用
> **place utility** utility created by making a product available at a location where customers wish to purchase it
>
> 时间效用
> **time utility** utility created by making a product available when customers wish to purchase it
>
> 拥有效用
> **possession utility** utility created by transferring title (or ownership) of a product to a buyer

Figure 4-1 Types of Utility

Form utility is created by the production process, but marketing creates place, time, and possession utility.

Wanted: One pair of size 8 shoes in Duluth, immediately. Will pay $50.

	CAN SATISFY THE NEED WITH:	BUT CANNOT SATISFY THE NEED WITH:
Form utility	Size 8 shoes	Size 10 shoes
Place utility	Size 8 shoes in Duluth	Size 8 shoes in Los Angeles
Time utility	Size 8 shoes in Duluth available now	Size 8 shoes in Duluth available next month
Possession utility	Size 8 shoes in Duluth available now for $50	Size 8 shoes in Duluth available now for $80

Place, time, and possession utility have real value in terms of both money and convenience. This value is created and added to goods and services through a wide variety of marketing activities—from research suggesting desired features to advertising those features to product warranties ensuring that customers get what they pay for. Overall, these marketing activities account for about half of every dollar spent by consumers. When they are part of an integrated marketing program that delivers maximum utility to the customer, many would agree that they are worth the cost.

> **Concept Check**
> - Explain the four kinds of utility.
> - Provide an example of each.

营销理念
4-3 The Marketing Concept

> **Learning Objective**
> **4-3** Discuss the development of the marketing concept and how it is implemented.

The **marketing concept** is a business philosophy that a firm should provide goods and services that satisfy customers' needs through a coordinated set of activities that allow the firm to achieve its objectives. Initially, the firm communicates with potential customers to assess their product needs. Then, the firm develops a good or service to satisfy those needs. Finally, the firm continues to seek ways to provide customer satisfaction. This process is an application of the marketing concept or marketing orientation. Consider the century-old Nordstrom department store chain. Long renowned for its customer service, the company continues to innovate by developing and acquiring technology to improve its customer experience both in stores and online. It also satisfies regular customers with a rewards program and curbside pickup. Through partnerships, the company has brought in many new products to appeal to diverse consumers, especially Millennials. While other retailers are faltering and shuttering stores, Nordstrom is experimenting with new store concepts, like its inventory-free Nordstrom Local stores where customers can try on products, pick up Style Board orders that have been curated for them, and more. These efforts help Nordstrom learn what customers want now so that it can satisfy them and keep them coming back.[6] It is important to recognize that all functional areas—research and development, production, finance, human resources, and, of course, marketing—play a role in providing customer satisfaction.

营销理念
marketing concept a business philosophy that a firm should provide goods and services that satisfy customers' needs through a coordinated set of activities that allow the firm to achieve its objectives.

营销理念的演变
4-3a Evolution of the Marketing Concept

From the start of the Industrial Revolution until the early 20th century, business effort was directed mainly toward the production of goods. Consumer demand for manufactured products was so great that manufacturers could almost bank on selling everything they produced. Business had a strong *production orientation*, which placed an emphasis on increased output and production efficiency. Marketing activities were limited to taking orders and distributing finished goods.

In the 1920s, production caught up with and began to exceed demand. Producers had to direct their efforts toward selling goods rather than just producing them. This new *sales orientation* was characterized by increased advertising, enlarged sales forces, and, occasionally, high-pressure selling techniques. Manufacturers produced the goods they expected consumers to want, and marketing consisted primarily of promoting products through personal selling and advertising, taking orders, and delivering goods.

During the 1950s, however, businesspeople started to realize that even enormous advertising expenditures

Putting products at the customer's fingertips. Firms try to provide customers with products when and where they need them.

and proven sales techniques were not sufficient to gain a competitive edge. It was then that business managers recognized that they were not primarily producers or sellers, but were in the business of satisfying customers' needs. Marketers realized that the best approach was to adopt a *customer orientation*—in other words, the organization had to first determine what customers need and then develop goods and services to fill those particular needs (refer to Table 4-2).

The marketing concept is dynamic and has continued to evolve. In the late 1990s, marketers increasingly focused their efforts on building and maintaining long-term relationships with customers. This *relationship orientation* adopted customer relationship management tools and technology to try to retain and increase long-term profitability through customer loyalty. In today's digital world where consumers can find just about anything they want at the touch of a smartphone button, the marketing concept continues to evolve to include social media and mobile technology. As an example, Zappos, the online shoe store renowned for its customer service, uses social media to respond to consumer queries, resolve issues, elicit consumer feedback, and highlight customers, all of which help it refine its marketing strategies.[7] Marketers also must adopt multiple distribution channels to reach customers wherever and whenever they might choose to shop—in stores, online, and through smart device apps. Nonetheless, all marketers still must focus on providing products that satisfy customers' needs and wants as well as their own objectives.

Tell us what you *really* think. Customer satisfaction is a major element of the marketing concept. Many businesses attempt to measure customer satisfaction through surveys. Surveys can be conducted in a variety of ways: in person, by mail or phone, or online. Online surveys have made it very inexpensive for firms to gather customer feedback.

营销理念的实施
4-3b Implementing the Marketing Concept

To implement the marketing concept, a firm first must obtain information about its present and potential customers. The firm must determine not only what customers' needs are, but also how well these needs are satisfied by products currently in the market—both its own products and those of competitors. It must ascertain how its products might be improved and what opinions customers have about the firm and its marketing efforts.

The firm then must use this information to pinpoint the specific needs and potential customers toward which it will direct its marketing activities and resources.

Table 4-2 Evolution of Customer Orientation

Business managers recognized that they were not primarily producers or sellers, but were in the business of satisfying customers' wants.

Production Orientation	Sales Orientation	Customer Orientation	Relationship Orientation
Take orders	Increase advertising	Determine customer needs	Use all possible media to build relationships
Distribute goods	Enlarge sales force	Develop products to fill those needs	Increase value to customer over time
	Intensify sales techniques	Achieve the organization's goals	Gain customer loyalty and increase long-term profitability

Next, the firm must mobilize its marketing resources to (1) provide a product that will satisfy its customers, (2) price the product at a level that is acceptable to buyers and will yield a profit, (3) promote the product so that potential customers will be aware of its existence and its ability to satisfy their needs, and (4) ensure that the product is distributed so that it is available to customers where and when it is needed.

Finally, the firm must again obtain marketing information—this time regarding the effectiveness of its efforts. Can the product be improved? Is it being promoted effectively? Is it being distributed efficiently? Is the price too high or too low? The firm must be ready to modify any or all of its marketing activities based on information about its customers and competitors. Consider Zara, the fashion retailer owned by Spain-based Inditex, which employs a strategy of quickly designing, manufacturing, and stocking small quantities of fashion items—in as little as two weeks—and then nimbly updating inventories in response to customer reaction and requests. The firm's strategy and strong customer focus allow it to maintain fresh and exciting product assortments that keep customers happy.[8]

> ✓ **Concept Check**
> ▸ Identify the major components of the marketing concept.
> ▸ How did the customer orientation evolve?
> ▸ What steps are involved when implementing the marketing concept?

市场及其分类
4-4 Markets and Their Classification

Learning Objective
4-4 Define what markets are and classify them.

A **market** is a group of individuals or organizations, or both, that need products in a given category and that have the ability, willingness, and authority to purchase them. Markets are broadly classified as consumer or business-to-business, and marketing efforts vary depending on the intended market. Marketers should understand the general characteristics of these two groups.

Consumer markets consist of purchasers and/or household members who intend to consume or benefit from the purchased products and who do not buy products to make profits. *Business-to-business (B2B) markets*, also called *industrial markets*, are grouped broadly into producer, reseller, governmental, and institutional categories. These markets purchase specific kinds of products for use in making other products for resale or for day-to-day operations. *Producer markets* consist of individuals and business organizations that buy certain products to use in the manufacture of other products. *Reseller markets* include intermediaries, such as wholesalers and retailers, that buy finished products and sell them for a profit. *Government markets* consist of federal, state, county, and local governments that buy goods and services to maintain internal operations and to provide citizens with such products as highways, education, water, energy, and national defense. Government purchases total billions of dollars each year. *Institutional markets* include churches, not-for-profit private schools and hospitals, civic clubs, fraternities and sororities, charitable organizations, and foundations. Their goals are different from the typical business goals of profit, market share, or return on investment.

> ✓ **Concept Check**
> ▸ What is a market?
> ▸ Identify and describe the major types of markets.

制定营销策略
4-5 Developing Marketing Strategies

Learning Objective
4-5 Describe the two major components of a marketing strategy—target market and marketing mix.

市场
market a group of individuals or organizations, or both, that need products in a given category and that have the ability, willingness, and authority to purchase them

A **marketing strategy** is a plan that will enable an organization to make the best use of its resources and advantages to meet its objectives. A marketing strategy consists of (1) the selection and analysis of a target market and (2) the creation and maintenance of an appropriate **marketing mix**, a combination of product, price, distribution, and promotion developed to satisfy a particular target market.

目标市场的选择和评估
4-5a Target Market Selection and Evaluation

A **target market** is a group of individuals or organizations, or both, for which a firm develops and maintains a marketing mix suitable for the specific needs and preferences of that group. In selecting a target market, marketing managers examine potential markets for their possible effects on the firm's sales, costs, and profits. The managers attempt to determine whether the organization has the resources to produce a marketing mix that meets the needs of a particular target market and whether satisfying these needs is consistent with the firm's overall objectives. They also analyze the strengths and number of competitors already marketing to the target market. A target market can range in size from millions of people to only a few, depending on the product and the marketer's objectives. Consider Zipcar, a car-sharing company that targets people who live in cities and do not want to own a car, as well as those who cannot afford a car or only need one occasionally. Its target market treats cars as a sustainable option for getting around, not as a status symbol.[9] On the other hand, Rolls-Royce targets its automobiles toward a small, very exclusive market: wealthy people who want the ultimate in prestige in an automobile. Some companies target multiple markets with different products, prices, distribution systems, and promotions for each one. Some high-end clothing designers, for instance, target multiple markets when they introduce more affordable lines distributed at mass market retail outlets, such as Target and Walmart. This strategy allows designers to reach customers with varying needs and levels of disposable income. Target has partnered with such high-end designers as Victoria Beckham, Marimekko, and Lily Pulitzer to offer affordable versions of high-end products.[10] The strategy has introduced the normally elite brands to a much larger market, enhancing Target's stylish image.

Reaching the right market segments. The market for fragrances is segmented based on gender. Some fragrances are aimed at men while others, such as the perfume in this photo, are aimed at women.

Undifferentiated Approach A company that designs a single marketing mix and directs it at the entire market for a particular product is using an **undifferentiated approach** (refer to Figure 4-2). This approach assumes that individual customers in the target market for a specific kind of product have similar needs and that the organization can satisfy most customers with a single marketing mix, which consists of one type of product with little or no variation, one price, one promotional program aimed at everyone, and one distribution system to reach all customers in the total market. Products that can be marketed successfully with the undifferentiated approach include staple food items, such as sugar and salt, and some produce. An undifferentiated approach is useful in only a limited number of situations because buyers have varying needs for most product categories, which requires the market segmentation approach.

Market Segmentation Approach Market segmentation is required because different consumers have different needs. A firm that markets 40-foot yachts would not direct its marketing effort toward every person in the total boat market, for instance, because not all boat buyers have the same needs. Marketing efforts directed at the wrong target market are wasted.

Instead, the firm should direct its attention toward a particular portion, or segment, of the total market for boats. A **market segment** is a group of individuals or organizations within a market that shares one or more common characteristics. The process of dividing a market into segments is called **market segmentation**. As shown in Figure 4-2, there are two market segmentation approaches: concentrated and differentiated. When an organization uses *concentrated* market segmentation, a single marketing mix is directed at a single market segment. Pair Eyewear, for example, targets its direct-to-consumer eyeglasses at children (and their parents) with fun colors and patterns, along with a child-friendly home tryout process.[11]

营销策略
marketing strategy a plan that will enable an organization to make the best use of its resources and advantages to meet its objectives

营销组合
marketing mix a combination of product, price, distribution, and promotion developed to satisfy a particular target market

目标市场
target market a group of individuals or organizations, or both, for which a firm develops and maintains a marketing mix suitable for the specific needs and preferences of that group

无差别方法
undifferentiated approach directing a single marketing mix at the entire market for a particular product

细分市场
market segment a group of individuals or organizations within a market that shares one or more common characteristics

市场细分
market segmentation the process of dividing a market into segments and directing a marketing mix at a particular segment or segments rather than at the total market

Figure 4-2 General Approaches for Selecting Target Markets

The undifferentiated approach assumes that individual customers have similar needs and that most customers can be satisfied with a single marketing mix. When customers' needs vary, the market segmentation approach—either concentrated or differentiated—should be used.

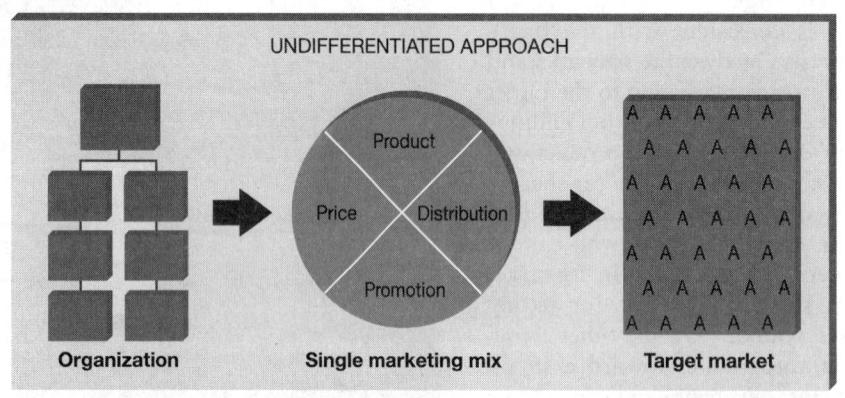

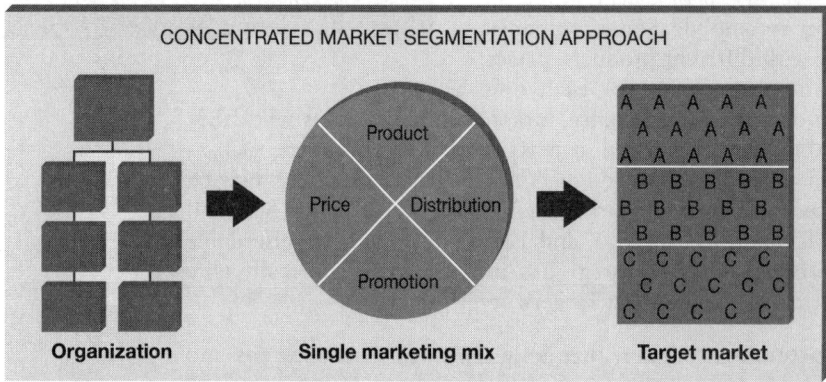

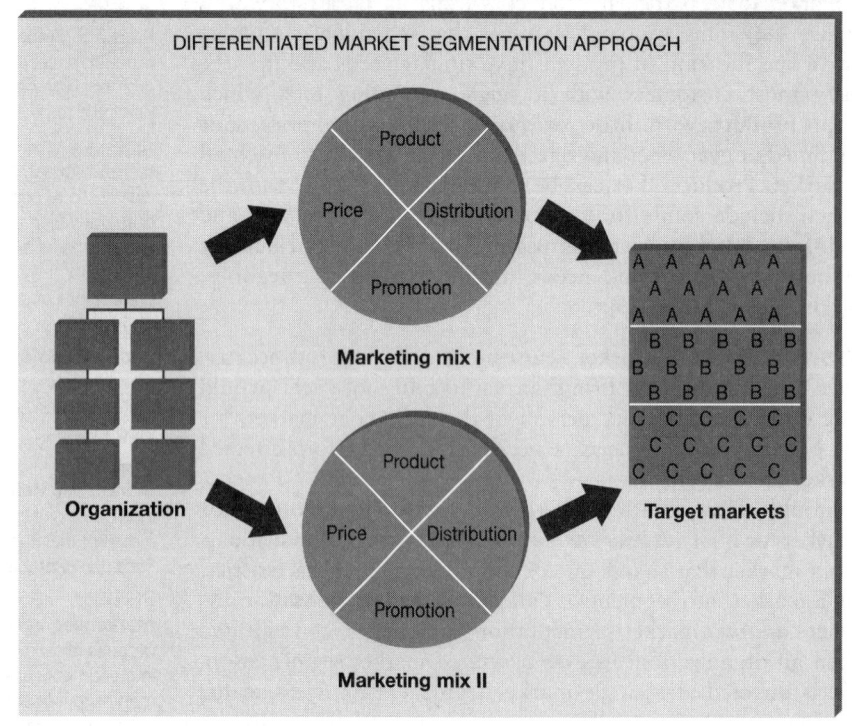

UNDIFFERENTIATED APPROACH

Organization → Single marketing mix (Product, Price, Distribution, Promotion) → Target market

CONCENTRATED MARKET SEGMENTATION APPROACH

Organization → Single marketing mix (Product, Price, Distribution, Promotion) → Target market

DIFFERENTIATED MARKET SEGMENTATION APPROACH

Organization → Marketing mix I (Product, Price, Distribution, Promotion) and Marketing mix II (Product, Price, Distribution, Promotion) → Target markets

Note: The letters in each target market represent potential customers. Customers that have the same letters have similar characteristics and similar product needs.

If *differentiated* market segmentation is used, multiple marketing mixes are focused on multiple market segments. Kellogg's employs a differentiated approach; for instance, it targets health-conscious consumers with Special K and Smart Start cereals, and parents of young children with Apple Jacks and Fruit Loops cereals and Pop-Tarts.

In our boat example, one common characteristic, or *basis*, for segmentation might be end use of a boat. The firm would be interested primarily in the market segment whose uses for a boat could lead to the purchase of a 40-foot yacht. Other bases for segmentation might be income or geographic location. Variables can affect the type of boat an individual might purchase. When choosing a basis for segmentation, it is important to select a characteristic that relates to differences in customers' needs for a product. The yacht producer, for example, would not use religion to segment the boat market because people's needs for boats do not vary based on religion.

Differentiated targeting strategy. Gillette employs a differentiated targeting strategy for its razors. The company uses multiple marketing mixes and aims them at multiple target markets. As shown here, Gillette aims its razor on the left at men and its razor on the right at women.

Marketers use a wide variety of segmentation bases. Those most commonly applied to consumer markets are shown in Table 4-3. Each may be used as a single basis for market segmentation or in combination with other bases. For example, Honda and Toyota use gender and family life cycle as bases for marketing their respective minivans, the Odyssey and the Sienna, with features and advertising designed to appeal to parents.

创建营销组合
4-5b Creating a Marketing Mix

A business controls four important elements of marketing that it combines in a way that reaches the firm's target market. These are the *product* itself, the *price* of the product, the means chosen for its *distribution*, and the *promotion* of the product. When combined, these four elements form a marketing mix (refer to Figure 4-3). A firm can vary its marketing mix by changing any one or more of the ingredients. Thus, a firm may use one marketing mix to reach one target market and another

▶ **Table 4-3** Common Bases of Market Segmentation

Demographic	Psychographic	Geographic	Behavioristic
Age	Personality attributes	Region	Volume usage
Gender	Motives	Urban, suburban, rural	End use
Race	Lifestyles	Market density	Benefit expectations
Ethnicity		Climate	Brand loyalty
Income		Terrain	Price sensitivity
Education		City size	
Occupation		County size	
Family size		State size	
Family life cycle			
Religion			
Social class			

Chapter 4   Building Customer Relationships Through Effective Marketing

Figure 4-3 The Marketing Mix and the Marketing Environment

The marketing mix consists of elements that the firm controls—product, price, distribution, and promotion. The firm generally has no control over forces in the marketing environment.

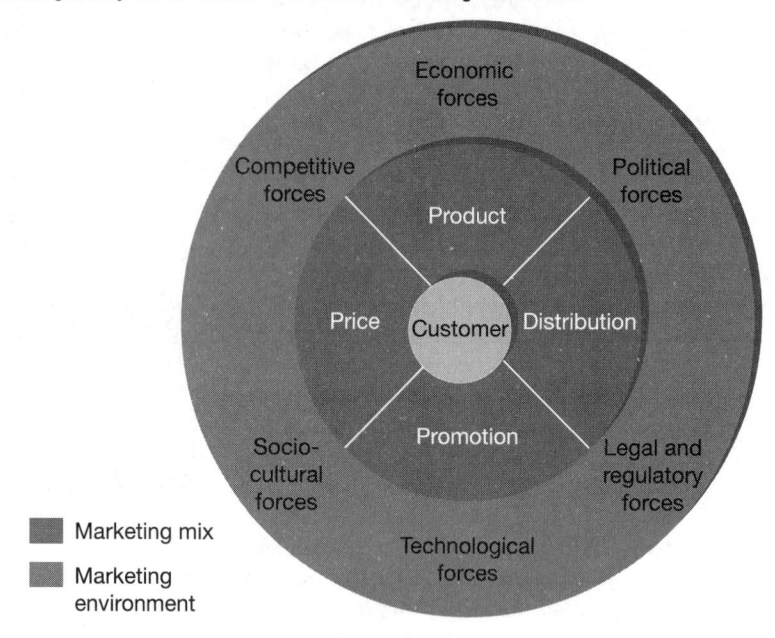

- Marketing mix
- Marketing environment

Marketing mix: Product, Price, Distribution, Promotion — centered on Customer.

Marketing environment: Economic forces, Political forces, Legal and regulatory forces, Technological forces, Sociocultural forces, Competitive forces.

Developing the right marketing mix. Firms have little control over the marketing environment. However, they *can* control the marketing mixes for their products—that is, the nature of the products themselves and how they are priced, distributed, and promoted. Marketers at PepsiCo have developed a specific marketing mix for regular Pepsi.

marketing mix to reach a different target market. For example, most automakers produce several different types and models of vehicles and aim them at different market segments based on the potential customers' age, income, family life-cycle stage, and other factors.

The most visible ingredient of the marketing mix is obviously the *product*. Product decisions typically relate to the product's design, functions, features, brand name, packaging, and warranties. When McDonald's decides on new menu items, brand names, package designs, sizes of orders, flavors of sauces, and recipes, these choices are all part of the product ingredient.

The *pricing* ingredient is concerned with both base prices and discounts. Consider the Samsung Galaxy Fold Z2 smartphone, which is priced at $2,000.[12] Pricing decisions are intended to achieve particular goals, such as to maximize profit or to make room for new models. The rebates offered by automobile manufacturers are a pricing strategy developed to boost low auto sales. Product and pricing are discussed in more detail in Chapter 5.

The *distribution* ingredient involves not only transportation and storage, but also intermediaries. How many levels of intermediaries are appropriate in the distribution of a particular product and should it be distributed as widely as possible or restricted to specialized outlets? Companies may have to alter the distribution ingredient over time. For example, as customers' consumption habits shift, retailers are adapting their distribution to include online and mobile sales. Retailers are increasingly developing their own apps to have greater control over their customer experience and to allow customers to order products whenever and wherever they might think about it. Sephora customers, for example, can use its app to shop for products and see their past purchases so they can reorder just the right shade. The app also lets shoppers "try on" various facial products so they can find the ideal products.[13]

The *promotion* ingredient focuses on providing information to target markets. The major forms of promotion are advertising, personal selling, sales promotion, and public relations. Careful planning and implementation of promotional tools is crucial to ensure their effectiveness. Distribution and promotion are discussed in more detail in Chapter 6.

These ingredients of the marketing mix are controllable elements. A firm can vary each of them to suit its organizational and marketing goals and target market needs. For instance, it can add new features to a product or reduce its price to reach a particular segment or to boost its *market share*—the percentage of a market that actually buys a specific product from a particular company. Microsoft, for example, added Microsoft Editor, Teams for Consumers, and greater cloud storage to its Microsoft 365 subscription office software suite for personal use.[14] As we extend our discussion of marketing strategy, we will see that the marketing environment includes a number of *uncontrollable* elements as well.

✓ Concept Check

▶ What are the major components of a marketing strategy?

▶ Describe the major approaches used in target market selection.

▶ Identify the four elements of the marketing mix.

营销策略与营销环境

4-6 Marketing Strategy and the Marketing Environment

The marketing mix consists of elements that a firm controls and uses to reach its target market. The firm also has control of organizational resources, such as finances and data, which can be utilized to accomplish marketing goals and refine the marketing mix. All of a firm's marketing activities can be affected by external forces, which are generally uncontrollable. As Figure 4-3 illustrates, the following forces make up the external *marketing environment*:

- *Economic forces*—the effects of economic conditions on customers' ability and willingness to buy;
- *Sociocultural forces*—influences in a society and its culture that result in changes in attitudes, beliefs, norms, customs, and lifestyles;
- *Political forces*—influences that arise through the actions of political figures;
- *Competitive forces*—the actions of competitors, who are in the process of implementing their own marketing plans;
- *Legal and regulatory forces*—laws that protect consumers and competition and government regulations that affect marketing; and
- *Technological forces*—technological changes that can create new marketing opportunities or cause products to become obsolete rapidly.

Learning Objective

4-6 Explain how the marketing environment affects strategic market planning.

These forces influence decisions about marketing mix ingredients. Changes in the environment can affect existing marketing strategies. Consider the challenges faced by marketers during the COVID-19 pandemic and the resulting economic downturn. While many Americans slashed their spending after losing their jobs, many others began to work from home. Consumers bought more laptops, desk

> **Concept Check**
>
> ▸ Describe the environmental forces that affect a firm's marketing decisions and activities.
>
> ▸ How are marketing decisions affected by environmental forces?

chairs, and baking supplies, but spent less on gasoline and cosmetics. All consumers spent more on cleaning supplies and pantry staples, but stopped going to movie theaters and gyms. Marketers had to shift gears to ensure they were offering the products consumers were willing to buy, pricing and promoting them appropriately, and distributing far more of them via online outlets, while navigating supply chain challenges and a shifting regulatory environment. In addition, changes in environmental forces may lead to dramatic shifts in customers' needs or wants. Consider the effect technological forces have had on printed newspapers. Years ago, very few people would have predicted that consumers would one day read the news on their phone, yet most people now do exactly that.

制订营销计划

4-7 Developing a Marketing Plan

Learning Objective

4-7 Examine the major components of a marketing plan.

A **marketing plan** is a written document that specifies an organization's resources, objectives, marketing strategy, and implementation and control efforts to be used in marketing a specific product or product group. The marketing plan describes the firm's current position or situation, establishes marketing objectives for the product, and specifies how the organization will attempt to achieve these objectives. Marketing plans vary with respect to the time period involved. Short-range plans are for one year or less, medium-range plans cover from over one year to five years, and long-range plans cover periods of more than five years.

营销计划
marketing plan a written document that specifies an organization's resources, objectives, strategy, and implementation and control efforts to be used in marketing a specific product or product group

Although time-consuming, developing a clear, well-written marketing plan is important. The plan helps establish a unified vision for an organization and is used for communication among the firm's employees. It covers responsibilities, tasks, and schedules for implementation, specifies how resources are to be allocated to achieve marketing objectives, and helps marketing managers monitor and evaluate

Table 4-4 Components of the Marketing Plan

Plan Component	Component Summary	Highlights
Executive summary	One- to two-page synopsis of the entire marketing plan	1. Stress key points 2. Include one to three key points that make the company unique
Environmental analysis	Information about the company's current situation with respect to the marketing environment	1. Assessment of marketing environment factors 2. Assessment of target market(s) 3. Assessment of current marketing objectives and performance
SWOT analysis	Assessment of the organization's strengths, weaknesses, opportunities, and threats	1. Strengths of the company 2. Weaknesses of the company 3. Opportunities in the environment and industry 4. Threats in the environment and industry
Marketing objectives	Specification of the firm's marketing objectives	1. Qualitative measures of what is to be accomplished 2. Quantitative measures of what is to be accomplished
Marketing strategies	Outline of how the firm will achieve its objectives	1. Target market(s) 2. Marketing mix
Marketing implementation	Outline of how the firm will implement its marketing strategies	1. Marketing organization 2. Activities and responsibilities 3. Implementation timetable
Performance evaluation	Explanation of how the firm will measure and evaluate the results of the implemented plan	1. Performance standards 2. Financial controls 3. Monitoring procedures (audits)

the performance of the marketing strategy. Because the forces of the marketing environment are subject to change, marketing plans have to be updated frequently. Consider Coca-Cola's Powerade sports drink brand, which has experienced lagging sales in recent years as exercise patterns shifted and consumers turned to other options like coconut water and enhanced waters after exercise. The company responded by adjusting its marketing mix to introduce new products, such as Power Water, a line of electrolyte-enhanced flavored water targeted at casual exercisers, and Powerade Ultra, targeted at more serious athletes with 50 percent more electrolytes and creatine, to compete.[15] Such changes in strategy will likely be reflected in the firm's marketing plan.

The major components of a marketing plan are shown in Table 4-4.

4-8 Market Measurement and Sales Forecasting

Measuring the sales potential of specific market segments can help an organization make important decisions. An accurate measure of a market segment can help a firm to determine the feasibility of entering new segments and how best to allocate marketing resources and activities among market segments in which it is already active. All such estimates should identify the relevant time frame. As with marketing plans, these plans may be short-range for periods of less than one year, medium-range for one to five years, or long-range for more than five years. The estimates should also define the geographic boundaries of the forecast, such as a city, county, state, or group of nations. Finally, analysts should indicate whether their estimates are for a specific product item, a product line, or an entire product category.

A **sales forecast** is an estimate of the amount of a product that an organization expects to sell during a certain period of time based on a specified level of marketing effort. Managers may rely on sales forecasts when they purchase raw materials, schedule production, secure financial resources, consider plant or equipment purchases, hire personnel, and plan inventory levels. Because the accuracy of a sales forecast is so important, organizations often use several forecasting methods, including executive judgments, surveys of buyers or sales personnel, time-series analyses, correlation analyses, and market tests. The specific methods used depend on the costs involved, type of product, characteristics of the market, time span of the forecast, purposes for which the forecast is used, stability of historical sales data, availability of the required information, and expertise and experience of forecasters. To assist with complicated predictions, many companies utilize sales forecasting software.

4-9 Marketing Information

Developing effective marketing strategies requires understanding target markets. Marketers therefore require accurate and timely information about customers' needs and desires, new marketing opportunities, and changing customer attitudes and purchase patterns, as well as changes in the forces of the marketing environment. The availability and analysis of marketing information improve a firm's ability to make informed decisions and respond to a changing environment, which can lead to better performance. Thanks to the proliferation of information-gathering technology, marketers can obtain a wealth of data to support decision making.

4-9a Collecting and Analyzing Marketing Information

Marketers have greater access to reliable data and tools for analyzing them than ever before. **They often** use the term *big data* to refer to the massive amounts of data that come from a variety of sources. Data from *internal* sources include sales figures,

✓ Concept Check
- What are the major components of a marketing plan?
- Why is developing a well-written marketing plan important?

Learning Objective
4-8 Describe how market measurement and sales forecasting are used.

✓ Concept Check
- Why is sales forecasting important?
- What methods do businesses use to forecast sales?

Learning Objective
4-9 Explain how marketers collect and analyze information useful for marketing decision making.

sales forecast an estimate of the amount of a product that an organization expects to sell during a certain period of time based on a specified level of marketing effort

Chapter 4 Building Customer Relationships Through Effective Marketing   115

Exploring Careers

职业探索：趋势提醒——市场研究分析师需求量很大

Trend Alert: Market Research Analysts Are in High Demand

Data analysis and analytical reasoning are two of the most in-demand skills in the job market. Big data analytics—mining insights from large amounts of data to identify trends—has given rise to the market research analyst role in the United States. According to the U.S. Bureau of Labor Statistics, this role is projected to grow 18 percent within the next 10 years, significantly faster than the 4 percent average growth for all occupations.

Big data can come in the form of social media comments, online product reviews, transaction data, and much more. Marketers have a vast amount of data at their fingertips, but it's not always easy to know what to do with it or how to use it effectively. Analysts will be needed to identify customer needs and wants, establish key performance indicators (KPIs), monitor the impact of marketing strategies, and more. Problem-solving, identifying new opportunities, and monitoring and forecasting trends using statistical software and internal systems are just a few of the duties at the core of the market research analyst job.

Analytical skills, communication skills, critical thinking skills, and a detail-oriented mindset are important soft skills for data analysts. Analysts must be able to digest large amounts of data as well as have strong interpersonal skills to communicate their findings. A variety of employers such as marketing agencies, financial institutions, universities, and government agencies will seek out professionals matching this skill set as the market research analyst role becomes increasingly important.

Sources: Based on information in Mara Leighton, "5 Skills LinkedIn Say Will Help You Get Hired in 2020 - and Where to Learn Them," *World Economic Forum*, September 3, 2020; U.S. Bureau of Labor Statistics, "Market Research Analysts".

---

product and marketing costs, inventory levels, and activities of the sales force. The savviest marketers also collect data from following every move consumers make on their websites and their social media interactions. Data from *external* sources relate to the organization's suppliers, intermediaries, and customers. It can also come from competitors' marketing activities and economic conditions.

Typically, these data are stored in one or more databases that allow marketers to access both internal and external sources. Many marketers also subscribe to commercial databases, such as LEXISNEXIS and Dun & Bradstreet's Data Cloud, to obtain information for marketing decisions. A great deal of information that used to be attainable only for a high price from companies specializing in producing commercial databases is now available via the internet.

Information provided by a single firm on household demographics, purchases, television-viewing and online behavior, and responses to promotions such as coupons and free samples is called *single-source data*. Consumers often use multiple devices to view shows and movies, including televisions, smartphones, and computers, making it difficult for companies to track media consumption habits and needs. To solve this problem, Nielsen has formed partnerships with Facebook, Twitter, and Instagram to compile accurate single-source data about what and how people are watching shows and when, as well as when they are talking about shows in social media. The partnerships represent a step forward in helping marketers track consumer media consumption over multiple devices.[16]

The internet, of course, is a powerful communication medium that links customers and organizations around the world and provides affordable data to help better understand customers. Companies like Lands' End and Paula's Choice that sell online accumulate data by tracking customers' purchases as well as the items they browse. By collecting and analyzing this data, the marketing information system helps the company track the buying habits of its most valued customers and informs decision making in response to these changes.

Businesses increasingly are using **marketing analytics**, the collection, organization, and interpretation of data about marketing performance, to mine useful insights from the huge amounts of data they collect. Marketing analytics begins with collecting and organizing the massive amounts of data obtained from customer contacts, retailer scanning, inventory management, and production. For instance, frequent-user programs like Marriott's Bonvoy not only collect data about customers' usage patterns by time of day, week, month, and year, but they can also ask loyal customers to participate in surveys about their needs and desires. Supermarkets and other retailers may offer store discount cards, which allow them to gain data on purchases through checkout scanners. These can be combined with other information a firm can acquire such as industry forecasts, business trends, and search data. The size and complexity of the diverse data requires sophisticated computer programs to store, organize, and analyze it. Many firms use customer relationship management (CRM) technologies and cloud computing to network technologies and organize the marketing data available to them.

Marketing analytics can allow marketers to look at patterns of purchase and consumption to discover trends that predict future buying behaviors. Not all of these patterns would be as visible through traditional marketing research methods. Identifying these trends and patterns can result in more precise adjustments to marketing strategies or entirely new ones. Consider the Coca-Cola Company, which crunches numbers not only from sales but also from social media, vending machines, and self-serve soft drink fountains that permit customers to mix their own drinks. Analysis of these data identified that the most popular combination mixed at fountains was Sprite with cherry shots, so the company introduced Cherry Sprite as a new flavor of soft drink. The company has also installed some vending machines with artificial intelligence that can adapt to their location and personalize customer

营销分析
marketing analytics the collection, organization, and interpretation of data about marketing performance

Technology and Innovation

技术与创新：抖音使用人工智能和大数据留住用户

TikTok Uses AI and Big Data to Keep Users Coming Back for More

China-based TikTok, an app for sharing short-form videos, is one of the world's fastest-growing social networking platforms. With a reported 500 million active global users, TikTok knows a thing or two about keeping its users engaged. TikTok's parent company, ByteDance, is a multinational technology company that works with artificial intelligence (AI) algorithm development and big data analysis to understand and impact user behavior.

TikTok videos, which range from 5 to 60 seconds long, cater to a short attention span. The app defaults to the "For You" tab, a curated, seemingly never-ending feed of lip-syncing, storytelling, memes, makeup tutorials, cooking instructions, dancing, and more. Videos play automatically, quickly sucking users in. Users can easily swipe up to load new videos. The algorithm learns from user engagement—from watch time and likes to shares and comments—to personalize video recommendations in real time, getting better and better as time goes on. The average user opens the app eight times a day, consuming 46 minutes of content.

These personalization algorithms are at the heart of the app's technology. TikTok found that when app users are shown previews and given a choice of what to watch, such as on the YouTube app, they often disengage from the platform, overwhelmed by determining what to watch next. By delivering a hyper-personalized feed that immediately immerses users, TikTok answers the user's question of "What should I watch?" for them and better satisfies users with a frictionless experience.

Sources: "Explaining TikTok's Machine Learning Algorithm," *Jumpstart Mag*, June 22, 2020; Katie Sehl, "20 Important TikTok Stats Marketers Need to Know in 2020," *Hootsuite*, May 7, 2020; "How Cutting-Edge AI Is Making China's TikTok the Talk of Town," *Medium*, November 15, 2018.

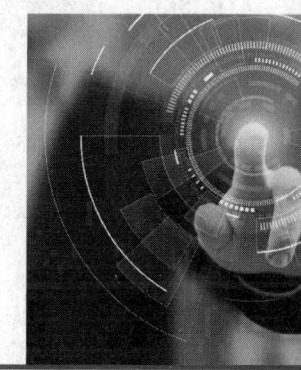

Chapter 4 Building Customer Relationships Through Effective Marketing

selections as well as report sales data back to the company.[17] Marketing analytics provides new understanding of customer behavior that has the potential to help firms create competitive advantage.

市场调研
4-9b Marketing Research

Although analyzing marketing information yields useful insights, it does not always provide specific information to solve a problem or refine a strategy, in which case research may be called for. **Marketing research** is the process of systematically gathering, recording, and analyzing data concerning a particular marketing problem. Marketing research is an important step of the marketing process because it involves collecting and analyzing data on what consumers want and need, their consumption habits, trends, and changes in the marketing environment. Information obtained from research increases marketers' ability to respond to those changes. For instance, many marketers would be interested in recent research that found that consumers are more likely to trust product recommendations from a family member, friend, or social media influencer than from brands on social media.[18] Such research can point marketers to new marketing channels for reaching particular target market segments.

Marketers collect *primary data* directly from consumers when they conduct mail, telephone, personal interview, online, focus group, or social networking surveys or conduct direct observation of consumer behavior. For example, focus groups are often used to test actual consumer reactions to advertisements, product modifications, and even movie endings. Marketers use *secondary data* from sources compiled inside or outside of the firm to help support marketing research initiatives. These sources often include commercial and government reports as well as internal databases. Marketing researchers are increasingly monitoring blogs and social networks to discover what consumers are saying about their products—both positive and negative. Many companies use social media outlets to solicit feedback from customers on their existing or upcoming products. While there is always a risk that customers will give a company or its products bad reviews online, most firms deem the risk worthwhile to conduct the low-cost research they need to be successful. If handled correctly, consumer complaints can be an important source of data on how to improve products and services. Indeed, the internet has made marketing research easier and cheaper than ever. Social media sites such as Facebook and Twitter can help small firms gauge potential market demand and try out product ideas for little or no cost. The internet also offers numerous databases and other sources of valuable information on competitors, target markets, and the marketing environment.

Table 4-5 lists a variety of useful resources for secondary information, which is existing information that has been gathered by other organizations. As can be seen in Table 4-5, secondary information can come from a variety of sources, including governments, trade associations, general publications and news outlets, and corporate information.

Table 4-6 outlines a six-step procedure for conducting marketing research. It is particularly well suited to test new products, determine various characteristics of consumer markets, and evaluate promotional activities. Even when marketers outsource marketing research to external firms such as IQVIA, Nielsen, and IRI, these firms generally apply this process.

市场调研
marketing research the process of systematically gathering, recording, and analyzing data concerning a particular marketing problem

Focus groups. Many business organizations use focus groups as one method of doing marketing research. A variety of different types of information can be collected through focus groups.

Table 4-5 Sources of Secondary Information

Government Sources	
U.S. Census	https://www.census.gov/
International Trade Administration—country market research	https://www.trade.gov/research-country
National Technical Information Services	https://www.ntis.gov/
Canadian trade	https://strategis.ic.gc.ca/
Trade Associations and Shows	
Center for Association Leadership	https://www.asaecenter.org/
Directory of Associations	https://directoryofassociations.com/
Trade Show News Network	https://www.tsnn.com/
U.S. Chamber of Commerce	https://www.uschamber.com/
Magazines, Newspapers, Video, and Audio News Programming	
Google Video Search	https://www.google.com/videohp?hl=en
Google News Directory	https://news.google.com/
Yahoo! Video Search	https://video.search.yahoo.com/
Corporate Information	
The Public Register Online—corporate annual reports	http://www.publicregister.com/
Bitpipe	https://www.bitpipe.com/
Business Wire—press releases	https://www.businesswire.com/
PR Newswire—press releases	https://www.prnewswire.com/

Source: Adapted and updated from "Data Collection: Low-Cost Secondary Research," KnowThis.com.

> ✓ **Concept Check**
> ▶ How can marketing analytics improve marketing decisions?
> ▶ What are the major reasons for conducting marketing research?
> ▶ Identify and describe the six steps of the marketing research process.

Table 4-6 The Six Steps of Marketing Research

1. Define the problem.	The problem is stated clearly and accurately, as it will determine the research issues and approaches, the right questions to ask, and the types of solutions that are acceptable. This is a crucial step that should not be rushed.
2. Make a preliminary investigation.	The preliminary investigation aims to develop a sharper definition of the problem and a set of tentative answers, which are developed by examining internal information and published data and by talking with persons who have experience with the problem. These answers will be tested by further research.
3. Plan the research.	At this stage, researchers know what facts are needed to resolve the identified problem and what facts are available. They make plans on how to gather needed but missing data.
4. Gather factual information.	Once a plan is in place, researchers can collect primary data from surveys and/or observation, and get secondary data from commercial or government data sources. The choice depends on the plan and the available sources of information.
5. Interpret the information.	Facts by themselves do not always provide a sound solution to a marketing problem. They must be interpreted and analyzed to determine the choices available to management.
6. Reach a conclusion.	Once the data have been evaluated, researchers seek to draw conclusions and make recommendations. These may be obvious or not, depending on intangible factors and whether data used were complete. When there are gaps in the data, it is important for researchers to state this.

Ethics and Social Responsibility

商业伦理与社会责任：营销人员必须遵守数据伦理

Marketers Must Embrace Data Ethics

Privacy and data collection have become increasingly important issues, yet less than half of major brands have data ethics policies in place. Research from the World Federation of Advertisers (WFA) revealed that data ethics is a priority for marketers, but major gaps still exist between what companies should be doing to protect data versus what they are currently doing. The WFA hopes its findings will encourage businesses to be more proactive in their data practices and establish their own ethics policies.

Many companies have been criticized for the way they collect, store, and use customer data. The possibility of racial bias in artificial intelligence (AI), for example, raises ethical concerns. Humans are susceptible to bias, which can lead to the unintentional creation of discriminatory algorithms. IBM shut down its facial recognition programs due to concerns the AI-enabled algorithms would be used for mass surveillance, racial profiling, and human rights violations.

Individuals entrust businesses with vast amounts of personal information, from credit card data and mailing addresses to Social Security numbers and shopping preferences. Organizations should take the utmost care to protect consumer data with proper data handling and security measures to fend off breaches. Breaches can quickly erode consumer trust. Ancestry.com, a family history search company, faced a leak that exposed sensitive data belonging to 60,000 customers. Unlike other countries, the United States lacks general consumer data privacy laws, leaving businesses to self-regulate. According to the WFA, respect, fairness, accountability, and transparency should be at the center of data ethics policies.

Sources: Based on information in Rebecca Stewart, "CMOs Accept Data Ethics Falls on Their Shoulders, but Brands' Policies Are Lacking," *The Drum*, June 1, 2020; Eugene Bekker, "2020 Data Breaches | The Most Significant Breaches of the Year," Identity Force, January 3, 2020; "IBM Abandons 'Biased' Facial Recognition," BBC, June 9, 2020.

购买行为的类型

4-10 Types of Buying Behavior

Learning Objective
4-10 Identify the major steps in the consumer buying decision process and the sets of factors that may influence this process.

Buying behavior may be defined as the decisions and actions of people involved in buying and using products. **Consumer buying behavior** refers to the purchasing of products for personal or household use, not for business purposes. **Business buying behavior** is the purchasing of products by producers, resellers, governmental units, and institutions. Because a firm's success depends in large part on buyers' reactions to a marketing strategy, it is important to understand buying behavior. Marketing managers are better able to predict customer responses to marketing strategies and to develop a satisfying marketing mix if they are aware of the factors that affect buying behavior.

消费者购买行为
4-10a Consumer Buying Behavior

购买行为
buying behavior the decisions and actions of people involved in buying and using products

消费者购买行为
consumer buying behavior the purchasing of products for personal or household use, not for business purposes

企业购买行为
business buying behavior the purchasing of products by producers, resellers, governmental units, and institutions

Consumers' buying behaviors differ for different types of products. For frequently purchased low-cost items, a consumer uses *routine decision making* which involves very little search or decision-making effort. The buyer uses *limited decision making* for purchases made occasionally, or when they need more information about an unknown product in a well-known product category. When buying an unfamiliar or expensive item, or one that is seldom purchased, the consumer engages in *extended decision making*. Consumers have become empowered by information available on the internet that allows them to compare prices and features and read reviews about goods and services without stepping into a store. Increasingly, buyers feel sufficiently informed by their online research to proceed with buying decisions without the help of a salesperson. In this environment, marketing and customer service are increasingly important.

A person deciding on a purchase goes through some or all of the steps shown in Figure 4-4. First, the consumer recognizes that a problem exists that might be solved by a good or service. The "problem" might be something the person desires but does not possess, like the latest iPhone or Xbox. Second, the buyer looks for information, which may include brand names, product characteristics, warranties, and other features, as well as product reviews. Next, the buyer weighs the various alternatives, makes a choice, and acquires the item. In the after-purchase stage, the consumer evaluates the suitability of the product, which will affect future purchases. Consider the Geico advertisement, which highlights the fact that its product can solve the problem of paying too much for insurance. The ad further informs potential consumers of the benefits of Geico's customer service in addition to saving them money on insurance products. As Figure 4-4 depicts, the buying process is influenced by situational factors (physical surroundings, social surroundings, time, purchase reason, and buyer's mood and condition), psychological factors (perception, motivation, learning, attitudes, personality, and lifestyle), and social factors (family, roles, reference groups, digital influences, social class, culture, and subculture).

Consumer buying behavior is also affected by the ability to buy, called one's *buying power*, which is largely determined by income. As every taxpayer

SAVINGS IS JUST THE START

It starts with getting a quote to see if you could save 15% or more on car insurance. From there, you'll discover the comfort of 24/7 service with a licensed agent, the fast, fair, professional claim handling and why, for over 75 years, GEICO has been the choice of millions of drivers for all their insurance needs.

GEICO.COM   1-800-947-AUTO   LOCAL AGENT

Problem recognition. This Geico advertisement attempts to stimulate problem recognition. What's the problem? How can I save money on my insurance?

▶ **Figure 4-4 Consumer Buying Decision Process and Possible Influences on the Process**

A buyer goes through some or all of these steps when making a purchase.

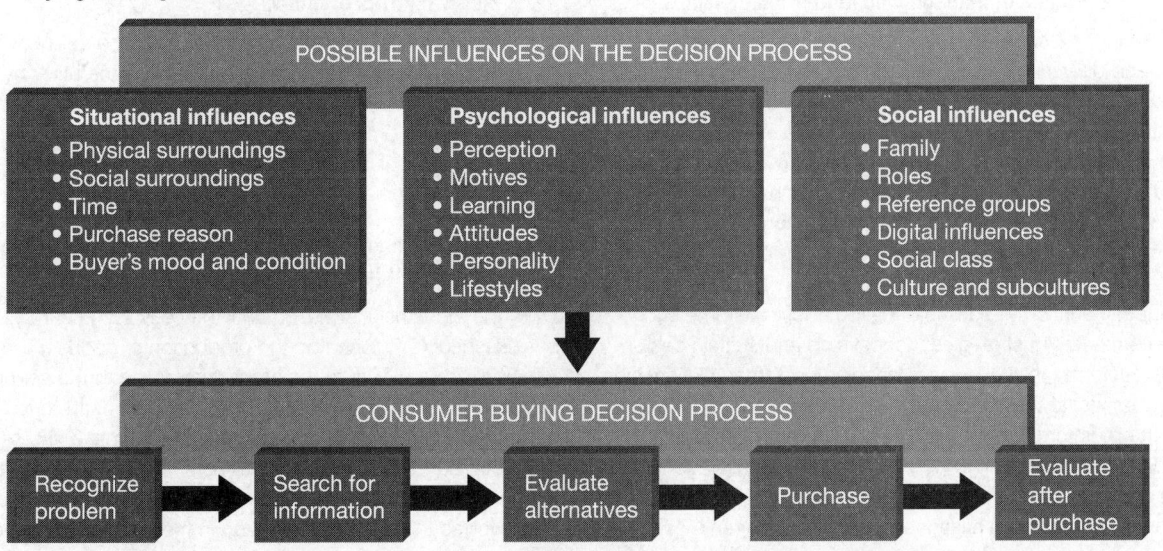

POSSIBLE INFLUENCES ON THE DECISION PROCESS

Situational influences
- Physical surroundings
- Social surroundings
- Time
- Purchase reason
- Buyer's mood and condition

Psychological influences
- Perception
- Motives
- Learning
- Attitudes
- Personality
- Lifestyles

Social influences
- Family
- Roles
- Reference groups
- Digital influences
- Social class
- Culture and subcultures

CONSUMER BUYING DECISION PROCESS

Recognize problem → Search for information → Evaluate alternatives → Purchase → Evaluate after purchase

Chapter 4   Building Customer Relationships Through Effective Marketing

✓ Concept Check

- Why is it important to understand buying behavior?
- How does a customer's decision-making time vary with the type of product?
- What are the five stages of the consumer buying decision process?
- What are the possible influences on this process?
- What is the difference between disposable income and discretionary income?

个人收入
personal income the income an individual receives from all sources

可支配收入
disposable income personal income *less* all personal taxes

可自由支配收入
discretionary income disposable income *less* savings and expenditures on food, clothing, and housing

knows, not all income is available for spending. For this reason, marketers consider income in three different ways. **Personal income** is the income an individual receives from all sources. **Disposable income** is personal income *less* all personal taxes. These taxes include income, estate, gift, and property taxes levied by local, state, and federal governments. **Discretionary income** is disposable income *less* savings and expenditures on food, clothing, and housing. Discretionary income is of particular interest to marketers because consumers have the most choice in spending it. Consumers use their discretionary income to purchase a wide variety of items ranging from automobiles and vacations to movies and pet food. In China, for example, a growing middle class with rising discretionary income is more interested than ever in Western brands. To capitalize on this demand, Walmart plans to open 14 more Sam's Club membership stores in China, bringing its total stores there to more than 40, all stocking popular Western brands alongside store branded Chinese products. It also plans to invest hundreds of millions of dollars in renovating existing stores and improving its supply chain there.[19]

企业购买行为
4-10b Business Buying Behavior

The business buying decision process is similar to the consumer process, but business buyers are generally better informed than consumers and consider a product's quality, its price, and the service provided by suppliers. Business purchases can be large, and a committee or a group of people, rather than just one person, often decides on purchases. Committee members must consider the organization's objectives, purchasing policies, resources, and personnel. The process of business buying is different than consumer buying. It occurs through description, inspection, sampling, or negotiation. Because business transactions can be more complicated and orders tend to be larger, obtaining complete and correct information on buyers and sellers is important.

Summary 小 结

4-1 Describe the meaning of *marketing* and the importance of managing customer relationships.

Marketing is a set of processes for creating, communicating, and delivering value to customers and for managing customer relationships in ways that benefit the organization and its stakeholders. Value is a customer's estimation of the worth of a product based on a comparison of its costs and benefits, including quality, relative to other products. Maintaining positive relationships with customers is crucial. Relationship marketing is establishing long-term, mutually satisfying buyer–seller relationships. Customer relationship management (CRM) uses information about customers to create marketing strategies that develop and sustain desirable customer relationships. Managing customer relationships requires identifying patterns of buying behavior and focusing on the most profitable customers. Customer lifetime value (CLV) is a combination of purchase frequency, average value of purchases, and brand-switching patterns over the entire span of a customer's relationship with the company.

4-2 Explain how marketing adds value by creating several forms of utility.

Marketing adds value in the form of utility, or the ability of a product to satisfy a human need. It creates place utility by making products available where customers want them, time utility by making products available when customers want them, and possession utility by transferring the ownership of products to buyers.

4-3 Discuss the development of the marketing concept and how it is implemented.

From the Industrial Revolution until the early 20th century, businesspeople focused on the production of goods. From the 1920s to the 1950s, the emphasis moved to the selling of goods. During the 1950s, businesspeople began to recognize that they were in business not only to make and sell products, but also to satisfy customers' needs. They began to implement the marketing concept, a business philosophy that involves the entire organization in the dual processes of

122   Part 2   Marketing

meeting the customers' needs and achieving the organization's goals. The marketing concept is dynamic and continues to evolve. Marketers today strive to build long-term relationships with customers wherever and whenever their needs arise.

Implementation of the marketing concept begins and ends with customers. A firm must first determine what customers' needs are and then pinpoint the specific needs and potential customers toward which it will direct its marketing activities and resources. Finally, the firm must evaluate the effectiveness of its efforts in meeting these needs.

4-4 Define what markets are and classify them.

A market is a group of individuals or organizations, or both, that need products in a given category and that have the ability, willingness, and authority to purchase them. Consumer markets include purchasers and/or household members who intend to consume or benefit from the purchased products and who do not buy products to make profits. Business-to-business or industrial markets, which include producers, resellers, governments, and institutions, purchase specific kinds of products for use in making other products for resale or for day-to-day operations.

4-5 Describe the two major components of a marketing strategy—target market and marketing mix.

A marketing strategy is a plan for the best use of an organization's resources to meet its objectives. Developing a marketing strategy involves selecting and analyzing a target market and creating and maintaining a marketing mix that will satisfy the target market.

A target market is a group of individuals or organizations, or both, for which a firm develops and maintains a marketing mix suitable for the specific needs and preferences of that group. Businesses that use an undifferentiated approach design a single marketing mix and direct it at the entire market for a particular product. The market segmentation approach directs a marketing mix at a segment of a market. A market segment is a group of individuals or organizations within a market that have similar characteristics and needs. A concentrated segmentation approach directs a single marketing mix at a single market segment, while a differentiated segmentation approach directs multiple marketing mixes at multiple market segments. Marketers use a wide variety of segmentation bases.

The four elements of a firm's marketing mix are product, price, distribution, and promotion. The product ingredient includes decisions about the product's design, brand name, packaging, and warranties. The pricing ingredient is concerned with base prices and various types of discounts. Distribution involves not only transportation and storage but also the selection of intermediaries. Promotion focuses on providing information to target markets. The elements of the marketing mix can be varied to suit broad organizational goals, marketing objectives, and target markets.

4-6 Explain how the marketing environment affects strategic market planning.

Marketing activities are affected by the external forces that make up the marketing environment. These forces include economic, sociocultural, political, competitive, legal and regulatory, and technological forces. These forces influence marketing strategy decisions and can be dramatic.

4-7 Examine the major components of a marketing plan.

A marketing plan is a written document that specifies an organization's resources, objectives, strategy, and implementation and control efforts to be used in marketing a specific product or product group. The marketing plan describes a firm's current position, establishes marketing objectives, and specifies the methods the organization will use to achieve these objectives. Marketing plans can be short-range, medium-range, or long-range.

4-8 Describe how market measurement and sales forecasting are used.

Market measurement and sales forecasting are used to estimate sales potential and predict product sales in specific market segments. A sales forecast is an estimate of the amount of a product that an organization expects to sell during a certain period of time based on a specified level of marketing effort.

4-9 Explain how marketers collect and analyze information useful for marketing decision making.

Marketers require information about customers' needs and desires, marketing opportunities, and changing customer attitudes and purchase patterns, as well as changes in the marketing environment. They acquire big data from both internal and external sources, store and organize them, and analyze them. Marketing analytics—the collection, organization, and interpretation of data about marketing performance—helps them mine useful insights from the huge amounts of data they collect. This analysis can allow marketers to look at patterns of purchase and consumption to discover trends that predict future buying behaviors and thereby improve marketing strategies. When this information is insufficient for solving a problem or refining a strategy, marketers turn to marketing research. Marketing research is the process of systematically gathering, recording, and analyzing data concerning a particular marketing problem. Marketers collect primary data directly from consumers through marketing research. Secondary data are compiled inside or outside of the firm to help support marketing research initiatives.

4-10 Identify the major steps in the consumer buying decision process and the sets of factors that may influence this process.

Buying behavior consists of the decisions and actions of people involved in buying and using products. Consumer buying behavior refers to the purchase of products for personal or household use. Organizational buying behavior is the purchase of products by producers, resellers, governments, and institutions. Understanding buying behavior helps marketers predict how buyers will respond to marketing strategies. The consumer buying decision process consists of five steps: recognizing the problem, searching for information, evaluating alternatives, purchasing, and post-purchase evaluation. Factors affecting the consumer buying decision process fall into three categories: situational influences, psychological influences, and social influences. Consumer buying power is further influenced by personal, disposable, and discretionary income.

Key Terms   关键术语

You should now be able to define and give an example relevant to each of the following terms:

marketing	form utility	target market	marketing research
value	place utility	undifferentiated approach	buying behavior
relationship marketing	time utility	market segment	consumer buying behavior
customer relationship management (CRM)	possession utility	market segmentation	business buying behavior
customer lifetime value (CLV)	marketing concept	marketing plan	personal income
utility	market	sales forecast	disposable income
	marketing strategy	marketing analytics	discretionary income
	marketing mix		

Discussion Questions   讨论题

1. Define marketing in your own words.
2. Why are companies so interested in relationship marketing?
3. How is a customer-oriented firm different from a production-oriented firm or a sales-oriented firm?
4. What are the major requirements for a group of individuals and organizations to be a market? How does a consumer market differ from a business-to-business market?
5. What are the major components of a marketing strategy?
6. What is the purpose of market segmentation? What is the relationship between market segmentation and the selection of target markets?
7. Describe the forces in the marketing environment that affect an organization's marketing decisions.
8. What is a marketing plan, and what are its major components?
9. What new information technologies are changing the ways that marketers keep track of business trends and customers?
10. Why do marketers need to understand buying behavior?
11. Is it a good strategy to focus most marketing efforts on the most profitable customers?
12. How might adoption of the marketing concept benefit a firm? How might it benefit the firm's customers?
13. How can marketing analytics help marketers improve marketing performance?
14. How does the marketing environment affect a firm's marketing strategy?

Case 4   案例4：星巴克"酿造"客户满意度

Starbucks Brews Customer Satisfaction

With more than 32,000 stores across more than 80 markets, Starbucks is the world's largest coffeehouse chain. In 50 years of business, the company grew from a single coffee shop in Seattle to a booming $80 billion business that holds a 57 percent share of the U.S. café market. Zev Siegl, Jerry Baldwin, and Gordon Bowker opened the first Starbucks location in Seattle's historic Pike Place Market in 1971 under the guidance of Alfred Peet, the founder of Peet's Coffee.

Starbucks faced many challenges on its way to the top, including overexpansion and shifting consumer preferences.

Interestingly, the first Starbucks locations didn't serve coffee, selling whole and ground beans exclusively. At the time, Starbucks enticed consumers who were more accustomed to instant or canned coffee by offering high-quality beans. It wasn't until Howard Schultz joined Starbucks in the 1980s as director of retail operations and marketing that Starbucks evolved. After visiting Italy, Schultz had a vision of recreating the Italian coffeehouse concept in the United States. In 1984, the company opened its first downtown Seattle café and served the first Starbucks Caffè Latte.

The concept proved to be a success. Schultz worked with investors in 1987 to buy Starbucks for $3.8 million and pursued an aggressive expansion strategy. When the company went public in 1992, it had 265 stores. By the time Schultz left Starbucks in 2000, it had more than 2,000 locations, a number that quadrupled by 2007. At the height of its growth, it seemed there was a Starbucks on nearly every corner in densely populated urban areas. This clustering strategy proved to be a misstep that resulted in fewer transactions at individual locations. After the Great Recession began in 2007, Starbucks realized its mistake. Though people loved their daily Starbucks fix, the financial crisis caused consumers to tighten their purse strings.

With Starbucks' stock price plummeting, Schultz returned to the helm. He slowed expansion in the United States, closing redundant locations and focusing more on international growth and enhancing the customer experience. For one day, Schultz closed all U.S. stores to retrain baristas in the art of espresso to improve quality. The stores reintroduced in-house coffee grinding to bring back the café ambiance. Schultz's strategy worked, and same-store sales rebounded. It wasn't until 2012 that the company set its sights on domestic expansion once again.

Now, Starbucks is focusing on adjusting its product mix to accommodate changing consumer preferences. The Frappuccino, for example, was one of the company's most popular beverages, but a sharp drop in sales reflected the fact that consumers have become more health-conscious, moving away from sugary drinks. Starbucks has since focused on drinks such as its Refreshers and cold brew to adapt to changing consumer preferences.

Starbucks is also investing in delivery as an avenue for growth, entering into partnerships in the United States with Brightloom and Uber Eats. Online orders, especially delivery orders, tend to result in higher checks, which could be good news for Starbucks. Another major undertaking is the opening of upscale Starbucks Reserve Roastery stores. These 20,000-square foot stores, located in Shanghai, Tokyo, Manhattan, Chicago, Seattle, New York, and Milan, are designed to be tourist destinations. The roasteries serve a wide array of coffee and experiment with coffee beverages. The high-end experiential stores contribute to the so-called halo effect, which elevates Starbucks in the minds of consumers.

Under the leadership of Starbucks' current CEO Kevin Johnson, the company opened a 20,000-square foot facility called the Tryer Center at its headquarters in Seattle where employees test new concepts using rapid prototyping. Employees quickly test new concepts and deploy ideas in just a matter of months. For example, a single-cup brewing prototype was created with the lab's 3D printer and deployed a month later. Starbucks employees from every level of the business submit ideas. The innovation lab makes Starbucks more agile in developing, testing, and releasing new products and systems.

Starbucks has tackled challenges head-on on its path to the top, demonstrating its ability to identify and adapt to changes in the market. With a heightened focus on innovation, Starbucks can refine the customer experience, improve its systems and processes, and introduce new, relevant products.[20]

Questions

1. Discuss the result of Starbucks' aggressive expansion strategy.
2. In what ways has Starbucks created products that satisfy consumer wants and needs?
3. How does Starbucks support innovation?

Building Skills for Career Success   为成功的职业生涯培养技能

1. Social Media Exercise

Comcast, the cable and communications provider, was one of the first companies to use Twitter* for customer service. The ComcastCares feed on Twitter was developed by Frank Eliason, the company's first Director of Digital Care, and is currently managed by Bill Gerth. Gerth and the Comcast team scan Twitter for complaints about service and contact the customers to see how Comcast can remedy the situation. This has altered the culture of the organization and prompted other companies to utilize Twitter for customer service. Visit @comcastcares on Twitter.

1. After exploring @comcastcares on Twitter, do you think that this helps with customer service? Why or why not?
2. Do you see other applications for Twitter for a communications giant like Comcast?

---

* 编者注：Twitter 于 2023 年 7 月更名为 X。

Chapter 4　Building Customer Relationships Through Effective Marketing

2. Building Team Skills

Review the text definitions of *market* and *target market*. Markets can be classified as consumer or industrial. Buyer behavior consists of the decisions and actions of those involved in buying and using products or services. By examining aspects of a company's products, you can determine the company's target market and the characteristics important to members of that target market.

Assignment

1. Working in teams of three to five, identify a company and a few of its most popular products.
2. List and discuss characteristics that customers may find important, including price, quality, brand name, variety of services, salespeople, customer service, special offers, promotional campaign, packaging, convenience of use, convenience of purchase, location, guarantees, store/office decor, and payment terms.
3. Write a description of the company's primary customer (target market).

3. Researching Different Careers

Before interviewing for a job, you should learn all you can about the company to help prepare you to ask meaningful questions during the interview. To find out more about a company, you can conduct market research before you interview.

Assignment

1. Choose at least two local companies for which you might like to work.
2. Contact your local Chamber of Commerce. (The Chamber of Commerce collects information about local businesses, and most of its services are free.) Ask for the information you desire.
3. Call the Better Business Bureau in your community (or check online) to determine if there are any complaints against the companies you are researching.
4. Prepare a report summarizing your findings.

Chapter 5

Creating and Pricing Products That Satisfy Customers

创造和定价让顾客满意的产品

Learning Objectives

Once you complete this chapter, you will be able to:

5-1 Explain what a product is and how products are classified..

5-2 Describe the product life cycle and how it leads to new-product development.

5-3 Define product line and product mix and distinguish between the two.

5-4 Identify the methods available for managing a product mix.

5-5 Examine the uses and importance of branding, packaging, and labeling.

5-6 Describe the economic basis of pricing and the means by which sellers can control prices and buyers' perceptions of prices.

5-7 Specify the major pricing objectives used by businesses.

5-8 Compare the three major pricing methods that businesses employ.

5-9 Explain the different strategies available to companies for setting prices.

5-10 Recognize three major types of pricing associated with business products.

Why Should You Care?

To be successful, a businessperson must understand how to develop and manage a mix of appropriately priced products and to change the mix of products as customers' needs change.

Inside Business

商业透视：Petco 的品牌重塑专注于宠物健康

Petco Rebrand Focuses on Pet Health and Wellness

In a push to center itself as a leading pet health and wellness company, Petco rebranded itself from Petco Animal Supplies to Petco, The Health + Wellness Co. This is part of a greater strategy to stand out from the competition and fend off online retailer Chewy's impressive growth. Petco competes with Chewy as well as other traditional retailers such as PetSmart, Pet Supermarket, Walmart, and a growing number of independent healthy pet stores.

A significant element of the rebranding is the expansion of its in-store veterinary hospitals. The company's 100 veterinary hospitals are integrated with PetCoach, its digital pet medical advice service. To increase revenue from this side of its business, Petco introduced Vital Care, a vet service membership program with perks such as unlimited nail trims and teeth-brushing for dogs. To further support its image as a pet health and wellness company, Petco announced it would stop selling shock collars, a controversial product category that is worth $10 million a year. This follows a $100 million decision to eliminate food with artificial ingredients.

Petco's pivot into health and wellness demonstrates that pet food and basic pet supplies have become commoditized, which means the products are just one more in a sea of similar products. This happens when customers begin to perceive competing products as offering roughly the same benefits. This makes price increasingly important, which is bad news for pet supply retailers. In this reality, Petco's growth must come from other product categories, such as its veterinary services and fresh and frozen pet food offerings.

By shifting into pet health and wellness, Petco is following the money. U.S. consumers spend approximately $30 billion per year on vet care and products alone, according to the American Pet Products Association. Because online retailers like Chewy and Amazon don't have brick-and-mortar locations to offer vet services, Petco believes this is the perfect area for growth.[1]

Did You Know?

Petco operates more than 1,500 stores in the United States, Mexico, and Puerto Rico.

产品
product everything one receives in an exchange, including all tangible and intangible attributes and expected benefits; it may be a good, a service, or an idea

Brands, like Petco, are an important way that consumers recognize products. A **product**, like Twisted Mango Diet Coke, has everything one receives in an exchange, including all tangible and intangible attributes and expected benefits. A car includes tangible benefits, such as comfortable seats, a warranty, and Apple CarPlay or Android Auto interface, as well as intangible attributes, such as status and the memories generated from road trips. Developing and managing products effectively, including these tangible and intangible benefits, are crucial to an organization's ability to maintain successful marketing mixes.

A product can be a good, a service, or an idea. A *good* is a real, physical thing that we can touch, such as an Oreo cookie. A *service* is the result of applying human or mechanical effort to a person or thing. A service is a change we pay others to make for us. A real estate agent's services result in a change in the ownership of real property. A hair stylist's services result in a change in your hairstyle. An *idea* may take the form of philosophies, lessons, concepts, or advice. Often ideas are bundled with a good or service. Thus, we might buy a book (a good) that provides ideas on how to lose weight. Alternatively, we might join Weight Watchers for ideas on how to lose weight and for help (service) in doing so.

In this chapter, we first look at the different aspects of products. We examine product classifications and describe the four stages of the product life cycle through which every product progresses. Next, we examine how companies manage products by modifying or deleting existing ones and developing new products. We also discuss branding, packaging, and labeling. Then our focus shifts to pricing. We explain competitive factors that influence sellers' pricing decisions and explore buyers' perceptions of prices. After considering organizational objectives that can be accomplished through pricing, we outline several methods for setting prices. Finally, we describe pricing strategies by which sellers can reach target markets successfully.

产品分类

5-1 Classification of Products

Different classes of products are directed at different target markets according to their varying needs and wants. A product's classification largely determines what kinds of distribution, promotion, and pricing are appropriate in marketing it.

Products can be grouped into two general categories: consumer and business (also called *business-to-business* or *industrial products*). A product purchased to satisfy personal and family needs is a **consumer product**. A product bought by a business for resale, for making other products, or for use in a firm's operations is a **business product**. The same item can be both a consumer and a business product, depending on the buyer's end use. LED light bulbs are a consumer product when you use them in your home, but are a business product if you purchase them for use in an office.

消费品的分类
5-1a Consumer Product Classifications

The traditional and most widely accepted system of classifying consumer products consists of four categories: convenience, shopping, specialty, and unsought products. These groupings are based primarily on characteristics of buyers' purchasing behavior.

A **convenience product** is a relatively inexpensive, frequently purchased item for which buyers want to exert only minimal effort to procure. Examples include bread, gasoline, newspapers, soft drinks, and chewing gum. The buyer spends little time in planning the purchase of a convenience item or in comparing available brands or sellers.

A **shopping product** is an item for which buyers are willing to expend considerably more effort on planning and purchasing. Shopping products cost more than convenience products and buyers allocate ample time for comparing prices, product features, qualities, services, and warranties between different stores and brands. Appliances, upholstered furniture, men's suits, bicycles, and mobile phones are examples of shopping products. These products are expected to last for a fairly long time and thus are purchased less frequently than convenience items.

A **specialty product** possesses one or more unique characteristics for which a group of buyers is willing to expend considerable purchasing effort. Buyers know exactly what they want and will not accept a substitute. When seeking out specialty products, purchasers do not compare alternatives. Examples include unique sports cars, a rare imported beer, or original artwork.

Unsought products are those that people do not plan on purchasing, such as products that address a sudden problem or that customers are unaware of until they see them in a store or online. Emergency medical services and automobile repairs are examples of products needed quickly and suddenly to solve a problem. A consumer who is sick or injured has little time to plan to go to an emergency medical center or hospital and will find the closest location to receive service. In such cases, speed of problem resolution is more important than price or other features a buyer might normally consider if there were more time for making a decision.

Learning Objective

5-1 Explain what a product is and how products are classified.

消费品
consumer product a product purchased to satisfy personal and family needs

工业品
business product a product bought for resale, for making other products, or for use in a firm's operations

便利产品
convenience product a relatively inexpensive, frequently purchased item for which buyers want to exert only minimal effort

选购产品
shopping product an item for which buyers are willing to expend considerable effort on planning and making the purchase

特色产品
specialty product an item that possesses one or more unique characteristics for which a significant group of buyers is willing to expend considerable purchasing effort

非求购产品
unsought product an item that people do not plan on purchasing, such as one that addresses a sudden problem or that customers are unaware of until they see it in a store or online

Consumer products can be classified into convenience, shopping, and specialty. Cheetos, a convenience product, is an item you are likely to grab off the shelf without much thought as you walk through the snack aisle of a supermarket. By contrast, people may spend a considerable amount of time and effort engaged in comparison shopping behavior when buying a shopping product, like a pair of Nike shoes.

原材料
raw material a basic material that becomes part of a physical product; usually comes from mines, forests, oceans, or recycled solid wastes

主要设备
major equipment large tools and machines used for production purposes

附属设备
accessory equipment standardized equipment used in a firm's production or office activities

零部件
component part an item that becomes part of a physical product and is either a finished item ready for assembly or a product that needs little processing before assembly

工艺材料
process material a material that is used directly in the production of another product but is not readily identifiable in the finished product

供应品
supply an item that facilitates production and operations but does not become part of a finished product

✓ Concept Check

- Identify the general categories of products.
- Describe the classifications of consumer products.
- Based on their characteristics, business products can be classified into what categories?

工业品的分类
5-1b Business Product Classifications

Based on their characteristics and intended uses, business products can be classified into the following categories: raw materials, major equipment, accessory equipment, component parts, process materials, supplies, and services.

A **raw material** is a basic material that becomes part of a physical product. It usually comes from mines, forests, oceans, or recycled solid wastes. Raw materials are generally bought and sold according to grades and specifications.

Major equipment includes large tools and machines used for production purposes. Examples of major equipment are lathes, cranes, and stamping machines. Some major equipment is custom-made for a particular organization, but other items are standardized products that perform one or several tasks for many types of organizations.

Accessory equipment is standardized equipment used in a firm's production or office activities. Examples include hand tools, photocopiers, fractional horsepower motors, and calculators. Compared with major equipment, accessory items are usually less expensive and are purchased routinely with less negotiation.

A **component part** becomes part of a physical product and is either a finished item ready for assembly or a product that needs little processing prior to assembly. Although it becomes an element of a larger product, a component part can often be identified easily. Clocks, tires, computer chips, and switches are examples of component parts.

A **process material** is used directly in the production of another product. Unlike a component part, a process material is not readily identifiable in the finished product. Like raw materials, process materials are purchased according to industry standards or to the specifications of the individual purchaser. Examples include industrial glue and food preservatives.

A **supply** facilitates production and operations but does not become part of a finished product. Paper, pencils, oils, and cleaning agents are examples.

A **business service** is an intangible product that an organization uses in its operations. Examples include financial, legal, online, janitorial, and marketing research services. Purchasers must decide whether to provide their own services internally or to hire a contractor from outside the organization.

产品生命周期
5-2 The Product Life Cycle

In a way, products are like people. They are born, they live, and they die. Every product progresses through a **product life cycle**, a series of stages in which a product's sales revenue and profit increase, reach a peak, and then decline. A firm must be able to launch, modify, and delete products from its offering in response to changes in product life cycles. Otherwise, the company's profits will disappear, and the firm will fail. Depending on the product, life-cycle stages vary in length. In this section, we discuss the stages of the life cycle and how marketers can use this information.

> Learning Objective
>
> **5-2** Describe the product life cycle and how it leads to new-product development.

产品生命周期的各阶段
5-2a Stages of the Product Life Cycle

Generally, the product life cycle is composed of four stages—introduction, growth, maturity, and decline—as shown in Figure 5-1. Some products progress through these stages rapidly, in a few weeks or months, while others can take years. The Koosh Ball, popular in the late 1980s, had a short life cycle. In contrast, Parker Brothers' Monopoly game, which was introduced nearly a century ago, is still going strong.

Introduction In the *introduction stage*, customer awareness and acceptance of the new product are low. Sales rise gradually as a result of promotion and distribution activities. There are no competitors at this stage. High development and marketing costs result in low profit, or even in a loss, initially. The price can be high as the company recoups research and development expenses and ramps up production. Customers are primarily people who want to be at the forefront of owning the new product. Examples of products in the introductory stage include self-driving cars and smart glasses such as Amazon's Echo frames. The marketing challenge at this stage is to make potential customers aware of the product's existence and its features, benefits, and uses. Marketers may make the product available to social media influencers so that they will share information about the product with their followers.

> **Figure 5-1** Product Life Cycle
>
> The graph shows sales volume and profits during the life cycle of a product.
>
> [Graph with x-axis "Time" and y-axis "Money" showing four stages: Introduction, Growth, Maturity, Decline. Two curves labeled "Industry sales volume" and "Industry profits" rising through growth, peaking at maturity, and declining.]

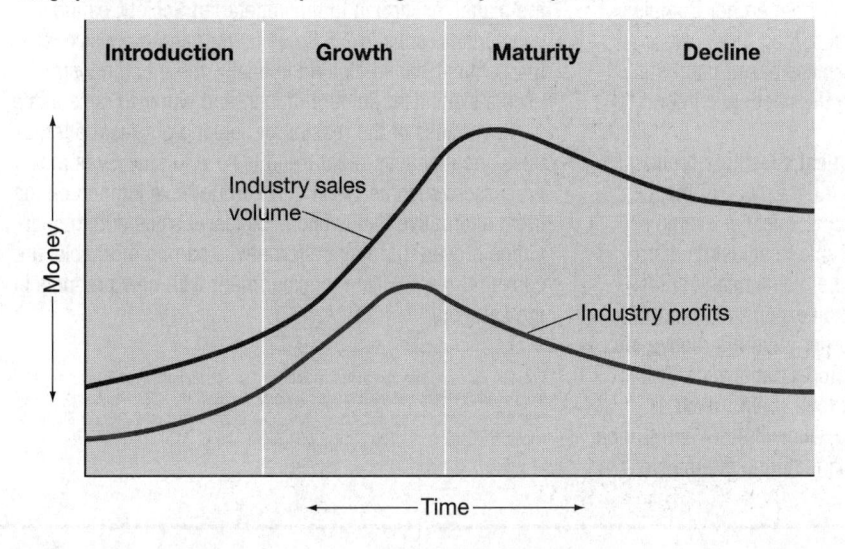

商业服务
business service an intangible product that an organization uses in its operations

产品生命周期
product life cycle a series of stages in which a product's sales revenue and profit increase, reach a peak, and then decline

Chapter 5   Creating and Pricing Products That Satisfy Customers   131

A new product is seldom an immediate success. Marketers must monitor early buying patterns and be prepared to modify the product promptly if necessary. The company should attempt to price the product to attract the market segment that has the greatest desire and ability to purchase it. Plans for distribution and promotion should suit the targeted market segment. All ingredients of the marketing mix may need to be adjusted quickly to maintain sales growth during the introduction stage.

Growth In the *growth stage*, sales increase rapidly as consumers gain awareness of the product. Other companies have begun to market competing products. The competition and decreased unit costs (owing to mass production) result in a lower price, which reduces the profit per unit. Industry profits reach a peak and begin to decline during this stage. To meet the needs of the growing market, the originating firm offers modified versions of the product and expands distribution. Virtual reality headsets, esports, and products with CBD are currently in the growth stage.

Marketers' goal in the growth stage is to stabilize and strengthen the product's position by encouraging brand loyalty. To beat the competition, the company may further improve the product or expand the product line to appeal to additional market segments. For example, to compete with the Amazon Echo smart speaker with Alexa the voice assistant, Google and Apple introduced their own smart speakers with voice assistants aimed at capturing different market segments and gaining market share in the growing industry.

A firm also may compete by lowering prices if increased production efficiency has resulted in sufficient savings. As the product becomes more widely accepted,

Sustaining the Planet

保护地球：消费者选择肉食替代品而成为弹性素食者

Consumers Go Flexitarian with Fake Meat

The alternative protein category has experienced skyrocketing growth in recent years with the widespread availability of brands such as Beyond Meat and Impossible Foods. Supply chain disruptions during the COVID-19 pandemic led many consumers to try so-called fake meat products for the first time in the face of meat shortages. According to research from Archer Daniels Midland, one of the world's largest food producers, 97 percent of people who tried plant-based meat substitutes for the first time during the pandemic intend to purchase them again.

Many plant-based meat substitute brands found themselves in the right place at the right time during the pandemic. For example, Impossible Foods was able to adjust its distribution strategy when the global health crisis struck, speeding up retail expansion and getting its plant-based burger meat alternative into thousands of grocery stores nationwide. This was paired with major food chains, such as Starbucks, Burger King, Dunkin', KFC, and Qdoba, introducing menu items featuring alternative meats.

Though Americans aren't becoming full-fledged vegetarians in large numbers, there is a significant trend toward a flexitarian diet, which is a veggie-centric way of eating. Consumers often cite health, safety, and convenience as top reasons for eating meat alternatives, while others believe that eating a plant-based diet is better for the planet. According to the Vegetarian Society, eating vegetarian results in 2.5 times fewer carbon emissions than a meat-based diet. Additionally, the meat industry uses a significant amount of land and water to raise cattle.

Regardless of the reason for seeking out meat alternatives, the meatless-meat trend is here to stay. Even meat processors such as Tyson and Perdue have jumped on the meat alternative bandwagon. Explosive sales during quarantine proved that meat alternatives can be profitable, and consumers are willing to experiment with new products in the category.

Sources: Based on information in T. L. Stanley, "Lockdown Fake Meat Buyers Turned Into Full-Blown Plant-Based Converts," *Adweek*, October 30, 2020; Vegetarian Society, "Eat to Beat Climate Change"; Rhian Hunt, "Can't Find Burger Meat? Kroger Stocks Impossible Burgers in 1,700 Stores," *USA Today*, May 6, 2020.

marketers may be able to broaden the network of distributors. Marketers can also emphasize customer service and prompt credit for defective products. During this period, promotional efforts attempt to build brand loyalty among customers.

Maturity Sales are still increasing at the beginning of the *maturity stage*, but the rate of increase has slowed. Later, the sales curve peaks and begins to decline, as do industry profits. Product lines are simplified, markets are segmented more carefully, and price competition increases, which forces weaker competitors to leave the industry. Marketers continue to introduce refinements and extensions of the original product to the market, like Samsung's folding Galaxy smartphone. Yes, smartphones have entered the maturity stage.

During a product's maturity stage, its market share may be strengthened by redesigned packaging or style changes. As an example, J.M. Smucker Company introduced Jif peanut butter in squeezable upright pouches to give consumers more flexibility when using the product. The new package lets consumers spread the product without a knife, measure precise amounts for recipes, or facilitate children serving themselves.[2] Redesigned packaging may convince consumers to use the product more often or in new ways, improving flagging sales.

Pricing strategies are flexible during the maturity stage. Markdowns and price incentives are not uncommon, although price increases may work to offset production and distribution costs. Marketers may offer incentives and assistance of various kinds to dealers to encourage them to support mature products, especially in the face of competition from private-label brands. New promotional efforts and aggressive personal selling may be necessary during this period of intense competition.

Decline During the *decline stage*, sales volume decreases sharply, and profits continue to fall. The number of competing firms declines, and the only survivors in the marketplace are businesses that specialize in marketing the product. Production and marketing costs become the most important determinant of profit. Mp3 players and landlines are examples of declining products.

When a product adds to the success of the overall product line, the company may retain it. Otherwise, marketers must determine when to eliminate it. A product usually declines because of technological advances, environmental factors, or consumers switching to alternative products. Therefore, few changes are made in the product itself during this stage. Instead, managers may raise the price to cover costs, reprice to maintain market share, or lower the price to reduce inventory. They will narrow distribution to the most profitable existing markets. During this period, the company probably will not spend heavily on promotion, although it may use some advertising and sales incentives to slow the product's decline. The company may choose to eliminate less-profitable versions of the product from the product line or may decide to drop the product entirely. Coca-Cola, for example, discontinued its Tab diet soft drink as part of a companywide strategic culling of underperforming products and brands. The nearly 60-year-old Tab brand languished after the introduction of Diet Coke, which went on to become one of Coca-Cola's best-selling soft drinks.[3]

Saying "goodbye" to the pay telephone. The pay telephone is in the decline stage of the product life cycle. Do you recall seeing one? If so, when and where? You might have a hard time remembering.

产品生命周期的运用
5-2b Using the Product Life Cycle

When making marketing strategy decisions, managers must be aware of the life-cycle stage of each product for which they are responsible and to estimate how long the product is expected to remain in that stage. For example, if a product is expected to remain in the maturity stage for a long time, there is no rush to develop a replacement product. A company risks speeding the decline of an existing product by releasing a replacement before the earlier product has reached the decline stage. Even so, a firm will be willing to take that risk in some cases. In other situations, a company will attempt to extend a product's life cycle. Extending its life can be an important tool in maintaining a product's profitability. A condiment staple since its introduction more than 140 years ago, Heinz Ketchup has extended its life through packaging innovations, such as squeeze bottles and single-serving containers, releasing different flavors like balsamic and sriracha, and even experimenting with purple and green-colored ketchup.

> ✓ **Concept Check**
> ▸ Explain the four stages of the product life cycle.
> ▸ How does knowledge of the product life cycle relate to the introduction of new products?

产品线和产品组合
5-3 Product Line and Product Mix

> **Learning Objective**
> **5-3** Define *product line* and *product mix* and distinguish between the two.

A **product line** is a group of similar products that differ only in relatively minor characteristics. Generally, the products within a product line are related to each other in the way they are produced, marketed, or used. Procter & Gamble, for example, manufactures and markets several shampoos, including Pantene, Head & Shoulders, and Herbal Essences.

While organizations may start a new product line, many opt to introduce new products within existing product lines. It is less costly than starting a new product line and permits them to apply the experience and knowledge they have acquired to the production and marketing of new products. FritoLay, for example, regularly introduces new flavors of its popular potato chips, such as Flamin' Hot and Kettle Cooked Jalapeno.

An organization's **product mix** consists of all the products the firm offers for sale. For example, Procter & Gamble has about 60 brands—some of which are well known, like Gillette and Febreze, and others that are less familiar in the United States, such as Lenor and Ariel—that fall into several product lines.[4] Two "dimensions" are often applied to a firm's product mix. The *width* of the mix is the number of product lines it contains. The *depth* of the mix is the average number of individual products within each line. These measures are general—no exact numbers correspond to these categories. Some organizations offer a broad product mix as a means of trying to be competitive in many different categories.

> ✓ **Concept Check**
> ▸ How does a product line differ from a product mix?
> ▸ Can a product line be a product mix?

产品组合的管理
5-4 Managing the Product Mix

> **Learning Objective**
> **5-4** Identify the methods available for managing a product mix.

To provide products that satisfy people in a firm's target market or markets and that also achieve the organization's objectives, a marketer must develop, adjust, and maintain an effective product mix. The same product mix is rarely effective for long. As customers' product preferences and attitudes change, their desire for a product may diminish or grow. A company may also need to alter its product mix to adapt to changes in the competition. For example, a marketer may have to introduce a new product, modify an existing one, or eliminate a product from the mix because one or more competitors have grown more dominant in the market segment. A marketer may also expand the firm's product mix to take advantage of excess marketing and production capacity. Panera, for instance, introduced three flavors of flatbread pizzas to help bring customers into its casual dining restaurants at dinnertime.[5] A company must be careful when altering the product mix that the

产品线
product line a group of similar products that differ only in relatively minor characteristics

产品组合
product mix all the products a firm offers for sale

134 Marketing

changes made bring about improvements in the mix. There are three major ways to improve a product mix: change an existing product, delete a product, or develop a new product.

现有产品的管理
5-4a Managing Existing Products

A product mix can be changed by deriving additional products from existing ones. This can be accomplished through product modifications and by line extensions.

Product Modifications **Product modification** refers to changing one or more of a product's characteristics. For this approach to be effective, several conditions must be met. First, the product must be modifiable. Second, existing customers must be able to perceive that a modification has been made, assuming that the modified item is still directed at the same target market. Third, the modification should make the product more consistent with customers' desires so that it provides greater satisfaction. For example, after being acquired by Ferrero Group, Keebler reformulated a number of its cookies to capitalize on the growing consumer demand for "cleaner" foods. The company replaced high-fructose corn syrup and artificial vanilla with more natural ingredients. It also redesigned the packaging to improve freshness, highlight the ingredient changes, and unify designs across the Keebler brand.[6]

Existing products can be altered in three primary ways: in quality, function, and aesthetics. *Quality modifications* are changes that relate to a product's dependability and durability and are usually achieved by alterations in the materials or production process. *Functional modifications* affect a product's versatility, effectiveness, convenience, or safety. They usually require redesign of the product. Typical product categories that have undergone extensive functional modifications include home appliances, office and farm equipment, and consumer electronics. *Aesthetic modifications* change the sensory appeal of a product by altering its taste, texture, sound, smell, or visual characteristics. Because a buyer's purchasing decision is affected by sensory stimuli, an aesthetic modification may impact purchases. Through aesthetic modifications, a company can differentiate its product from competing brands and gain market share if customers find the modified product more appealing.

Line Extensions A **line extension** is the development of a product closely related to one or more products in the existing product line but designed specifically to meet somewhat different customer needs. For example, Hostess Brands introduced new flavors of its perennial snack cakes, including caramel-filled Ding Dongs and mixed berry Twinkies, as well as several holiday themed versions of Twinkies, Hostess CupCakes, SnoBalls, and Donettes.[7]

Many of the so-called new products introduced each year are in fact line extensions. Line extensions are more common than new products because they are a less-expensive, lower-risk alternative for increasing sales. A line extension may focus on a different market segment or be an attempt to increase sales within the same market segment by more precisely satisfying that segment's needs, hopefully taking away market share from competitors.

Part of a product line. These products are part of Lay's potato chip product line.

产品改进
product modification the process of changing one or more of a product's characteristics

产品线延伸
line extension development of a new product that is closely related to one or more products in the existing product line but designed specifically to meet somewhat different customer needs

Line extensions help companies to be more competitive and to maintain or increase their market shares. There are 40 flavors of Oreos in the United States, and more than 85 worldwide. Each flavor is a line extension derived from the original product.

Chapter 5   Creating and Pricing Products That Satisfy Customers   135

Exploring Careers

职业探索：您准备好从事产品管理工作了吗

Are You Ready for a Career in Product Management?

Product managers are responsible for coordinating activities related to understanding customers' needs, the development of products, and product design. While product managers are not necessarily charged with product development specifically, they guide decision making across teams by communicating customer pain points and helping identify solutions. Product managers may come from a variety of backgrounds, which creates many types of product management.

Customer-focused product managers often have a background in sales or customer support and are focused on how to best serve the needs of customers. These product managers ask questions such as "Who is the customer?" "What is the customer problem or opportunity?" and "What does the customer experience look like?" On the other end of the spectrum is business-focused product management. These managers usually have a sales background and focus on how to develop, fund, and improve products and how the products will affect the business.

Technical product managers come from the areas of information technology and software engineering and focus on how a product is developed. These managers work on technical products such as Software-as-a-Service (SaaS, a software licensing and delivery model) products. Lastly, design-focused product managers focus on elements such as packaging, labeling, and functionality. Many more types of product managers exist, and more often than not, these types of product management blend together. Apple, for instance, hires product managers to drive design and work with engineering to differentiate its customer-centric products.

There is no "one size fits all" career path to becoming a product manager, so there are several ways to enter the field. Regardless of their background, a product manager must be a team player with a creative mind and excellent communication, organization, problem-solving, interpersonal, and technical skills. Technical skills, such as the ability to develop product strategies, are learned along the way.

Sources: Based on information in Kristen Baker, "How to Start Your Career in Product Management," *Hubspot*, November 6, 2019; Karthik Sankar, "How to Do Customer-Focused Product Management," *Products That Count*, April 13, 2020; Roi Lavan, "Are You an Apple-Like or Google-Like Product Manager," *Medium*, February 22, 2017.

淘汰产品

5-4b Deleting Products

To maintain an effective product mix, an organization often has to eliminate some products. This is called **product deletion**. A weak and unprofitable product costs a company time, money, and resources that could be used to modify other products or develop new ones. A weak product's unfavorable image can negatively affect the customer perception and sales of other products sold by the firm.

Most organizations find it difficult to delete a product because of the costs associated with bringing the product to market or for more emotional reasons. Some companies drop weak products only after they have become severe financial burdens. A better approach is to conduct a systematic review of the product's impact on the overall effectiveness of a firm's product mix. Such a review should analyze a product's contribution to a company's sales for a given period and should include estimates of future sales, costs, and profits. This review should help a firm to determine whether changes in the marketing strategy might improve the product's performance.

A product-deletion program can improve a company's performance. The Canadian aircraft maker Bombardier surprised the aviation world when it announced that it would stop selling Learjet small private aircraft, which have seen declines in demand and profits in recent years. Celebrities and wealthy customers have been turning away from the 60-year-old brand in recent years in favor of larger, more long-range aircraft. Discontinuing Learjet will allow the company to cut costs and

产品淘汰
product deletion the elimination of one or more products from a product line

improve cash flow, which the company will channel into its more lucrative, larger business jet aircraft.[8]

开发新产品
5-4c Developing New Products

Developing and introducing new products is frequently time consuming, expensive, and risky. Joby Aviation, for example, has spent a decade and more than $100 million developing a fast, electric air taxi that it hopes one day will compete with Uber and Lyft for short trips.[9] Thousands of new products are introduced annually. For most firms, more than half of new products will fail. Although developing new products is risky, failing to introduce new products can be just as hazardous. Successful new products can produce benefits for an organization, including survival, profits, a sustainable competitive advantage, and a favorable public image.

New products are generally grouped into three categories on the basis of their degree of similarity to existing products. *Imitations* are products designed to compete with existing products of other companies. The success of Mark Anthony Brand's White Claw hard seltzer, for instance, spawned many competitors such as Truly (Boston Beer), Bud Light Seltzer (Anheuser-Busch InBev), and Vizzy (Molson Coors). *Adaptations* are variations of existing products that are intended for an established market. Product refinements and line extensions are the adaptations considered most often, although imitative products may also include some refinement and extension. *Innovations* are entirely new products. They may give rise to a new industry or disrupt an existing one, like Chime's no-fee, app-based financial service did for the banking industry. Innovative products take considerable time, effort, and money to develop. They are by far the riskiest new product to develop and launch and are therefore less common than adaptations and imitations. While other companies market basic hair straighteners that cost $13–$200, the $500 Dyson Corrale flat iron uses proprietary technology and design that makes it operate cooler and safer, easier to use, and less damaging to hair. Dyson spent seven years and $43 million dollars developing the new product.[10] As shown in Figure 5-2, the process of developing a new product consists of seven phases.

Idea Generation Idea generation involves looking for product ideas that will help a firm achieve its objectives. Although some organizations get their ideas almost by chance, companies trying to maximize product-mix effectiveness develop systematic approaches for generating new-product ideas. Ideas may come from virtually any stakeholder associated with the firm, including managers, employees, researchers, engineers, competitors, advertising agencies, management consultants, private research organizations, customers, salespersons, or top executives. Sometimes, large companies with superior experience and resources may mentor small firms and help them generate ideas to help their businesses grow. Business incubators exist all over the country that pair new businesses with established ones so that the new business can learn about marketing and branding from experts. Goldman Sachs, Walmart, Chase Bank, and Staples have all hosted events and programs to counsel start-ups. Jim Koch of Boston Beer Company, maker of Sam Adams, partners with the small business lender, Accion, for the Brewing the American Dream program, which offers speed coaching sessions and loans to small businesses.[11]

Screening During screening, ideas that do not match organizational resources and objectives are rejected. In this phase, a firm's managers consider whether the organization has the financial resources and personnel with the correct expertise to develop and market the proposed product. Additionally, the company will assess whether the idea can address some need or want of buyers. Marketers may reject a good idea because the company lacks the necessary skills and abilities to make the product a success or because there is no apparent market for the product. The largest number of product ideas is rejected during the screening phase.

> **Figure 5-2** Phases of New-Product Development
>
> Generally, marketers follow these seven steps to develop a new product.
>
> 1. Idea generation
> 2. Screening
> 3. Concept testing
> 4. Business analysis
> 5. Technical development
> 6. Test marketing
> 7. Commercialization

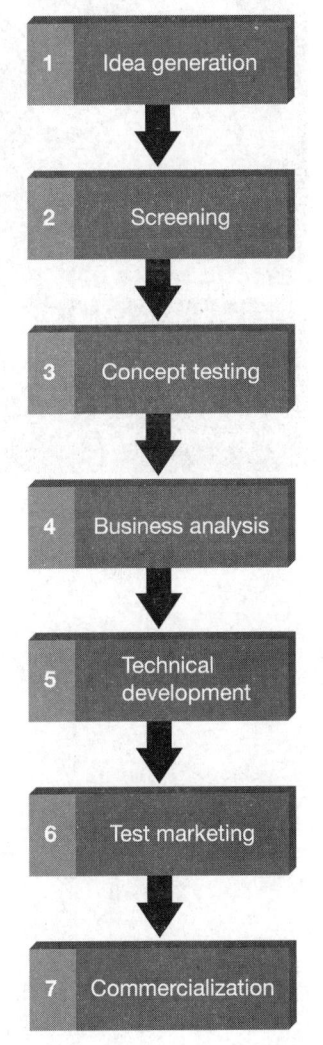

Chapter 5 Creating and Pricing Products That Satisfy Customers

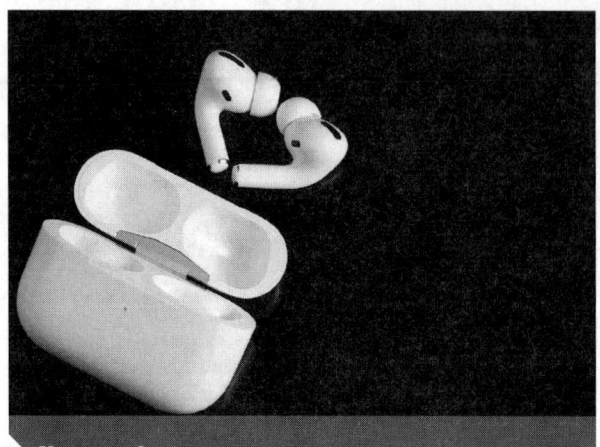

New product. Apple AirPods Pro are a new product that allow users to connect wirelessly to their cell phones through Bluetooth technology. There are also different levels of noise cancellation that now allow you to be fully in tune with your music, podcasts, and calls whenever and wherever you desire.

Concept Testing Concept testing is a phase in which a product idea is presented to a sample of potential buyers through a written or oral description (and perhaps drawings) to determine their attitudes and initial buying intentions. An organization may test one or several concepts when developing a product idea. Concept testing is a low-cost means for an organization to determine consumers' initial reactions to an idea before investing considerable resources in product research and development (R&D). Product development personnel use the results of concept testing to make product attributes and benefits reflect the characteristics and features most important to potential customers. The questions asked vary considerably depending on the type of product idea being tested. The following are typical:

- Which benefits of the proposed product are especially attractive to you?
- Which features are of little or no interest to you?
- What are the primary advantages of the proposed product over the one you currently use?
- If this product were available at an appropriate price, how often would you buy it?
- How could this proposed product be improved?

Business Analysis Business analysis generates tentative ideas about a potential product's financial performance, including profitability. During this stage, the firm considers how the new product, if it were introduced, would affect the firm's overall sales, costs, and profits. Marketing personnel usually work up preliminary sales and cost projections at this point, with the help of R&D and production managers.

Technical Development In the technical development phase, the company must determine whether it is technically feasible to produce the product and if the product can be made at a low enough cost for the company to generate a profit. If a product idea makes it to this point, it is transformed into a working model, or *prototype*. Often, this step is time consuming and expensive for the organization. When James Dyson was working to invent his first cyclonic, bagless vacuum cleaner, he went through more than 5,000 prototypes before he found the right one; his company continues to go through many prototypes throughout the research and development process of creating new products that solve problems.[12] If a product moves through this step successfully, then it is ready for test marketing.

Test Marketing Test marketing is the limited introduction of a product in several towns or cities that are representative of the intended target market. Its aim is to determine buyers' probable reactions. Marketers experiment with advertising, pricing, and packaging in different test markets and measure the extent of brand awareness, brand switching, and repeat purchases that result from alterations in the marketing mix. As an example, Chick-fil-A, test marketed a new Honey Pepper Pimento Chicken sandwich in restaurants in some cities in North and South Carolina. The fast-food chain has been testing new chicken sandwich flavors to broaden its appeal and compete with new chicken sandwich offerings from Popeyes, KFC, and even McDonald's.[13]

Commercialization During commercialization, the organization completes plans for full-scale manufacturing and marketing and prepares project budgets. In the

Technology and Innovation

技术与创新：高科技就是高级时尚

High-Tech Is High Fashion

By and large, the fashion industry is incredibly unsustainable. Fast fashion—mass-producing low-priced, trendy clothing at a low cost—in particular, comes at an extraordinary environmental cost. According to the World Economic Forum (WEF), the fashion industry emits more carbon than international flights and maritime shipping combined. Improvements driven by new technologies, however, have the power to turn the industry around.

Major brands are pledging to make sustainability a greater priority. Zara, one of the largest fast-fashion brands, pledged to use only organic, sustainable, or recycled cotton, linen, and polyester by 2025. By the same year, Nike said its plants will be powered by 100 percent renewable energy. Other companies, such as Wrangler, have developed new processes that reduce or eliminate water waste.

Many of these changes are enabled by advances in technology. Consumers are demanding that fashion brands become more transparent with their supply chains. They want to know where and how clothing is made. To achieve this, some brands have begun using blockchain technology to track their supply chains. For example, H&M partnered with VeChain to provide consumers with detailed supply chain tracing data. With just a click, consumers can view the suppliers and factories that contributed to a particular piece of clothing. With blockchain technology, the ledger creates permanent, time-stamped records of each step in a product's journey.

It can be challenging for companies to measure their social and environmental impact, but the growing demand for social accounting has given rise to new technology that will make it easier. Google Cloud partnered with designer Stella McCartney to create a tool powered by data analytics and machine learning to help do just that. The tool will give companies better insights into the environmental impact of their production processes.

Sustainability is the future of fashion. Circular business models, which aim to reduce waste through the continual use of resources, as well as supply chain tracing will become mainstream in the long run as technology accelerates. Consumers increasingly demand transparency, sustainability, and accountability across industries, and fashion is no exception.

Sources: Based on information in Nell Lewis and Max Burnell, "Look and Feel Good: How Tech Could Save the Fashion Industry," *CNN*, September 30, 2019; Morgan McFall-Johnsen, "These Facts Show How Unsustainable the Fashion Industry Is," *World Economic Forum*, January 31, 2020; "H&M Head of Sustainability Praises VeChain's Traceability Solution," *Crypto News Flash*, September 1, 2020.

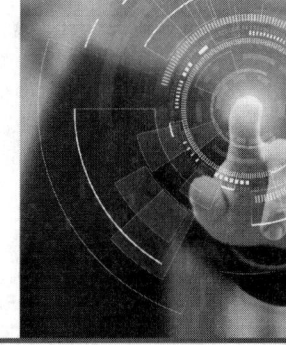

---

early part of the commercialization phase, marketing management analyzes the results of test marketing to determine necessary changes in the marketing mix. Test marketing may reveal, for example, that marketers need to change the product's physical attributes, modify the distribution plan, alter promotional efforts, or change the price. Most new products are marketed in stages, beginning in selected geographic areas and expanding into adjacent areas over a period of time.

为什么产品会失败
5-4d Why Do Products Fail?

Despite this rigorous process for developing product ideas, most new products end up as failures. In fact, many well-known companies have produced market failures (refer to Table 5-1).

Why does a new product fail? Mainly because the product and its marketing program are not planned and tested as thoroughly as they should be. For example, Samsung's Galaxy Note S7 phablet—a supersized smartphone—failed because some of the phones' batteries caught on fire. After the phones were banned from domestic flights, Samsung recalled the phones and ultimately opted to discontinue the model rather than lose more money on its investment.[14] To save on development costs, a firm may market-test a product before the kinks are worked out, or may not test its entire marketing mix. Or, when problems show up in the testing stage, a

Chapter 5 Creating and Pricing Products That Satisfy Customers

Concept Check

- What are some ways to improve a product mix? Describe two approaches to use existing products to strengthen a product mix.
- Why is it important to delete certain products? The largest number of product ideas are rejected during which stage?
- What is the aim of test marketing?
- Describe the seven phases of new-product development.

Table 5-1 Examples of Product Failures

Company	Product
Microsoft	Zune (2006)
Apple	Newton (1993)
Amazon	Fire Phone (2014)
Coca-Cola	New Coke (1985)
Frito-Lay	WOW! Chips (1998)

Sources: Adapted from: "When Corporate Innovation Goes Bad—The 160 Biggest Product Failures of All Time," *CBInsights*, April 7, 2020; Ben Gilbert, "25 of the Biggest Failed Product from the World's Biggest Companies," *Business Insider*, October 17, 2019.

company may try to recover its product development costs by pushing ahead with full-scale marketing anyway. Finally, some companies try to market new products with inadequate financing.

品牌、包装和标签
5-5 Branding, Packaging, and Labeling

Learning Objective

5-5 Examine the uses and importance of branding, packaging, and labeling.

Three important features of a product (particularly a consumer product) are its brand, package, and label. These features may be used to associate a product with a successful product line or to distinguish it from existing products. They may be designed to attract customers at the point of sale or to provide information to potential buyers. Because the brand, package, and label are integral elements of the product, they deserve careful attention during product planning.

什么是品牌
5-5a What Is a Brand?

A **brand** is a name, term, symbol, design, or any combination that identifies a seller's products and distinguishes it from other sellers' products. A **brand name** is the part of a brand that can be spoken. It may include letters, words, numbers, or pronounceable symbols, such as the ampersand in *Procter & Gamble*. A **brand mark**, on the other hand, is the part of a brand that is a symbol or distinctive design, such as the Nike "swoosh." A **trademark** is a brand name or brand mark that is registered with the U.S. Patent and Trademark Office and thus is legally protected from use by anyone except its owner. A **trade name** is the complete and legal name of an organization, such as Pizza Hut or Cengage (the publisher of this text).

品牌的类型
5-5b Types of Brands

Brands are often classified according to who owns them: manufacturers or stores. A **manufacturer (or producer) brand**, as the name implies, is a brand that is owned by the manufacturer. Many foods (Kellogg's Frosted Flakes), major appliances (Whirlpool), gasolines (Chevron), automobiles (Honda), and clothing (American Eagle) are sold as manufacturers' brands. Some consumers prefer manufacturer brands because they are usually nationally known, offer consistent quality, and are widely available.

A **store (or private) brand** is a brand that is owned by an individual wholesaler or retailer. Among the better-known store brands are Cat & Jack (Target), Kirkland Signature (Costco), and Trader Joe's. Owners of store brands claim that they can offer lower prices, earn greater profits, and improve customer loyalty by offering their own brands. Target, the first company to have ten billion-dollar store brands, uses them to help distinguish itself from rivals and to build loyalty among customers.[15]

品牌
brand a name, term, symbol, design, or any combination of these that identifies a seller's products as distinct from those of other sellers

品牌名称
brand name the part of a brand that can be spoken

品牌标志
brand mark the part of a brand that is a symbol or distinctive design

商标
trademark a brand name or brand mark that is registered with the U.S. Patent and Trademark Office and thus is legally protected from use by anyone except its owner

经营名称
trade name the complete and legal name of an organization

制造商（或生产商）品牌
manufacturer (or producer) brand a brand that is owned by a manufacturer

商店（或私人）品牌
store (or private) brand a brand that is owned by an individual wholesaler or retailer

Some companies that manufacture private brands also produce their own manufacturer brands. They often find such operations profitable because they can use excess capacity and avoid most marketing costs. Many private-branded grocery products are produced by companies that specialize in making private-label products. Most supermarkets rely heavily on their store brands. In the United States, store brands account for about 18 percent of all consumer packaged goods sales, and these private brand sales are rising faster than large manufacturer brand sales.[16]

A **generic product** (sometimes called a **generic brand**) is a product with no brand at all. Its plain package carries only the name of the product—applesauce, peanut butter, or potato chips. Generic products, available in supermarkets since 1977, are sometimes made by the major producers that manufacture name brands.

品牌化的好处
5-5c Benefits of Branding

Consumer confidence is the most important element in the success of a branded product, whether the brand is owned by a producer or by a retailer. Because branding identifies each product, customers can easily repurchase products that provide satisfaction, performance, and quality. Moreover, they can just as easily avoid or ignore unsatisfactory products. In supermarkets, the products most likely to keep their shelf space are the brands with large market shares and strong customer loyalty.

Both buyers and sellers benefit from branding. Because brands are easily recognizable, they reduce the amount of time buyers spend on shopping, as they can quickly identify the brands they prefer. Choosing particular brands, such as Chanel, Polo, Patagonia, or Nike, can be a way of expressing oneself and identifying with certain lifestyle characteristics and values. Brands also help reduce the perceived risk of purchase. Finally, customers may receive a psychological reward from owning a brand that symbolizes status. The Lexus brand is an example.

Branding helps a firm introduce a new product that carries a familiar brand name because buyers already know the brand. Branding aids sellers in their promotional efforts because promotion of each branded product indirectly promotes other products of the same brand. H.J. Heinz, for example, markets many products with the Heinz brand name, such as ketchup, vinegar, gravies, barbecue sauce, and steak sauce.

One chief benefit of branding is the creation of **brand loyalty**, the extent to which a customer is favorable toward buying a specific brand. The stronger the brand loyalty, the greater is the likelihood that buyers will consistently choose the brand. There are three levels of brand loyalty: recognition, preference, and insistence. *Brand recognition* is the level of loyalty at which customers are aware that the brand exists and will purchase it if their preferred or familiar brands are unavailable. This is the weakest form of brand loyalty. *Brand preference* is the level of brand loyalty at which a customer prefers one brand over competing brands. However, if the preferred brand is unavailable, the customer is willing to substitute another brand. *Brand insistence* is the strongest and least common level of brand loyalty. Brand-insistent customers will not buy substitutes. Apple is a brand known for having brand-insistent customers. Every time Apple releases a new product, customers will stand in line for hours, even days, just to be among the first to purchase it. Brand loyalty in general seems to be declining, partly due to marketers' increased dependence on discounted prices, coupons, and other short-term promotions, and partly because of the enormous array of new products with similar characteristics. It is also easier than ever to comparison shop for products that meet customers' needs at the lowest possible price.

You can easily recognize a manufacturer's brand because it is not sold by just one retailer. This brand was initiated by the manufacturer and is owned and supported by the manufacturer. Pop-Tarts are sold in many supermarkets.

一般产品（或通用品牌）
generic product (or generic brand) a product with no brand at all

品牌忠诚度
brand loyalty extent to which a customer is favorable toward buying a specific brand

Chapter 5   Creating and Pricing Products That Satisfy Customers

Table 5-2 Top Ten Most Valuable Brands in the World

Brand	Brand Value (billion $)
1. Apple	323.0
2. Amazon	200.7
3. Microsoft	166.0
4. Google	165.4
5. Samsung	62.3
6. Coca-Cola	56.9
7. Toyota	51.6
8. Mercedes-Benz	49.3
9. McDonald's	42.8
10. Disney	40.8

Source: "Best Global Brands Rankings," *Interbrand*.

Brand equity is the marketing and financial value associated with a brand's strength in a market. Although difficult to measure, brand equity represents the value of a brand to an organization. The top ten most valuable brands in the world are shown in Table 5-2. The four major factors that contribute to brand equity are brand awareness, brand associations, perceived brand quality, and brand loyalty. Brand awareness leads to brand familiarity—buyers are more likely to select a familiar brand. The symbolic associations of a brand connect it to a personality type or lifestyle. For example, customers associate Michelin tires with protecting family members, Nike products with pushing yourself athletically ("Just Do It"), and Dr Pepper with a unique taste. When consumers are unable to judge for themselves the quality of a product, they may rely on a brand's perceived level of quality. Finally, brand loyalty is a valued element of brand equity because it reduces both a brand's vulnerability to competitors and the need to spend tremendous resources to attract new customers. Loyalty also increases brand visibility and encourages retailers to carry the brand. Sometimes, large firms opt to purchase a well-known brand to diversify or complement their existing brands. As an example, Mohawk Group, a consumer products conglomerate, acquired the Spiralizer, PurSteam, and Pohl Schmitt brands in order to diversify its portfolio of brands with small appliance options.[17]

选择和保护品牌
5-5d Choosing and Protecting a Brand

A number of issues should be considered when selecting a brand name. The name should be easy for customers to say, spell, and recall. Short, one-syllable names such as *Tide* often satisfy this requirement. Words, numbers, and letters can be combined to yield brand names such as Samsung's Galaxy S21 Ultra phone or BMW's Z4 Roadster. The brand name should suggest, in a positive way, the product's uses, special characteristics, and major benefits, and should be distinctive enough to set it apart from competing brands.

It is important that a company select a brand that can be protected through registration, reserving it for exclusive use by that firm. Some brands, because of their designs, are infringed on more easily than others. Registration protects trademarks domestically for ten years and can be renewed indefinitely. To protect its exclusive right to the brand, the company must ensure that the selected brand will not be considered an infringement on any existing brand already registered with the U.S. Patent and Trademark Office. This task may be complicated by the fact that courts determine infringement and base their decisions on whether a brand causes consumers to be confused, mistaken, or deceived about the source of the product. McDonald's is one company that is known for aggressively protecting its trademarks against infringement. It has brought charges against a number of companies with *Mc* names because of concerns that the use of the prefix might give consumers the impression that these companies are associated with or owned by McDonald's.

A business does not want a brand name to become a generic term that refers to a general product category. Generic terms cannot be legally protected as exclusive brand names. For example, names such as *yo-yo*, *aspirin*, *escalator*, and *thermos*—all exclusively brand names at one time—eventually were declared generic terms that refer to product categories. As such, they can no longer be protected. To ensure that a brand name does not become a generic term, the firm should spell the name with a capital letter and use it as an adjective to modify the name of the general product class, as in Jell-O Brand Gelatin. An organization can deal directly with this problem by advertising that its brand is a trademark and should not be used generically. Firms also can use the registered trademark symbol ® to indicate that the brand is trademarked.

品牌资产
brand equity marketing and financial value associated with a brand's strength in a market

品牌战略
5-5e Branding Strategies

The basic branding decision for any firm is how to brand its products. A producer may market its products under its own brands, private brands, or both. A retail store may carry only producer brands, its own brands, or both. Once either type of firm decides to brand, it chooses one of two branding strategies: individual branding or family branding.

Individual branding is the strategy in which a firm uses a different brand for each of its products. For example, Procter & Gamble uses individual branding for its line of bar soaps, which includes Ivory, Safeguard, and Olay. Individual branding offers two major advantages: a problem with one product will not affect the good name of the firm's other products and the different brands can be directed toward different market segments.

Family branding is the strategy in which a firm uses the same brand for all or most of its products. Sony, Dell, IBM, and Xerox use family branding for their product mixes. A major advantage of family branding is that successful promotion for any one item that carries the family brand can help all other products with the same brand name. In addition, a new product has a head start when its brand name is already known and accepted by customers. As an example, when Anheuser-Busch InBev introduced a new seltzer product to compete with White Claw, it called the line Bud Light Seltzer to capitalize on the name recognition of its Bud Light brand.[18]

品牌延伸
5-5f Brand Extensions

A **brand extension** occurs when an organization uses one of its existing brands to brand a new product in a different product category. The French fashion house Louis Vuitton, for example, extended its brand when it opened an LV branded chocolate shop and café in a new glass tower in Ginza in Tokyo.[19] A brand extension should not be confused with a line extension. A *line extension* refers to using an existing brand on a new product in the same product category, such as a new flavor or new sizes. Pringles engages in line extension when releasing a new flavor, such as Nashville Hot Chicken flavor. Marketers must be careful not to extend a brand too many times or extend too far outside the original product category. Either action may weaken the brand.

包装
5-5g Packaging

Packaging consists of all the activities involved in developing and providing a container with graphics for a product. The package is a vital part of the product. It can make the product more versatile, safer, or easier to use. Through its shape, size, appearance, and printed message, a package can influence purchasing decisions.

Packaging Functions Effective packaging is a combination of function and aesthetics. The basic function of packaging materials is to protect the product and maintain its functional form. Fluids such as milk, orange juice, and hair spray need packages that preserve and protect the product inside. Packaging should prevent damage that would affect the product's usefulness and increase costs. Because product tampering has become a problem for marketers of many types of goods, packaging techniques have been developed to counter this danger. Some packages are also designed to foil shoplifting.

独立品牌
individual branding the strategy in which a firm uses a different brand for each of its products

家族品牌
family branding the strategy in which a firm uses the same brand for all or most of its products

品牌延伸
brand extension using an existing brand to brand a new product in a different product category

包装
packaging all the activities involved in developing and providing a container with graphics for a product

Another function of packaging is to offer consumer convenience. For example, individual-serving boxes or plastic bags that contain liquids and do not require refrigeration appeal strongly to parents of small children and to young adults with active lifestyles. The size or shape of a package may relate to the product's storage, convenience of use, or replacement rate. Small, single-serving cans of vegetables, for instance, may prevent waste and make storage easier.

A third function of packaging is to promote a product by communicating its features, uses, benefits, and image. Sometimes a firm develops a reusable package to make its product more desirable. For example, CleanPath multi-surface cleaners employ Replenish technology which allows them to be sold as cleaner concentrate in pods that screw onto the bottom of a spray bottle. Consumers purchase the bottle once, add water, and the pod releases the correct amount of cleaner concentrate. The system saves on plastic and water waste and is cheaper than many competitors' products.[20]

Package Design Considerations Many factors must be weighed when developing packages. Obviously, one major consideration is cost. Expensive packaging can affect the final cost of a product.

Marketers must also decide whether to package the product in single or multiple units. Multiple-unit packaging can increase demand by increasing the amount of the product available at the point of consumption (in the home, for example). Multiple-unit packaging does not work for infrequently used products because buyers generally prefer not to have an excess supply or to store products for a long time. However, multiple-unit packaging can make storage and handling easier (as in the case of twelve-packs used for soft drinks). It can also facilitate special price offers, such as two-for-one sales. Multiple-unit packaging may encourage customers to try a product several times, but it may also backfire and deter them from trying the product if they cannot purchase just one.

Marketers should consider how much consistency is desirable among an organization's package designs. To promote an overall company image, a firm may decide that all packages must be similar or include a distinct design element. This approach, called *family packaging* is often used only for lines of products, as with Campbell's soups, Weight Watchers foods, and Planters nuts. The best policy is sometimes no consistency, especially if a firm's various products are unrelated or aimed at different target markets.

Packages also play an important promotional role. Through verbal and nonverbal symbols, the package informs potential buyers about the product's content, uses, features, advantages, and hazards. Businesses can create desirable images and associations by choosing particular colors, designs, shapes, and textures. Many cosmetics manufacturers, for example, design their packages to create impressions of richness, luxury, and exclusivity. The package performs another promotional function when it is designed to be safer or more convenient to use than competitors'.

Packaging also must meet the needs of intermediaries. Wholesalers and retailers consider whether a package is easy to transport, handle, and store. Resellers may refuse to carry certain products if their packages are too cumbersome.

Finally, firms must consider the issue of environmental responsibility when developing packages. Companies must balance consumers' desires for convenience against the need to preserve the environment. Reducing packaging will help with global waste problems because about one-half of all garbage consists of plastic packaging. As part of its long-term World Without Waste initiative, Coca-Cola introduced a new soft drink bottle made from 100 percent recycled plastic. It first rolled out the new 13.2-ounce bottles for Coke, Diet Coke, and Fanta in some areas, gradually expanding the geographic distribution and number of brands using the new recycled bottles. The new bottles are part of Coke's goal of making 100 percent of its packaging recyclable by 2025 and to use 50 percent recycled content by 2030.[21]

标签
labeling the presentation of information on a product or its package

质量保证书
express warranty a written explanation of the producer's responsibilities in the event that a product is found to be defective or otherwise unsatisfactory

标签
5-5h Labeling

Labeling is the presentation of information on a product or its package. The *label* is the part of a package that contains information, including the brand name and mark, the registered trademark symbol®, the package size and contents, product claims, directions for use and safety precautions, ingredients, the name and address of the manufacturer, and the Universal Product Code (UPC) symbol, which is used for automated checkout and inventory control. Labels are significant during the consumer buying decision process. Researchers have found that 60 percent of consumers will bypass a product when its label fails to present sufficient details, and 33 percent will reject a product if they don't like the design of the label.[22]

A number of federal regulations specify information that *must* be included in the labeling for certain products:

- Garments must be labeled with the name of the manufacturer, country of manufacture, fabric content, and cleaning instructions.
- Food labels must contain the most common term for ingredients and indicate whether the item contains common allergens.
- Any food product for which a nutritional claim is made must have nutrition labeling that follows a standard format.
- Food product labels must state the number of servings per container, the serving size, the number of calories per serving, the number of calories derived from fat, and the amounts of specific nutrients.
- Nonedible items such as shampoos and detergents must carry safety precautions and instructions for use.

Such regulations are aimed at protecting customers from misleading product claims and the improper (and thus unsafe) use of products. Food manufacturers are not allowed to make misleading health claims about their products.

Labels also may carry the details of written, or express, warranties. An **express warranty** is a written explanation of the producer's responsibilities in the event that a product is found to be defective or otherwise unsatisfactory.

Heinz turns the ketchup bottle on its head. The original design of the ketchup bottle made it difficult for customers to get the ketchup out. To solve this problem, Heinz put the cap on the bottom of the bottle and made the opening larger. In addition, Heinz made the bottle squeezable.

✓ Concept Check

▶ Describe the major types of brands.

▶ How do brands help customers in product selection? How do brands help companies introduce new products? Explain the three levels of brand loyalty.

▶ Define brand equity and describe the four major factors that contribute toward brand equity. What issues must be considered while choosing a brand name?

▶ What are the major functions of packaging?

产品定价
5-6 Pricing Products

A product is a set of attributes and benefits that has been designed to satisfy its market while earning a profit for its seller. Pricing is an integral part of this equation. Each product has a price at which consumers' desires and expectations are balanced with a firm's need to make a profit. We will now look more closely at how businesses go about determining a product's price.

Learning Objective

5-6 Describe the economic basis of pricing and the means by which sellers can control prices and buyers' perceptions of prices.

价格的含义和用途
5-6a The Meaning and Use of Price

The **price** of a product is the amount of money a seller is willing to accept in exchange for the product at a given time and under given circumstances. At times, the price results from negotiations between buyer and seller. In many business situations, however, the price is fixed by the seller. Suppose that a seller

价格
price the amount of money a seller is willing to accept in exchange for a product at a given time and under given circumstances

Chapter 5   Creating and Pricing Products That Satisfy Customers   145

sets a price of $10 for a product. The seller is saying, "Anyone who wants this product can have it here and now in exchange for $10." Each interested buyer then makes a personal judgment regarding the product's utility, often in terms of a dollar value. People who feel that they will get at least $10 worth of want satisfaction (or value) from the product are likely to buy it. If they believe they can get more want satisfaction by spending $10 in some other way, they will not buy the product.

Price thus serves the function of *allocator*. First, it allocates goods and services among those who are willing and able to buy them. (The answer to the economic question "For whom to produce?" depends primarily on prices.) Second, price allocates financial resources (sales revenue) among producers according to how well they satisfy customers' needs. Third, price helps customers allocate their own financial resources among various want-satisfying products.

价格竞争和非价格竞争
5-6b Price and Non-Price Competition

Before a product's price can be set, an organization must determine whether it will compete on the basis of price alone, or on a combination of factors. The choice influences pricing decisions as well as other marketing-mix variables.

Price competition occurs when a seller emphasizes a product's low price and sets a price that equals or beats competitors' prices. Planet Fitness, for example, experienced dramatic growth by offering $10/month gym memberships when other sport club memberships average $50 a month. Although Planet Fitness offers fewer amenities, its lower price is appealing to consumers who don't use most gym amenities—or simply forget to cancel.[23] To use this approach most effectively, a seller must have the flexibility to change prices often, rapidly, and aggressively in response to competitors' price changes. Price competition allows a marketer to set prices based on product demand or in response to changes in the firm's finances. Competitors can do likewise, however, which is a major drawback of price competition. If circumstances force a seller to raise prices, competing firms may be able to maintain their lower prices. The internet has made it more difficult than ever for sellers to compete on the basis of price, as consumers can quickly and easily conduct comparison-shopping online.

Non-price competition is competition based on factors other than price. It is used most effectively when a seller can make its product stand out through distinctive product quality, customer service, promotion, packaging, or other features. Buyers must be able to perceive these characteristics and consider them desirable. Once customers have chosen a brand for non-price reasons, they may not be as attracted to competing businesses and brands. In this way, a seller can build customer loyalty to its brand. A method of non-price competition, **product differentiation**, is the process of developing and promoting differences between one's product and all similar products. Consider the direct-to-consumer hair care company Prose, which creates customized shampoo and conditioner formulas for each customer, based on hair texture, local weather and water conditions, and what styling treatments they use. Although the products are offered at prices considerably higher than mass shampoos sold in stores, customers do not seem to mind paying more for products personalized just for them.[24]

价格竞争
price competition an emphasis on setting a price equal to or lower than competitors' prices to gain sales or market share

非价格竞争
non-price competition competition based on factors other than price

产品差异化
product differentiation the process of developing and promoting differences between one's product and all similar products

How low can you go? Price competition is fierce among fast-food restaurants. Value pricing has been used by some fast-food organizations for more than 20 years.

Ethics and Social Responsibility

商业伦理与社会责任：企业为了对种族和文化更加敏感而重塑品牌

Companies Rebrand to Be More Sensitive

Over the years, critics have called for brands that use symbols that perpetuate racial stereotypes or are culturally insensitive to abandon them or remake them to convey more positive images. In recent years, social unrest and heightened calls for racial justice sparked a new national conversation about race in America. Many companies saw this as an opportunity to support people of color by ending brand imagery with insensitive connotations.

PepsiCo, the parent company for Quaker Oats, announced that it would rebrand its 130-year-old Aunt Jemima syrup brand, including the name and symbol. Although the Aunt Jemima brand mark had evolved over the decades, the company acknowledged in its statement that "Aunt Jemima's origins are based on a racial stereotype." The line of pancake mixes and syrups was reintroduced a year later as the Pearl Milling Company. Mars, Inc., which owns the Uncle Ben's brand of rice products, quickly followed with its own announcement, renaming the brand to Ben's Original.

The owners of other brands, including Cream of Wheat and Mrs. Butterworth, also pledged to examine their products and packaging for racially and culturally insensitive symbols. Land O'Lakes redesigned its packaging and dropped the Native American "butter maiden." Likewise, Dreyer's Grand Ice Cream announced that it would rebrand the century-old Eskimo Pie chocolate-covered ice cream and discontinue its Eskimo character symbols. Changing a brand, including its name and symbols, can be very expensive, but these companies recognize that rebranding positions them as being part of the solution to racial inequality.

Sources: Based on information in Maria Cramer, "After Aunt Jemima, Reviews Underway for Uncle Ben, Mrs. Butterworth and Cream of Wheat," *The New York Times*, June 17, 2020; Maria Cramer, "Maker of Eskimo Pie Ice Cream Will Retire 'Inappropriate' Name," *The New York Times*, June 20, 2020; Ben Kesslen, "Aunt Jemima Brand to Change Name, Remove Image that Quaker Says Is 'Based on a Racial Stereotype,'" *NBCNews*, June 17, 2020.

购买者对价格的看法

5-6c Buyers' Perceptions of Price

In setting prices, managers should consider the price sensitivity of the target market. Members of one market segment may be more influenced by price than members of another. Consumer price sensitivity can also vary between products. For example, buyers may be more sensitive to price when purchasing gasoline than when purchasing running shoes.

Buyers will tolerate a narrow range of prices for certain items and a wider range for others. Consider the varying prices of soft drinks—from 15 cents per ounce at the movies down to 1.5 cents per ounce on sale at the grocery store. Managers should be aware of consumers' price limits and the products to which they apply. The company also should take note of buyers' perceptions of a given product relative to competing products. A premium price may be appropriate if a product is considered superior to others in its category, or if the product has inspired strong brand loyalty. On the other hand, a lower price may be necessary if buyers have even a slightly negative product perception.

Sometimes buyers equate price and quality. Managers involved in pricing decisions should determine whether this outlook is widespread in the target market. If it is, a higher price may improve a product's image, making it more desirable.

> **Concept Check**
> - What factors must be considered when pricing products?
> - How does a change in price affect the demand and supply of a product?
> - Differentiate price competition and non-price competition.
> - Why is it important to consider the buyer's sensitivity to price when pricing products?

定价目标

5-7 Pricing Objectives

Before setting prices for a firm's products, marketers must establish pricing objectives that are aligned with organizational and marketing objectives. Of course,

Learning Objective
5-7 Specify the major pricing objectives used by businesses.

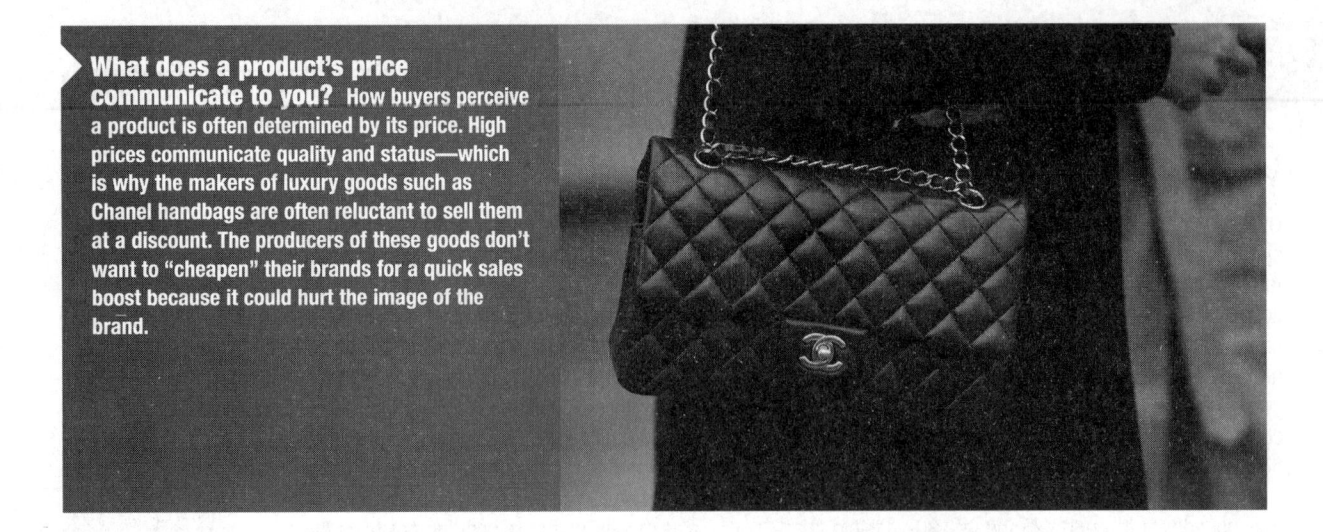

What does a product's price communicate to you? How buyers perceive a product is often determined by its price. High prices communicate quality and status—which is why the makers of luxury goods such as Chanel handbags are often reluctant to sell them at a discount. The producers of these goods don't want to "cheapen" their brands for a quick sales boost because it could hurt the image of the brand.

one objective of pricing is to make a profit, but this may not be a firm's primary objective. One or more of the following factors may be just as important.

基于生存目标
5-7a Survival

A firm may have to price its products to survive—either as an organization or as a player in a particular market. This usually means that the company will cut its price to attract customers, even if it must operate at a loss for a while. Obviously, such a goal cannot be pursued on a long-term basis, for consistent losses would cause the business to fail.

基于利润最大化目标
5-7b Profit Maximization

Many businesses may state that their goal is to maximize profit, but this goal is impossible to define (and thus impossible to achieve). What, exactly, is the *maximum* profit? How does a company know when it has been reached? Firms that wish to set profit goals should express them as either specific dollar amounts, or percentage increases, over previous profits.

基于投资回报率目标
5-7c Target Return on Investment

The *return on investment* (ROI) is the amount earned as a result of a financial investment. Some businesses set an annual percentage ROI as a quantifiable means to gauge the success of their pricing goal.

基于市场份额目标
5-7d Market-Share Goals

A firm's *market share* is its proportion of total industry sales. Some companies attempt, through pricing, to maintain or increase their market shares. Both U.S. cola giants, Coke and Pepsi, continually try to gain market share through aggressive pricing and other marketing efforts.

为了维持现状而定价
5-7e Status-Quo Pricing

In pricing their products, some businesses are guided by a desire to maintain the status quo. This is especially true in industries that depend on price stability. If such a firm can maintain its profit or market share simply by matching the competition—charging about the same price as competitors for similar products—then it will do so.

✓ **Concept Check**
- Explain the various types of pricing objectives.
- Which ones will usually result in a firm having lower prices?

定价方法
5-8 Pricing Methods

Once a firm has developed its pricing objectives, it must select a pricing method to reach that goal. Two factors are important to every company engaged in setting prices. The first is recognition that the market, and not the firm's costs, ultimately determines the price at which a product will sell. The second is awareness that costs and expected sales can be used only to establish a *price floor,* the minimum price at which the firm can sell its product without incurring a loss. In this section, we look at three kinds of pricing methods: cost-based, demand-based, and competition-based pricing.

Learning Objective

2-8 Compare the three major pricing methods that businesses employ.

成本导向定价
5-8a Cost-Based Pricing

Using the simplest method of pricing, *cost-based pricing,* the seller first determines the total cost of producing (or purchasing) one unit of the product. The seller then adds an amount to cover additional costs (such as insurance or interest) and profit. The amount that is added is called the **markup**. The total of the cost plus the markup is the product's selling price.

Marketers can calculate markup as a percentage of total costs. Suppose, for example, that the total cost of manufacturing and marketing 1,000 headsets is $100,000, or $100 per unit. If the manufacturer wants a markup that is 20 percent above costs, the selling price will be $100 plus 20 percent of $100, or $120 per unit.

Markup pricing is easy to apply and is used by many businesses (mostly retailers and wholesalers). However, it has two major flaws. The first is the difficulty of determining the best markup percentage. If the percentage is too high, the product may be overpriced for its market and too few units will be sold to cover the cost of producing and marketing it. If the markup percentage is too low, the seller forgoes profit it could have earned by assigning a higher price.

The second problem with markup pricing is that it separates pricing from other business functions. The product is priced *after* production quantities are determined, *after* costs are incurred, and almost without regard for the market or the marketing mix. To be most effective, the cost of various business functions should be integrated. *Each* should have an impact on all marketing decisions.

Cost-based pricing can also be calculated through breakeven analysis. For any product, the **breakeven quantity** is the number of units that must be sold for the total revenue (from all units sold) to equal the total cost (of all units sold). **Total revenue** is the total amount received from the sales of a product. We estimate projected total revenue as the selling price multiplied by the number of units expected to be sold.

The costs involved in operating a business can be broadly classified as either fixed or variable. A **fixed cost** is a cost incurred no matter how many units of a product are produced or sold. Rent, for example, is a fixed cost because it remains the same whether 1 or 1,000 units are produced. A **variable cost** is a cost that depends on the number of units produced. The cost of fabricating parts for a stereo receiver is a variable cost. The more units produced, the more efficient production will be and the per-unit cost of the parts will go down. The **total cost** of producing a certain number of units is the sum of the fixed costs and the variable costs attributed to those units.

If we assume a particular selling price, we can find the breakeven quantity either graphically or by using a formula. Figure 5-3 graphs the total revenue earned and the total cost incurred by the sale of various quantities of a hypothetical product. With fixed costs of $40,000, variable costs of $60 per unit, and a selling price of $120, the breakeven quantity is 667 units (represented in Figure 5-3 as the intersection of the total revenue and total cost curves). To find the breakeven quantity, first deduct the variable cost from the selling price to determine how much money the sale of

加价
markup the amount a seller adds to the cost of a product to determine its basic selling price

盈亏平衡量
breakeven quantity the number of units that must be sold for the total revenue (from all units sold) to equal the total cost (of all units sold)

总收入
total revenue the total amount received from the sales of a product

固定成本
fixed cost a cost incurred no matter how many units of a product are produced or sold

可变成本
variable cost a cost that depends on the number of units produced

总成本
total cost the sum of the fixed costs and the variable costs attributed to a product

Chapter 5 Creating and Pricing Products That Satisfy Customers 149

Figure 5-3 Breakeven Analysis

Breakeven analysis answers the question: What is the lowest level of production and sales at which a company can break even on a particular product?

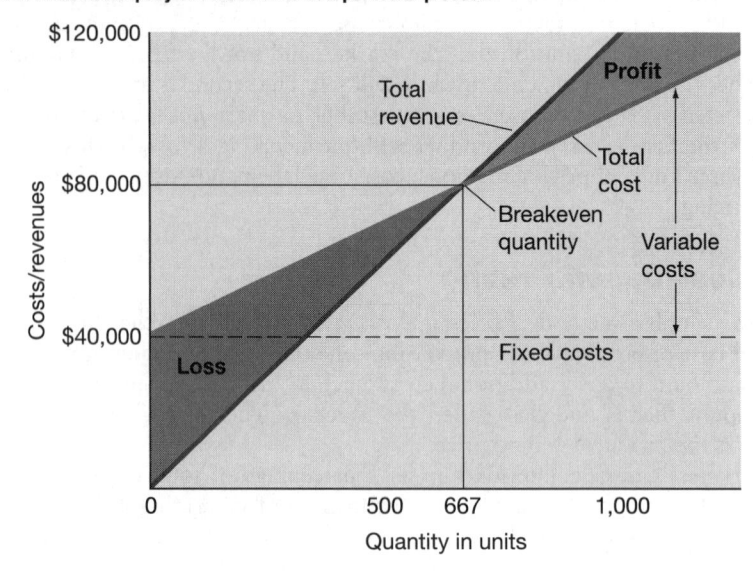

one unit contributes toward offsetting fixed costs. Divide that contribution into the total fixed costs to arrive at the breakeven quantity. If the firm sells more than 667 units at $120 each, it will earn a profit. If it sells fewer units, it will suffer a loss.

需求导向定价
5-8b Demand-Based Pricing

Rather than basing the price of a product on its cost, companies sometimes use a pricing method based on the level of demand for the product: *demand-based pricing*. This method results in a higher price when product demand is strong and a lower price when demand is weak. To use this method, a marketer estimates the amount of a product that customers will demand at different prices and then chooses the price that should generate the highest total revenue. Obviously, the effectiveness of this method depends on the firm's ability to estimate demand accurately.

A company may favor a demand-based pricing method called *price differentiation* if it wants to use more than one price in the marketing of a specific product. Price differentiation can be based on such considerations as time of the purchase, type of customer, or type of distribution channel. The use of so-called *dynamic pricing*—which raises prices during periods of high demand—is growing, especially for services such as car ride-hailing apps like Uber and Lyft as well as restaurants looking for a more even flow of customers throughout the day. For instance, all tickets for Los Angeles Dodgers' baseball games are sold using dynamic pricing. Ticket prices are adjusted based on real-time market conditions that include seat location, the popularity of time and day, as well as whether there are special promotions like bobblehead giveaways.[25] For price differentiation to work, the company must be able to segment a

Did you pay twice as much for your plane ticket as the person sitting next to you? Airlines use demand-based pricing. The sophisticated software the companies use constantly re-prices seats based on historical data, as well as how many customers are purchasing tickets at any given time on a specific flight.

150   Marketing

market on the basis of different strengths of demand. The company must then be able to keep the segments separate enough so that those who buy at lower prices cannot sell to buyers in segments that are charged a higher price. This isolation can be accomplished, for example, by selling to geographically separated segments. However, the internet has made price differentiation for products more difficult.

Compared with cost-based pricing, demand-based pricing places a firm in a better position to attain higher profit levels, assuming that buyers value the product at levels sufficiently above the product's cost. To use demand-based pricing, however, management must be able to estimate demand at different price levels, which may be difficult to assess accurately.

竞争导向定价
5-8c Competition-Based Pricing

In using *competition-based pricing*, an organization considers costs and revenue secondary to competitors' prices. The importance of this method increases if competing products are similar and the organization is serving markets in which price is the crucial variable of the marketing strategy. A firm that uses competition-based pricing may choose to sell below competitors' prices, slightly above competitors' prices, or at the same level. The price that your bookstore paid to the publishing company of this text was determined using competition-based pricing. Competition-based pricing can help to attain a pricing objective to increase sales or market share. Competition-based pricing may also be combined with other cost approaches to arrive at a profitable level.

> **Concept Check**
> - List and explain the three kinds of pricing methods.
> - Give an advantage and a disadvantage for each method.

定价策略
5-9 Pricing Strategies

A *pricing strategy* is a course of action designed to achieve pricing objectives. The extent to which a business uses any of the following strategies depends on its pricing and marketing objectives, the markets for its products, the degree of product differentiation, the product's life-cycle stage, and other factors. Figure 5-4 is a list of the major types of pricing strategies. We discuss these strategies in the remainder of this section.

> **Learning Objective**
> **5-9** Explain the different strategies available to companies for setting prices.

新产品定价
5-9a New-Product Pricing

The two primary types of new-product pricing strategies are price skimming and penetration pricing. An organization can use either one, or even both, over a period of time.

Figure 5-4 Types of Pricing Strategies

Companies have a variety of pricing strategies available to them.

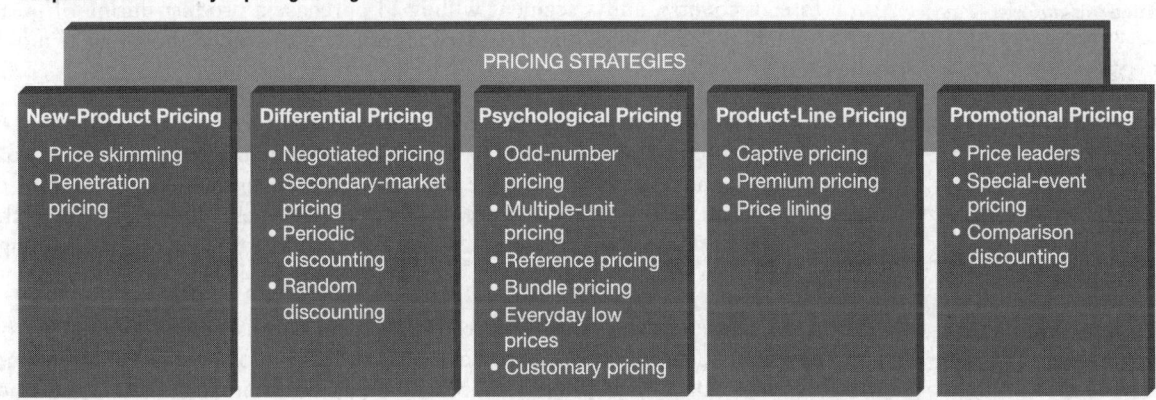

PRICING STRATEGIES

New-Product Pricing	Differential Pricing	Psychological Pricing	Product-Line Pricing	Promotional Pricing
• Price skimming • Penetration pricing	• Negotiated pricing • Secondary-market pricing • Periodic discounting • Random discounting	• Odd-number pricing • Multiple-unit pricing • Reference pricing • Bundle pricing • Everyday low prices • Customary pricing	• Captive pricing • Premium pricing • Price lining	• Price leaders • Special-event pricing • Comparison discounting

Price Skimming Some consumers are willing to pay a high price for an innovative product, either because of its novelty or because of the prestige or status that ownership confers. **Price skimming** is the strategy of charging the highest possible price for a product during the introduction stage of its life cycle. This strategy helps to recover the high costs of R&D quickly. In addition, a skimming policy may hold down demand for the product, which is helpful if the firm's production capacity is limited during the introduction stage. A danger is that a price-skimming strategy may make the product appear more lucrative than it actually is to potential competitors, encouraging more competitors to enter the market.

Penetration Pricing At the opposite extreme, **penetration pricing** is the strategy of setting a low price for a new product to build market share quickly. The seller hopes that building a large market share will discourage competitors from entering the market. If the low price stimulates sales, the business may also be able to order longer production runs, which usually results in lower production costs per unit. A disadvantage of penetration pricing is that it places a firm in a less flexible position on pricing. It is more difficult to raise prices significantly than it is to lower them.

差别定价
5-9b Differential Pricing

An important issue in pricing decisions is whether to use a single price or different prices for the same product. *Differential pricing* means charging different prices to different buyers for the same quality and quantity of product. For example, many theaters offer discounted tickets for daytime matinee performances, and airlines have different pricing tiers for airline seats depending on whether customers paid extra to board early or other perks. For differential pricing to be effective, the market must consist of multiple segments with different price sensitivities. When this method is employed, caution should be used to avoid confusing or antagonizing customers. Differential pricing can take several forms, including negotiated pricing, secondary-market pricing, periodic discounting, and random discounting.

Negotiated Pricing **Negotiated pricing** occurs when the final price is established through bargaining between the seller and the customer. Negotiated pricing occurs at all levels of distribution and is common in a variety of industries. Even when there is a predetermined stated price or a price list, manufacturers, wholesalers, and retailers may negotiate to establish the final sales price. Consumers commonly negotiate prices for houses, cars, and used equipment.

Secondary-Market Pricing **Secondary-market pricing** means setting one price for the primary target market and a different price for another market. The price charged in the secondary market is often, but not always, lower. Examples of secondary markets include a geographically isolated domestic market, a market in a foreign country, and a segment willing to purchase a product during off-peak times (such as "early bird" dinners at restaurants and matinee showings at movie theaters).

Periodic Discounting **Periodic discounting** is the temporary reduction of prices on a patterned or systematic basis. For example, many retailers have annual holiday sales, and apparel stores have seasonal sales. From the marketer's point of view, a problem with periodic discounting is that customers can predict when the reductions will occur and may delay their purchases until they can take advantage of the lower prices.

Random Discounting To alleviate the problem of customers holding off on purchases until a discount period, some organizations employ **random discounting**. That is, they reduce their prices temporarily on a nonsystematic basis. When price

---

撇脂定价
price skimming the strategy of charging the highest possible price for a product during the introduction stage of its life cycle

渗透定价
penetration pricing the strategy of setting a low price for a new product to build market share quickly

协议定价
negotiated pricing establishing a final price through bargaining

二级市场定价
secondary-market pricing setting one price for the primary target market and a different price for another market

定期折扣
periodic discounting temporary reduction of prices on a patterned or systematic basis

随机折扣
random discounting temporary reduction of prices on an unsystematic basis

reductions of a product occur randomly, current users of that brand are not able to predict when reductions will occur. They therefore will not delay their purchases in anticipation of purchasing the product at a lower price. Marketers also use random discounting to attract new customers.

心理定价
5-9c Psychological Pricing

Psychological pricing strategies encourage purchases based on emotional responses rather than on economically rational ones. These strategies are used primarily for consumer products rather than business products.

Odd-Number Pricing Many retailers believe that consumers respond more positively to odd-number prices such as $4.99 than to whole-dollar prices such as $5. **Odd-number pricing** is the strategy of setting prices using odd numbers that are slightly below whole-dollar amounts. Nine and five are the most popular ending figures for odd-number prices.

Multiple-Unit Pricing Many retailers (supermarkets in particular) practice **multiple-unit pricing**, setting a single price for two or more units, such as two cans for 99 cents, rather than 50 cents per can. Especially for frequently purchased products, this strategy can increase the amount of an item that is sold. Customers who see the single price and who expect eventually to use more than one unit of the product will purchase multiple units to save money.

Reference Pricing **Reference pricing** means pricing a product at a moderate level and positioning it next to a more expensive model or brand in the hope that the customer will use the higher price as a reference price (i.e., a comparison price). Because of the comparison, the customer is expected to view the moderate price favorably.

Bundle Pricing **Bundle pricing** is the packaging together of two or more products, usually of a complementary nature, to be sold for a single price. To be attractive to customers, the single price usually is considerably less than the sum of the prices of the individual products. Because the products are complementary, such as shampoo and conditioner, the customer will also find convenience value from purchasing them together. The firm may find bundling to be a valuable strategy because, by bundling slow-moving products with more popular ones, an organization can stimulate sales and increase revenues. Selling products as a package rather than individually also may result in cost savings for the organization. It is common for telecommunications providers to sell service bundles of cable, internet, and phone service for one price.

Everyday Low Prices (EDLPs) To reduce or eliminate frequent short-term price reductions, some organizations use an approach referred to as **everyday low prices (EDLPs)**. When EDLPs are used, a marketer sets a low price for its products on a consistent basis, rather than setting high prices and frequently discounting them. EDLPs, though not deeply discounted, are set far enough below competitors' prices to make customers feel confident that they are receiving a good deal. EDLPs are employed by retailers such as Walmart and by manufacturers such as Procter & Gamble. A company that uses EDLPs benefits from reduced promotional costs, reduced losses from frequent markdowns, and more stability in sales. However, customers may not trust the EDLP and assume the deal is merely a marketing gimmick.

Customary Pricing In **customary pricing**, certain goods are priced primarily on the basis of tradition. It is not as common as it once was, but examples of customary, or traditional, prices are those set for candy bars and chewing gum.

奇数定价
odd-number pricing the strategy of setting prices using odd numbers that are slightly below whole-dollar amounts

多单位定价
multiple-unit pricing the strategy of setting a single price for two or more units

参考定价
reference pricing pricing a product at a moderate level and positioning it next to a more expensive model or brand

捆绑定价
bundle pricing packaging together two or more complementary products and selling them for a single price

每日低价
everyday low prices (EDLPs) setting a low price for products on a consistent basis

习惯性定价
customary pricing pricing on the basis of tradition

Chapter 5 Creating and Pricing Products That Satisfy Customers 153

产品线定价
5-9d Product-Line Pricing

Rather than considering products on an item-by-item basis when determining pricing strategies, some marketers employ product-line pricing. *Product-line pricing* means establishing and adjusting the prices of multiple products within a product line. Product-line pricing can provide marketers with flexibility in price setting. For example, marketers can set prices high so that one product is highly profitable, whereas another has a low price to increase market share.

When marketers employ product-line pricing, they have several strategies from which to choose. These include captive pricing, premium pricing, and price lining.

Captive Pricing When **captive pricing** is used, the basic product in a product line is priced low, but the price on the items required to operate or enhance it are higher. Two common examples of captive pricing are razor blades and printer ink. The razor handle and the printer are generally priced quite low, but the razor blades and the printer ink replacement cartridges are usually very expensive.

Premium Pricing **Premium pricing** occurs when the highest-quality product or the most-versatile version of similar products in a product line is assigned the highest price. Other products in the line are priced to appeal to more price-sensitive shoppers, or to those seeking product-specific features. Marketers that employ premium pricing often realize a significant portion of profits from the premium-priced products. Examples of product categories in which premium pricing is common are small kitchen appliances, beer, ice cream, and television cable service.

Price Lining **Price lining** is the strategy of selling goods only at certain predetermined prices that reflect definite price breaks. For example, a shop may sell men's ties only at $22 and $37. This strategy is used in clothing and accessory stores. It eliminates minor price differences from the buying decision—both for customers and for managers who buy merchandise to sell in these stores.

促销价
5-9e Promotional Pricing

Price, as an ingredient in the marketing mix, often is coordinated with promotions. The two variables sometimes are so interrelated that the pricing policy is promotion-oriented. Examples of promotional pricing include price leaders, special-event pricing, and comparison discounting.

Price Leaders Sometimes, a firm prices a few products below the usual markup, near cost, or below cost, which results in **price leaders**. This type of pricing is used most often in supermarkets and restaurants to attract customers by giving them especially low prices on a few items. Management hopes that customers will purchase regularly priced items as well, which will offset the reduced revenues from the price leaders.

Special-Event Pricing To increase sales volume, many organizations coordinate price with advertising or sales promotions for seasonal or special occasions. **Special-event pricing** involves advertised sales or price cutting linked to a holiday, season, or event. If the pricing objective is survival, then special sales events may be designed to generate the necessary operating capital.

Comparison Discounting **Comparison discounting** sets the price of a product at a specific level and compares it with a higher price. The higher price may be the product's previous price, the price of a competing brand, the product's price at another retail outlet, or a manufacturer's suggested retail price. Comparison discounting can significantly influence customers' decisions. Because this pricing

---

附属产品定价
captive pricing pricing the basic product in a product line low, but pricing related items at a higher level

溢价定价
premium pricing pricing the highest-quality or most-versatile products higher than other models in the product line

分级定价
price lining the strategy of selling goods only at certain predetermined prices that reflect definite price breaks

价格领导者
price leaders products priced below the usual markup, near cost, or below cost

特殊事件定价
special-event pricing advertised sales or price cutting linked to a holiday, season, or event

比较折扣
comparison discounting setting a price at a specific level and comparing it with a higher price

strategy can lead to deceptive pricing practices, the Federal Trade Commission (FTC) has established guidelines for comparison discounting. If the higher price against which the comparison is made is the price formerly charged for the product, sellers must have made the previous price available to customers for a reasonable period of time. If sellers present the higher price as the one charged by other retailers in the same trade area, they must be able to demonstrate the veracity of the claim. When they present the higher price as the manufacturer's suggested retail price, then the higher price must be similar to the price at which a reasonable proportion of the product was sold.

> ✓ **Concept Check**
> - Identify the five categories of pricing strategies.
> - Describe two specific pricing strategies in each category.

工业品定价

5-10 Pricing Business Products

Many of the pricing issues discussed thus far in this chapter deal with pricing in general. However, setting prices for business products is different from setting prices for consumer products because of factors such as the size of purchases, transportation considerations, and geographic issues. We examine three types of pricing associated with business products: geographic pricing, transfer pricing, and discounting.

> **Learning Objective**
> **5-10** Recognize three major types of pricing associated with business products.

地理定价
5-10a Geographic Pricing

Geographic pricing strategies deal with delivery costs. The pricing strategy that requires the buyer to pay the delivery costs is called *FOB origin pricing*. This stands for "free on board at the point of origin," which means that the price does not include freight charges. Thus, the buyer must pay the transportation costs from the seller's warehouse to the buyer's place of business. *FOB destination* indicates that the price does include freight charges, and thus the seller pays these charges.

转让定价
5-10b Transfer Pricing

When one unit within an organization sells a product to another unit, **transfer pricing** occurs. The price is determined by calculating the cost of the product. A transfer price can vary depending on the types of costs included in the calculations. The choice of the costs to include depends on the company's management strategy and the nature of the units' interactions. An organization also must ensure that transfer pricing is fair to all units involved in the purchases.

折扣
5-10c Discounting

A **discount** is a deduction from an item's price. Producers and sellers may offer a wide variety of discounts to their customers, including trade, quantity, cash, and seasonal discounts and allowances. *Trade discounts* are reductions taken off the list prices that are offered to marketing intermediaries, or middlemen. *Quantity discounts* are discounts given to customers who buy in large quantities, which makes the seller's per-unit selling cost lower for larger purchases. *Cash discounts* are concessions offered for prompt payment. A seller may offer a discount of "2/10, net 30," meaning that the buyer receives a 2 percent discount if full payment occurs within ten days; otherwise, payment in full is due within 30 days. A *seasonal discount* is a price reduction to buyers that purchase out of season. This discount encourages off-season sales and ensures steady production throughout the year. An *allowance* is a reduction in price to achieve a desired goal. Trade-in allowances, for example, are price reductions granted for turning in used equipment when purchasing new equipment. Table 5-3 describes some of the reasons for using these discounting techniques and some examples.

转让定价
transfer pricing prices charged in sales between an organization's units

折扣
discount a deduction from the price of an item

> ✓ **Concept Check**
> - Describe the three types of pricing associated with business products.
> - Differentiate between FOB origin and FOB destination pricing.
> - Explain the five types of discounts for business products.

Table 5-3 Discounts Used for Business Markets

Type	Reasons for Use	Examples
Trade (functional)	To attract and retain effective resellers by compensating them for performing certain functions, such as transportation, warehousing, selling, and providing credit.	A college bookstore pays about one-third less for a new textbook than the retail price a student pays.
Quantity	To encourage customers to buy large quantities when making purchases and, in the case of cumulative discounts, to encourage customer loyalty.	Large department store chains purchase some women's apparel at lower prices than do individually owned specialty stores.
Cash	To reduce expenses associated with accounts receivable and collection by encouraging prompt payment of accounts.	Numerous companies serving business markets allow a 2 percent discount if an account is paid within ten days.
Seasonal	To allow a marketer to use resources more efficiently by stimulating sales during off-peak periods.	Florida hotels provide companies, holding national and regional sales meetings, with deeply discounted accommodations during the summer months.
Allowance	In the case of a trade-in allowance, to assist the buyer in making the purchase and potentially earn a profit on the resale of used equipment. In the case of a promotional allowance, to ensure that dealers participate in advertising and sales support programs.	A farm equipment dealer takes a farmer's used tractor as a trade-in on a new one. Nabisco pays a promotional allowance to a supermarket for setting up and maintaining a large end-of-aisle display for a two-week period.

Summary 小 结

5-1 Explain what a product is and how products are classified.

A product is everything one receives in an exchange, including all attributes and expected benefits. The product may be a manufactured item, a service, an idea, or a combination.

Products are classified according to their ultimate use. Classification affects a product's distribution, promotion, and pricing. Consumer goods, which include convenience, shopping, specialty, and unsought products, are purchased to satisfy personal and family needs. Business products are purchased for resale, in making other products, or for use in a firm's operations. Business products can be classified as raw materials, major equipment, accessory equipment, component parts, process materials, supplies, and services.

5-2 Describe the product life cycle and how it leads to new-product development.

Every product moves through a series of four stages—introduction, growth, maturity, and decline—which together form the product life cycle. As the product progresses through these stages, its sales and profitability increase, peak, and decline. Marketers keep track of the life-cycle stage of products in order to determine appropriate strategies and to estimate when a new product should be introduced to replace a declining one.

5-3 Define *product line* and *product mix* and distinguish between the two.

A product line is a group of similar products marketed by a firm. They are related to each other in the way they are produced, marketed, and consumed. The firm's product mix includes all the products it offers for sale. The width of a mix is the number of product lines it contains. The depth of the mix is the average number of individual products within each line.

5-4 Identify the methods available for managing a product mix.

Customer satisfaction and organizational objectives require marketers to develop, adjust, and maintain an effective product mix. Marketers may improve a product mix by changing existing products, deleting products, and developing new products. A product mix can be changed by deriving additional products from existing ones through product modifications and by line extensions. Deleting a weak and unprofitable product that costs a company resources may be necessary to modify other products or develop new ones. Developing new products is expensive and potentially risky. New products are developed through a series of seven steps. The first step, idea generation, involves developing a pool of product ideas. Screening, the second step, removes from consideration those product ideas that do not match organizational goals or resources. Concept testing, the third step, is a phase in which a sample of potential buyers is exposed to a proposed product through a written or oral description in order to determine their initial reactions and buying intentions. The fourth step, business analysis, generates information about potential sales, costs, and profits. During the technical development step, the product idea is transformed into mock-ups and prototypes to determine if product production is technically feasible and can be produced at reasonable costs. Test marketing is an actual launch of the product in selected cities chosen for their representativeness of target markets. Finally, during commercialization, plans for full-scale production and marketing are refined and implemented. Most product failures result from inadequate product planning and development.

5-5 Examine the uses and importance of branding, packaging, and labeling.

A brand is a name, term, symbol, design, or any combination of these that identifies a seller's products as distinct from those of other sellers. Brands can be identified by a brand name, brand mark, and trademark, and they can be classified as manufacturer brands, store brands, or generic brands. Buyers and sellers both benefit from branding, and branding can foster loyalty and confer value. Brands should be chosen carefully to set them apart and protected to preserve their exclusive use. A firm can choose between two branding strategies—individual or family branding—which are used to associate (or *not* associate) particular products with existing products, producers, or intermediaries. Brands can also be extended to new product categories.

Packaging protects goods, increases consumer convenience, and enhances marketing efforts by communicating product features, uses, benefits, and image. Marketers must consider factors such as cost, consistency, promotional use, and sustainability when designing packaging.

Labeling provides customers with product information, some of which is required by law.

5-6 Describe the economic basis of pricing and the means by which sellers can control prices and buyers' perceptions of prices.

The price of a product is the amount of money a seller is willing to accept in exchange for the product at a given time and under given circumstances. Price thus serves the function of allocating goods and services among those who are willing and able to buy them, financial resources among producers according to how well they satisfy customers' needs, and customers' own financial resources among products.

Price competition occurs when a seller emphasizes a product's low price and sets a price that equals or beats competitors' prices. To use this approach most effectively, a seller must have the flexibility to change prices often. Nonprice competition is based on factors other than price. It is used most effectively when a seller can make its product stand out from the competition by differentiating product quality, customer service, promotion, packaging, or other features. Buyers' perceptions of prices are affected by the importance of the product to them, the range of prices they consider acceptable, their perceptions of competing products, and their association of quality with price.

5-7 Specify the major pricing objectives used by businesses.

Objectives of pricing include survival, profit maximization, target return on investment, achieving market goals, and maintaining the status quo. Firms sometimes have to price products to survive, which usually requires cutting prices to attract customers. The return on investment (ROI) is the amount earned as a result of the investment in developing and marketing the product. Some businesses set an annual percentage ROI as the pricing goal. Other firms use pricing to maintain or increase their market share. In industries in which price stability is important, companies often price their products by charging about the same as competitors.

5-8 Compare the three major pricing methods that businesses employ.

The three major pricing methods are cost-based pricing, demand-based pricing, and competition-based pricing. When cost-based pricing is employed, a proportion of the cost is added to the total cost to determine the selling price. It can be added as an amount called a markup or calculated through breakeven analysis by understanding the costs involved. When demand-based pricing is used, the price will be higher when demand is higher, and the price will be lower when demand is lower. A firm that uses competition-based pricing may choose to price below competitors' prices, at the same level as competitors' prices, or slightly above competitors' prices.

5-9 Explain the different strategies available to companies for setting prices.

Pricing strategies fall into five categories: new-product pricing, differential pricing, psychological pricing, product-line pricing, and promotional pricing. Price skimming and penetration pricing are two strategies used for pricing new products. Differential pricing can be accomplished through negotiated pricing, secondary-market pricing, periodic discounting, and random discounting. Types of psychological pricing strategies are odd-number pricing, multiple-unit pricing, reference pricing, bundle pricing, everyday low prices, and customary pricing. Product-line pricing can be achieved through captive pricing, premium pricing, and price lining. The major types of promotional pricing are price-leader pricing, special-event pricing, and comparison discounting.

5-10 Recognize three major types of pricing associated with business products.

Setting prices for business products is different from setting prices for consumer products because of several factors, including the size of purchases, transportation considerations, and geographic issues. The three types of pricing associated with business products are geographic pricing, transfer pricing, and discounting.

Key Terms 关键术语

You should now be able to define and give an example relevant to each of the following terms:

product	line extension	labeling	random discounting
consumer product	product deletion	express warranty	odd-number pricing
business product	brand	price	multiple-unit pricing
convenience product	brand name	price competition	reference pricing
shopping product	brand mark	non-price competition	bundle pricing
specialty product	trademark	product differentiation	everyday low prices (EDLPs)
unsought product	trade name	markup	customary pricing
raw material	manufacturer (or producer) brand	breakeven quantity	captive pricing
major equipment	store (or private) brand	total revenue	premium pricing
accessory equipment	generic product (or generic brand)	fixed cost	price lining
component part		variable cost	price leaders
process material	brand loyalty	total cost	special-event pricing
supply	brand equity	price skimming	comparison discounting
business service	individual branding	penetration pricing	transfer pricing
product life cycle	family branding	negotiated pricing	discount
product line	brand extension	secondary-market pricing	
product mix	packaging	periodic discounting	
product modification			

Discussion Questions 讨论题

1. What major factor determines whether a product is a consumer or a business product?
2. What are the four stages of the product life cycle? How can a firm determine which stage a particular product is in?
3. Under what conditions does product modification work best?
4. Some companies do not delete products until they become financially threatening. What problems may result from this practice?
5. Why should businesses introduce new products?
6. What is the difference between manufacturer brands and store brands? Between family branding and individual branding?
7. What is the difference between a line extension and a brand extension?
8. For what purposes is labeling used?
9. Compare and contrast the characteristics of price and non-price competition. Under what conditions would a firm be most likely to use non-price competition?
10. How might buyers' perceptions of price influence pricing decisions?
11. What are the five major categories of pricing strategies? Give at least two examples of specific strategies that fall into each category.
12. Identify and describe the main types of discounts that are used in the pricing of business products.
13. Under what conditions would a business most likely decide to employ one of the differential pricing strategies?
14. For what types of products are psychological pricing strategies most likely to be used?

Case 5   案例 5：值得关注的 Shinola

Shinola Is One to Watch

Shinola Watch Company is a luxury design brand that sells timepieces, leather goods, jewelry, and more. The Shinola brand dates back to 1877 when it was a shoe polish company in Rochester, New York. It operated for nearly 100 years before going out of business in 1960. Tom Kartsotis, the founder of Fossil Group, a multi-billion-dollar watch company, decided to create Shinola Watch Company in 2011 with investment group Bedrock Manufacturing. Kartsotis's goal was to create a high-quality American watch brand that could compete with Swiss watchmakers at a lower price point. The company introduced its first watch in 2013, producing 2,500 watches and selling them for $550 each. The watches sold out in two weeks. Shinola was creating timepieces in a way that hadn't been done in the United States since the 1960s.

The company's watch and leather factory is located in Detroit, Michigan. Inside, artisans assemble Shinola's timepieces and other products by hand. The company employs more than 500 people and is committed to delivering the highest quality products. Shinola creates opportunities for its employees with extensive training. Employees meticulously assemble watches by hand. The Shinola team assembles between 500 and 700 watches per day and cuts and sews up to 550 leather watch straps per day. From start to finish, each watch may touch the hands of more than 30 people.

A commitment to quality is at the core of Shinola Watch Company. For example, its watches and leather straps that are produced in-house are done so using labor-intensive methods and custom Italian machinery. For its other leather goods, Shinola partnered with hand-selected manufacturers to scale production. The watchmaker creates products that last and stands behind its craftsmanship with industry-leading guarantees. Shinola offers a limited lifetime warranty of its core watch styles and a best-in-class three-year-limited warranty on its Detrola Watch Collection.

Shinola has promoted itself as an American-made brand and a supporter of Detroit. Its watches are even labeled "Detroit." However, the company's American pride was called into question when the Federal Trade Commission (FTC) discovered that some of its watches were made almost entirely out of foreign parts. The FTC is charged with protecting consumers from deceptive advertising. In response, Shinola changed its labeling to read "built in Detroit" and "Swiss & imported parts."

The company has also been criticized for using Detroit as a marketing tool and exploiting the city's hardships to sell watches. Supporters of the company say this is not the case and highlight the fact that Shinola has supported the local economy by adding jobs and helping to make Detroit a cleaner and safer place. However, recently, the company laid off several employees and announced plans to outsource leather design and product development to keep costs down, remain competitive in the watch industry, and clear a path to profitable growth.

Shinola's customers are its top supporters. Notable customers include former Michigan governor Rick Snyder, Oscar-winning director Peter Farrelly, and former presidents Bill Clinton and Barack Obama. Today, Shinola continues to match its high-quality timepieces along with a variety of other luxury goods. The company operates boutiques in 14 cities in the United States, Canada, and the United Kingdom along with its own boutique hotel in downtown Detroit.[26]

Questions

1. How does Shinola Watch Company back up its commitment to quality?
2. What measures has Shinola taken to keep its prices lower than Swiss competitors?
3. Why do you think Shinola advertises itself as being an American brand?

Building Skills for Career Success   为成功的职业生涯培养技能

1. Social Media Exercise

Casper is a direct-to-consumer company that makes and sells memory foam mattresses through its website. Unlike many mattress retailers, Casper sells just four mattresses, though in all available sizes, plus one for dogs. It prices the mattresses below that of most brick-and-mortar mattress stores and offers a 100-day trial period to help nudge customers into clicking the "buy" button. The young company doesn't spend a lot on advertising, so building brand recognition and preference is key to achieving sales. One way the firm does so is through its @Casper Twitter account, which regularly tweets in the persona of a Casper mattress, especially late at night when those having trouble sleeping are likely to be perusing social media. The tweets are often amusing and timely one-liners about sleep, though followers are likely to find humorous memes, GIFs, and videos, as well as links to information about sleep and insomnia in the timeline.

1. Go to Twitter.com and search for @Casper and look through recent tweets in the account's timeline. How is Casper using humor and pop culture to build brand loyalty?
2. What is the role of humor in Casper's tweets? In what ways does humor move customers closer to making a purchase, if at all?

2. Building Team Skills

In his book, *The Post-Industrial Society*, Peter Drucker wrote:

> Society, community, and family are all conserving institutions. They try to maintain stability and to prevent, or at least slow down, change. But the organization of the post-capitalist society of organizations is a destabilizer. Because its function is to put knowledge to work—on tools, processes, and products; on work; on knowledge itself—it must be organized for constant change. It must be organized for innovation.

New product development is important in this process of systematically abandoning the past and building a future. Current customers can be sources of ideas for new products and services and ways of improving existing ones.

Assignment

1. Working in teams of five to seven, brainstorm ideas for new products (goods, services, or ideas) for your college.
2. Construct questions to ask currently enrolled students (your customers). Sample questions might include:
   a. Why did you choose this college?
   b. How can this college be improved?
   c. What products do you wish were available?
3. Conduct the survey and review the results.
4. Prepare a list of improvements and/or new products for your college.

3. Researching Different Careers

Marketing involves creating, delivering, and communicating about products that have value for customers. Within this exciting and evolving field are many jobs that may offer a lucrative and rewarding career path.

Assignment

1. Research marketing careers. You may find sites such as flexjobs.com, indeed.com, thebalancecareers.com, and https://www.bls.gov/ooh/helpful.
   a. Identify three jobs within the marketing field that interest you.
   b. What type of work do each of these jobs involve?
   c. What are the potential earnings of these jobs?
   d. What is the long-term outlook for these jobs?
   e. How can you qualify for each of them?
2. Prepare a report of your findings.

Chapter 6

Distributing and Promoting Products
产品分销和产品促销

Learning Objectives

Once you complete this chapter, you will be able to:

6-1 Examine the various distribution channels and market coverage of products.

6-2 Explain how supply chain management facilitates partnering among channel members.

6-3 Describe the types of wholesalers and the services they provide.

6-4 Distinguish among the major types of retailers and shopping centers.

6-5 Identify the five most important logistics activities.

6-6 Define integrated marketing communications.

6-7 List the basic elements of the promotion mix.

6-8 Examine advertising, including types of advertising, the advertising campaign, and social and legal considerations.

6-9 Explore personal selling, including the types of salespersons, the personal-selling process, and major sales management tasks.

6-10 Identify sales promotion objectives and methods.

6-11 Describe the types and uses of public relations.

Why Should You Care?

Not only is it important to create and maintain a mix of products that satisfies customers but also to make these products available at the *right place* and *time* and to communicate with customers effectively.

Chapter 6 Distributing and Promoting Products

Inside Business

商业透视：沃尔玛整合了采购团队

Walmart Brings Its Buying Teams Together

To increase e-commerce profits and streamline in-store and online operations, Walmart combined its online and store product-buying teams. Before the merger, product manufacturers that wanted the retail giant to carry their products both on Walmart.com and in stores had to pitch their goods to two separate buying teams. Not only were these two functions split, but also the teams worked in different offices. E-commerce teams worked in Arkansas and store teams worked in California and New Jersey.

This inefficiency often created conflict between the units related to pricing. Having separate buying teams became a more prominent issue as Walmart started to use stores to facilitate online home delivery sales. In about 4,700 U.S. locations, Walmart offers a service that allows its customers to buy online and pickup orders from the store parking lot. Additionally, 1,600 currently offer online grocery delivery. The company has been hard at work figuring out how to blend online and in-store inventory and make hard-to-manage categories, such as apparel, available both in-store and online. Bringing its buying teams together follows a move to combine its online and store supply chains and finance teams.

In the new structure, Walmart created six category teams (e.g., food, consumables, apparel, and entertainment) that are each managed by an executive. Restructuring and centralizing merchandising added to the company's product assortment online and made prices as well as the shopper experience more consistent. Walmart's expansion of its online-meets-in-store strategy facilitates its ability to offer a seamless experience on mobile, desktop, or traditional retail spaces. If Walmart can perfect this omnichannel strategy, it will have a major leg up on e-commerce competitor Amazon.[1]

Did you know?

There are approximately 10,500 Walmart stores in 24 countries.

Successful companies like Walmart use multiple avenues of distribution, which helps give them a sustainable competitive advantage. Nearly 2 million firms in the United States help to move products from producers to consumers. Store chains such as Dollar General, Starbucks, Forever 21, and Target operate retail outlets where consumers make purchases. Some retailers, such as Avon Products and Arbonne, send their salespeople to the homes of customers. Other retailers, such as Lands' End and REI, sell in stores, online, through catalogs, or a combination of the three. Still others, such as Amazon, sell primarily online.

In this chapter, we first examine the various distribution channels through which products move as they progress from producer to ultimate user as well as supply chain management. Then we discuss wholesalers, including their types and the services they provide. Next, we focus on retailers, including online retailing, retail stores, shopping centers, and nonstore retailing. We then explore the logistics function and the major modes of transportation that are used to move goods. We then turn our attention to integrated marketing communication and the elements of the promotion mix. Finally, we discuss each element of the promotion mix: advertising, personal selling, sales promotion, and public relations.

分销渠道及市场覆盖

6-1 Distribution Channels and Market Coverage

A **distribution channel** (or **marketing channel**) is a sequence of marketing organizations that directs a product from the producer to the ultimate user. Every marketing channel begins with the producer and ends with either the consumer or the business user. A marketing organization that links a producer and user within a marketing channel is called a **middleman (or marketing intermediary)**. For the most part, middlemen are concerned with the transfer of *ownership* of products along their journey from producer to customer. In many cases, intermediaries handle the product, including its ownership, and add their own value as they move it along the distribution channel. Let's take a closer look at these channels and intermediaries.

常用分销渠道
6-1a Commonly Used Distribution Channels

Different channels of distribution generally are used to move consumer and business products. Figure 6-1 illustrates the most common distribution channels for consumer and business products.

Producer to Consumer This channel, often called the *direct channel*, has no marketing intermediaries. Most services and a few consumer goods are distributed through a direct channel. If you buy a laptop directly from Apple's or Dell's website, you are using a direct channel. Direct marketing via the internet has become a critically important part of many companies' distribution strategies, often as a complement to selling products in retail stores. A growing number of companies have disrupted their industries by selling directly to consumers online using a *direct-to-consumer (D2C)* strategy, including Warby Parker, Casper, Bonobos, and Glossier.

Producers sell directly to consumers for several reasons. They can better control the quality and price of their products. They can maintain closer relationships with customers and better understand their needs. Also, they do not have to pay (through discounts) for the services of intermediaries.

> **Learning Objective**
> **6-1** Examine the various distribution channels and market coverage of products.

> 分销渠道（或营销渠道）
> **distribution channel** (or **marketing channel**) a sequence of marketing organizations that directs a product from the producer to the ultimate user
>
> 中间商（或营销中介）
> **middleman** (or **marketing intermediary**) a marketing organization that links a producer and user within a marketing channel

▶ **Figure 6-1** Distribution Channels

CONSUMER PRODUCTS				BUSINESS PRODUCTS	
Producer	Producer	Producer	Producer	Producer	Producer
			Agents or brokers		
		Wholesalers	Wholesalers		Agent middlemen
	Retailers	Retailers	Retailers		
Consumers	Consumers	Consumers	Consumers	Organizational buyers	Organizational buyers

Chapter 6 Distributing and Promoting Products

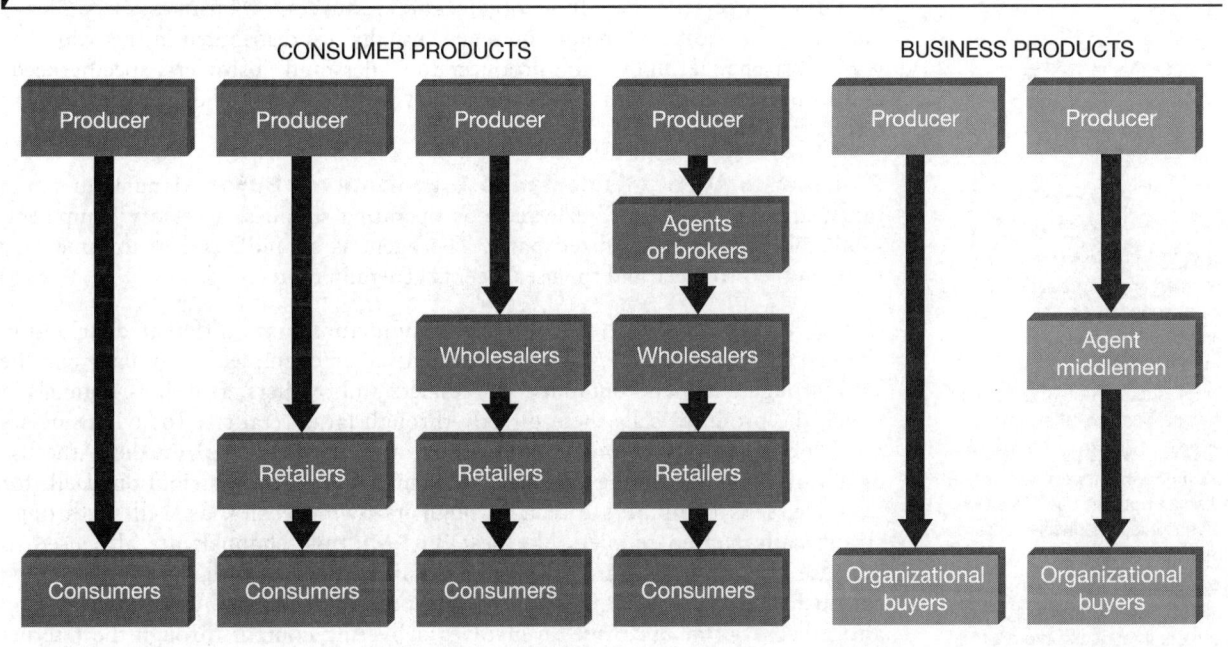

Using multiple marketing channels. Sometimes, companies use multiple marketing channels rather than just one. College textbook publishers often sell their products through multiple marketing channels. This textbook can be purchased directly from the publisher. It can also be purchased at a campus bookstore, or through Amazon.

Producer to Retailer to Consumer A **retailer** is an intermediary that buys from producers or other middlemen and sells to consumers. Producers sell directly to retailers when the retailers are large enough to buy in large quantities. This channel is used most often for products that are bulky, such as furniture and automobiles, for which additional handling would increase marketing costs. It is also the usual channel for perishable products, such as fruits and vegetables, and for clothing.

Producer to Wholesaler to Retailer to Consumer This channel is known as the *traditional channel* because many consumer goods (especially convenience goods) pass through wholesalers to retailers. A **wholesaler** is an intermediary that sells products to other firms. These businesses may be retailers, industrial users, or other wholesalers. A producer uses wholesalers when its products are carried by so many retailers that the producer cannot manage and distribute all of them. For example, chewing gum and candy manufacturers often use this type of channel.

Producer to Agent to Wholesaler to Retailer to Consumer Producers can use agents to reach wholesalers. Agents are functional middlemen that do not take title to products and are compensated by commissions paid by producers. Often the products with which agents deal are inexpensive, frequently purchased items. For example, to reach a large number of potential customers, a small manufacturer of gas-powered lawn trimmers might choose to use agents to market them to wholesalers. The wholesalers then sell the product to a large network of retailers. This channel is also used for seasonal products (such as Christmas decorations) and by producers that do not have in-house sales forces.

Producer to Organizational Buyer In this direct channel, the manufacturer's own sales force sells directly to organizational buyers, or business users. Heavy machinery, aircraft, and major equipment usually are distributed in this way. The very short channel allows the producer to understand customers' specific needs and to provide them with expert and timely services, such as delivery, machinery installation, and repairs.

Producer to Agent Middleman to Organizational Buyer Manufacturers use this channel to distribute such items as operating supplies, accessory equipment, small tools, and standardized parts. The agent is an independent intermediary between the producer and the user. Agents generally represent sellers.

Using Multiple Channels Often a manufacturer uses different distribution channels to reach different market segments. For example, candy bars may be sold through channels containing wholesalers and retailers, as well as channels in which the producer sells them directly through large retailers. Today, businesses are likely to engage in **multichannel (or omnichannel) distribution**—the use of a variety of marketing channels to ensure maximum distribution. Dell, for example, sells computers direct, through its own website, as well as through strategically chosen retailers like Best Buy. Multiple channels are also used to increase sales or to capture a larger share of the market with the goal of selling as much merchandise as possible. Some products forgo physical distribution altogether: **Digital distribution** involves delivering content through the internet to a computer or other device. For example, when you stream content on Netflix

零售商
retailer an intermediary that buys from producers or other middlemen and sells to consumers

批发商
wholesaler an intermediary that sells products to other firms

多渠道（或全渠道）分销
multichannel (or omnichannel) distribution the use of a variety of marketing channels to ensure maximum distribution

数字分销
digital distribution delivering content through the internet to a computer or other device

or Spotify, subscribe to Office 365 software, or book a rental through Airbnb, you are making use of a digital distribution channel.

市场覆盖水平
6-1b Level of Market Coverage

As with other marketing decisions, producers must analyze all relevant factors when deciding which distribution channels and intermediaries to use. Marketers should weigh the firm's production capabilities and marketing resources, the target market and buying patterns of potential customers, and the product itself. After evaluating these factors, the producer chooses the appropriate level of *intensity of market coverage*. Then the producer selects channels and intermediaries to implement that coverage.

Intensive distribution is the use of all available outlets for a product. It gives a product the widest possible exposure in the marketplace. The manufacturer reaches the market by selling to any intermediary of good financial standing that is willing to stock and sell the product. For the consumer, intensive distribution means being able to shop at a convenient store and spend minimum time selecting and buying the product. Many convenience goods, including candy, gum, and soft drinks, are distributed intensively.

Selective distribution is the use of only a portion of the available outlets for a product in each geographic area. Manufacturers of goods such as furniture, major home appliances, and clothing typically prefer selective distribution. For instance, you may prefer Hanes brand socks, which are distributed through retailers such as Target and Kohl's.

Exclusive distribution is the use of only a single retail outlet for a product in a large geographic area. Exclusive distribution usually is limited to prestigious products. It is appropriate, for instance, for specialty goods such as grand pianos, fine china, and expensive jewelry. The producer usually places many requirements (such as inventory levels, sales training, service quality, and warranty procedures) on exclusive dealers. For example, Patek Philippe watches, which may sell for $500,000 or more, are available in only a few select locations.

通过供应链管理建立伙伴关系
6-2 Partnering Through Supply Chain Management

Supply chain management refers to the coordination of all marketing channel activities associated with the flow and transformation of supplies, products, and information throughout the supply chain to the ultimate consumer. It requires cooperation throughout the entire marketing channel, including manufacturing, research, sales, advertising, and shipping. Supply chains focus not only on producers, wholesalers, retailers, and customers, but also on component-parts suppliers, shipping companies, communication companies, and other organizations that participate in product distribution. Suppliers strongly influence what items retail stores carry.

Supply chain management encourages cooperation in reducing the costs of inventory, transportation, administration, and handling. It also accelerates order-cycle times and increases profits for all channel members. When buyers, sellers, marketing intermediaries, and facilitating agencies work together, customers' needs regarding delivery, scheduling, packaging, and other requirements are better met. As an example, Procter & Gamble developed new packaging for its leading laundry brands to make them easier to ship to customers who order them from online retailers. The new packaging for Tide laundry detergent concentrates the liquid in a sealed bag with a dripless spout inside of a shoe-box sized container, which Amazon and other online retailers can ship without additional packaging. The new designs are environmentally friendlier and provide greater value for retailers, shippers, and customers.[2]

密集分销
intensive distribution the use of all available outlets for a product

✓ Concept Check

▶ How do the different types of intermediaries link a producer to a user within a marketing channel?

▶ Describe the six distribution channels. Give an example of each.

▶ Explain the three intensities of market coverage. Which types of products are generally associated with each of the different intensity levels?

Learning Objective

6-2 Explain how supply chain management facilitates partnering among channel members.

选择性分销
selective distribution the use of only a portion of the available outlets for a product in each geographic area

独家经销
exclusive distribution the use of only a single retail outlet for a product in a large geographic area

供应链管理
supply chain management the coordination of all marketing channel activities associated with the flow and transformation of supplies, products, and information throughout the supply chain to the ultimate consumer

Sustaining the Planet

保护地球：千禧一代青睐符合伦理的钻石

Millennials Take a Shining to Ethically Sourced Diamonds

Diamonds are thought to be synonymous with love, but it's love for planet Earth that's leading to their downfall. Diamonds, which are mined from the earth, are inherently unsustainable. A new wave of jewelry makers is using lab-grown and recycled diamonds as well as recycled metals to appeal to Millennials. De Beers, an international diamond mining company, popularized the diamond engagement ring in the 1940s, a time when the company controlled 90 percent of the diamond market. Millennials often see through marketing ploys and are more focused on ethics, social responsibility, and sustainability than prior generations, a trend that seems likely to continue with Generation Z.

Man-made diamonds are chemically the same as natural diamonds. They both have the same crystal structure and are assigned the same grades based on the four Cs: carat, cut, clarity, and color. Plus, lab-grown diamonds tend to be more affordable than diamonds that are mined from the earth. The Diamond Producers Association implied that lab-grown diamonds are not real in its "Real Is Rare, Real Is a Diamond" smear campaign, but the Federal Trade Commission responded by issuing new guidelines that established lab-grown diamonds are in fact "real."

This new crop of sustainable jewelry makers is forcing old-school jewelry companies to adapt. Though retailers initially attempted to discredit and disparage lab-grown diamonds, the tactic flopped. Kay Jewelers and Jared, for example, now offer lab-created diamond jewelry as well. Despite the rise in sustainable diamond sales, the jewelry industry as a whole is grappling with declining consumer demand. Every segment (mass, premium, and luxury) has been affected. Eco-friendly jewelry companies and traditional jewelers alike have been negatively affected by declining marriage rates. Traditional jewelers are now on board with the eco-friendly alternative because it could spark more excitement and attract a new generation of customers.

Sources: Based on information in Pamela N. Danziger, "Lab-Grown and Natural Diamond Industries End Hostilities, as Declining Jewelry Demand Threatens All," *Forbes*, July 19, 2020; Lane Florsheim, "For Engagement Rings, Are Natural Diamonds on the Way Out?" *The Wall Street Journal*, September 25, 2020; Stephanie Osmanski, "Why You Should Consider Ethical and Sustainable Diamonds," *Green Matters*, May 20, 2019.

Technology has enhanced the implementation of supply chain management significantly. Through computerized integrated information sharing, channel members reduce costs and improve customer service. Additionally, technologies such as blockchain, artificial intelligence (AI), and robotics can help improve efficiency, responsiveness, and transparency throughout the supply chain. DHL, for example, has invested more than $300 million in AI and robotics technologies for the benefits of its customers. AI helps the shipping company analyze its supply chain to identify areas for improvement, while specialized robots have increased the company's productivity and safety by reducing mistakes and shortening the time required for routine or physically demanding activities.[3] As many major industries transform their processes, the end result is increased productivity by reducing inventory, shortening cycle time, and reducing wasted human effort.

营销中介：批发商

6-3 Marketing Intermediaries: Wholesalers

Wholesalers are possibly the most misunderstood of marketing intermediaries. Producers sometimes try to cut out wholesalers in favor of dealing directly with retailers or consumers. However, wholesalers increase distribution efficiency. The marketing activities performed by wholesalers *must* be performed by other channel members if wholesalers are eliminated, which means that cutting out wholesalers may not reduce distribution costs.

✓ Concept Check

▶ How does supply chain management encourage cooperation between buyers and sellers?

▶ How has technology enhanced the implementation of supply-chain management?

Learning Objective

6-3 Describe the types of wholesalers and the services they provide.

Wholesalers facilitate trade by connecting manufacturers with retailers. A general-merchandise wholesaler buys many types of products from a broad range of manufacturers, warehouses the products, and then sells them to retailers. So, instead of having to contact hundreds of different manufacturers to stock their shelves, retailers need to contact only a small number of wholesalers.

批发商向零售商和制造商提供服务
6-3a Wholesalers Provide Services to Retailers and Manufacturers

Wholesalers help retailers by:

- Buying in large quantities and selling to retailers in smaller quantities and delivering goods to retailers.
- Stocking in one place the variety of goods that retailers otherwise would have to buy from many producers.
- Providing assistance in other vital areas, including promotion, market information, and financial aid.

Wholesalers help manufacturers by:

- Performing functions similar to those provided to retailers.
- Providing a sales force, reducing inventory costs, assuming credit risks, and furnishing market information.

批发商的类型
6-3b Types of Wholesalers

Wholesalers generally fall into two categories: merchant wholesalers, and agents and brokers. Of these, merchant wholesalers constitute the largest portion. They account for about four-fifths of all wholesale establishments and employees.

Merchant Wholesalers A **merchant wholesaler** is an intermediary that purchases goods in large quantities and sells them to other wholesalers or retailers and to institutional, farm, government, professional, or industrial users.

Merchant wholesalers have the following characteristics:

- They usually operate one or more warehouses at which they receive, take title to, and store goods. These wholesalers are sometimes called *distributors* or *jobbers*.
- Most merchant wholesalers are businesses composed of salespeople, order takers, receiving and shipping clerks, inventory managers, and office personnel.
- The successful merchant wholesaler must analyze available products and market needs. It must be able to adapt the type, variety, and quality of its products to changing market conditions.
- Merchant wholesalers may be classified as full-service or limited-service wholesalers depending on the number of services they provide. A **full-service wholesaler** performs the entire range of wholesaler functions. These functions

批发销售商
merchant wholesaler an intermediary that purchases goods in large quantities and sells them to other wholesalers or retailers and to institutional, farm, government, professional, or industrial users

全方位服务批发商
full-service wholesaler an intermediary that performs the entire range of wholesaler functions

Chapter 6　Distributing and Promoting Products

167

一般商品批发商
general-merchandise wholesaler an intermediary that deals in a wide variety of products

有限产品线批发商
limited-line wholesaler an intermediary that stocks only a few product lines but carries numerous product items within each line

专业批发商
specialty wholesaler an intermediary that carries a select group of products within a single line

代理人
agent an intermediary that expedites exchanges, represents a buyer or a seller, and often is hired permanently on a commission basis

经纪人
broker an intermediary that specializes in a particular commodity, represents either a buyer or a seller, and is likely to be hired on a temporary basis

线上零售
online retailing retailing that makes products available to buyers through computer or mobile connections

✓ Concept Check

▶ What services do wholesalers provide to producers and to retailers?

▶ Identify and describe the various types of wholesalers.

Learning Objective

6-4 Distinguish among the major types of retailers and shopping centers.

include delivering goods, supplying warehousing, arranging for credit, supporting promotional activities, and providing general customer assistance.

A full-service wholesaler can be of the following three different types:

- A **general-merchandise wholesaler** deals in a wide variety of products, such as over-the-counter medications, hardware, nonperishable foods, cosmetics, detergents, and tobacco.
- A **limited-line wholesaler** stocks only a few product lines but carries numerous product items within each line.
- A **specialty wholesaler** carries a select group of products within a single line. Food delicacies, such as shellfish, represent a product handled by this type of wholesaler. One type of specialty wholesaler you may encounter is a *rack jobber*, which owns and stocks display racks in supermarkets, drugstores, and discount and variety stores.

Agents and Brokers Agents and brokers perform a small number of marketing activities and are paid a commission that is a percentage of the sales price. They do not take ownership of the products they carry.

An **agent** is an intermediary that expedites exchanges, represents a buyer or a seller, and often is hired permanently on a commission basis. When agents represent producers, they are known as *sales agents* or *manufacturer's agents*. As long as the products represented do not compete, a sales agent may represent one or several manufacturers on a commission basis. The agent solicits orders for the manufacturers within a specific territory. As a rule, the manufacturers ship the merchandise and bill the customers directly. The manufacturers also set the prices and other conditions of the sales. The sales agent provides immediate entry into a territory, regular calls on customers, selling experience, and a known, predetermined selling expense (a commission that is a percentage of sales revenue).

A **broker** is an intermediary that specializes in a particular commodity, represents either a buyer or a seller, and is likely to be hired on a temporary basis. Food brokers that sell grocery products to resellers are the exception to this rule. They generally have long-term relationships with clients. Brokers may perform only the selling function or both buying and selling using their established contacts and specialized knowledge of their fields.

营销中介：零售商

6-4 Marketing Intermediaries: Retailers

Retailers are the final link between producers and consumers. Retailers may buy from either wholesalers or producers. They can sell goods, services (such as auto repairs or haircuts), or both. Home Depot, for instance, sells consumer goods, financial services, and installation and repair services for home appliances purchased at Home Depot.

The U.S. Bureau of Labor Statistics reports that the United States has about 1 million retail establishments ringing up total sales of more than $4 trillion.[4] Most retailers are small, with annual revenues well under $1 million. However, some retailers are quite large, with hundreds or even thousands of stores. Table 6-1 lists the ten largest retail organizations in the United States, their sales revenues, and number of stores. In recent years, conventional retail stores have faced numerous challenges, including changing consumer habits, the growth of online shopping, and the COVID-19 pandemic.

线上和多渠道零售

6-4a Online and Multichannel Retailing

As you probably know from firsthand experience, **online retailing** makes products available to buyers through computer or mobile connections. Online retailing is a rapidly growing segment with sales expected to exceed $1 trillion by 2023;

Table 6-1 The Ten Largest U.S. Retailers

Rank	Company	Sales (in billions)	# of Stores
1	Walmart	$524.0	5,355
2	Amazon	$250.5	564
3	Costco	$152.7	542
4	Walgreens Boots Alliance	$136.9	9,168
5	Kroger	$122.3	3,003
6	Home Depot	$110.5	1,973
7	CVS Health	$88.5	9,909
8	Target	$77.1	1,868
9	Lowe's	$72.2	1,727
10	Albertsons	$62.4	2,258

Source: National Retail Federation, "Top 100 Retailers 2020 List".

online purchases now account for 19 percent of all retail sales and are expected to grow to 33 percent by 2030.[5] Business and consumer spending on sites like Amazon, Alibaba, and Jet have come at the expense of conventional stores. To remain competitive, most retailers today have websites to sell products, provide information about their company, and offer incentives. Nordstrom, for example, gets more than one-half of its sales online, and its online presence supports its conventional stores.[6] Larger retailers like Starbucks, Best Buy, and Kohl's also have their own apps for customers to carry out retailing activities on their tablets or smartphones wherever they may be. Starbucks' app, for example, allows customers to order and pay right from their phone as well as accumulate loyalty reward points, while Target's app lets customers shop online and arrange for pickup or delivery or to find products in the store and identify coupons and other savings.

Many retailers today actually engage in **multichannel retailing** by employing multiple types of retailing. These retailers integrate a particular combination of brick-and-mortar stores, websites, apps, catalogs, direct-response marketing, telemarketing, and even vending so that a customer can research a product and purchase it from home, work, or in the car. D2C mattress retailer Casper, for example, has opened brick-and-mortar stores where customers can try out its mattresses before they buy. The company also has partnerships with retailers such as Sam's Club and Ashley HomeStore so that consumers can try out mattresses. These stores complement Casper's online efforts by opening more avenues for interacting with customers wherever they want to shop.[7]

多渠道零售
multichannel retailing employing multiple types of retailing

独立零售商
independent retailer a firm that operates only one retail outlet

连锁零售商
chain retailer a company that operates more than one retail outlet

零售店的类型
6-4b Types of Retail Stores

One way to classify retailers is by the number of stores owned and operated by the firm.

1. An **independent retailer** is a firm that operates only one retail outlet. Most retailers are independent, one-store operators that generally provide personal service and a convenient location.

2. A **chain retailer** is a company that operates more than one retail outlet. By adding outlets, chain retailers reach new geographic markets. As sales increase, chains usually buy merchandise in larger

Utilizing multiple retail approaches. Many retailers use multichannel retailing to reach potential customers. IKEA operates more than 455 retail stores in 52 countries. It also engages in direct marketing through online retailing.

Accessing customers through different types of retailers. When people are asked to name a retailer, they often think of brick-and-mortar establishments like the one shown in this photo. However, retailing goes on in all kinds of places, including in people's homes and workplaces, online, over the phone and on TV, and even on the streets.

quantities and thus take advantage of quantity discounts. They also wield more power in their dealings with suppliers. There are many fewer chain retail organizations than independent retailers.

Another way to classify retail stores is by store size and the kind and number of products carried. We will now take a closer look at store types based on these dimensions.

Department Stores These large retail establishments consist of several sections, or departments, that sell a wide assortment of products. The U.S. Census Bureau defines a **department store** as a retail store that (1) employs 25 or more persons and (2) sells at least home furnishings, appliances, family apparel, and household linens and dry goods, each in a different part of the store. Macy's, Kohl's, Selfridges, and Printemps are examples of large, international, department stores. Traditionally, department stores have been service-oriented. Along with the goods they sell, these retailers provide credit, personal assistance, liberal return policies, and pleasant shopping atmospheres.

Discount Stores A **discount store** is a self-service general-merchandise outlet that sells products at lower-than-usual prices. Stores like Target and Walmart operate on smaller markups and higher merchandise turnover than other retailers and offer minimal customer services. There has been a rise of extreme-value stores like Dollar General and Dollar Tree, which are a fraction of the size of conventional discount stores and typically offer very low prices on smaller-size name-brand nonperishable household items.

Warehouse Showrooms A **warehouse showroom** is a retail facility with five basic characteristics: (1) a large, low-cost building, (2) warehouse materials-handling technology, (3) vertical merchandise displays, (4) a large, on-premises inventory, and (5) minimal service. Some of the best-known showrooms are operated by big furniture retailers, including IKEA. These operations employ few personnel and offer few services. Most customers carry away purchases in the manufacturer's carton and assemble the products themselves, although some warehouse showrooms will deliver for a fee.

Convenience Stores A **convenience store** is a small food store that sells a limited variety of products but remains open well beyond normal business hours. Because convenience stores are common, most patrons of a particular store live within a mile of it. 7-Eleven, Circle K, Turkey Hill, and Open Pantry stores, for example, are convenience stores found either regionally or nationally in the United States. Limited product mixes and higher prices keep convenience stores from threatening the business of other grocery retailers. There are more than 150,000 convenience stores in the United States.[8]

Supermarkets A **supermarket** is a large self-service store that sells primarily food and household products. It stocks fresh, canned, frozen, and processed foods, paper products, and cleaning supplies. Sometimes called grocery stores, supermarkets also may sell such items as housewares, toiletries, toys and games, pharmacy products, stationery, books and magazines, plants and flowers, and a few clothing items. Supermarkets like Kroger, Albertsons, and H-E-B are large-scale operations that emphasize low prices and one-stop shopping for household needs.

Superstores A **superstore** is a large retail store that carries not only food and nonfood products ordinarily found in supermarkets, but also additional product lines

---

百货商店
department store a retail store that (1) employs 25 or more persons and (2) sells at least home furnishings, appliances, family apparel, and household linens and dry goods, each in a different part of the store

折扣店
discount store a self-service general-merchandise outlet that sells products at lower-than-usual prices

仓储式展厅
warehouse showroom a retail facility in a large, low-cost building with a large on-premises inventory and minimal service

便利店
convenience store a small food store that sells a limited variety of products but remains open well beyond normal business hours

超市
supermarket a large self-service store that sells primarily food and household products

大型超级商场
superstore a large retail store that carries not only food and nonfood products ordinarily found in supermarkets but also additional product lines

such as housewares, hardware, small appliances, clothing, personal-care products, garden products, and automotive merchandise. Superstores also provide services, including automotive repair, snack bars and restaurants, photo printing, and banking. Target, Walmart, and H-E-B operate some superstores.

Warehouse Clubs The **warehouse club** is a large-scale members-only establishment that combines features of cash-and-carry wholesaling with discount retailing. For an annual fee, small retailers or individuals may become members and purchase products at low prices for business use, for resale, or for personal use. Because their product lines are shallow and sales volumes are high, warehouse clubs like Sam's Club and Costco can offer a broad range of merchandise, including perishable and nonperishable foods, beverages, books, appliances, housewares, automotive parts, hardware, and furniture.

Traditional Specialty Stores A **traditional specialty store** carries a narrow product mix with deep product lines. Traditional specialty stores are sometimes called *limited-line retailers*. If they have depth in one product category, such as baked goods or jewelry, they may be called *single-line retailers*. Specialty stores usually offer deeper product mixes than department stores. They attract customers by emphasizing service, atmosphere, and location. Consumers who are dissatisfied with the impersonal atmosphere of large retailers often find the attention offered by specialty stores appealing. Specialty stores include chains such as the Gap, Bath and Body Works, and Foot Locker, as well as many independent stores.

Off-Price Retailers An **off-price retailer** is a store that buys manufacturers' seconds, overruns, returns, and off-season merchandise at below-wholesale prices and sells them to consumers at deep discounts. Off-price retailers sell limited lines of national-brand and designer merchandise, usually clothing, shoes, or housewares. Off-price retailers include T.J. Maxx, Burlington, and Ross. Off-price stores charge up to 50 percent less than department stores for comparable merchandise but offer few customer services. They often include community dressing rooms and central checkout counters. Some off-price retailers have a no-returns, no-exchanges policy.

Category Killers A **category killer** is a very large specialty store that concentrates on a single product line and competes by offering low prices and an enormous number of products. These stores are called *category killers* because they take business away from smaller, higher-priced retail stores. Category killers such as PetSmart and Office Depot are seeing increased competition from online retailing. The cost of maintaining such large stores can drain a company of its profits.

购物中心的类型
6-4c Types of Shopping Centers

There are several different types of shopping centers where retailers can choose to locate. A *planned shopping center* is a self-contained retail facility operated by independent owners and consisting of various stores. Shopping centers are designed and promoted to serve diverse groups of customers with widely differing needs. The management of a shopping center strives for a coordinated mix of stores, a comfortable atmosphere, adequate parking, pleasant landscaping, and special events to attract customers. The convenience of shopping for most family and household

Killing the competition? Or not? Home Depot is an example of a category killer. Category killers aren't likely to annihilate all of the competition though. Small retailers with less product variety and higher prices have found it difficult to compete against category killers. However, small retailers that carry a smaller inventory of products that are different from those stocked by category killers and compete on the basis of service, rather than price, can survive.

仓储会员店
warehouse club a large-scale members-only establishment that combines features of cash-and-carry wholesaling with discount retailing

传统专卖店
traditional specialty store a store that carries a narrow product mix with deep product lines

低价零售店
off-price retailer a store that buys manufacturers' seconds, overruns, returns, and off-season merchandise for resale to consumers at deep discounts

品类杀手
category killer a very large specialty store that concentrates on a single product line and competes on the basis of low prices and product availability

Lifestyle shopping center. Lifestyle shopping centers include specialty retailers, restaurants, and areas for cultural activities in an open-air setting.

needs in a single location is an important element of shopping-center appeal. There are several types of shopping centers: lifestyle, neighborhood, community, or regional.

A **lifestyle shopping center** is a shopping center that has an open-air configuration and is occupied primarily by upscale national chain specialty stores. The lifestyle shopping center model is popular because it combines shopping with the feel of strolling along Main Street. Some lifestyle shopping centers, like The Domain in Austin, Texas, include residences and offices above the stores, as well as activities and culture in their design in order to attract a wide variety of people.

A **neighborhood shopping center**, also called a *strip mall,* typically consists of several small convenience and specialty stores. Businesses in neighborhood shopping centers might include small grocery stores, drugstores, gas stations, and fast-food restaurants. These retailers serve consumers who live less than ten minutes away, usually within a two- to three-mile radius. Unlike in a lifestyle shopping center, most purchases in the neighborhood shopping center are based on convenience or personal contact. These retailers generally make only limited efforts to coordinate their promotional activities.

A **community shopping center** includes one or two department stores and some specialty stores, along with convenience stores. It attracts consumers from a wider geographic area who will drive longer distances to find products and specialty items unavailable in neighborhood shopping centers. Community shopping centers, which are carefully planned and coordinated, generate traffic with special events such as art exhibits, automobile shows, and sidewalk sales. The management of a community shopping center maintains a mix of tenants so that the center offers wide product mixes and deep product lines.

A **regional shopping center** usually has large department stores, numerous specialty stores, restaurants, movie theaters, and sometimes even hotels. It carries a similar mix of merchandise to that available in a downtown shopping district. Regional shopping centers carefully coordinate management and marketing activities to reach the 150,000 or more customers in their target market. These large centers usually advertise, hold special events, and may even provide transportation for customers. National chain stores can gain leases in regional shopping centers more easily than small independent stores because they are better able to meet the centers' financial requirements.

In addition to these types of shopping centers, outlet malls feature discount and factory outlet stores carrying traditional manufacturer brands, such as Polo Ralph Lauren, Nike, Guess, and Sunglass Hut. Some outlet centers feature upscale products from last season, discounted for quick sale. Manufacturers own these stores and make a special effort to avoid conflict with traditional retailers of their products. Manufacturers place these stores in noncompetitive locations, often outside of metropolitan areas. Factory outlet centers attract value-conscious customers seeking quality and major brand names. They operate in much the same way as regional shopping centers, but usually draw customers, some of whom may be tourists, from a larger shopping radius.

无店铺零售
6-4d Nonstore Retailing

Nonstore retailing is selling that does not take place in conventional store facilities. Consumers may purchase products without ever visiting a store. This form of retailing accounts for an increasing percentage of total retail sales. Nonstore retailers use direct selling, direct marketing, and vending.

生活方式购物中心
lifestyle shopping center an open-air-environment shopping center with upscale chain specialty stores

邻里购物中心
neighborhood shopping center a planned shopping center consisting of several small convenience and specialty stores

社区购物中心
community shopping center a planned shopping center that includes one or two department stores and some specialty stores, along with convenience stores

区域性购物中心
regional shopping center a planned shopping center containing large department stores, numerous specialty stores, restaurants, movie theaters, and sometimes even hotels

无店铺零售
nonstore retailing selling that does not take place in conventional store facilities

Direct Selling **Direct selling** is the marketing of products to customers through face-to-face sales presentations at home or in the workplace. Traditionally called *door-to-door selling,* direct selling in the United States began with peddlers more than a century ago and is now a major industry with $35 billion in U.S. sales annually.⁹ Instead of the door-to-door approach, many companies today—such as Mary Kay, Amway, and Avon—use other approaches. They can identify customers by mail, telephone, or the internet and then set up appointments. Direct selling sometimes involves the "party plan," which can occur in the customer's home or workplace. Direct selling through the party plan requires effective salespeople who identify potential hosts and provide encouragement and incentives for them to organize a gathering. Companies that commonly use the party plan are Tupperware, Cutco, and Pampered Chef.

Direct Marketing **Direct marketing** is the use of the telephone, internet, and nonpersonal media to communicate product and organizational information to customers, who then can purchase products via mail, telephone, or the internet. Direct marketing can occur online (discussed earlier) and through catalog marketing, direct-response marketing, telemarketing, and television home shopping.

In **catalog marketing**, an organization provides a catalog from which customers make selections and place orders by mail, telephone, or the internet. Catalog marketing began in 1872 when Montgomery Ward issued its first catalog to rural families. There are thousands of catalog marketing companies in the United States, many of which publish online. Some catalog marketers sell products spread over multiple product lines, while others are more specialized. Catalog companies, such as Burpee (seeds and plants) and Coldwater Creek (women's apparel), offer considerable depth in only one major product line. The advantages of catalog marketing include efficiency and convenience for customers because they do not have to visit a store. The retailer benefits by being able to locate in remote, low-cost areas, save on expensive store fixtures, and reduce both personal selling and store operating expenses. Disadvantages are that catalog marketing is inflexible, provides limited service, and is most effective for only a selected set of products.

Direct-response marketing occurs when a retailer advertises a product and makes it available through mail, telephone, or online orders. This marketing method has resulted in some products gaining widespread popularity. You may have heard of the Shamwow, Snuggie, and Magic Bullet—all of which became popular through direct response television marketing campaigns. Direct-response marketing can also be conducted by sending letters, samples, brochures, or booklets to prospects on a mailing list.

Telemarketing is the performance of marketing-related activities by telephone. Some organizations use a prescreened list of prospective clients. Telemarketing has many advantages, such as generating sales leads, improving customer service, speeding up payments on past-due accounts, raising funds for nonprofit organizations, and gathering market data. However, many consumers do not like being contacted by marketers via the phone and increasingly restrictive telemarketing laws have made it a less appealing marketing method. In 2003, U.S. Congress implemented a national do-not-call registry, which lists more than 241 million people who wish to opt out of telemarketing calls. Companies that make telemarketing phone calls must pay for access to the do-not-call registry and must obtain updated numbers from the registry at least every three days. The Federal Trade Commission (FTC) enforces violations, and companies are subject to fines of up to $16,000 for each call made to numbers on the list. The Federal Communications Commission (FCC) further outlaws prerecorded calls—"robocalls"—from companies for marketing purposes. However, new technologies mean that some unscrupulous firms are increasingly ignoring the National Do Not Call Registry and using robocalls for telemarketing purposes.¹⁰

Television home shopping presents products to television viewers, encouraging them to order through toll-free numbers and pay with credit cards.

直销
direct selling the marketing of products to customers through face-to-face sales presentations at home or in the workplace

直接营销
direct marketing the use of the telephone, internet, and nonpersonal media to introduce products to customers, who then can purchase them via mail, telephone, or the internet

目录营销
catalog marketing a type of marketing in which an organization provides a catalog from which customers make selections and place orders by mail, telephone, or the internet

直复营销
direct-response marketing a type of marketing in which a retailer advertises a product and makes it available through mail, telephone, or online orders

电话营销
telemarketing the performance of marketing-related activities by telephone

电视家庭购物
television home shopping a form of selling in which products are presented to television viewers, who can buy them by calling a toll-free number and paying with a credit card

✓ Concept Check

- Describe the major types of retail stores. Give an example of each.
- What are the most common types of shopping centers, and what types of store does each typically contain?
- How does nonstore retailing occur?

Learning Objective

6-5 Identify the five most important logistics activities.

自动售货机
vending the use of machines to dispense products

物流
logistics all those activities concerned with the efficient flow and storage of products from the producer to the ultimate user

Home Shopping Network (HSN) originated and popularized this format. Most homes in the United States receive at least one home shopping channel.

Vending Vending is the use of machines to dispense products. Vending, which accounts for less than 2 percent of all retail sales, is one of the most impersonal forms of retailing. Small, standardized, routinely purchased products can be sold in machines because they do not readily spoil and consumers appreciate the convenience. Customers can now find a wide variety of products dispensed via vending machine, even high-end items such as gold bars, cars, and iPods as well as cosmetics and food.

6-5 Logistics 物流

Logistics, also known as physical distribution, is all those activities concerned with the efficient flow and storage of products from the producer to the ultimate user. Logistics, therefore, is the movement of the products themselves—both goods and services—through their channels of distribution. The annual cost of business logistics in the United States is tremendous, at $1.63 trillion. To put this in perspective, logistics costs are 7.6 percent of gross domestic product (GDP).[11] It combines several interrelated business functions, the most important of which are inventory management, order processing, warehousing, materials handling, and transportation. Because these functions and their costs are highly interrelated, marketers view logistics as an integrated effort that supports other marketing activities. The overall goal of logistics is to get the right product to the right place at the right time and at minimal total cost.

Technology and Innovation

技术与创新：开启无人机送货时代

Drone Delivery Takes Off

Drones, which have grown rapidly in popularity, have many potential applications for business such as inventory management, package delivery, surveillance, and aerial photography. While commercial deployment has been slow due to regulation issues, society has begun to realize, thanks to the COVID-19 pandemic, that the utility of these unmanned aerial vehicles may outweigh potential risks.

During the pandemic, when social distancing was an imperative, drone delivery pilot programs experienced a surge. For example, Wing, operated by Alphabet, has been working on making drone delivery a reality since 2012. It doubled deployment rates during the global health crisis, working with FedEx and Walgreens to deliver household goods and select food items from a local bakery in Christiansburg, Virginia. This afforded customers greater access to necessities. Likewise, JD.com, the largest retailer in China, made deliveries to rural villages and semi-isolated islands. The crisis drove changes in policy because drones were seen as a way to reduce human contact during the pandemic. For delivery programs to become widespread, regulations need to advance even further.

The Federal Aviation Administration (FAA) pushed the commercial drone market forward by creating a regulatory framework with its consumer drone registry. The pace of adoption has been slow because until recently, operators who wanted to fly a drone over people or at night needed a waiver. Drones must still be flown within the visual line of sight unless the FAA says otherwise. Wing was the first drone service to receive permission from the FAA to allow multiple pilots to operate multiple drones making deliveries simultaneously to the public. As we enter the Golden Age of drone delivery, commercial drone operators will have to work together to demonstrate to the public as well as regulators how drones benefit society.

Sources: Based on information in Harrison Wolf, "We're About to See the Golden Age of Drone Delivery – Here's Why," *World Economic Forum,* July 6, 2020; "Drone Technology Uses and Applications for Commercial, Industrial and Military Drones in 2021 and the Future," *Business Insider,* January 12, 2021; "FAA Outlines New Rules for Drones and Their Operators," *Los Angeles Times,* December 30, 2020.

库存管理
6-5a Inventory Management

We define **inventory management** as the process of managing inventories in such a way as to minimize inventory costs, including both holding costs and potential stock-out costs. *Holding costs* are the expenses of storing products until they are purchased or shipped to customers. *Stock-out costs* are sales lost when items are not in inventory. Marketers seek to balance these two costs so that the company always has sufficient inventory to satisfy customer demand, but with little surplus because storing unsold products can be very expensive.

Holding costs include the money invested in inventory, the cost of storage space, insurance costs, and inventory taxes. Often even a relatively small reduction in inventory can generate a large increase in available working capital. Sometimes firms discover that risking some stockout costs can be cheaper than having too much inventory. Generally speaking, inventory management software helps companies maintain the correct levels of inventory and know when to place orders.

订单处理
6-5b Order Processing

Order processing consists of activities involved in receiving and filling customers' purchase orders. It may include not only the means by which customers order products but also procedures for billing and granting credit.

Fast, efficient order processing can provide a dramatic competitive edge. Those in charge of purchasing goods for intermediaries are especially concerned with their suppliers' promptness and reliability in order processing. To them, promptness and reliability mean minimal inventory costs as well as the ability to order goods when they are needed rather than weeks in advance. The internet is providing new opportunities for improving services associated with order processing.

仓储
6-5c Warehousing

Warehousing is the set of activities involved in receiving and storing goods and preparing them for reshipment. Goods are stored to create time utility, meaning they are held until they are needed for use or sale. Warehousing includes the following activities:

- *Receiving goods.* The warehouse accepts delivered goods and assumes responsibility for them.
- *Identifying goods.* Records are made of the quantity of each item received. Items may be marked, coded, or tagged for identification.
- *Sorting goods.* Delivered goods may have to be sorted before being stored.
- *Dispatching goods to storage.* Items must be moved to storage areas, where they can be found later.
- *Holding goods.* The goods are protected in storage until needed.
- *Recalling, picking, and assembling goods.* Items that are to leave the warehouse must be selected from storage and assembled efficiently.
- *Dispatching shipments.* Each shipment is packaged and directed to the proper transport vehicle. Shipping and accounting documents are prepared.

A firm may use its own private warehouses or rent space in public warehouses. A *private warehouse,* owned and operated by a particular firm, can be designed to serve the firm's specific needs. However, the organization must take on the task of financing the facility and determining the best location for it.

Public warehouses are open to all individuals and firms. Most are located on the outskirts of cities, where rail and truck transportation is easily available. They provide storage facilities, areas for sorting and assembling shipments, and office and display spaces for wholesalers and retailers. Public warehouses also will hold—and issue receipts for—goods used as collateral for borrowed funds.

库存管理
inventory management the process of managing inventories in such a way as to minimize inventory costs, including both holding costs and potential stock-out costs

订单处理
order processing activities involved in receiving and filling customers' purchase orders

仓储
warehousing the set of activities involved in receiving and storing goods and preparing them for reshipment

Chapter 6 Distributing and Promoting Products

物料搬运
6-5d Materials Handling

Materials handling is the actual physical handling of goods—in warehouses as well as during transportation. Proper materials-handling procedures and techniques can increase the efficiency and capacity of a firm's warehouse and transportation system, as well as reduce product breakage and spoilage. Increasingly, companies use technology such as robotics and *radio frequency identification (RFID)*—a system of tags and readers that use radio waves to identify and track materials tagged with special microchips—to facilitate efficient handling.

Materials handling attempts to reduce the number of times a product is handled. One method is called *unit loading*. Several smaller cartons, barrels, or boxes are combined into a single standard-size load that can be moved efficiently by forklift, conveyer, robot, or truck. Another is *containerization*, which involves consolidating many items into single, large containers that are sealed at their point of origin and opened at their destination. Their uniform size means they can be stacked and shipped via train, barge, or ship.

运输
6-5e Transportation

As a part of logistics, **transportation** is simply the shipment of products to customers. Transportation in the United States costs $1.06 trillion a year, 65 percent of total logistics activities' costs.[12] The greater the distance between seller and purchaser, the more important is the choice of the mode of transportation and the particular carrier. In recent years, the internet has emerged as a mode of transportation for digital products like streamed entertainment products such as songs and TV shows and downloadable products such as software.

A firm that offers transportation services is called a **carrier**. A *common carrier* is a transportation firm whose services are available to all shippers. Railroads, airlines, and most long-distance trucking firms are common carriers. A *contract carrier* is available for hire by one or several shippers. Contract carriers do not serve the general public and the number of firms they can handle at a time is limited by law. A *private carrier* is owned and operated by the shipper.

There are six major criteria that marketers use for selecting transportation modes: cost, speed, dependability, load flexibility, accessibility, and frequency. Table 6-2 compares these.

Obviously, the *cost* of a transportation mode is an important consideration. However, it is not the only one. Higher-cost modes of transportation can convey important benefits. *Speed* is measured by the total time that a carrier possesses the products, including time

物料搬运
materials handling the actual physical handling of goods, in warehouses as well as during transportation

运输
transportation the shipment of products to customers

承运商
carrier a firm that offers transportation services

Table 6-2 Characteristics of Transportation Modes

Selection Criteria	Railroads	Trucks	Pipelines	Waterways	Airplanes	Internet
Cost	Moderate	High	Low	Very low	Very high	Very low
Speed	Average	Fast	Slow	Very slow	Very fast	Very fast
Dependability	Average	High	High	Average	High	High
Load flexibility	High	Average	Very low	Very high	Low	Low
Accessibility	High	Very high	Very limited	Limited	Average	Very high
Frequency	Low	High	Very high	Very low	Average	Very high
Products carried	Coal, grain, lumber, heavy equipment, paper and pulp products, chemicals	Clothing, computers, books, groceries and produce, livestock	Oil, processed coal, natural gas, wood chips	Chemicals, bauxite, grain, motor vehicles, agricultural implements	Flowers, food (highly perishable), technical instruments, emergency parts and equipment, overnight mail	Information, songs, TV shows, movies, software, services

Marketing

required for pickup and delivery, handling, and movement between point of origin and destination. Usually there is a direct relationship between cost and speed, meaning faster modes of transportation are more expensive. A transportation mode's *dependability* is determined by its consistency of service. *Load flexibility* is the degree to which a transportation mode can be adapted for moving different kinds of products with varying requirements, such as controlled temperatures or humidity levels. *Accessibility* refers to a transportation mode's ability to move goods over a specific route or network. *Frequency* refers to how frequently a marketer can ship products by a specific transportation mode. While pipelines provide continuous shipments, railroads and waterways follow specific schedules for moving products from one location to another. Table 6-2 compares each transportation mode according to these six selection criteria.

Railroads Shipping by railroad remains one of the most important modes of transportation in the United States. Rail is also the least expensive mode for many products. Almost all railroads are common carriers, although a few coal-mining companies operate their own lines. Many commodities carried by railroads could not be transported easily by any other means.

Trucks The trucking industry consists of common, contract, and private carriers. Trucks are a very popular transportation mode because they have the advantage of being able to move goods to areas not served by railroads. They can handle freight quickly and economically, and they can carry a wide range of shipments. Many shippers favor this mode because it offers door-to-door service, less stringent packaging requirements than ships and airplanes, and flexible delivery schedules. Railroad and truck carriers sometimes team up to provide a form of transportation called *piggyback*, wherein truck trailers are loaded onto railroad flatcars for much of the distance and then pulled by trucks to the final destination.

Airplanes Air transport is the fastest, but most expensive, means of transportation. All certified airlines are common carriers. Supplemental or charter lines are contract carriers. Because of the high cost, uneven geographic distribution of airports, and reliance on weather conditions, airlines carry only a tiny fraction of intercity freight. Usually, only high-value, perishable items or goods that are needed immediately are shipped by air.

Waterways Cargo ships and barges offer the least expensive, but slowest, form of transportation. They are used mainly for bulky, nonperishable goods such as iron ore, bulk wheat, motor vehicles, and agricultural implements. Of course, shipment by water is limited to ports and cities located on navigable waterways. Many international distributors will combine this mode with a land mode to transport products to their destination.

Pipelines Pipelines are a highly specialized mode of transportation. They are used primarily to carry petroleum and natural gas. Such products as semiliquid coal and wood chips also can be shipped through pipelines, although their use can be controversial when they cut across animal migratory pathways or spring a leak in remote areas.

Internet In recent years, the internet has emerged as a mode of transportation for digital products. Examples include streamed entertainment products such as songs and TV shows and downloadable products such as software.

什么是整合营销传播

6-6 What Is Integrated Marketing Communications?

Integrated marketing communications is the coordination of promotion efforts to ensure maximum informational and persuasive impact on customers. A major goal of integrated marketing communications is to send a consistent message to customers. Unilever's Dove brand, for example, ran the successful Dove Campaign for Real Beauty,

> ✓ **Concept Check**
>
> ▸ How is inventory management a balancing act between stockout costs and holding costs?
>
> ▸ Explain the seven major warehousing activities.
>
> ▸ What is the goal of materials handling?
>
> ▸ Describe the major characteristics of the primary transportation modes.

整合营销传播
integrated marketing communications coordination of promotion efforts to ensure maximal informational and persuasive impact on customers

Learning Objective
6-6 Define integrated marketing communications.

which employed variations on the message in advertising on billboards, television, and online for more than a decade, with some ads being watched and shared millions of times. The brand also paired the Real Beauty messaging with its Dove Self-Esteem Project used by parents and educators to help promote confidence in children. The integrated campaign helped increase the brand's sales by $1.5 billion over ten years.[13]

Integrated marketing communications helps organizations coordinate and manage promotions in order to convey a consistent message. This approach fosters long-term customer relationships as well as the efficient use of promotional resources. The concept of integrated marketing communications has been increasingly accepted for several reasons. Mass-media advertising, a very popular promotional method in the past, is used less today because of its high costs and variable audience sizes. Marketers now take advantage of highly targeted promotional tools, such as social media, cable TV, direct mail, DVDs, the internet, special-interest magazines, and podcasts. These vehicles let marketers be more precise in targeting individual customers. As an example, affordable beauty firm e.l.f. Cosmetics uses TikTok and Instagram to reach its diverse customer base with fun and creative messaging that reinforces its brand and depicts ways customers use its products.[14]

Because the overall costs of marketing communications are significant, managers demand systematic evaluations of communications efforts to ensure that promotional resources are being used efficiently. Although the fundamental role of promotion has not changed, the specific communication vehicles employed and the precision with which they are used are evolving.

> ✓ **Concept Check**
>
> ▸ What is the major goal of integrated marketing communications?
>
> ▸ Why are integrated marketing communications being increasingly accepted?

促销组合：概述

6-7 The Promotion Mix: An Overview

Learning Objective

6-7 List the basic elements of the promotion mix.

Promotion is communication about an organization and its products that is intended to inform, persuade, or remind target-market members. Promotion is not limited to business. Charities use promotion to inform us about their cause or issue, to persuade us to donate, and to remind us to do so. Even the Internal Revenue Service uses promotion (in the form of publicity) to remind us of the mid-April deadline for filing tax returns.

A **promotion mix** (sometimes called a *marketing-communications mix*) is the particular combination of promotion methods a firm uses to reach a target market. The makeup of a mix depends on many factors, including the firm's promotional resources and objectives, the nature of the target market, the product characteristics, and the feasibility of the various promotional methods. The four elements of the promotion mix are advertising, personal selling, sales promotion, and public relations, as illustrated in Figure 6-2.

Advertising is a paid nonpersonal message communicated to a select audience through a mass medium. Advertising is flexible and can reach a very large or a small, carefully chosen target group. **Personal selling** is personal communication aimed at

▸ **Figure 6-2 Possible Elements of a Promotion Mix**

Depending on the type of product and target market involved, one or more of these ingredients are used in a promotion mix.

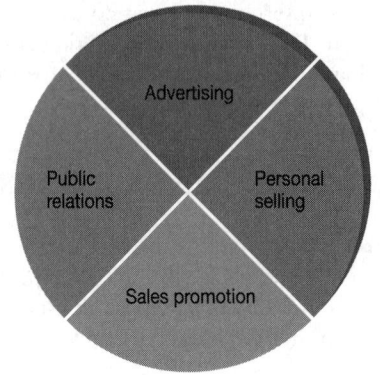

促销
promotion communication about an organization and its products that is intended to inform, persuade, or remind target-market members

促销组合
promotion mix the particular combination of promotion methods a firm uses to reach a target market

广告
advertising a paid nonpersonal message communicated to a select audience through a mass medium

人员推销
personal selling personal communication aimed at informing customers and persuading them to buy a firm's products

Marketing

informing customers and persuading them to buy a firm's products. It is more expensive to reach a consumer through personal selling than through advertising, but this method provides immediate feedback and often is more persuasive than advertising. **Sales promotion** is the use of activities or materials as direct inducements to customers or salespersons, which can add value to the product and increase the customer's incentive to make a purchase. **Public relations** is a broad set of communication activities used to create and maintain favorable relationships between an organization and various public groups, both internal and external. Public relations activities are numerous and varied and can be a very effective form of promotion.

In addition to deciding which combination of promotional methods is most appropriate for a marketing strategy, marketers must decide whether to use a push or pull strategy. With a *push policy*, a producer promotes the product only to the next organization down the marketing channel, and each channel member in turn promotes to the next. In a marketing channel with wholesalers and retailers, the producer promotes to the wholesaler because, in this case, the wholesaler is the channel member just below the producer. As an example, a paper wholesaler might offer an office-supply store $3 off every box of paper purchased for sale in the store; an appliance manufacturer's sales representatives might use personal selling to encourage retailers to carry a new model. Indeed, a push policy normally stresses personal selling. With a *pull policy*, however, a marketer promotes directly to consumers to spur strong consumer demand for its products. It does so primarily through advertising and sales promotion. Because consumers are persuaded to seek the products in retail stores, retailers in turn go to wholesalers or the producers to buy the products. An example of a pull policy is the Apple iPhone. Apple uses advertising to tease each new iPhone or Apple Watch, which creates demand through word-of-mouth. Consumers hear about Apple's new product and are encouraged to seek out more information. Push and pull policies are not mutually exclusive. At times, an organization uses both simultaneously.

While it is possible for a marketer to only use one ingredient of the promotion mix, it is more likely that two, three, or even all four of these ingredients will be used, depending on the type of product and target market involved.

6-8 Advertising

Advertising is a very important element of the promotion mix. Organizations currently spend around $169.9 billion annually on advertising in the United States.[15] In this section, we discuss the types of advertising and how to develop an advertising campaign.

6-8a Types of Advertising by Purpose

Depending on its purpose and message, advertising may be classified into one of three groups: primary demand, selective demand, or institutional.

Primary-Demand Advertising **Primary-demand advertising** is advertising aimed at increasing the demand for all brands of a product within a specific industry. Trade and industry associations, such as the National Pork Producers Council and the California Milk Processor Board, use primary-demand advertising. To reach out to a new generation of potential home buyers, the National Association of Realtors launched a multimedia campaign, "That's Who We R," to highlight stories of professional realtors helping all kinds of families buy homes and start businesses.[16]

Selective-Demand Advertising **Selective-demand (or brand) advertising** is advertising that is used to sell a particular brand of product. It is by far the most common type of advertising, and it accounts for the majority of advertising expenditures. As an example, Burger King used radio ads to introduce its Impossible Whopper, humorously highlighting the confusion people experience eating a plant-based burger that tastes just like a Whopper made with beef.[17]

---

sales promotion the use of activities or materials as direct inducements to customers or salespersons

Concept Check

▶ What are the major elements of a promotion mix?

▶ How can each element help a firm reach a target market?

▶ How does a push strategy differ from a pull strategy?

Learning Objective

6-8 Examine advertising, including the types of advertising, the advertising campaign, and social and legal considerations.

---

public relations communication activities used to create and maintain favorable relationships between an organization and various public groups, both internal and external

primary-demand advertising advertising whose purpose is to increase the demand for *all* brands of a product within a specific industry

selective-demand (or brand) advertising advertising that is used to sell a particular brand of product

Chapter 6 Distributing and Promoting Products

Harnessing the power of social media. Social media allows a business to reach out to customers in a context that is familiar and comfortable to them. Firms attempt to measure the effectiveness of their social media efforts by gathering statistics on the number of followers and fans they have, traffic to their websites, and mentions of their products on social networking sites.

Selective-demand advertising that aims at persuading consumers to make purchases within a short time is called *immediate-response advertising*. Most local advertising is of this type. Often local advertisers promote products with immediate appeal. Selective advertising aimed at keeping the public aware of a firm's name or product is called *reminder advertising*. *Comparative advertising* compares the sponsored brand with one or more identified competing brands. The association shows the sponsored brand to be as good as or better than the other identified competing brands. Marketers must be careful when using this technique to present information truthfully and not to obscure or distort facts.

Institutional Advertising **Institutional advertising** is advertising designed to enhance a firm's image or reputation. Some large firms allocate a portion of advertising dollars to build goodwill, rather than to stimulate sales directly. As an example, McDonald's ran commercials thanking healthcare workers, firefighters, and other first responders for their service during the COVID-19 pandemic. The fast-food chain also gave away "Thank You Meals" that included a thank you note to first responders.[18] A positive public image helps an organization to attract customers, employees, and investors.

开展广告活动的主要步骤
6-8b Major Steps in Developing an Advertising Campaign

An advertising campaign is developed in several stages, which can vary in the order in which they are implemented. Factors affecting a campaign include the company's resources, products, and target audiences. The development of a campaign in any organization includes the following steps in some form:

1. Identify and Analyze the Target Audience The target audience is the group toward which a firm's advertisements are directed. To pinpoint the organization's target audience and develop an effective campaign, marketers analyze various factors, such as the geographic distribution of potential customers, their age, gender, race, income, and education, and their attitudes toward the product, the nature of the competition, and the product's features. It is crucial to identify the target market correctly because all subsequent efforts will fail if not directed at the right audience.

2. Define the Advertising Objectives The goals of an advertising campaign should be stated precisely and in quantifiable terms. Objectives should give specific details about the actual and desired position of the company and how it will arrive there, including a timetable for achieving goals. For example, advertising objectives that focus on sales will stress increasing sales by a certain percentage or dollar amount, or expanding the firm's market share by a specific amount.

3. Create the Advertising Platform An advertising platform includes the important selling points, or features, that an advertiser will incorporate into the advertising campaign. These should be features that are lacking in competitors' products and that are important to customers. Although research into what consumers view as important issues is expensive, it is the most productive way to determine what to include in an advertising platform.

4. Determine the Advertising Appropriation The advertising appropriation is the total amount of money designated for advertising in a given time period. Developing an acceptable advertising appropriation is critical—too little and promotional efforts will not meet demand, too much will waste resources and

商誉广告
institutional advertising
advertising designed to enhance a firm's image or reputation

reduce the funds available for other activities. Advertising appropriations may be based on historical or forecasted sales, what competitors spend on advertising, or executive judgment. Companies that spend the most on advertising in the United States include Amazon, Procter & Gamble, L'Oréal, Samsung, and Unilever.[19]

5. Develop the Media Plan A media plan includes media selection and media scheduling. This involves deciding which media vehicles to use: internet and mobile, television, radio, out of home, magazines, newspapers, or some combination. Although cost-effectiveness is not easy to measure, the primary concern of the media planner is to reach the largest proportion of the target audience possible for each dollar spent. Media planners must also consider the location and demographics of the target market, the content of the message, and the characteristics of the audiences reached by various media. The media planner begins with general media decisions, selects subclasses within each medium, and chooses specific media vehicles for the campaign. The advantages and disadvantages of the major media classes are shown in Table 6-3.

Table 6-3 Advantages and Disadvantages of Major Media Classes

	Advantages	Disadvantages
Internet/Digital Media	Immediate response, potential to reach a precisely targeted audience, ability to track customers and build databases, highly interactive medium, real-time analytics	Costs of precise targeting can be high, inappropriate ad placement, effects difficult to measure, concerns about security and privacy
Social Media	Target, interact, and connect more personally with customers, receive real-time feedback, direct messages to specific individuals, effectively reach target market/followers	Restricted number of contacts per message because of highly targeted nature, new media—unsure of best applications and how to calculate ROI, large time commitment to monitor
Television	Reaches large audiences, high frequency available, dual impact of audio and video, highly visible, high prestige, geographic and demographic selectivity, difficult to ignore, on-demand capabilities	Very expensive, highly perishable message, size of audience not guaranteed, amount of prime time limited, lack of selectivity in target market
Radio	Reaches a large proportion of consumers, mobile and flexible, low relative costs, ad can be changed quickly, high level of geographic and demographic selectivity, encourages use of imagination	Lacks visual imagery, short life of message, listeners' attention limited, market fragmentation, difficult buying procedures, limited media and audience research
Out of Home	Allows for frequent repetition, low cost, message can be placed close to point of sale, geographic selectivity, operable 24 hours a day, high creativity	Message must be short and simple, no demographic selectivity, seldom attracts readers' full attention, criticized as traffic hazard and blight on landscape, much wasted coverage, limited capabilities
Magazines	Demographic selectivity, good reproduction, long life, prestige, geographic selectivity when regional issues available	High costs, 30- to 90-day average lead time, high level of competition, limited reach, communicates less frequently
Newspapers	Reaches large audience, purchased to be read, geographic flexibility, short lead time, frequent publication, favorable for cooperative advertising	Not selective for socioeconomic groups or target market, short life, limited reproduction capabilities, large advertising volume limits exposure
Direct Mail	Little wasted circulation, highly selective, circulation controlled by advertiser, few distractions, personal, stimulates actions, easy to measure performance, hidden from competitors	Very expensive, lacks editorial content to attract readers, often thrown away unread as junk mail, criticized as invasion of privacy, consumers must choose to read the ad

Sources: Adapted from William F. Arens and Michael Weigold, *Contemporary Advertising & Integrated Communications*, 16th ed. (Burr Ridge, IL: Irwin/McGraw-Hill, 2021); George E. Belch and Michael Belch, *Advertising and Promotion: An Integrated Marketing Communications Perspective*, 12th ed. (Burr Ridge, IL: Irwin/McGraw-Hill, 2021).

6. Create the Advertising Message The content and form of a message are influenced by the product's features, the characteristics of the target audience, the objectives of the campaign, and the choice of media. An advertiser must consider these factors to choose words and illustrations that will be meaningful and appealing to the target audience. The copy, or words, of an advertisement will vary depending on the media choice, but attempt to engage the audience and move them through attention, interest, desire, and action. Artwork and visuals should complement copy by being visually attractive and communicating an idea quickly.

7. Execute the Campaign Execution of an advertising campaign requires extensive planning, scheduling, and coordinating because the tasks are carried out by many people and organizations and must be completed on time. Production companies, research organizations, media firms, printers, photoengravers, and commercial artists are just a few of the potential contributors to a campaign. Advertising managers must constantly assess the quality of the work and take corrective action when necessary. In some instances, advertisers must make changes in the middle of the campaign to meet objectives.

8. Evaluate Advertising Effectiveness A campaign's success should be compared against original objectives at regular intervals before, during, and after campaign launch. An advertiser should be able to track the impact of the campaign on sales and market share, as well as changes in customer attitudes and brand awareness. Data from past and current sales and responses to coupon offers and customer surveys administered by research organizations are some of the ways in which advertising effectiveness can be evaluated. Table 6-4 shows the five advertisers with the most effective campaigns according to the Effie Effectiveness Index, a global ranking system for advertising effectiveness. This ranking takes into account factors such as ROI, sales growth, and brand awareness in relation to money spent on promotional activities.

广告公司
6-8c Advertising Agencies

Advertisers can plan and produce their own advertising with help from in-house media personnel, or they can hire advertising agencies. An **advertising agency** is an independent firm that plans, produces, and places advertising for clients. Many large

Table 6-4 Most Effective Advertisers

Ranking	Advertiser
1	Unilever
2	Coca-Cola
3	Nestlé
4	AB InBev
5	PepsiCo

Source: Effie Worldwide, "2020 Effie Effectiveness Index: Overview".

广告公司
advertising agency an independent firm that plans, produces, and places advertising for its clients

Exploring Careers

职业探索：如何在广告公司找到工作

How to Land a Job in an Advertising Agency

Advertising, personal selling, sales promotion, and public relations are the four elements of the promotion mix. Advertising alone is a multibillion-dollar industry in the United States and offers exciting career opportunities. Instead of working for an individual company, many people seek employment at advertising agencies, independent firms that plan, produce, and place advertising for their clients. Some of the largest advertising agencies include BBDO, Deloitte Digital, Dentsu, Ogilvy, and TBWA Worldwide.

An early step toward starting a career in advertising is seeking a degree in a related field such as business, marketing, or communications. Some universities specifically offer a bachelor's degree in advertising that focuses on the principles of advertising, communication theory and analysis, creative strategy, media planning, ad sales, and more. Beyond college, one way to get a foot in the door of an agency is to apply for an internship. Internships provide valuable, hands-on experience in the fast-paced world of advertising. Many internships end with a job offer for an entry-level position.

Jobs in advertising include account coordination, copywriting, media buying, and more. To build a portfolio of work, freelancing can be an effective way to break into copywriting and graphic design in particular.

In addition to traditional person-to-person networking, websites like Fiverr and Upwork can help individuals land clients. Even without engaging in freelancing, job seekers can hone their skills by creating spec ads by either reimagining existing print, digital, mobile, outdoor, or radio advertisements or conceptualizing an original campaign from the ground up. The important element is to show an understanding of the brand or product being promoted and demonstrate creativity and effective communication.

Though print advertising is in decline, the advertising industry as a whole is flourishing as companies invest in digital and mobile. Digital advertising will continue to grow at a greater rate than traditional media, accounting for more than 50 percent of ad spending. The changing landscape of advertising makes this career path both exciting and lucrative.

Sources: Based on information in Apryl Duncan, "How to Work for an Advertising Agency," *The Balance Careers*, January 4, 2020; "US Digital Ad Spending Will Surpass Traditional in 2019," *eMarketer*, February 19, 2019; "How to Get Into Advertising: Step-by-Step Career Guide," *Masterclass*, November 8, 2020.

---

ad agencies also help with sales promotion and public relations. The cost of using an advertising agency can be moderate, especially for large campaigns. It is usually around 15 percent commission. Some firms opt to use a combination of in-house advertising talent and outside specialists.

广告中的社会和法律因素
6-8d Social and Legal Considerations in Advertising

Critics of U.S. advertising have two main complaints—that it is wasteful and that it can be deceptive. Although advertising (like any other activity) can be performed inefficiently, evidence shows that it is not wasteful:

- Advertising is the most effective and least expensive means of communicating product information to a large number of individuals and organizations.
- Advertising encourages competition. It thus leads to the development of new and improved products, wider product choices, and lower prices.
- Advertising revenues support mass-communication media—internet, television, newspapers, magazines, and radio, effectively paying for news coverage and entertainment programming.
- Advertising provides job opportunities in fields ranging from sales to film production.

Concept Check

▶ Describe the major types of advertising by purpose.

▶ Explain the eight major steps in developing an advertising campaign.

Learning Objective

6-9 Explore personal selling, including the types of salespersons, the personal-selling process, and major sales management tasks.

订单开发者
order getter a salesperson who is responsible for selling a firm's products to new customers and increasing sales to current customers

创造性销售
creative selling selling products to new customers and increasing sales to current customers

订单接单员
order taker a salesperson who handles repeat sales in ways that maintain positive relationships with customers

销售支持人员
sales support personnel employees who aid in selling but are more involved in locating prospects, educating customers, building goodwill for the firm, and providing follow-up service

A number of government and private agencies scrutinize advertising for false or misleading claims or offers that might harm consumers. At the national level, the Federal Trade Commission (FTC), the Food and Drug Administration (FDA), and the Federal Communications Commission (FCC) oversee advertising practices. Advertising also may be monitored by state and local agencies, better business bureaus, and industry associations.

人员推销
6-9 Personal Selling

Personal selling is the most adaptable of all promotional methods because the person presenting the message can modify it to suit the individual buyer. However, it is also the most expensive method because it involves salespeople communicating with customers one at a time or in small groups. Many selling situations demand the face-to-face contact and adaptability of personal selling. This is especially true of industrial sales, in which a single purchase may amount to millions of dollars. Obviously, sales of that size must be based on carefully planned presentations, personal contact with customers, and thorough negotiations.

销售人员的种类
6-9a Kinds of Salespersons

Because most businesses employ different salespersons to perform different functions, marketing managers need to select the kinds of sales personnel that will be most effective in selling the firm's products. Salespersons may be identified as order getters, order takers, and support personnel. A single individual can, and often does, perform all three functions.

Order Getters An **order getter** is responsible for what is sometimes called **creative selling**—selling a firm's products to new customers and increasing sales to current customers. An order getter must be able to perceive buyers' needs, supply customers with information about the product, and persuade them to buy it.

Order Takers An **order taker** handles repeat sales and customer demands to maintain positive relationships. *Inside order takers* receive incoming mail, online, and telephone orders for businesses. Salespersons in retail stores are also inside order takers. *Outside* (or *field*) *order takers* travel to customers. Often the buyer and the field salesperson develop a mutually beneficial relationship of placing, receiving, and delivering orders. Both inside and outside order takers are active salespersons and produce a large proportion of their companies' sales.

Support Personnel **Sales support personnel** aid in selling but are more involved in locating prospects (likely first-time customers), educating customers, building goodwill for the firm, and providing follow-up service. The most common categories of support personnel are missionary, trade, and technical salespersons.

A **missionary salesperson**, who usually works for a manufacturer, visits retailers to persuade them to buy the manufacturer's products. If the retailers agree, they buy the products from wholesalers, who are the manufacturer's actual customers.

The pros and cons of personal selling. Personal selling is sometimes more effective than advertising. It's easy to ignore an advertisement. Saying "no" to a salesperson is much harder. The main drawback of personal selling is that it's expensive, which is why it's generally used to sell high-dollar goods and services.

A **trade salesperson**, who generally works for a food producer or processor, assists customers in promoting products, especially in retail stores. A trade salesperson may obtain additional shelf space for the products, restock shelves, set up displays, and distribute samples. Because trade salespersons usually are order takers as well, they are not strictly support personnel.

A **technical salesperson** assists a company's current customers in technical matters. Technical salespeople may explain how to use a product, how it is made, how to install it, or how a system is designed. They should have degrees in science or engineering.

Firms usually need to employ sales personnel from several of these categories. Factors that affect which sales personnel are hired include the number of customers and their characteristics; the product's attributes, complexity, and price; the distribution channels used by the company; and the company's approach to advertising.

人员推销过程
6-9b The Personal-Selling Process

No two selling situations are exactly alike, and no two salespeople perform their jobs in exactly the same way. Most salespeople, however, follow the six-step procedure illustrated in Figure 6-3.

Prospecting The first step in personal selling is to research potential buyers and choose the most likely customers, or prospects. Business associates and customers, social media contacts, public records, telephone and trade-association directories, and company files can all be good sources of new prospects. The salesperson also assesses whether prospects have the financial resources, willingness, and authority to buy the product, a process known as *qualifying*.

Approaching the Prospect First impressions are often lasting. Therefore, a salesperson's first contact with a prospect is crucial to successful selling. A salesperson should be friendly and knowledgeable about the product, the prospect's needs, and how the product can meet those needs. Those salespeople who demonstrate an understanding of and sensitivity to a customer's situation are more likely to make a good first impression and make a sale.

Making the Presentation The next step is actual delivery of the sales presentation, which often includes a product demonstration. The salesperson points out the product's features, its benefits, and how it is superior to competitors' merchandise. The salesperson may list other clients (if given permission) during the presentation.

During a demonstration, the salesperson may suggest that the prospect try out the product personally. The demonstration and product trial should underscore specific points made during the presentation.

Answering Objections The prospect may raise objections or ask questions at any time during the process. This is the salesperson's chance to eliminate objections that could prevent a sale, to point out additional features, or to mention special services the company offers.

Closing the Sale To close the sale, the salesperson asks the prospect to buy the product. This is the critical point in the selling process. Many experienced salespeople employ a *trial closing*, in which they ask questions before the actual close in a tone that assumes a successful sale. Typical questions are: "When would you want delivery?" and "Do you want the standard model or the one with the special options package?" They allow the salesperson to gauge the likelihood and imminence of a sale.

Following Up The salesperson's job does not end with a sale. They must follow up to ensure that the product is delivered on time, in the right quantity, and in proper

Figure 6-3 The Six Steps of the Personal-Selling Process

Personal selling is not only the most adaptable of all promotional methods but also the most expensive.

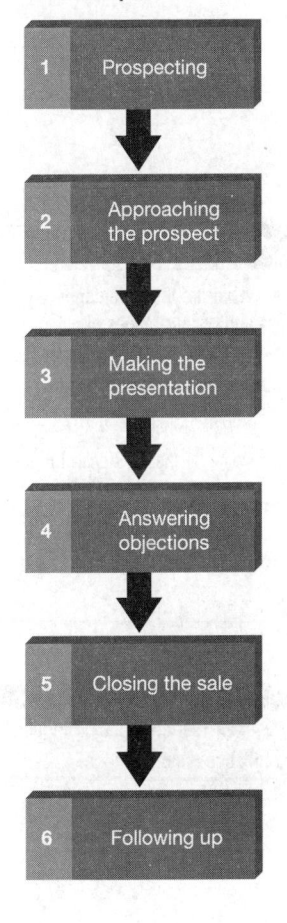

1. Prospecting
2. Approaching the prospect
3. Making the presentation
4. Answering objections
5. Closing the sale
6. Following up

推销式销售人员
missionary salesperson a salesperson—generally employed by a manufacturer—who visits retailers to persuade them to buy the manufacturer's products

快消品销售人员
trade salesperson a salesperson—generally employed by a food producer or processor—who assists customers in promoting products, especially in retail stores

技术销售人员
technical salesperson a salesperson who assists a company's current customers in technical matters

Chapter 6 Distributing and Promoting Products

operating condition. During follow-up, salespeople should also make it clear that they are available in case problems develop. Follow-up is essential to the selling process because it leaves a good impression and helps to increase the likelihood of future sales.

主要的销售管理工作
6-9c Major Sales Management Tasks

A firm's success often hinges on the competent management of its sales force. Although some companies operate efficiently without one, most firms rely on a strong sales force—and the revenue it brings in—for their success.

Sales managers must:

- Set sales objectives in concrete, quantifiable terms and specify a period of time and geographic area;
- Adjust the size of the sales force to meet changes in the firm's marketing plan and the marketing environment;
- Attract and hire effective salespersons;
- Develop a training program and decide where, when, how, and for whom to conduct the training;
- Formulate a fair and adequate compensation plan to retain qualified employees;
- Motivate salespersons to keep their productivity high;
- Define sales territories and determine scheduling and routing of the sales force; and
- Evaluate the operation holistically, through sales reports, communications with customers, and invoices.

> **✓ Concept Check**
> ▸ What are the advantages and disadvantages of using personal selling?
> ▸ Identify the three types of salespersons.
> ▸ Describe the six steps of the personal-selling process.

销售促销
6-10 Sales Promotion

> **Learning Objective**
> **6-10** Identify sales promotion objectives and methods.

Sales promotion consists of activities or materials that are direct inducements to customers or salespersons. Receiving a free sample at the supermarket or using a frequent flier program are examples of sales promotions. Sales promotion techniques can significantly affect sales and are often used to enhance and supplement other promotional methods. Firms have dramatically increased spending on sales promotions as they increase their importance as part of the promotion mix.

促销目标
6-10a Sales Promotion Objectives

Sales promotion activities may be used singly or in combination to achieve one goal or a set of goals. Marketers use sales promotion activities and materials for a number of purposes, including:

1. To attract new customers;
2. To encourage trial of a new product;
3. To invigorate the sales of a mature brand;
4. To boost sales to current customers;
5. To reinforce advertising;
6. To increase traffic in retail stores;
7. To smooth out customer demand;
8. To build up reseller inventories;
9. To neutralize the competition's promotional efforts; and
10. To increase the attractiveness of shelf placement and displays.

Sales promotion objectives should be consistent with the organization's general goals and with its marketing and promotional objectives.

促销方法
6-10b Sales Promotion Methods

Most sales promotion methods can be classified as promotional techniques for either consumer sales or trade sales.

A **consumer sales promotion method** attracts consumers to particular retail stores and motivates them to purchase certain new or established products. A **trade sales promotion method** encourages wholesalers and retailers to stock and actively promote a manufacturer's product. Incentives such as money, merchandise, marketing assistance, and gifts may provide incentives to resellers to purchase products or support a firm in other ways. Of the combined dollars spent on sales promotion and advertising, about one-half is spent on trade promotions, one-fourth on consumer promotions, and one-fourth on advertising.

Do you use coupons? Companies give away coupons to increase the sales of their products and encourage consumers who are unfamiliar with their products to give them a try.

Rebates A **rebate** is a return of part of the purchase price of a product. Usually the rebate is offered by the producer to consumers who submit proof of purchase and perhaps other documents. Rebating is a relatively low-cost promotional method, but consumers may not be attracted by it because they view it to be too complicated or time consuming.

Coupons A **coupon** reduces the retail price of a particular item by a stated amount at the time of purchase. Coupons may be worth anywhere from a few cents to a few dollars. Customers can find coupons online, through apps, and in newspapers, magazines, direct mail, and shelf dispensers in stores. After declining throughout the 1990s, the popularity of coupons has rebounded, largely because consumers can visit coupon websites, and companies send coupons via email or smartphone to loyal customers. Target, for instance, offers customers customized coupons and more via its Target app. RetailMeNot gives consumers access to digital coupon offers and promo codes from 70,000 stores and restaurants via a website or smartphone app.[20]

Samples A **sample** is a free product given to customers to encourage trial and purchase. Marketers utilize samples to increase awareness of a product, which can increase sales volume in the early stages of a product's life cycle and improve distribution. Samples may be offered via online coupons or direct mail or in stores. It is the most expensive sales promotion technique. Established brands, such as cosmetics companies, may use free samples to attract customers and renew interest in a brand. Club Demonstration Services, which operates sampling tables for Costco, reported that its sampling of a frozen pizza product at many retailers boosted sales by an average of 600 percent.[21] Organizations must consider such factors as seasonal demand for the product, market characteristics, and prior advertising when designing a free sample campaign.

Premiums A **premium** is a gift that a producer offers a customer in return for buying its product. It is used to attract competitors' customers, introduce different sizes of established products, add variety to other promotional efforts, and stimulate consumer loyalty. Creativity is essential when using premiums. To stand out and achieve a significant number of redemptions, the premium must suit the target audience and the brand's image. The premium must also be recognizable and desirable to customers. Premiums are generally placed on or inside packages.

Frequent-User Incentives A **frequent-user incentive** is a program developed to reward customers who engage in repeat (frequent) purchases. These are often called customer loyalty programs, and increasingly, they are app-based. Such programs are used commonly by service businesses such as airlines, hotels, auto

消费者促销法
consumer sales promotion method a sales promotion method designed to attract consumers to particular retail stores and to motivate them to purchase certain new or established products

贸易促销法
trade sales promotion method a sales promotion method designed to encourage wholesalers and retailers to stock and actively promote a manufacturer's product

回扣
rebate a return of part of the purchase price of a product

优惠券
coupon reduces the retail price of a particular item by a stated amount at the time of purchase

样品
sample a free product given to customers to encourage trial and purchase

Chapter 6 Distributing and Promoting Products

赠品
premium a gift that a producer offers a customer in return for buying its product

常客激励
frequent-user incentive a program developed to reward customers who engage in repeat (frequent) purchases

购买点展台
point-of-purchase display promotional material placed within a retail store

行业展会
trade show an industry-wide exhibit at which many sellers display their products

购买折让
buying allowance a temporary price reduction to resellers for purchasing specified quantities of a product

合作广告
cooperative advertising an arrangement whereby a manufacturer agrees to pay a certain amount of a retailer's media cost for advertising the manufacturer's products

rental agencies, and coffee shops. Frequent-user incentives foster customer loyalty because the customer is given an additional reason to continue patronizing the company or group of companies. A well-structured program can also generate significant data about customer usage and preferences that companies can use to refine their marketing strategies.

Point-of-Purchase Displays A **point-of-purchase display** is promotional material placed within a retail store. The display is usually located near the product being promoted. It may hold merchandise or information and encouragements to buy the product. Most point-of-purchase displays are prepared and set up by manufacturers and wholesalers.

Trade Shows A **trade show** is an industry-wide exhibit at which many sellers display their products. Many trade shows are organized exclusively for dealers—to permit manufacturers and wholesalers to show their latest lines to retailers. Others are promotions designed to stimulate consumer awareness and interest, such as annual home or bridal shows.

Buying Allowances A **buying allowance** is a temporary price reduction to resellers for purchasing specified quantities of a product. A laundry detergent manufacturer might give retailers $1 for each case of detergent purchased. A buying allowance is an incentive to resellers to handle new products and may stimulate purchase of items in large quantities. A shortcoming of buying allowances is that competitors can counter quickly with their own buying allowances.

Cooperative Advertising **Cooperative advertising** is an arrangement whereby a manufacturer agrees to pay a certain amount of a retailer's media cost for advertising the manufacturer's products. To be reimbursed, a retailer must show proof that the advertisements did appear. Not all retailers take advantage of available cooperative advertising offers, either because they cannot afford to advertise or choose not to.

促销方式的选择
6-10c Selection of Sales Promotion Methods

Several factors affect a marketer's choice of sales promotion methods, including:

1. The objectives of the promotional effort;
2. Product characteristics—size, weight, cost, durability, uses, features, and hazards;
3. Target-market profiles—age, gender, income, location, density, usage rate, and buying patterns;
4. Distribution channels and availability of appropriate resellers; and
5. The competitive and regulatory forces in the environment.

公共关系
6-11 Public Relations

✓ Concept Check

▶ Why do marketers use sales promotion?

▶ What are the two classifications of sales promotion methods?

▶ What factors affect the choice of sales promotion used?

Learning Objective
6-11 Describe the types and uses of public relations.

As noted earlier, public relations is a broad set of communication activities used to create and maintain favorable relationships between an organization and various public groups, both internal and external. These groups may include customers, employees, stockholders, suppliers, educators, the media, government officials, and society in general.

公共关系工具的类型
6-11a Types of Public Relations Tools

Organizations use a variety of public relations tools to convey messages and to create images. Public relations professionals prepare written materials such as brochures,

Entrepreneurial Success

创业成功：BODEN 是一家屡获殊荣的拉美裔所有的公关公司

Inside BODEN, an Award-Winning, Latina-Owned PR Company

BODEN is an independent communications agency in Miami, Florida, which was founded by Honduran native Natalie Boden. Boden has received numerous accolades for her agency's successes, including being inducted into PRWeek's "Hall of Femme." She also serves on the board of directors for the Culture Marketing Council.

Boden started with a single client, the Miami Parking Authority. After building a small set of retainer clients (clients who pay a fee in advance for services over an extended period of time), Boden hired her first employee. Not long after, the agency landed its first Fortune 500 clients, Target and McDonald's. The company has been recognized by the Hispanic Public Relations Association as "PR Agency of the Year" and by PR News as being one of the "Best Places to Work."

Boden says that her public relations agency's competitive advantage is its independence. BODEN can offer the creativity and quick turnaround of a boutique agency while upholding the standards of a global agency. The agency, which includes communicators, strategists, creatives, and digital and social experts, focuses on building trust with multicultural and Hispanic communities. Rather than turning to paid media (i.e., advertising), BODEN's approach centers around earned media (i.e., public relations). The PR agency has built relationships with influencers, organizations, community leaders, and the media to generate publicity.

Boden discourages her clients from using clichéd tactics such as hiring Hispanic celebrities or developing a Spanish advertisement. To stand out to Hispanic audiences, BODEN's mission is to "help global brands lead with culture." This means standing out with bold, culturally strategic communications that are both authentic and inspiring. The agency stands behind long-term, purpose-driven strategies that will leave a legacy.

Sources: Based on information in Court Stroud, "How One Latina Entrepreneur Founded an Award-Winning, Female-Led PR Company," *Forbes*, April 29, 2020; Steve Barrett, "Cafecito Break with Boden PR's Natalie Boden," *PR Week*, October 14, 2020; BODEN, "About Us".

---

newsletters, company magazines, annual reports, and news releases. They also create corporate-identity materials such as logos, business cards, signs, and stationery. Speeches, YouTube videos, and social media accounts at TikTok, Twitter, Instagram, and Facebook are additional public-relations tools through which companies can communicate information and ideas, interact with customers and other brands, or respond to negative information about the firm. Consider the San Diego Zoo, which has nearly 2 million followers on TikTok and uses the platform to post humorous animal videos that keep the nonprofit organization on the public's mind.[22]

Another public relations tool is event sponsorship, in which a company pays for all or part of a special event such as a concert, sports competition, festival, or play. Sponsoring special events is an effective way for organizations to increase brand recognition and receive media coverage, sometimes with relatively little investment. The energy drink brand Red Bull, for example, underscores its reputation for giving consumers energy through sponsoring athletes and teams, acts of daring, concerts, and festivals such as Coachella.

Publicity is an important part of public relations, as it increases public awareness of a firm or brand through mass media communications at no cost to the business. **Publicity** is communication in news-story form about an organization, its products, or both. Organizations use publicity to provide information about products; to

Event sponsorships are intended to promote a positive image of a firm. Event sponsorships are a public relations tool. They are often used in conjunction with advertising, personal selling, and sales promotions.

宣传

publicity communication in news-story form about an organization, its products, or both

Chapter 6 Distributing and Promoting Products

新闻稿
news release a typed page of about 300 words provided by an organization to the media as a form of publicity

专题文章
feature article a piece (of up to 3,000 words) prepared by an organization for inclusion in a particular publication

带说明的照片
captioned photograph a picture accompanied by a brief explanation

新闻发布会
press conference a meeting at which invited media personnel hear important news announcements and receive supplementary textual materials and photographs

announce new product launches, expansions, or research; and to strengthen the company's image. Public relations personnel sometimes organize events, such as grand openings with prizes and celebrities, to generate news coverage of a company.

The most widely used tool of publicity is the **news release**. It is generally one typed page of about 300 words provided by an organization to the media as a form of publicity. The release includes the firm's name, address, phone number, and contact person. A **feature article**, which may run as long as 3,000 words, is usually written for inclusion in a particular publication. For example, a software firm might send an article about its new product to a computer magazine. A **captioned photograph**, a picture accompanied by a brief explanation, is an effective way to illustrate a new or improved product. A **press conference** allows invited media personnel to hear important news announcements and to receive supplementary materials and photographs. Finally, letters to the editor, special newspaper or magazine editorials, and videos may be prepared and distributed to appropriate media for possible use in news stories.

公共关系的运用
6-11b Uses of Public Relations

Public relations can be used to promote many things, including people, places, activities, and ideas. Public relations focuses on enhancing the reputation of the total organization by increasing public awareness of a company's products, brands, or activities and by fostering desirable company images, such as that of innovativeness, dependability, or social responsibility. By getting the media to report on a firm's accomplishments, public relations helps a company to maintain public visibility. Effective management of public relations efforts also can reduce the amount of unfavorable coverage surrounding negative events. For example, after KFC UK suffered negative publicity when it was unable to receive chicken supplies due to a delivery snafu, the company launched a mischievous campaign that included full-page ads and irreverent tweets to apologize and update British customers in a humorous way on when restaurants would resume normal operations.[23]

✓ Concept Check

- What are the common tools of public relations?
- What is publicity, and why do organizations use it?
- What are the four common types of publicity?

Summary 小 结

6-1 Examine the various distribution channels and market coverage of products.

A marketing channel is a sequence of marketing organizations that directs a product from producer to ultimate user. The marketing channel for a particular product is concerned with the transfer of ownership of that product.

The channels used for consumer products include the direct channel from producer to consumer, the channel from producer to retailer to consumer, the channel from producer to wholesaler to retailer to consumer, and the channel from producer to agent to wholesaler to retailer to consumer. There are two major channels of industrial products: producer to user and producer to agent middleman to user. Firms often use multichannel distribution that includes more than one channel. Products may also be distributed digitally via the internet.

Channels and intermediaries are chosen to implement a given level of market coverage. Intensive distribution is the use of all available outlets for a product, providing the widest market coverage. Selective distribution uses a portion of the available outlets in an area. Exclusive distribution uses only a single retail outlet for a product in a large geographic area.

6-2 Explain how supply chain management facilitates partnering among channel members.

Supply chain management refers to the coordination of all marketing channel activities associated with the flow and transformation of supplies, products, and information throughout the supply chain to the ultimate consumer. Cooperation is required among all channel members, including manufacturing, research, sales, advertising, and shipping. When all channel partners work together, delivery, scheduling, packaging, and other customer requirements are better met. Technology makes supply chain management easier to implement.

6-3 Describe the types of wholesalers and the services they provide.

Wholesalers—intermediaries that purchase from producers or other intermediaries and sell to industrial users, retailers, or other wholesalers—increase distribution efficiency. They perform many functions in a distribution channel. If they are eliminated, other channel members—such as the producer or retailers—will have to perform these functions. Wholesalers help retailers with promoting products, collecting information, and financing. They

Marketing

help manufacturers with sales assistance, reduce their inventory costs, furnish market information, and extend credit to retailers.

Wholesalers may be classified as merchant wholesalers, agents, or brokers, depending in part on whether they take title to merchandise. Merchant wholesalers buy and then sell products to other intermediaries. Agents and brokers expedite exchanges, represent a buyer or a seller, and may be hired permanently (agents) or temporarily (brokers) on a commission basis. Sales branches and offices are owned by the manufacturers and resemble merchant wholesalers and agents, respectively.

6-4 Distinguish among the major types of retailers and shopping centers.

Retailers are intermediaries that buy from producers or wholesalers and sell to consumers. Online retailing makes products available to buyers through computer or mobile connections. Multichannel retailing, which uses multiple types of retailing, is growing rapidly. In-store retailers include department stores, discount stores, warehouse showrooms, convenience stores, supermarkets, superstores, warehouse clubs, traditional specialty stores, off-price retailers, and category killers. Shopping centers can be classified into lifestyle, neighborhood, community, and regional, depending on their mix of stores and geographic area served. Nonstore retailers use direct selling, direct marketing, and vending. Types of direct marketing include online retailing, catalog marketing, direct-response marketing, telemarketing, and television home shopping.

6-5 Identify the five most important logistics activities.

Logistics, or physical distribution, consists of activities designed to move products from producers to ultimate users. Its five major functions are inventory management, order processing, warehousing, materials handling, and transportation. These interrelated functions are integrated into marketing efforts.

6-6 Define integrated marketing communications.

Integrated marketing communications is the coordination of promotion efforts to achieve maximum informational and persuasive impact on customers.

6-7 List the basic elements of the promotion mix.

Promotion is communication about an organization and its products that is intended to inform, persuade, or remind target market members. A promotion mix is the particular combination of promotion methods a firm uses to reach a target market—advertising, personal selling, sales promotion, and public relations. Organizations can use a push or pull strategy to promote their products.

6-8 Examine advertising, including types of advertising, the advertising campaign, and social and legal considerations.

Advertising is a paid nonpersonal message communicated to a specific audience through a mass medium. Primary-demand advertising promotes the products of an entire industry rather than just a single brand. Selective-demand advertising promotes a particular brand of product. Institutional advertising is image-building advertising for a firm.

An advertising campaign is developed in several stages. A firm first identifies and analyzes its advertising target. The goals of the campaign must be clearly defined. Then the firm develops the advertising platform and determines the size of advertising budget. The next steps are to develop a media plan, to create the advertising message, and to execute the campaign. Finally, promotion managers must evaluate the effectiveness of the advertising efforts before, during, and/or after the campaign. Although a firm can develop its own campaign, many firms employ advertising agencies to do so.

6-9 Explore personal selling, including the types of salespersons, the personal-selling process, and major sales management tasks.

Personal selling is personal communication aimed at informing customers and persuading them to buy a firm's products. It is the most adaptable promotional method because the salesperson can modify the message to fit individual buyers. The major types of salespersons are order getters, order takers, and support personnel. The six steps in the personal-selling process are prospecting, approaching the prospect, making the presentation, answering objections, closing the sale, and following up. Sales managers are involved directly in setting sales force objectives; recruiting, selecting, and training salespersons; compensating and motivating sales personnel; creating sales territories; and evaluating sales performance.

6-10 Identify sales promotion objectives and methods.

Sales promotion is the use of activities and materials as direct inducements to customers and salespersons. Sales promotions for consumers and business customers enhance and supplement other promotional methods. Methods of sales promotion include rebates, coupons, samples, premiums, frequent-user incentives, point-of-purchase displays, trade shows, buying allowances, and cooperative advertising.

6-11 Describe the types and uses of public relations.

Public relations is a broad set of communication activities used to create and maintain favorable relationships between an organization and various public groups, both internal and external. Organizations use a variety of public relations tools to convey messages and create images. Brochures, newsletters, company magazines, and annual reports are written public relations tools. Speeches, event sponsorship, and publicity are other public relations tools. Publicity is communication in news-story form about an organization, its products, or both. Types of publicity include news releases, feature articles, captioned photographs, and press conferences. Public relations can also be used to promote people, places, activities, and ideas. It can be used to enhance the reputation of an organization and reduce the unfavorable effects of negative events.

Key Terms 关键术语

You should now be able to define and give an example relevant to each of the following terms:

- distribution channel (or marketing channel)
- middleman (or marketing intermediary)
- retailer
- wholesaler
- multichannel (or omnichannel) distribution
- digital distribution
- intensive distribution
- selective distribution
- exclusive distribution
- supply chain management
- merchant wholesaler
- full-service wholesaler
- general-merchandise wholesaler
- limited-line wholesaler
- specialty wholesaler
- agent
- broker
- online retailing
- multichannel retailing
- independent retailer
- chain retailer
- department store
- discount store
- warehouse showroom
- convenience store
- supermarket
- superstore
- warehouse club
- traditional specialty store
- off-price retailer
- category killer
- lifestyle shopping center
- neighborhood shopping center
- community shopping center
- regional shopping center
- nonstore retailing
- direct selling
- direct marketing
- catalog marketing
- direct-response marketing
- telemarketing
- television home shopping
- vending
- logistics
- inventory management
- order processing
- warehousing
- materials handling
- transportation
- carrier
- integrated marketing communications
- promotion
- promotion mix
- advertising
- personal selling
- sales promotion
- public relations
- primary-demand advertising
- selective-demand (or brand) advertising
- institutional advertising
- advertising agency
- order getter
- creative selling
- order taker
- sales support personnel
- missionary salesperson
- trade salesperson
- technical salesperson
- consumer sales promotion method
- trade sales promotion method
- rebate
- coupon
- sample
- premium
- frequent-user incentive
- point-of-purchase display
- trade show
- buying allowance
- cooperative advertising
- publicity
- news release
- feature article
- captioned photograph
- press conference

Discussion Questions 讨论题

1. What are the most common marketing channels for consumer products? For industrial products?
2. What are the levels of market coverage? What types of products are each used for?
3. What services are performed by wholesalers for producers and for retailers?
4. Identify three kinds of full-service wholesalers. What factors are used to classify wholesalers into one of these categories?
5. Differentiate among the types of retailers.
6. What can nonstore retailers offer their customers that in-store retailers cannot?
7. What is logistics? Which major functions does it include?
8. Can a middleman be eliminated from a marketing channel? Explain.
9. What is integrated marketing communications, and why is it becoming increasingly accepted?
10. Identify and describe the major ingredients of a promotion mix.
11. Identify and give examples of the three major types of salespersons.
12. What are the major tasks involved in managing a sales force?
13. What is the difference between publicity and public relations? What is the purpose of each?
14. Why do firms use event sponsorship?

Case 6 案例 6：在箱子里思考的 Casper

Casper Thinks Inside the Box

Known for its "bed-in-a-box" concept, Casper Sleep Inc. was created in 2014 with the simple idea of selling a mattress online. The company's goal was to create an affordable foam mattress that could be shipped in a box.

The direct-to-consumer (D2C) mattress company wanted to bypass traditional mattress showrooms and deliver mattresses direct to its customer's doors.

Investors initially turned their nose up at Casper's concept. They thought no one would ever purchase a mattress online and didn't see a path for Casper to disrupt the $14 billion mattress market. The founders charged tens of thousands of dollars to their credit cards to bring the brand to life. Eventually, they caught the eye of an investor who had experience with other D2C brands. When Casper launched, it sold out of inventory on day one. The company expected to make $1.8 million in its first year, but it ended up hitting that goal within two months. The online mattress market is now crowded with competitors such as Leesa, Purple, and Tuft & Needle.

Excitement around the brand ramped up quickly, attracting the attention of celebrity investors such as actor Ashton Kutcher and rapper Nas. Casper became known for its quirky advertising, such as puzzles on subway ads, but its social media mentions, both paid and organic, became the company's bread and butter. Happy customers were excited to spread the word about Casper online. Casper implemented a referral program to capitalize on this word-of-mouth communication. The program took off, leading to a wave of unboxing videos on YouTube.

The popular mattress brand has run into its fair share of challenges. The company was initially considered a "unicorn" leading up to its initial public offering (IPO), meaning the privately held company was valued at more than $1 billion. This made Casper seem like a good investment, but things took a turn when Casper reduced its IPO price from $17 to $12. Shortly after the IPO, investors filed a lawsuit against the company for allegedly misleading them and not disclosing material information prior to the IPO. While Casper's revenue was up, so were losses. Additionally, the company spent more than $400 million in less than three years on marketing alone to maintain its edge over the competition. The bigger issue was that Casper was worth much less than $1 billion.

Some say Casper intentionally mislead investors, reporting steadily increasing profits when the reality was more dismal. Additionally, although Casper's registration statement detailed growth efforts with the introduction of retail stores in 20 countries, the company stated shortly after the IPO that it would reduce the size of its global operations and wind-down its European operations. This led to a reduction of its workforce by 21 percent. Lastly, Casper also failed to disclose that it was unloading large amounts of old inventory to customers at steep discounts.

Despite these challenges, the CEO and co-founder of Casper, Philip Krim, continues to be enthusiastic about the company's future. Krim says that by opening more stores and initiating more retail partnerships, the company could spend less on sales and marketing.[24]

Questions

1. How does Casper's distribution strategy differ from traditional mattress companies?
2. Casper disrupted the mattress industry. Why do you think investors were initially hesitant to back Casper?
3. Describe Casper's promotion mix.

Building Skills for Career Success　为成功的职业生涯培养技能

1. Social Media Exercise

Social media allows brands to share their personalities and culture as well as their products with others. Some brands are more successful than others at this. Wendy's has gained a reputation on Twitter for not only promoting its products and interacting with its followers but also savagely roasting its competitors, especially McDonald's. It has also poked fun at other brands on #NationalRoastDay. The fast-food giant has established a presence on other social media platforms, including Animal Crossing, via Twitch. Find Wendy's Twitter page or search for the company in your favorite social media platform.

1. Do you think that social media buzz is an effective way to promote a product? Why or why not?
2. Have you ever interacted with a brand's social media campaign like Wendy's roasts of its competitors? If so, how did your interaction influence your feelings about the brand?

2. Building Team Skills

Surveys are a common tool in marketing research. The information they provide can reduce business risk and facilitate decision making. Retail outlets often survey their customers' wants and needs by distributing comment cards or questionnaires.

The following is an example of a customer survey that a local photography shop might distribute to its customers.

Assignment

1. Working in teams of three to five, choose a local retailer.
2. Classify the retailer according to the major types.
3. Design a survey to help the retailer improve customer service. (You may find it beneficial to work with the retailer and actually administer the survey to customers. Prepare a report of the survey results.)
4. Present your findings to the class.

Customer Survey

To help us to serve you better, please take a few minutes to answer the following questions. Your opinions are important to us.

1. Do you live/work in the area? (Circle one or both if they apply.)
2. Why did you choose us? (Circle all that apply.)

    Close to home Quality

    Close to work Full-service photography shop

    Convenience Other

    Good service

3. How did you learn about us? (Circle one.)

    Newspaper

    Flyer/coupon

    Passing by

    Recommended by someone

    Other

4. How frequently do you have photos printed? (Please estimate.)

    ___ Times per month

    ___ Times per year

5. Which aspects of our photography shop do you think need improvement?
6. Our operating hours are from 8:00 a.m. to 7:00 p.m. weekdays and from 9:30 a.m. to 6:00 p.m. Saturdays. We are closed on Sundays and legal holidays. If changes in our operating hours would serve you better, please specify your preferences.
7. Age (Circle one.)

    Under 25

    25–39

    40–60

    Over 60

    Comments:

3. Researching Different Careers

When you are looking for a job, the people closest to you can be a great resource. Family members and friends may be able to answer your questions directly or put you in touch with someone else who can. This type of "networking" can lead to an "informational interview," in which you meet with someone who will answer your questions about a career or a company and who can provide inside information on related fields and other helpful hints.

Assignment

1. Choose a retailer or wholesaler and identify a position within the company that interests you.
2. Call the company and ask to speak to the person in that particular position. Explain that you are a college student interested in the position and ask to set up an informational interview.
3. Prepare a list of questions to ask in the interview. The questions should focus on:

    a. The training and experience recommended for the position

    b. How the person entered the position and advanced within the organization

    c. What the person likes and dislikes about the work

    d. Present your findings to the class

Running a Business 经营企业

Graeter's 是 "冰淇淋的代名词"
Graeter's Is "Synonymous with Ice Cream"

When a 150-year-old company finally redesigns its logo and launches its first national ad campaign, that's big news. Graeter's, the beloved Cincinnati-based maker of premium, hand-packed ice cream, is still managed by direct descendants of its founders. Its new logo is just one part of a major rebranding effort to support the company's first big planned expansion. "If we don't continue to improve and innovate, somebody will come and do it better than us," says Chip Graeter, the company's vice president of retail stores. "And we don't want that to happen."

Quality Builds the Brand

Graeter's considers as its competitors not only the Häagen-Dazs and Ben & Jerry's brands, national premium ice-cream brands that have much bigger marketing budgets, but also all kinds of premium-quality desserts and edible treats. Taking that wide-angle view means its competition is both broad and fierce. One thing the company is firm about, however, is maintaining the quality of its dense, creamy product (it's so dense that one pint of Graeter's ice cream weighs about a pound). Graeter's quality standards call for adhering to its simple, original family recipe—which now includes more all-natural ingredients, like beet juice instead of food dye and dairy products from hormone-free cows—and an original, artisanal production process that yields only about two gallons per machine every 20 minutes. "We were always all-natural," says CEO Richard Graeter II, "but now we're being militant about it."

That hard-earned premium quality is what built the Graeter's brand from its earliest days when refrigeration was unknown and ice cream was a true novelty. Today, "Graeter's in Cincinnati is synonymous with ice cream," says a company executive. "People will say, 'Let's go get a Graeter's.' They don't say, 'Let's go get an ice cream.'" Quality is also what the current management team hopes will propel Graeter's beyond its current market, which consists of 55 company-owned retail stores in Ohio, Missouri, Kentucky, and nearby states, and the freezer cases of about 6,000 supermarkets and grocery stores, particularly the Kroger chain. Graeter's is also on the menu in some fine restaurants and country clubs. The company operates an online store and will ship ice cream overnight via UPS to any of the 48 continental states (California is its biggest shipping market). Graeter's also sells a limited line of candies, cakes, and other bakery goods, and its ice-cream line includes smoothies and sorbets.

Expanding to New Markets

Graeter's ambitious expansion plans are backed by a recent increase in production capacity from one factory to three (one of the new factories was built, and the other purchased). The plans call for distributing Graeter's delectable, seasonal flavors to even more supermarkets and grocery stores, and for gradually opening new retail stores, perhaps as far away as Los Angeles and New York. The Kroger chain is Graeter's biggest distribution partner. Of the tens of thousands of brands Kroger carries, says the chain, pricey Graeter's commands the strongest brand loyalty. It was through Kroger, in fact, that Graeter's managers hit upon the idea of conducting a trial expansion to Denver, a new market for the brand.

Kroger owns the King Soopers chain of grocery stores in Denver, and research showed that more Denver ice-cream buyers choose premium brands than cheaper choices, suggesting that Graeter's might do well there. So Graeter's chose 12 flavors to send to 30 King Soopers stores in Denver as a test market, with the goal of selling two or three gallons a week. The test was an unqualified success. Within a few weeks, the company was selling an average of five gallons a week per store.

"I'd like to be coast to coast," admits Graeter's CEO. In fact, the management team would like to explore selling Graeter's in Canada, perhaps within the next five years. "The challenge, of course, is to preserve the integrity of the product as we grow. But we have done that for more than 100 years, and I'd argue that it's better now than ever."

Promoting the Brand

Graeter's had already gotten a big free boost from a positive mention on the *Oprah Winfrey Show*, when the influential talk-show host called it the best ice cream she had ever tasted. "We were shipping about 40 orders a day," says CEO Richard Graeter II. "After her show, the next day we probably shipped 400." National attention continues with occasional exposure on the Food Network, the Travel Channel, and even the History Channel. "How does that happen?" asks one of the firm's executives. "It happens because we have a product and a process and a growth that is exciting."

Still, says George Denman, the company's vice president of sales and marketing, Graeter's faces the same challenge in new markets as any "small, regional niche player" and one with a limited marketing budget: "establishing a relationship with the consumer, building brand awareness [through] trial and repeat. . . . So obviously when we roll into a marketplace one of the first things we do is we sample the product. We get it out in front of the consumer and get them to taste it, because the product sells itself." The company has also been reducing its price to distributors, who pass the savings along to stores that can then advertise that Graeter's pints are on sale. "If a consumer has maybe been buying Ben & Jerry's and never considered ours, because maybe that dollar price point difference was too high, this gives her the opportunity to try us. And once she tries us, we know we've brand-switched that consumer right then," says Denman.

Marketing Communications

Through its Cincinnati-based ad agency, Graeter's does some local advertising, including attractive point-of-sale displays in supermarkets and grocery stores and some radio ads, occasional print ads, and billboards. The company launches small-scale promotions for the introduction of a new flavor or to celebrate National Ice Cream Month or other occasions. To support the brand's nationwide presence in grocery stores, the company began airing commercials nationally for the first time in 2014. The company has also received good publicity from its strategic partnerships with The Cure Starts Now Foundation and the Cincinnati Zoo. After the zoo had a baby hippo born premature, Graeter's introduced a new flavor called Chunky Hunky Hippo, with part of the revenue from the flavor going to help support the zoo and baby Fiona the hippo.

However, brand loyalty for this family business has grown mostly through word of mouth that endures across generations. "We are the beneficiary of that loyalty that our customers have built up over so many years, multiple generations," says one of the company's executives. "Our customers have told us they were introduced to the product through their grandmother, or a special time. . . . They don't come to our stores because they have to; they come because they want to."

"We use the traditional [marketing] methods," says Denman. "We are also doing nontraditional methods. We are looking at electronic couponing, where consumers will be able to go to our website as a new consumer . . . and secure a dollar-off coupon to try Graeter's, just for coming to our website or joining up on Facebook. We've done loyalty programs with Kroger where they have actually direct-mailed loyal consumers and offered . . . discounts as well. . . . So far it's worked well for us. We've had to go back and look at the return on investment on each of these programs and cut some things out and improve on some other things, but in the end we have been very pleased with the results."

"Quality . . . We Never Changed"

"We ship our product, and that was something that for the first hundred years you never thought about. I mean, who would think about shipping ice cream from Cincinnati to California? But it is our number-one market for shipping, so all those things you can change," says Richard Graeter, the CEO. "The most important thing, the quality of the product and how we make it, that we never changed."[25]

Questions

1. What are the elements of Graeter's marketing mix? Which are most likely to be affected by external forces in the marketing environment?
2. Graeter's ice-cream line includes smoothies and sorbets. Do you think it should consider other brand extensions such as yogurt, low-fat ice cream, coffee drinks, or other related products? Why or why not?
3. How might Graeter's capitalize on its valuable capacity for word-of-mouth promotion in expanding to new markets where, despite some national publicity from Oprah Winfrey, its name is still not widely known?

Building a Business Plan 制订商业计划

This part is one of the most important components of your business plan. In this part, you will present the facts that you have gathered on the size and nature of your market(s). State market size in dollars and units. How many units and what is the dollar value of the products you expect to sell in a given time period? Indicate your primary and secondary sources of data and the methods you used to estimate total market size and your market share. This book covers all marketing-related topics. These chapters should help you answer the questions in this part of the business plan.

The Marketing Plan Component

The marketing plan component is and should be unique to your business. Many assumptions or projections used in the analysis may turn out differently; therefore, this component should be flexible enough to be adjusted as needed.

The marketing plan should include answers to at least the following questions:

1.1. What are your target markets, and what common identifiable need(s) can you satisfy?

1.2. What are the competitive, legal, political, economic, technological, and sociocultural factors affecting your marketing efforts?

1.3. What are the current needs of each target market? Describe the target market in terms of demographic, geographic, psychographic, and product-usage characteristics. What changes in the target market are anticipated?

1.4. What advantages and disadvantages do you have in meeting the target market's needs?

1.5. How will your product distribution, promotion, and price satisfy customer needs?

1.6. How effectively will your products meet these needs?

1.7. What are the relevant aspects of consumer behavior and product use?

1.8. What are your company's projected sales volume, market share, and profitability?

1.9. What are your marketing objectives? Include the following in your marketing objectives:
- Product introduction, improvement, or innovation
- Sales or market share
- Profitability
- Pricing
- Distribution
- Advertising

Make sure that your marketing objectives are clearly written, measurable, and consistent with your overall marketing strategy.

1.10. How will the results of your marketing plan be measured and evaluated?

Review of Business Plan Activities

Remember that even though it will be time-consuming, developing a clear, well-written marketing plan is important. Therefore, make sure that you have checked the plan for any weaknesses or problems. Also, make certain that all your answers to the questions in this and other parts are consistent throughout the business plan. Finally, write a brief statement that summarizes all the information for this part of the business plan.

Chapter 7

Exploring Social Media and e-Business

探索社交媒体和电子商业

Learning Objectives

Once you complete this chapter, you will be able to:

7-1 Examine why it is important for a business to use social media.

7-2 Discuss how businesses use social media tools.

7-3 Explain the business objectives for using social media.

7-4 Describe how businesses develop a social media plan.

7-5 Explain the meaning of e-business.

7-6 Define the fundamental models of e-business.

7-7 Identify the factors that will affect the future of the internet, social media, and e-business.

Why Should You Care?

Question: How important are social media and e-business for a business today? Answer: Today, more and more businesses are using social media and e-business to reach new customers and increase sales and profits.

Inside Business

商业透视：Netflix 在客户保留率方面领先于竞争对手

Netflix Tops the Competition in Customer Retention

Netflix, the world's largest subscription-based streaming service, is deep in the trenches of the streaming war. Although it may have been the first successful entertainment company to stream programming, Netflix's advantage is quickly fading because of new competitors, including Amazon Prime Video, Hulu, Disney+, HBO Max, Apple TV+, and Peacock. In order to maintain its standing as the largest streaming service, Netflix must continue to build its content library, provide exceptional customer service, create original programming, retain existing customers, and add new subscribers to stay ahead of competitors.

While Netflix faces stiff competition, one measurement—churn rate—indicates that Netflix is likely to remain the leader in streaming services. Churn rate refers to the percentage of subscribers who do not renew their subscriptions during a given time frame. As competition heats up, one would expect Netflix's churn rate to increase because subscribers have more choices, but that hasn't been the case. The company's churn rate is between 2 and 3 percent, which is below the same measurement for all of its rivals. Competitors like HBO and Showtime often see a temporary increase in subscribers because viewers want to watch a new series that has been heavily marketed to build subscriber interest. Once subscribers see the series finale, streaming companies often experience a churn rate spike because they don't have additional content subscribers want. On the other hand, Netflix is able to retain customers because of its extensive content library that enables subscribers to always find something interesting that they want to watch.

Netflix also adds value to its service through personalization, an area where other streaming competitors lag behind. By considering the viewer's previous content choices and investing in search site algorithms, text analytics, and filtering to power its search function, Netflix is able to improve the subscriber's browsing experience and help viewers choose the content they will enjoy.

Is Netflix winning the war for subscribers? With 200 million subscribers worldwide and year-over-year subscriber growth rates in the double digits, it is beating the competition—for now. Still, Netflix knows the war is far from over. To maintain its number one position, Netflix knows it must retain existing customers and find ways to reach new customers. It must also continue to innovate and to build on the business and marketing practices that enabled it to become the leader in the subscription-based streaming service market.[1]

Did You Know?

Netflix has more than 200 million subscribers.

Take a moment to think about how social media and e-business affect your own life. In just a few short years, it has changed the way we communicate with each other, it has changed the way we meet people, and it has changed the way we shop. It has also changed the way we watch television. Netflix, the company profiled in the Inside Business feature for this chapter, is the leader in subscription streaming services. And yet, Netflix has big-name competitors that want a share of this market. The fact there are so many companies competing for a share of a large global market is evidence of how important streaming services (and e-business) have become. In this chapter, we explore how these trends affect both individuals and businesses.

We begin this chapter by examining why social media is important for both individuals and business firms. Next, we discuss how companies can use social media to build relationships with customers, the objectives for social media, the steps to build a social media plan, and ways to measure the effectiveness of a firm's social media activities. In the last part of this chapter, we take a close look at how firms use e-business and technology to conduct business using computers and the internet and what growth opportunities and challenges affect both social media and e-businesses.

为什么社交媒体很重要

7-1 Why Is Social Media Important?

Next time you go to lunch at your favorite restaurant or go to a ball game or the shopping mall, take a look at the number of people using their smartphones or even a tablet *and* social media to communicate with friends and relatives. In fact, if you are under the age of 40, you know exactly what social media is because you have grown up with computers and technology and are comfortable sharing information about yourself. If you are anyone else, social media seems like a strange (but exciting) phenomenon where millions of people freely share, create, vote, and connect with other people effortlessly using internet-based technologies.

Learning Objective

7-1 Examine why it is important for a business to use social media.

什么是社交媒体，它有多受欢迎

7-1a What Is Social Media and How Popular Is It?

Today, there are many definitions of social media because it is still developing and continually changing. For our purposes, **social media** represents the online interactions that allow people and businesses to communicate and share ideas, personal information, and information about products and services. Simply put, social media is about people. It is about a culture of participation, meaning that people can now discuss, vote, create, connect, and advocate much easier than ever before. For example, you can post your plans for a weekend trip on Facebook. Then you can share a travel itinerary and chronicle your trip through videos, photos, and ratings on Facebook, Snapchat, Pinterest, Twitter, and other social media sites. While it's hard to imagine, many popular social media sites like Facebook and Google were only created in the past 25 years (refer to Figure 7-1). Because early social media sites were so successful, more sites were developed. For example, TikTok was launched in 2016 and had more than 675 million monthly users at the beginning of 2021.

So, how popular are social media sites? A recent Pew Internet Research study found that 70 percent of Facebook users visit the site each day as part of their daily routine. Other sites including Instagram (59 percent), Snapchat (59 percent), YouTube (54 percent), and Twitter (46 percent) also have a large percentage of users that visit each site every day.[2] Among the most popular worldwide social media sites are Facebook, which has approximately 2.7 billion users, YouTube, which has more than 2 billion users, and Instagram, which has more than 1 billion users.[3] These numbers increase daily as people log onto social media from home, from work, and from smartphones to stay in touch with family and friends, reconnect with old friends or classmates, share photos and videos, and obtain information available on the internet.

社交媒体
social media the online interactions that allow people and businesses to communicate and share ideas, personal information, and information about products and services

企业为什么要使用社交媒体

7-1b Why Businesses Use Social Media

Social media has completely changed the business environment. Just the sheer number of people using social media makes using social media a top priority for many business firms. Today, a business can use social media to:

- Connect with its customers and stakeholders;
- Provide information that is valuable to customers; and
- Provide another means of customer service.

Now many companies, large and small, are using social media to learn about customers' likes and dislikes, seek public input about products and marketing, and promote specific products. Macy's, for example, is active on Facebook, Twitter, Pinterest, YouTube, and a blog designed

The leader! When it comes to social media, Facebook is the most popular site in the world and has more than 2.7 billion users. For many people, Facebook is the go-to site to keep up with friends and relatives or reconnect with people they haven't talked to in years. Other people just want to see what's happening in someone else's life.

Chapter 7 Exploring Social Media and e-Business

Figure 7-1 Timeline for Many Popular Social Media Sites

Ever wonder when your favorite social media site was created? To answer that question, look at the timeline below.

	SOCIAL MEDIA BREAKTHROUGH
1998	• Google
2003	• LinkedIn
2004	• Facebook, Yelp
2005	• YouTube, Mashable
2006	• Twitter
2007	• Tumblr
2010	• Pinterest, Instagram
2011	• Snapchat, Twitch
2012	• Tinder
2013	• Vine, Telegram
2014	• Periscope
2016	• TikTok
The Future	• Who knows what the next generation of social media will mean for both individuals and business?

Note: Although there have been fewer internet and social media startups since 2016, they are usually small and when successful are often acquired by larger companies—many of the same companies listed in this figure.

to be read on mobile screens. The company uses its Facebook site, for example, to provide fashion tips and news about new products and special events to communicate with its 14.6 million-plus Facebook fans. Often it uses the Twitter hashtag #Macys to highlight special in-store events and announce discounts and clearance sales. A **hashtag** is either a word or a short phrase, preceded by the pound sign (#), to identify different topics. On Pinterest, Macy's lets pictures do the talking with "pinned" images of the latest in beauty products, fashions, bridal registry items, and home decor. Its YouTube channel includes Macy's commercials, coverage of the annual Thanksgiving Day Parade, behind-the-scenes designer interviews, and videos about fashion trends.

The fact that so many people are actively sharing information about themselves and their likes and dislikes online for all to see was a driving force for many companies to develop a social media presence. Unlike social media, traditional marketing and advertising messages were top-down because companies used television, newspapers, and magazine ads to promote their product to a large audience without any opportunity for feedback. With social media, customers can and do provide feedback. If people have bad experiences with a product or service, they tend to let the world know by writing about it on a blog, mentioning it on Facebook, or tweeting about it. A recent survey by Customer Care Measurement and Consulting found that 66 percent of households experienced a problem with a product or service in the last 12 months, and many of the survey respondents used social media to complain. In addition, the survey also discovered that 55 percent of the respondents expect a response to a complaint posted on social media and nearly half of the same respondents got no response. Seventeen percent of customers who experience poor customer service tell their friends and neighbors to raise public awareness of their experience.[4] While companies no longer have much

话题标签
hashtag a word or a short phrase, preceded by the pound sign (#), to identify different topics

Figure 7-2 The Six Most Important Benefits for a Business That Uses Social Media

While there are many reasons a business uses social media, the number one reason is that social media generates increased exposure for a business.

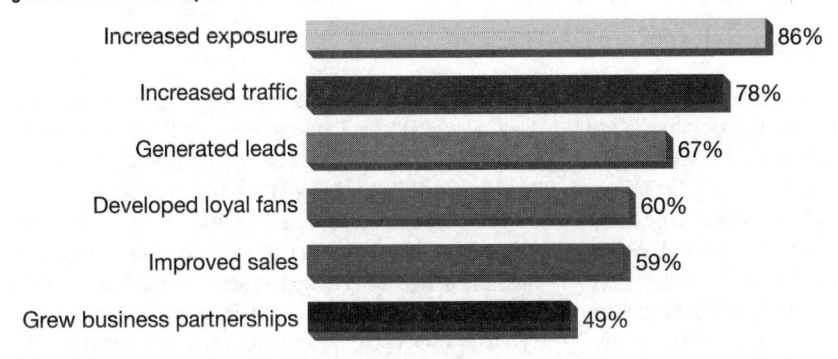

Benefit	Percentage
Increased exposure	86%
Increased traffic	78%
Generated leads	67%
Developed loyal fans	60%
Improved sales	59%
Grew business partnerships	49%

Source: Michael A. Stelzner, "2020 Social Media Marketing Industry Report," The Social Media Examiner.

control over what is said about their products or services, many still respond to negative comments about the company and its products or services made by their customers. Even if the company's response doesn't completely resolve the issue, customers appreciate the company's effort to improve customer service.

In addition to complaints, companies often use social media to respond to questions and positive customer feedback to provide additional information and build customer goodwill. The bottom line: If businesses aren't using social media to see what customers are saying about their products or services, they are missing an opportunity to increase sales and profits. For more information about why businesses use social media (and the benefits for a business), refer to Figure 7-2.

> ✓ **Concept Check**
> - According to material in this section, what are the reasons why people use social media?
> - How has social media changed the environment for business firms?

商用社交媒体工具
7-2 Social Media Tools for Business Use

For a business, part of what makes social media so challenging is the sheer number of ways to interact with other businesses and existing and potential customers. For example, companies can use **social content sites** to create and share information about their products. Commercials, for example, can go viral on social media, especially when linked to major sporting events like the Super Bowl or the World Cup. Jeep, Doritos, and Facebook used social media to generate millions of online views for their Super Bowl commercials both before and after the game.[5] For businesses selling to other businesses, social content sites can also include webinars and online promotional materials. In addition to social content sites, businesses can use blogs, photos, videos, podcasts, and social media ratings to increase customer awareness of their products and services.

> **Learning Objective**
> **7-2** Discuss how businesses use social media tools.

博客的商业用途
7-2a Business Use of Blogs

A **blog** is a website that allows a company to share information to increase customers' knowledge about its products and services, as well as to build trust. Once a story or information is posted, customers can provide feedback through comments, which is one of the most important ways of creating a conversation with customers, not just as existing or potential customers, but as people.

Blogs are effective at developing better relationships with customers, attracting new customers, telling stories about the company's products or services, and providing an active forum for testing new ideas. For example, the Brooklyn-based online crafts marketplace Etsy uses its blogs to communicate with both buyers and

社交内容网站
social content sites websites which allow companies to create and share information about their products and services

博客
blog a website that allows a company to share information to increase the customer's knowledge about its products and services, and to build trust

Chapter 7 Exploring Social Media and e-Business

Exploring Careers

职业探索：HBO Max 实习生玩转抖音

HBO Max Interns Rock TikTok

Social media is an ever-changing landscape, making it challenging for companies to keep up with emerging trends and platforms. To bring in a fresh perspective, HBO Max hired five interns, Ashley Xu, Gray Fagan, Preeti Singh, Conor Driscoll, and Paravi Das, to create TikTok videos to promote the HBO Max subscription video on demand service. While each video was tied to HBO Max and its entertainment content, they were also created to entertain and make viewers laugh and at the same time increase HBO Max's TikTok following. The move paid off. Because of the videos created by the interns, HBO Max's TikTok following increased from 29,000 to more than 728,000 followers at the time of publication of your text.

TikTok is a short-form mobile video platform known for viral memes, dancing, educational content, challenges, and comedic sketches. The key for businesses like HBO Max to succeed on TikTok is to create content that feels in line with the app's culture and target viewers. While there are exceptions, the majority of TikTok viewers are Gen Z (people born after 1997) and Millennials (people born between 1981 and 1996). To reach the target audience, the five interns began by creating a makeup challenge video to promote the HBO Max show *Euphoria*. The video went viral, receiving more than 3 million views. Their first video was topped by another of their videos that got more than 32 million views.

HBO Max's competitive paid internship program is immersive and hands-on. While someone doesn't need a degree in business or marketing to work in social media, a wide variety of skills are valuable in this arena. For example, Fagan was a film production major, Driscoll was a business administration major, and Singh was a public relations and advertising major. The interns pooled their knowledge of public relations, advertising, business, film production, and, of course, social media to produce 60-second TikTok skits to engage users on the platform. Their creativity and ability to tell stories made them an asset to the company. Though their internship was set to end, the students successfully pitched a proposal to HBO Max leadership to extend their stay. And, in typical fashion, the five made a TikTok video to go along with their proposal. End result: Their internship was extended for another three months.

Sources: Based on information in Sarah Whitten, "HBO Max Activations Double to 17.2 Million in Fourth Quarter," *CNBC*, January 27, 2021; Kelsey Sutton, "HBO Max's Secret to Viral TikToks: Letting Their Interns Run the Account," *Adweek*, October 12, 2020; Michelle Anguka, "Savvy Storytelling, TikTok Skills Lead Chapman Film Students to HBO Max Internships," *Chapman University Newsroom*, October 7, 2020.

媒体共享网站
media sharing sites websites which allow users to upload photos, videos, and podcasts

sellers. Its blog posts, some written by artisans and some by Etsy personnel, profile online shops, highlight new fashion trends, teach do-it-yourself craft techniques, and showcase unusual and unique items for sale. Etsy also maintains a "Seller Handbook" blog to help sellers succeed on Etsy.

照片、视频和播客
7-2b Photos, Videos, and Podcasts

In addition to blogs, another tool for social content is **media sharing sites**, which allow users to upload photos, videos, and podcasts. Before creating a media sharing site, managers and employees should consider the following three factors:

- Who will create the photos, videos, and podcasts that will be used?
- How will the content be distributed to interested businesses and consumers?
- How much will it cost to create and distribute the material?

One increasingly popular form of media is photo sharing. Today, photo sharing provides a method for a company to tell a compelling story about its products or services through postings on either the company's website or a social media site. Target, Gap, and many other retailers, for example, post photos of clothing available in their stores or online on their Pinterest sites.

Videos have also gained popularity because of their ability to tell stories. Companies know that YouTube and other sites are useful because they are already recognized by other businesses and consumers as a source of both entertainment and information. For example, entertainment companies, like Disney and MGM, use YouTube to showcase movie trailers. Home Depot and Lowe's have also posted great do-it-yourself videos on their YouTube channels. For example, Martha Stewart has teamed up with Home Depot to create livestream videos that describe how you can create home décor. Other uses of livestream videos include online classes, interviews, and question and answer sessions with a social media influencer. An **influencer** is a person known on social media who has an influence over a large number of followers.

Podcasts are digital audio or video files that people listen to or watch online on tablets, computers, smartphones, or other mobile devices. Think of podcasts as programs that are distributed through various means and not linked to scheduled time periods. The great thing about podcasts is that they are available for download at any time. Shopify—an e-commerce site that provides e-commerce software and other management tools to help business start-ups and existing businesses—uses a series of podcasts to provide entrepreneurs with information that can be used to grow their businesses.

How do you find the best restaurant in town? Answer: Read the ratings social media users post on Yelp. While known for its restaurant reviews, the Yelp site also has ratings for shopping, automotive repairs, home services, and even nightlife. More than 175 million people visit the Yelp website each month to find out what other people think about local businesses.

社交媒体评级
7-2c Social Media Ratings

Social media enables shoppers to access ratings, reviews, opinions, recommendations, and referrals from others who have bought a product or service. Sites for reviews and ratings are based on the idea that consumers trust the opinions of others when it comes to purchasing products and services. According to a recent survey by BrightLocal, a marketing research company with locations in the United States and three other countries, 93 percent of consumers used the internet to find a local business in the last year.[6] Based on the early work of Amazon, eBay, Google, and Yelp, consumers can rate local businesses or compare products and services. In addition, individual businesses that range from retailers like Home Depot and Target to travel services like Priceline and Trip Advisor provide a way for consumers to share information about products and services.

According to consumers, the most important review factors are the overall star rating, if the review seems to be legitimate, if the reviews are current, and the number of reviews.[7] Consumer reviews are especially influential in certain purchase situations. For example, retailers, restaurants, medical services, repair services, and travel are types of businesses where ratings make a difference in consumer buying decisions. Knowing this, Wyndham Hotel Group puts the ratings of consumers who use TripAdvisor directly on its websites so travelers can see what others say about each individual hotel. By examining the reviews, Wyndham can get a good sense of its online reputation and identify specific areas for improvement.[8]

大咖
influencer a person known on social media who has an influence over a large number of followers

播客
podcasts digital audio or video files that people listen to or watch online on tablets, computers, smartphones, or other mobile devices

✓ Concept Check

▶ What is a blog? How can a business use a blog to develop relationships with customers?

▶ What types of content can be used on a media sharing site? What factors should be considered when developing content for a media sharing site?

▶ How important are social media ratings for consumers? For businesses?

Chapter 7   Exploring Social Media and e-Business

通过社交媒体实现商业目标

7-3 Achieving Business Objectives Through Social Media

Learning Objective
7-3 Explain the business objectives for using social media.

Although social media is a recent phenomenon, many businesses are already using it to achieve important objectives. Some of these goals are long term— such as building brand awareness and brand reputation—while others are more short term—such as increasing website traffic or generating sales leads. Regardless of how social media is used, there are a lot of business opportunities. In this section, we explore a few ways that companies have used social media effectively to achieve business objectives.

社交媒体社区
7-3a Social Media Communities

Social media communities are groups of people who share common interests and who want to use technology and the internet to connect with people with similar interests. People who are part of the communities can share information and even develop profiles. Individuals in a community can be called friends, fans, followers, or connections. Popular social networking sites include Facebook (the largest), LinkedIn (for professionals), Twitter, YouTube, Pinterest, and many others. To see how many businesses use the top six social media community sites, refer to Figure 7-3.

There are social communities for every interest, ethnic group, and lifestyle. Different types of social communities include forums and wikis. A **forum** is an interactive version of a community bulletin board that focuses on threaded discussions. These are particularly popular with people who share a common interest such as animal protection, health issues, or the latest movies. One of the most popular internet forums is Reddit, which is a massive collection of forums where people can share news and content and comment on other people's posts. Reddit is further broken down into subreddits, which are forums dedicated to specific topics. For example, there are subreddit communities for gaming, sports, television, travel, health and fitness, fashion, and many others. In reality, there are thousands of subreddits, and the number of subreddits continues to increase as more people with special interests interact on the Reddit site.

Another community based on social media is a wiki. A **wiki** is a collaborative online working space that enables members to contribute content that can be shared with other people. With wikis, members of the community are the editors and gatekeepers ensuring that the content is correct and updated. Wikipedia—the free online encyclopedia—is the best example of a wiki.

社交媒体社区
social media communities groups of people who share common interests and who want to use technology and the internet to connect with people with similar interests

论坛
forum an interactive version of a community bulletin board that focuses on threaded discussions

维基
wiki a collaborative online working space that enables members to contribute content that can be shared with other people

> **Figure 7-3** The Top Six Social Media Networking Sites Used by Businesses

For businesses using social media, the most popular social networking sites are Facebook and Instagram.

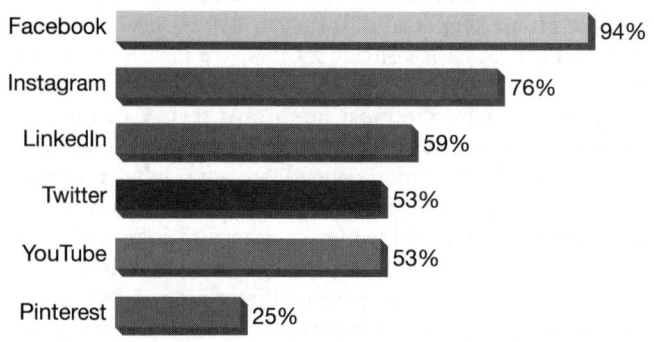

Site	Percentage
Facebook	94%
Instagram	76%
LinkedIn	59%
Twitter	53%
YouTube	53%
Pinterest	25%

Source: Michael A. Stelzner, "2020 Social Media Marketing Industry Report," The Social Media Examiner.

Today, many companies and nonprofit organizations are using social media to build communities to achieve important objectives. For a business, developing social media communities is a way to interact with customers. Coca-Cola uses many different types of social media to build a community for people who want more information about Coca-Cola products and stories about Coke's involvement in the community. Because companies like Coca-Cola recognize the value of this type of social media, the largest companies now have a team of professionals to develop and monitor their social media activities led by a social media community manager. A **social media community manager** is a high-level executive who is responsible for all of a company's social media activities. Nonprofit organizations also use social media to promote and fund their programs. The nonprofit organization Kiva has helped build communities around the globe by matching lenders and struggling would-be entrepreneurs. Using Kiva to identify potential borrowers, anyone who can lend $25 (or more) can loan money to people who need a bit of cash to go into business or keep a business running. To date, there are 1.9 million Kiva lenders that have funded loans of more than $1.6 billion to people in 77 different countries.[9]

危机与声誉管理

7-3b Crisis and Reputation Management

One of the most important reasons for listening to stakeholders is to determine whether there is a crisis brewing. Crises happen more often than most managers, employees, and customers realize. A recent survey by accounting firm PricewaterhouseCoopers (PWC) found that almost 70 percent of corporate managers have experienced a crisis in the last five years.[10] For example, consider the effect of the COVID-19 pandemic on businesses throughout the world. The pandemic quickly made its way to regions including Europe, South America, and North America. Businesses in the United States were especially hit hard when non-essential businesses were in lockdown during spring 2020. Then the virus made a resurgence toward the end of the year. In many cases, social media was used to let customers know if businesses were open and what precautions they were using to keep both customers and employees safe during the pandemic. For example:

- Many businesses, including Home Depot, Lowe's, and Ace Hardware, were open, but strict requirements for masks, social distancing, and reduced operating hours were announced on their social media sites.
- Restaurants including Saltgrass Steakhouses, the Olive Garden, Red Lobster, and other national chains used social media to inform people of their operating hours and if they were open for food pick-up, delivery, or if dine-in was an option at some of their locations.
- Many manufacturers used social media to communicate with their customers—wholesalers, distributors, and retailers—about plant closures, product availability, and expected delivery dates.

Although the previous examples highlight how companies used social media to inform customers, employees, and stakeholders of the steps they were taking to fight a pandemic, often they will use social media to respond to negative reviews about the company's products or services. The following illustrates how Jet Blue Airlines handled a negative Twitter post.[11]

> **Customer** – *My view during all the flight (4 hours). No movies, no TV. First complaint to one of my favorite airlines. [Followed by an image of a blank TV screen]*
> **Jet Blue Response** – *Oh no! That's not what we like to hear! Were all the TVs out on the plane or is it just yours?*
> **Customer** – *Just my TV. The ones I saw next to me, everything was working.*
> **Jet Blue Response** – *We always hate it when that happens. Send us a direct message with your confirmation code to get you a credit for the non-working TV.*

社交媒体社区经理
social media community manager a high-level executive who is responsible for all of a company's social media activities

The Jet Blue Twitter team did a great job responding to this customer's complaint. First, they quickly acknowledged the problem, and then they asked for more information. Finally, they apologized and offered a credit for the non-working TV.

Although most companies spend more time responding to negative reviews, they also respond to positive complements about their product or service. In either case, the goal is to build customer goodwill, increase customer retention, and ultimately increase sales. Even though businesses can't anticipate when and what type of crisis will occur or when they will receive negative reviews, planning should begin before a problem situation develops. Employees should already be trained in social media etiquette and be monitoring social media sites to see what is said about the company and its products. During a crisis, companies can use social media to answer questions with carefully worded posts, reassure the public, and present positive information to help rebuild their reputations.

听取利益相关者的意见
7-3c Listening to Stakeholders

Listening to people, whether they are customers or not, is always an important aspect of a company's social media plan. Indeed, listening is often the first step when developing a social media strategy. By monitoring Facebook, Twitter, or other social media sites, companies can determine what customers think about their products or services. If a company receives negative comments, it's important to respond

Technology and Innovation
技术与创新：大众在愚人节的恶作剧适得其反

VW's April Fools' Day Prank Backfires

While social media is a valuable tool to help brands recover in the wake of a reputational crisis, it can also be a threat to an organization's reputation. If a crisis is handled poorly, social media can amplify damage rather than restoring faith in the brand. Additionally, because of the viral nature of social media, news can quickly spread, putting a company in the global spotlight before a company even has time to respond to negative comments. Consider what happened with an April Fool's Day prank orchestrated by automaker Volkswagen.

April Fool's Day pranks often cause a stir on social media. VW discovered that's not always a good thing. The company leaked a phony press release saying it would change its name to Voltswagen to bring attention to its $86 billion push into the electric vehicle market. The company tweeted, "We know, 66 is an unusual age to change your name, but we've always been young at heart. Introducing Voltswagen. Similar to Volkswagen, but with a renewed focus on electric driving."

Unfortunately, many people, including reporters, did not realize it was a joke because it seemed authentic and was posted days ahead of April Fool's Day. The announcement was shared as a real news story on *USA Today*, *The Associated Press*, the *BBC*, *The Verge*, and dozens of other outlets. Social media users speculated about the press release for days before VW finally declared the announcement was a prank.

"What began as an April Fool's effort got the whole world buzzing," VW tweeted. "Turns out people are as passionate about our heritage as they are about our electric future. So, whether it's Voltswagen or Volkswagen, people talking about electric driving and our ID.4 can only be a good thing." (Note: ID.4 is VW's new electric SUV.) Consumers and the media did not agree, and the stunt was widely slammed.

The automaker, which was at the center of a previous emissions scandal where it lied to the public and regulators in 2015, has worked for years to repair its reputation. The April Fool's misstep dredged up memories of its unethical past. In fact, many media experts believe Volkswagen undermined its own efforts to move on from the emission scandal and eroded the company's trust and credibility.

Sources: Based on information in Aaron Gold, "How Volkswagen's 'Voltswagen' April Fools' Prank Backfired," *Motortrend*, April 5, 2021; Sean O'Kane, "Volkswagen of America Lied about Rebranding to 'Voltswagen'," *The Verge*, March 30, 2021; Volkswagen [@VW], *Twitter*, March 31, 2021; @RationalEtienne, *Twitter*, March 31, 2021.

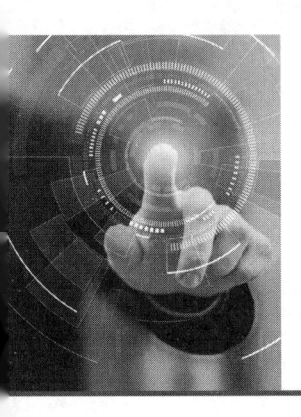

quickly. A personal response either on social media or a personal contact often will help resolve a complaint and at the same time restore customer goodwill. It also helps if the customer feels that the company will take action to correct the problem. For example, many companies encourage customers to complete quick surveys about products or services. Brinker International—parent company of Chili's and Maggiano's restaurants—provides customers with a link to a short survey on the bottom of their receipt. Customers are free to provide both positive and negative comments about their dining experience. Those comments are then used to fine-tune restaurant operations. In some cases, when negative reviews are justified, customers receive a personal note, a phone call, or an email reply that may be accompanied with a gift card to encourage customers to become return customers.

目标客户
7-3d Targeting Customers

Many companies are using social media to increase awareness and build their brand among customers. It is especially valuable to target people based on their age. Common population age groups are often referred to as generations. For example, Generation Z (people born after 1997) is America's largest generation and accounts for 27 percent of the U.S. population.[12] Other generations in the U.S. population include:

- Millennials—people born between 1981 to 1996 and represent 25 percent;
- Generation X—people born between 1965 to 1980 and represent 20 percent;
- Baby Boomers—people born between 1946 to 1964 and represent 21 percent;
- The Silent Generation—people born between 1928 to 1945 and represent 7 percent; and
- The Greatest Generation—people born before 1928 and represent less than 1 percent.

To reach people who are included in each generation, it helps to identify who the customer is and what characteristics make the customer unique. For example, many people in Generation Z are now teenagers and represent younger consumers compared to people in the other generations. People in Generation Z grew up with technology, the internet, and social media. Facebook, Instagram, Snapchat, and YouTube are popular social media sites for people in this age group. In fact, Generation Z is quickly surpassing Millennials as a key target group of customers for retailers and manufacturers. For example, Nike—one of the most well-known brands in the world—recognizes Generation Z as one of the most important groups to reach on social media. In fact, Nike uses Instagram, Facebook, Twitter, YouTube, and Pinterest to reach out to people in each generation.[13] Each of these social media sites is used to promote Nike athletic footwear, clothing, and other items with many posts, photos, and social media activities directed to specific age groups in different generations. As a result of social media and other promotion activities, the Nike swoosh and its marketing phrase "Just Do It" are known throughout the world. And yet, the real story is that the brand isn't using social media to just sell a specific product; Nike is selling the benefits and image of its products that literally become part of a person's lifestyle.[14] For the company, the investment in social media has increased brand awareness, but more importantly increased sales and profits.

社交媒体营销
social media marketing the utilization of software, computer technology, and the internet to provide information about a firm's products and services, increase sales revenues, and improve customer service

面向消费者的社交媒体营销
7-3e Social Media Marketing for Consumers

Social media marketing is the utilization of software, computer technology, and the internet to provide information about a firm's products and services, increase sales revenues, and improve customer service.

As companies become more comfortable with social media, we can expect even more companies to use social media to market products and services to their customers. Already, research indicates that companies are shifting their advertising money from traditional marketing (like television and magazines) to digital marketing (like internet search engines and social media). Experts now predict that companies will shift more marketing dollars to digital marketing over the next few years. And by 2024, some experts expect that spending on digital marketing will account for more than 50 percent of the marketing budget for many firms.[15] The primary reason is simple: People are spending more time on social media sites. Often the first step for a business that wants to use social media is to go to Facebook, Twitter, Snapchat, YouTube, LinkedIn, or some other popular social media site. As you can see from the information in Figure 7-4, companies like Snapchat make using their technology as easy as possible to connect with potential or existing customers.

其他业务的社交媒体营销
7-3f Social Media Marketing for Other Businesses

集客式营销
inbound marketing a marketing term that describes new ways of gaining attention, and ultimately customers, by creating content on a website that pulls customers in

Today, many companies have been quite successful using social media marketing not only to develop customer awareness, but also to obtain sales leads and increase actual sales to other businesses. HubSpot, for example, is a software company that helps companies develop inbound marketing programs. **Inbound marketing** is a marketing term that describes new ways of gaining attention, and ultimately customers, by

▶ **Figure 7-4** Snapchat's Marketing Solutions for Businesses

Like many social media sites, Snap's marketing tools help businesses connect with customers all over the globe. By using Snapchat, Domino's Pizza strengthened its brand awareness and surpassed both the company's and Snapchat's "success" benchmarks after a recent promotional campaign in Norway.

Source: Snapchat, https://forbusiness.snapchat.com/inspiration/dominos-strengthened-their-appeal-through-successful-campaign-on-snapchat, March 24, 2021.

creating content on a website that pulls customers in. Tools used for inbound marketing programs include search engine optimization, emails, blogging, videos, and social media. In order to market its software products, HubSpot shunned traditional advertising and began to practice what it preached. First, the company developed its own inbound marketing program by creating valuable content and marketing information that was then distributed through social media and search engine websites. Companies interested in HubSpot's software were required to enter contact information (name, phone number, and email address) in order to view the information because they believed the company's software could help them improve their marketing activities. As a result of HubSpot's inbound marketing program, the cost of generating new sales leads was reduced, the number of customers increased, and sales increased.

Companies also use social media marketing to sell goods and services, invite customer feedback, and reinforce a positive brand image. For General Electric (GE), social media marketing sets the stage for global sales of turbines, jet engines, and medical devices, among other products. GE is a social media innovator with award-winning videos, striking Instagram and Pinterest photos of its industrial products, followers on Facebook and Twitter, and a popular YouTube channel.

As important as social media marketing is, it is only one aspect of digital marketing. Indeed, digital marketing (sometimes referred to as online marketing) is comprised of several areas and also includes:

- *Search engine optimization*—using keywords in a company's website in order to rank higher in search engine results;
- *Search engine marketing*—buying advertising on sites like Google Ads to increase traffic to a company's website;
- *Display advertising*—buying banner ads; and
- *Email marketing*—targeting customers through opt-in email campaigns.

From an ethical perspective, all company employees should identify themselves during social media interactions with customers and be transparent about their role in digital marketing. For example, Intel, which makes computer chips, is one of many businesses that require disclosure of ties to the company when employees participate in different types of digital marketing.

众包
crowdsourcing outsourcing tasks to a group of people in order to tap into the ideas of the crowd

产生新产品创意
7-3g Generating New Product Ideas

Companies can use social media to conduct much of their consumer-based research. Using insight gained from Facebook or Twitter, for example, allows a company to modify existing products and services and develop new ones. Another method, **crowdsourcing** involves outsourcing tasks to a group of people in order to tap into the ideas of the crowd. In some cases, valuable information can be obtained by crowd voting. Frito-Lay, for example, has used crowd voting to determine which television commercials to advertise its popular Doritos brand. The company has also used crowdsourcing for product development. And in 2020, Frito-Lay used crowdsourcing to honor ordinary people who do extraordinary things to create joy in their communities. Family and friends were able to nominate someone who goes to great lengths to inspire joy. Once the crowd—a national sample of 5,000 adults—chose the winners, Frito-Lay then redesigned its famous potato chip bags to feature the smiles of the winners.[16]

The power of the crowd. LEGO—the Danish toymaker—uses crowdsourcing to generate new product ideas. Here's how it works. Customers can post and vote on ideas at https://ideas.lego.com. Ideas that get at least 10,000 votes are submitted to the company's review board. Then LEGO makes a final selection of promising ideas that begin the production process. For LEGO, the benefits include a new way to generate new product ideas and to build customer loyalty.

✓ Concept Check

- In your own words, describe how social media can help businesses to connect with other businesses and consumers.
- For a business, why are crisis and reputation management, listening to stakeholders, and targeting specific types of customers important activities?
- How can social media be used to market a firm's products or services to consumers and other businesses?
- How can social media help a firm generate new product ideas and recruit employees?

Companies can even build communities for specific brands in order to obtain information and new ideas from consumers. The Danish toymaker LEGO has created an online site called LEGO Ideas (https://ideas.lego.com) where brand enthusiasts can post and vote on new product ideas. LEGO benefits from its customers' creativity and the goodwill generated by seeking the community's input. Just as important, the creators receive credit for their ideas plus a small royalty from product sales.[17]

招聘员工
7-3h Recruiting Employees

For years, companies have used current employees to recruit new employees based on the theory that "birds of a feather flock together." The concept is simple: Current employees' friends and family may prove to be good job candidates. Social media takes that concept to a whole new level. LinkedIn, the largest social network for professionals, has been used quite effectively by large corporations, small businesses, nonprofit organizations, and government agencies that want to recruit new employees. Because LinkedIn hosts more than 750 million registered members, employers using the site can save time, reduce their recruiting costs, and see more information about individual candidates.[18] Companies like 3M, Coca-Cola, Four Seasons Hotels and Resorts, Hewlett Packard, IBM, Microsoft, Procter & Gamble, and many others have all had recruiting success with LinkedIn. Many other social media sites, including Glassdoor, Facebook, Instagram, and YouTube, can also be used for networking and to learn about a company where you might want to work.

制订社交媒体计划
7-4 Developing a Social Media Plan

Learning Objective
7-4 Describe how businesses develop a social media plan.

Before developing a plan to use social media, it is important to determine how social media can improve the organization's overall performance and how it "fits" with a company's objectives and other promotional activities. For example, if a social media plan attempts to improve customer service, it needs to link to the company's other efforts to improve customer service.

制订社交媒体计划的步骤
7-4a Steps to Build a Social Media Plan

Once it is determined how social media links to the company's other activities, there are several steps that should be considered.

Step 1: Listen to Determine Opportunities As pointed out earlier in this chapter, social media is often used to "listen" to what customers like and don't like about a company's products or services. For example, reading comments on social media sites can yield some insight into how consumers are reacting to a price increase for an existing product or service. Monitoring social media sites also allows managers and employees to not only listen but also to enter the conversation and tell the company's side of the story. In addition, companies can monitor social media sites to gather information about competitors as well as what is being said about the industry.

Step 2: Establish Social Media Objectives After listening to customers and analyzing the information obtained from social media sites, it is important to use that information to develop specific objectives. For social media, an objective is a statement about what a social media plan should accomplish. Each objective should be specific, measurable, achievable, realistic, and oriented toward the future. In addition, all objectives need to be linked to specific actions that can be used to accomplish each objective.

For most companies, the most popular objectives are:[19]

- Improving customer service
- Increasing brand awareness

212 Marketing

- Building brand presence
- Acquiring new customers
- Developing loyalty programs

Other objectives that are often important for many firms include introducing new products, improving search engine ranking, and increasing the number of people who visit the company's social media sites.

Step 3: Segment and Target the Social Media Customer Ideally, a company will have developed a customer profile that describes a typical customer in terms of age, income, gender, ethnicity, etc. When segmenting or targeting customers, it also helps to know how they think, how they spend their time, how much they buy, and how often they buy. Additionally, it is important to really understand how customers use social media.

- Do they create content like photos, videos, blog posts, etc.?
- Do they use social media for information, ratings, and reviews?
- Do they spend a lot of time using social media?

More information about potential customers will help you develop a social media plan to achieve a company's objectives. Lack of information about customers can lead to wasted time and money and the inability to successfully achieve the firm's social media objectives. For example, most companies feel that they must use Facebook, Instagram, and Twitter. But if their core customer does not use these social media sites, then it does not make sense to use them. Some of the information that can help you target just the "right" social media customer is illustrated in Figure 7-5.

▶ **Figure 7-5 Types of Information That Can Help Target Different Social Media Customers**

The more information you have about customers, the easier it is to develop a social media plan that targets the "right" customer.

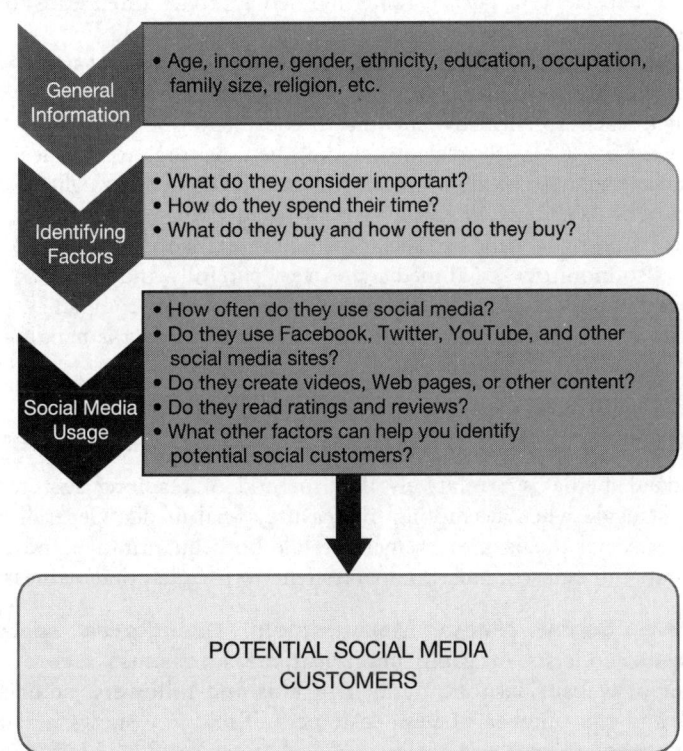

General Information
- Age, income, gender, ethnicity, education, occupation, family size, religion, etc.

Identifying Factors
- What do they consider important?
- How do they spend their time?
- What do they buy and how often do they buy?

Social Media Usage
- How often do they use social media?
- Do they use Facebook, Twitter, YouTube, and other social media sites?
- Do they create videos, Web pages, or other content?
- Do they read ratings and reviews?
- What other factors can help you identify potential social customers?

↓

POTENTIAL SOCIAL MEDIA CUSTOMERS

Step 4: Select Social Media Tools The search for the right social media tool(s) usually begins with the company's social media objectives, outlined in Step 2. It also helps to review the target customer or segment of the market the company is trying to reach (Step 3). With this information, the next step is to choose the right social media tools to reach the right customers. A company can use social media content sites, blogs, photos, videos, podcasts, or crowdsourcing to reach potential or existing customers. For example, if the goal is to recruit college graduates for sales positions for a large pharmaceutical company, LinkedIn may be a good choice. Remember, it is not necessary (or even advisable) to use all of the above tools. It is also possible for a business to build a social media community—especially when the objective is to fund business start-ups. Often money for worthwhile projects is obtained through crowdfunding. **Crowdfunding** is a method of raising money to fund a project for a business, a nonprofit organization, or an individual. The money raised can be an investment, a loan, or a donation. For example, a young startup company, Oculus VR, used Kickstarter—a crowdfunding site to raise $250,000. The money (along with later funding from venture capitalists) was used to build a virtual-reality headset, Oculus Rift, that puts players into their favorite games. Oculus VR was so successful that later Facebook bought the company for $2 billion.[20]

Step 5: Implement and Integrate the Plan Once social media tools have been identified, a company can implement and integrate the social media plan. Because a social media plan doesn't necessarily have a start and stop date, it is different from traditional advertising campaigns. Some social media activities continue and have a life of their own. For example, Zappos, a very successful online retailer, is a company that is always "on" in terms of its social media. Indeed, they do very little traditional advertising and instead rely on the company's website and social media to promote products, monitor customer service, and enhance the company's reputation. If a customer uses social media to complain, their customer service representatives will often contact the customer and try to resolve any problems the customer has experienced. This customer-focused approach often leads to increased customer satisfaction and increased sales.

Some companies, on the other hand, feel that it is important to have a mix of short- and long-term social media promotion. In this case, it's important to key the content to each social media site and to coordinate the timing of promotions. For example, Coca-Cola is constantly adding new features to its Facebook page, which has more than 105 million likes. One day, the company might post its latest video. The next day, it might invite visitors to participate in a survey. Knowing that customers post thousands of social media messages about its brand every day, Coca-Cola also monitors social media sites very carefully and responds quickly to questions and comments. Finally, like a growing number of companies, Coca-Cola integrates its social media and traditional marketing efforts for maximum impact and to get "more bang for the buck."

衡量和调整社交媒体计划
7-4b Measuring and Adapting a Social Media Plan

Because social media is a relatively new method of reaching customers, many companies struggle when attempting to measure social media. Generally, there are two types of social media measurement. While both quantitative and qualitative measurements can be used, most companies tend to use quantitative measurements.

Quantitative Social Media Measurement **Quantitative social media measurement** consists of using numerical measurements, such as counting the number of website visitors, number of fans and followers, number of leads generated, and the number of new customers. Table 7-1 shows a few popular quantitative ways to measure social media. A company like Macy's counts not

众筹
crowdfunding a method of raising money to fund a project for a business, a nonprofit organization, or an individual

量化社交媒体测量
quantitative social media measurement using numerical measurements, such as counting the number of website visitors, number of fans and followers, number of leads generated, and the number of new customers

Table 7-1 Quantitative Measurements for Selected Social Media Websites

Type of Social Media	Typical Measurements
Blogs	• Unique visitors • Number of views • Ratio of visitors to posted comments
Twitter	• Number of followers • Number of tweets and retweets • Click through rate (CTR) of tweeted links • Visits to website from tweeted links
Facebook	• Number of likes • Number of comments and responses • Visits to websites from Facebook links
YouTube	• Number of videos • Number of visitors • Ratio of comments to the number of videos • Watch time

only the number of social media likes and followers but also the number of times the company is mentioned each day. Although such measures help the company gauge brand awareness, determining how social media affects actual purchases of consumer products, like clothing and jewelry, can be difficult. Business-to-business marketers frequently set additional goals to track how social media activities lead to sales contacts and then to purchases. SAP North America, which markets software and technology services to corporations, uses social media to generate leads and facilitate the sales process. For example, SAP sponsors special events, workshops, and presentations that showcase the firm's software products. Both current and prospective customers often find out about these programs by accessing the firm's social media sites. To attend many of these events, people must register and provide basic contact information. Later, the person's contact information is used to initiate future sales calls.[21] By tracking such contacts, SAP can determine the effect of its programs on the company's sales revenues.

A number of companies are also using key performance indicators to measure their social media activities. **Key performance indicators (KPIs)** are measurements that define and measure the progress of an organization toward achieving its objectives. Generally, KPIs are *quantitative* (based on numbers like the number of YouTube views).

If measuring the success or failure of social media activities with KPIs, the first step is to connect KPIs with objectives. The second step is to set a benchmark—a number that shows what success should look like. Assume Mercedes-Benz sets a benchmark of 750,000 views for a new YouTube video that introduces a new S-Class model automobile. If at the end of a specified time period, 840,000 people have viewed the video, it would indicate the company's video campaign was successful.

Qualitative Social Media Measurement **Qualitative social media measurement** is the process of accessing the opinions and beliefs about a brand. This process primarily uses sentiment analysis to categorize what is being said about a company. **Sentiment analysis** is a measurement that uses technology to detect the mood,

关键绩效指标
key performance indicators (KPIs) measurements that define and measure the progress of an organization toward achieving its objectives

定性社交媒体测量
qualitative social media measurement the process of accessing the opinions and beliefs about a brand

情感分析
sentiment analysis a measurement that uses technology to detect the mood, attitudes, or emotions of people who experience a social media activity

Quantitative or qualitative measurements— Which one is best? That's a hard question to answer. Both methods can be used to measure the effectiveness of a company's social media plan. Quantitative measurements are numerical, like the number of visitors to a site. Qualitative measurements analyze a customer's sentiments, like what people think about a company's customer service. Sometimes just asking customers to check a box if they like a product or service or not is all it takes.

Chapter 7 Exploring Social Media and e-Business

attitudes, or emotions of people who experience a social media activity. Other measurements for determining customer sentiment include:

- *Customer satisfaction score*—the relative satisfaction of customers;
- *Issue resolution rate*—the percentage of customer service inquiries resolved satisfactorily using social media; and
- *Resolution time*—the amount of time taken to resolve customer service issues.

When compared to quantitative measurement, it should be noted that many of these qualitative social media measurements are more subjective in nature.

维护社交媒体计划的成本

7-4c The Cost of Maintaining a Social Media Plan

Basic assumption: Social media is not free and can be quite expensive. Because social media costs both time and money, it is important to measure the success of a social media plan and make adjustments and changes if needed. Based on quantitative and qualitative measurements, the company may also try to determine if it is getting a positive return on its investment in social media.

After reviewing results for social media activities against pre-established benchmarks, it may be necessary to make changes and update the plan to increase the effectiveness of the social media plan. A social media plan, for example, must provide current and up-to-date information in order to keep customers coming back to see what's new. Without updates, customers lose interest and the number of returning customers can drop dramatically. After all, one of the major objectives of social media activities is to provide customers and stakeholders with current and useful information about the company and its products or services. Once it is determined that updates and changes are needed, many of the same steps described in this section may be used to improve a firm's social media plan. It is also important to create future social media plans based on what worked and what didn't work in previous plans.

Social media is particularly important to businesses that use computers and the internet to sell their products and services online. In the next section, we take a close look at how e-business firms are organized, satisfy needs online, and earn profits.

电子商业的定义

7-5 Defining e-Business

In Chapter 1, we define *business* as the organized effort of individuals to produce and sell, for a profit, the goods and services that satisfy society's needs. Working from this original definition, then, **e-business (or electronic business)**, can be defined as the organized effort of individuals to produce and sell, for a profit, the goods and services that satisfy society's needs *through the facilities available on the internet*. Sometimes people use the term *e-commerce* instead of *e-business*. In a strict sense, e-business is used when you're talking about all business activities and practices conducted on the internet by an individual firm or industry. On the other hand, **e-commerce** is a part of e-business and usually refers only to buying and selling activities conducted online. Although actual statistics vary depending on the source, U.S. e-commerce retail sales already account for approximately $432 billion a year and are expected to increase to $563 billion by 2025.[22]

With the popularity of smartphones and tablet computers, many companies are also using **mobile marketing** to communicate with and sell to customers through mobile devices. Mobile marketing covers a range of activities, from optimizing websites for viewing on smartphones and tablets to delivering promotional messages and discounts via mobile devices. Because mobile devices are used in over 40 percent of online transactions, many businesses are investing more heavily in mobile marketing.[23] A growing number of companies have *apps* to make mobile

Concept Check

▶ What are the steps required to develop a social media plan?

▶ What is the difference between quantitative and qualitative measurements? Which type of measurement do you think is the most reliable when measuring the effectiveness of a company's social media plan?

Learning Objective

7-5 Explain the meaning of e-business.

电子商业
e-business (or electronic business) the organized effort of individuals to produce and sell, for a profit, the goods and services that satisfy society's needs through the facilities available on the internet

电子商务
e-commerce a part of e-business and usually refers only to buying and selling activities conducted online

移动营销
mobile marketing communicating with and selling to customers through mobile devices

transactions faster and more convenient for customers. For example, Starbucks offers an easy-to-use app for customers to pay for their lattes or espressos directly from a smartphone or tablet.

组织电子商业资源

7-5a Organizing e-Business Resources

As noted in Chapter 1, to be organized, a business must combine *human, material, informational,* and *financial resources*. This is true of e-business, too (refer to Figure 7-6), but in this case, the resources may be more specialized than in a typical business. For example, people who can design, create, and maintain websites are only a fraction of the specialized human resources required by e-businesses. Material resources often include customized computers and high-speed internet connections. Computer software programs that track the number of visitors who view a firm's website and customers who make online purchases are generally among the specialized informational resources required. Financial resources, the money required to start and maintain the firm and allow it to grow, usually reflect greater participation by individual entrepreneurs, venture capitalists, and investors willing to invest in a high-tech firm instead of conventional financial sources such as banks.

In an effort to reduce the cost of specialized resources that are used in e-business, many firms have turned to outsourcing. **Outsourcing** is the process of finding outside vendors and suppliers that provide professional help, parts, or materials at a lower cost. For example, a firm that needs computer programmers and specialized software to complete a project may turn to an outside firm located in another part of the United States, India, or an Eastern European country.

满足线上需求

7-5b Satisfying Needs Online

The internet has created some new customer needs that did not exist before its creation. Consider what happened during the second quarter (April, May, and June) of 2020. e-Commerce sales grew an average of 45 percent when compared to the same period the previous year.[24] The growth was the result of the COVID-19 pandemic. Because of a shutdown of non-essential businesses and fear for the health of not only themselves but also their families, customers turned to online shopping to obtain the products they needed. For the remainder of the year, the growth rate for e-commerce continued to rise to record levels. For example, 44 percent more

Figure 7-6 Combining e-Business Resources

While all businesses use four resources (human, material, informational, and financial), these resources are typically more specialized when used in an e-business.

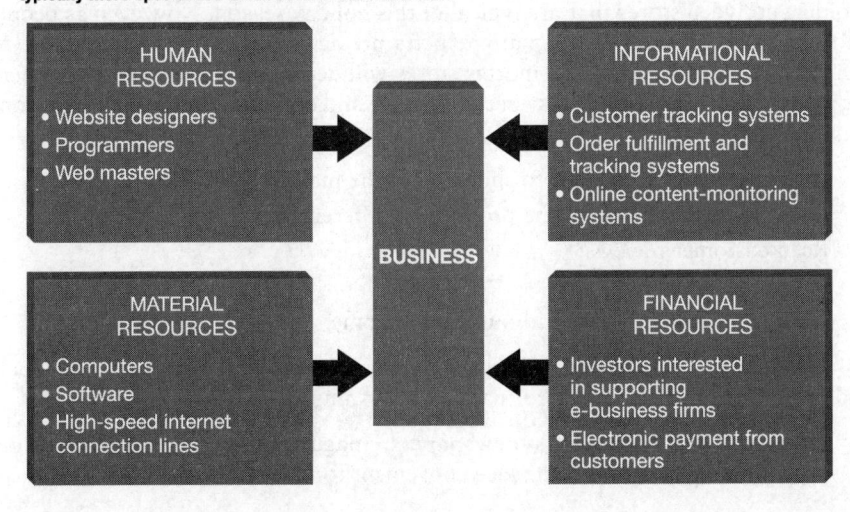

HUMAN RESOURCES
- Website designers
- Programmers
- Web masters

INFORMATIONAL RESOURCES
- Customer tracking systems
- Order fulfillment and tracking systems
- Online content-monitoring systems

MATERIAL RESOURCES
- Computers
- Software
- High-speed internet connection lines

FINANCIAL RESOURCES
- Investors interested in supporting e-business firms
- Electronic payment from customers

BUSINESS

外包
outsourcing the process of finding outside vendors and suppliers that provide professional help, parts, or materials at a lower cost

Entrepreneurial Success

创业成功：为什么小企业喜欢 Shopify

Why Small Businesses Like Shopify

In 2004, Tobias Lütke, Daniel Weinand, and Scott Lake came up with the idea for Shopify, a Canadian e-commerce platform, while opening a small online business for snowboarding equipment called Snowdevil. The three entrepreneurs were dissatisfied with existing e-commerce sites, so Lütke, a computer programmer, decided to build his own. Two years later, the platform hosting Snowdevil was launched as Shopify.

Now, more than 1 million businesses in 175 countries use Shopify to sell merchandise. One of the keys to Shopify's success is that instead of positioning itself as a traditional e-commerce platform, it markets itself as a one-stop-shop for business owners to start, run, and grow their businesses. Small business owners that use Shopify typically use a variety of services, including email marketing, website hosting, logistics management, and point-of-sale software. This all-in-one approach is attractive for small business owners who have limited time, resources, and technical expertise because it eliminates the need to deal with third parties to get the tools that they need to operate their businesses. For example, its customizable themes and drag-and-drop store builder tool eliminate the need for design skills. Another attractive feature allows Shopify users to sync online and in-store sales using its point-of-sales software. According to many users, Shopify offers solutions, tools, and services that were previously unavailable for many small business owners for a relatively small monthly fee.

Shopify was already growing steadily when the COVID-19 pandemic struck. With lockdown restrictions in place for many nonessential businesses and an increasing number of customers shopping online, many small business owners scrambled to get their businesses online. Shopify enticed new users by extending its 14-day free trial to 90 days for a limited time on select plans. Extending the free trial gave customers more time to determine if Shopify was the right e-commerce platform for them. As a result, Shopify experienced rapid growth.

Small business owners aren't the only ones enjoying everything Shopify has to offer. Major brands such as Pepsi, Heinz, and Staples also use the Shopify e-commerce platform. While it faces a variety of e-commerce competitors, including Adobe's Commerce, BigCommerce, WooCommerce, Wix, and even Amazon, Shopify stands out from the competition because of its ability to meet the needs of its small-business customers.

Sources: Based on information in Lauren Debter, "During Pandemic, Shopify Woos A Wave Of Small Businesses Eager To Get Online," *Forbes*, May 8, 2020; Matt Grossman and Kimberly Chin, "Shopify's Revenue Nearly Doubles as Covid-19 Pushes Shopping Online," *The Wall Street Journal*, July 30, 2020; Laura Forman, "Shopify's Business Sells Itself, for Now," *The Wall Street Journal*, July 29, 2020.

---

people made purchases online during the Thanksgiving to Cyber Monday period in 2020 when compared to the previous year.[25] This increase was caused by people avoiding crowded stores that are typical of this holiday season. Now even as people return to more normal times, many experts predict online sales will continue to increase and sales in brick-and-mortar stores will decline in the future. While there are many reasons for the increase in e-commerce and online shopping, major reasons include the ability to:

- Save time when compared to shopping at the mall or store;
- Compare prices for the same product on different websites;
- Read customer reviews;
- Avoid checkout lines; and
- Have products delivered without leaving home.

In addition to purchasing products, the internet can be used by both individuals and business firms to obtain information. For example:

- Internet users can access newspapers, magazines, radio, and television programming at a time and place convenient to them.

- The internet provides the opportunity for two-way interaction between an internet firm and the customer. For example, many new-car dealers have a "chat" option on their websites for customers who can ask specific questions or want more information about their automobiles or service.
- Finally, the internet allows customers to choose the content they are offered. For the advertiser, knowing that its advertisements are being directed to the most likely customers represents a better way to spend advertising dollars.

创造电子商业利润
7-5c Creating e-Business Profit

Business firms can increase profits either by increasing sales revenue or by reducing expenses through a variety of e-business activities.

Increasing Sales Revenue Each source of sales revenue flowing into a firm is referred to as a **revenue stream**. Today, there are many different ways to use the internet and technology to increase sales revenue. Because the opportunity to shop on the internet is virtually unrestricted, traditional retailers like Target (www.target.com) and Walmart (www.walmart.com) can obtain additional revenue by selling to a global customer base 24 hours a day, seven days a week. However, shifting revenues earned from customers inside a real store to revenues earned from these same customers online does not create any real new revenue for a firm. The goal is to find *new customers* that shop online and generate *new sales* so that *total revenues are increased*.

Intelligent information systems also can help to generate sales revenue for internet firms such as Amazon (www.amazon.com). Such systems store information about each customer's purchases, along with a variety of other information about the buyer's preferences. Using this information, the system can assist customers the next time they visit the website. For example, if the customer has bought a Carrie Underwood CD in the past, the system might suggest CDs by similar artists who have won awards from the Academy of Country Music.

Many internet firms generate revenue from commissions earned from sellers of products linked to their internet sites. For example, both Amazon and eBay earn revenue by providing a website where vendors can sell merchandise to buyers who may be located any place in the world.

Although some customers may not make a purchase online, the existence of the firm's website and the services and information it provides may lead to increased sales in the firm's physical stores. For example, Honda's website (www.honda.com) can provide basic comparative information for shoppers so that they are better prepared for their visit to an automobile showroom.

In addition to selling products or services online, e-business revenue streams are created by advertising placed on web pages and by subscription fees charged for access to online services and information. For example, Dun & Bradstreet (www.dnb.com/), a comprehensive source for company and industry information, makes some of its online content free for anyone who visits the site, but more detailed information is available only by paid subscription.

Reducing Expenses Reducing expenses is the second major way in which e-businesses can help to increase profitability. Providing online access to information

Who is the largest retailer in the world? Walmart is number one when you measure total sales from brick-and-mortar stores *and* e-commerce. And yet, if you *measure just e-commerce sales*, Amazon is larger. One of the reasons why Amazon is the leader in online retailing is that it is easy to purchase just about anything you want and have it delivered in a few days or even the same day in some locations. Now that's fast.

收入流
revenue stream a source of revenue flowing into a firm

Chapter 7 Exploring Social Media and e-Business

Concept Check

▶ What are the four major factors contained in the definition of e-business?

▶ How does e-business satisfy needs online?

▶ How do e-businesses generate revenue streams, reduce expenses, and earn a profit?

Learning Objective

7-6 Define the fundamental models of e-business.

that customers want can reduce the cost of dealing with customers. T-Mobile, for instance, is just one company that maintains an extensive website where potential customers can learn more about products and services, and where current customers can access personal account information, send questions to customer service, and purchase additional products or services. With such extensive online services, T-Mobile does not have to maintain as many physical store locations as it would without these online services. We examine more examples of how e-business contributes to profitability throughout this chapter, especially as we focus on some of the business models for activity on the internet.

电子商业的基本模式
7-6 Fundamental Models of e-Business

A **business model** represents a group of common characteristics and methods of doing business to generate sales revenues and reduce expenses. Each of the models discussed in the following text represents a primary e-business model. Regardless of the type of business model, planning often depends on if the e-business is a new firm or an existing firm adding an online presence—refer to Figure 7-7. It also helps to keep in mind that in order to generate sales revenues and profits, a business—especially an e-business—must meet the needs of its customers.

企业对企业（B2B）模式
7-6a Business-to-Business (B2B) Model

Some firms use the internet mainly to conduct business with other businesses. These firms are generally referred to as having a **business-to-business** (or **B2B**) **model**.

▶ **Figure 7-7** Planning for a New Internet Business or Building an Online Presence for an Existing Business

The approach taken to creating an e-business plan will depend on whether you are establishing a new Internet business or adding an online component to an existing business.

SUCCESSFUL E-BUSINESS PLANNING

Starting a new Internet business
- Will the new e-business provide a product or service that meets customer needs?
- Who are the new firm's potential customers?
- How do promotion, pricing, and distribution affect the new e-business?
- Will the potential market generate enough sales and profits to justify the risk of starting an e-business?

Building an online presence for an existing business
- Is going online a logical way to increase sales and profits for the existing business?
- Are potential online customers different from the firm's traditional customers?
- Will the new e-business activities complement the firm's traditional activities?
- Does the firm have the time, talent, and financial resources to develop an online presence?

商业模式
business model a model that represents a group of common characteristics and methods of doing business to generate sales revenues and reduce expenses

企业对企业（或 B2B）模式
business-to-business (or **B2B**) **model** a model used by firms that conduct business with other businesses

When examining B2B firms, two clear types emerge. In the first type, the focus is facilitating sales transactions between businesses. For example, Dell manufactures computers to specifications that customers enter on the Dell website (www.dell.com). A large portion of Dell's online orders are from corporate clients who are well informed about the products they need and are looking for fairly priced, high-quality computer products that will be delivered quickly. By dealing directly with Dell, customers eliminate costs associated with wholesalers and retailers, thereby helping to reduce the price they pay for equipment.

A second, more complex type of B2B model involves a company and its suppliers. Today, suppliers use the internet to bid on products and services they wish to sell to a business customer and learn about the customer's rules and procedures that must be followed. For example, Ford, General Motors, and Chrysler have developed a B2B model to link thousands of suppliers that sell the automobile makers parts, supplies, and raw materials worth millions of dollars each year. Although the B2B site is expensive to start and maintain, there are significant savings for all three automakers. Given the potential savings, it is no wonder that many other manufacturers and their suppliers are beginning to use the same kind of B2B systems that are used by the automakers.

Tired of standing in the checkout line at the grocery store? Then shop online. Many supermarket chains are experiencing an uptick in the number of consumers who are using their e-commerce sites to buy groceries. For consumers, the process is simple: Order your merchandise online, pay online, and then either pick up your groceries at the store's customer pickup location or have your purchases delivered to your home.

企业对消费者（B2C）模式
7-6b Business-to-Consumer (B2C) Model

In contrast with the B2B model, firms such as Amazon (www.amazon.com), Walmart (www.walmart.com), and Dick's Sporting Goods clearly are focused on individual consumers. These companies are referred to as having a **business-to-consumer (or B2C) model**. In a B2C situation, understanding how consumers behave online is critical to a firm's success. Typically, a business firm that uses a B2C model must answer the following questions:

- What sorts of products and services are best suited for online consumer shopping?
- Will consumers use websites to simplify and speed up comparison shopping?
- Will consumers purchase services and products online or end up buying at a traditional retail store?
- Are consumers willing to wait for purchases to be delivered, will they pay for next-day delivery, or will they collect online purchases from a convenient pickup site?

In addition to providing round-the-clock global access to all kinds of products and services, B2C firms often attempt to build long-term relationships with their customers. Often, firms will make a special effort to make sure that the customer is satisfied and that problems, if any, are solved quickly. Most B2C firms, for example, have liberal return policies and often pay for returning merchandise that the customer does not like. Specialized software can also help build good customer relationships. Tracking the decisions and buying preferences when customers shop online, for instance, helps a B2C business provide suggestions for additional merchandise or services the customer may want to consider. In essence, this is Orbitz's (www.orbitz.com) online selling

企业对消费者（或 B2C）模式
business-to-consumer (or B2C) model a model used by firms that focus on conducting business with individual consumers

Chapter 7 Exploring Social Media and e-Business

Table 7-2 Other Business Models That Perform Specialized e-Business Activities

Although modified versions of B2B or B2C, these business models perform specialized e-business activities to generate revenues.

Advertising e-business model	Advertisements that are displayed on a firm's website in return for a fee. Examples include pop-up and banner advertisements on search engines and other popular internet and social media sites.
Brokerage e-business model	Online marketplaces where buyers and sellers are brought together to facilitate an exchange of goods and services. One example is 1stDIBS (www.1stdibs.com), which provides a site for buying and selling furniture, lighting, home décor, antiques, jewelry, and fashion items.
Consumer-to-consumer model	Peer-to-peer software that allows individuals to share information over the internet. For example, Craigslist is a site where users can buy and sell all kinds of items.
Consumer to business model	Social media influencers, bloggers, or paid reviewers create content that promotes a company's products or services. In turn, the business pays either a predetermined dollar amount or a percentage of revenue for the promotion or information provided.
Subscription and pay-per-view e-business models	While some information may be free, detailed content is available only to users who pay a fee to gain access to a website. Examples include investment information provided by Morningstar (www.morningstar.com) and business research provided by Forrester Research, Inc. (www.forrester.com).

Concept Check

- What are the two-fundamental e-business models?
- Assume that you are the owner of a small company that produces outdoor-living furniture. Describe how you could use the B2C business model to sell your products to consumers.

approach. By tracking and analyzing customer data, the online travel company can provide individualized service to its customers. Although a "little special attention" may increase the cost of doing business for a B2C firm, the customer's repeated purchases will repay the investment many times over.

Today, B2B and B2C models are the most popular business models for e-business. And yet, there are other business models that perform specialized e-business activities to generate revenues. Most of the business models described in Table 7-2 are modified versions of the B2B and B2C models.

互联网、社交媒体和电子商业的未来

7-7 The Future of the Internet, Social Media, and e-Business

Learning Objective

7-7 Identify the factors that will affect the future of the internet, social media, and e-business.

Since the beginning of commercial activity on the internet, developments in computer technology, social media, and e-business have been rapid, with spectacular successes such as Facebook, Amazon, Google, eBay, and Pinterest. However, success is not guaranteed just because it is a "technology" firm. Even firms with a promising idea must develop a business plan to turn the idea into a reality—and a successful business. Today, most firms involved in the internet, social media, and e-business use a very intelligent approach to the initial start-up phase and expansion and development. The long-term view held by the vast majority of analysts is that the internet, social media, and e-business will continue to expand to meet the needs of businesses and consumers.

互联网的增长潜力

7-7a Internet Growth Potential

To date, only about 65 percent of the global population uses the internet. In late 2020, estimates suggest that about 5.1 billion of the 7.9 billion people in the world use the internet.[26] In the United States, 297 million, or about 90 percent of the nation's population use the internet. With approximately 90 percent of the U.S. population already using the internet, potential growth in the United States is

222   Marketing

limited.[27] On the other hand, the number of internet users in the world's developing countries is expected to increase dramatically.

Although the number of global internet users is expected to increase, that's only part of the story. Perhaps the more important question is why people are using the internet. Primary reasons for using the internet include the ability to connect with other people, to obtain information, or to purchase a firm's products or services. Of particular interest to business firms is the growth of social media. For example, Facebook now has approximately 2.7 billion users worldwide. And because only about 34 percent of the world population currently uses Facebook, the number of Facebook users is expected to continue to increase for years to come.[28] In fact, the number of users for other social media sites, like TikTok, YouTube, Twitter, Instagram, and Pinterest, is also expected to increase.

Experts also predict that the number of companies using e-business to increase sales and reduce expenses will continue to increase. Firms that adapt existing business models to an online environment will continue to dominate development. Although products or services will continue to be sold in the traditional way, more and more products will be sold online.

Even small businesses can sell merchandise online. While big retailers like Macy's, Walgreens, and Home Depot are increasing sales revenue from online sales, small businesses can also sell merchandise online. In fact, if a small business doesn't have a website, it's missing an opportunity to sell its products and services—especially unique or one-of-a-kind items.

伦理和法律问题
7-7b Ethical and Legal Concerns

The social and legal concerns for the internet, social media, and e-business extend beyond those shared by all businesses. Essentially, the internet is a new "frontier" without borders and with little control by governments or other organizations.

Ethics and Social Responsibility Socially responsible and ethical behavior by individuals and businesses on the internet are major concerns. For example, an ethically questionable practice in cyberspace is the unauthorized use of information discovered through computerized tracking of users once they are connected to the internet. Essentially, a user may visit a website and unknowingly receive a small piece of software code called a **cookie**. This cookie can track where the user goes on the internet and measure how long the user stays at any particular website. Although this type of software may produce valuable customer information, it also can be viewed as an invasion of privacy, especially since users may not even be aware that their movements are being monitored. AT&T, Verizon, and other cell phone service providers use cookies to track an individual's browsing on mobile devices for advertising purposes. Shoppers with smartphones and a retailer's app on their smartphones may even be tracked when they enter a store. Once the store knows your location in the store, it can send texts or posts about discounts and merchandise that is on sale. Unlike the situation with cookies, however, shoppers must download the app to be tracked—but in exchange, they benefit by receiving personalized discounts.

Some firms also practice data mining. **Data mining** refers to the practice of searching through data records looking for useful information. Customer registration forms typically require a variety of information before a user is given access to a site. Based on an individual's information, data mining analysis can then provide what might be considered private and confidential information about individuals. For instance, assume an individual frequents a website that provides information about a life-threatening disease. If this information is sent to an insurance company, the

网络跟踪软件
cookie a small piece of software sent by a website that tracks an individual's internet use

数据挖掘
data mining the practice of searching through data records looking for useful information

Chapter 7   Exploring Social Media and e-Business   223

The hackers are coming! Today it's hard to turn on your computer or read an email without worrying if you will get a computer virus that will enable hackers to steal your personal and financial information and then use it for their own personal gain. In fact, identity and computer security is such a big problem that it has created a whole new industry—the software security industry.

company might refuse to insure this individual, thinking that there is a higher risk associated with someone who wants more information about this disease.

Besides the unauthorized use of cookies and tracking your location and your online behavior, there are several other threats to users' privacy and confidentiality. Monitoring an employee's computer usage may be intended to help employers police unauthorized internet use on company time. However, the same records can also give a firm the opportunity to observe what otherwise might be considered private and confidential information. A recent survey of over 300 employers by the American Management Association and the ePolicy Institute found that two thirds of employers monitor employee usage.[29] Today, legal experts suggest that, at the very least, employers need to disclose the level of surveillance to their employees and consider the corporate motivation for monitoring employees' behavior.

Ethics and Social Responsibility

商业伦理与社会责任：加州加大隐私保护力度

California Ups the Ante on Privacy Protection

Data privacy is a major legal and ethical issue. In fact, 85 percent of U.S. internet users are concerned about how much information advertisers have collected about them. Even so, there is no comprehensive federal law that governs data privacy in the United States. Personal information, such as postal addresses, credit card numbers, email addresses, and browsing history, is a valuable marketing tool for companies, but the same information can open the door for identity thieves if it is not handled properly.

California took matters into its own hands with the California Consumer Privacy Act (CCPA). The act gave consumers more control over how their data is collected and used by businesses. The CCPA secured privacy rights for Californians, including the right to know what data is being collected and how it is used and shared, the right to have companies delete personal information (with some exceptions), the right to opt-out of having their personal information sold by one company to another, and the right to non-discrimination for exercising their CCPA rights.

California voters have also amended CCPA with the California Privacy Rights Act (CPRA). The CPRA amendment raised the privacy bar even higher. The original provisions put the burden on individuals to become aware of and protect their data instead of changing the way businesses collect, store, and use the data. The CPRA amendment created new requirements for businesses, such as limiting data retention, protecting data security, and minimizing data collection. It also strengthens accountability measures by requiring companies to conduct privacy risk assessments and cybersecurity audits.

Although the law was enacted in California, the importance of these laws goes beyond the state's boundaries because of the number of businesses that do business with California consumers. Also, the laws impact how marketers and ad publishers such as Facebook and Google personalize digital advertising. Finally, compliance will affect businesses financially when they hire data protection officers, implement new policies and procedures, train employees, modify processes, and monitor compliance.

Experts predict that California's privacy laws could become the national standard for data privacy, whether a federal law is created or not. Even if Congress enacts a national privacy law, it could face stiff opposition from Californians if the federal law does not meet or exceed the protections provided by the existing California law. The bottom line: Companies will need to find ways to help prevent identity theft and improve data protection now more than ever.

Sources: Based on information in Cameron F. Kerry and Caitlin Chin, "By Passing Proposition 24, California Voters up the Ante on Federal Privacy Law," *Brookings*, November 17, 2020; Yory Wurmser, "Election Impact: Why the Passing of California's Prop 24 Matters for Marketers and What to Expect in 2021," Business Insider, November 4, 2020; State of California Department of Justice, "California Consumer Privacy Act (CCPA)".

Internet Crime Because the internet is often regarded as an unregulated frontier, both individuals and business users must be particularly aware of online risks and dangers. For example, a general term that describes software designed to infiltrate a computer system without the user's consent is **malware**. Malware is often based on the creator's criminal or malicious intent and can include computer viruses, spyware, deceptive adware, and other software capable of criminal activities. According to TechJury, more than 30,000 websites are hacked each day.[30] In fact, the increase in internet crime and the devastating effects of both malware and computer viruses have given rise to a software security industry.

In addition to the risk of computer viruses and hackers, identity theft is one of the most common computer crimes that impacts both individuals and business users. A recent report by the United States Federal Trade Commission (FTC) determined that more than 1.4 million Americans reported identity theft in one year.[31] In recent years, major government entities including the United States government and many businesses such as Microsoft, MGM Resorts, Walgreens, T-Mobile, and many others have been hacked by thieves who stole sensitive data from tens of millions of people.[32]

Most consumers are also concerned about fraud. Because the internet allows easy creation of websites, access from anywhere in the world, and anonymity for the creator, it is almost impossible to know with certainty that the website, organization, or individuals that you believe you are interacting with are what they seem. As always, caveat emptor ("let the buyer beware") is a good suggestion to follow whether on the internet or not.

计算机技术、社交媒体和电子商业的未来挑战

7-7c Future Challenges for Computer Technology, Social Media, and e-Business

Today, more information and technology is available than ever before. Although individuals and business users may think we are at the point of information overload, the amount of information will only increase in the future. In order to obtain more information in the future, both business users and individuals must consider the cost of obtaining additional information and computer technology. In an effort to reduce expenses and improve accessibility, some companies and individuals are now using cloud computing. **Cloud computing** is a type of computer usage in which services stored on the internet are provided to users on a temporary basis. When cloud computing is used, a third party makes processing power, software applications, databases, and storage available for on-demand use from anywhere. Instead of running software and storing data on their employer's computer network or their individual computers, employees log onto the third party's system and use (and pay for) only the applications and data storage they actually need. Amazon Web Services (AWS), Microsoft, Google, IBM, Oracle, and many other firms in the technology industry offer cloud services. In addition to just cost, there are a number of external and internal factors that a business must consider.

Although the demands for a business are complex, it is useful to think of them as either *internal* or *external* forces that affect how a business uses computer technology. Internal forces are those that are closely associated with the actions and decisions taking place within a firm. As shown in Figure 7-8, typical internal forces include a firm's planning activities, organizational structure, human resources, management decisions, information database, and available financing. A shortage of skilled employees needed for a specialized project, for instance, can undermine a firm's ability to sell its services to clients. Unlike the external environmental forces affecting the firm, internal forces, such as this one, are more likely to be under the direct control of management. In this case, management can either hire the needed staff or choose to pass over a prospective project or outsource some of the work that is needed. In addition to the obvious internal factors that affect how a company operates, a growing number of firms are concerned about how their use of technology affects the environment. The term **green IT** is now used to describe all of a firm's activities to support a healthy environment

恶意软件
malware software designed to infiltrate a computer system without the user's consent

云计算
cloud computing a type of computer usage in which services stored on the internet are provided to users on a temporary basis

绿色 IT
green IT a term used to describe all of a firm's activities to support a healthy environment and sustain the planet

Figure 7-8 Internal and External Forces That Affect an e-Business

Today, managers and employees of an e-business must respond to internal forces within the organization and external forces outside the organization.

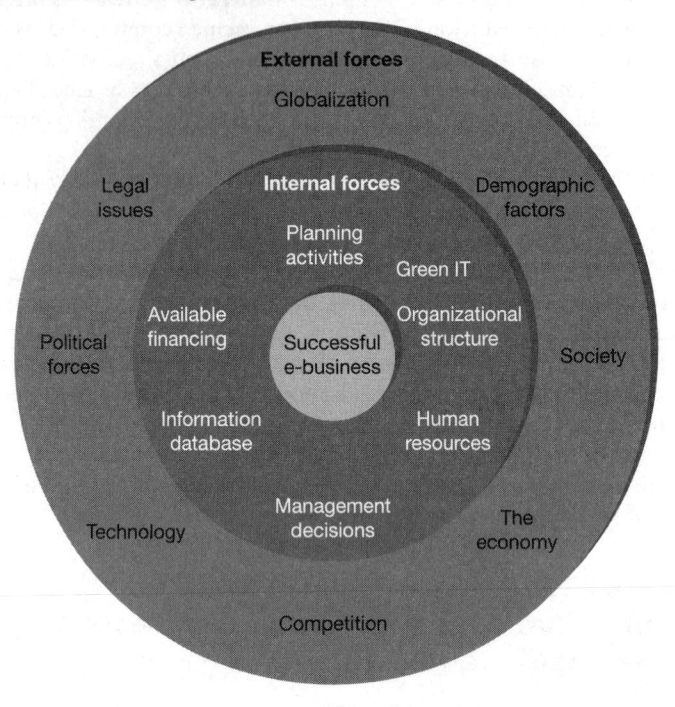

External forces: Globalization, Legal issues, Demographic factors, Political forces, Society, Technology, The economy, Competition

Internal forces: Planning activities, Green IT, Available financing, Organizational structure, Information database, Human resources, Management decisions

Successful e-business

✓ **Concept Check**

▶ Experts predict that the internet will continue to expand along with related technologies. What effect will this expansion have on society, business, and individuals in the future?

▶ Give an example of an unethical use of computer technology by a business.

▶ What is the difference between internal and external forces that affect an e-business?

---

and sustain the planet. Many offices, for example, are reducing the amount of paper they use by storing data and information on computers.

In contrast, external forces affect a company's use of technology and originate outside the organization. These forces are unlikely to be controllable by a company. Instead, managers and employees of a company generally will react to these forces, attempting to shield the organization from any negative effects and finding ways to take advantage of opportunities in an ever-changing technology environment. The primary external forces affecting a company's use of technology include globalization, demographic, societal, economic, competitive, technological, and political and legal forces.

In this chapter, we have explored how both individuals and businesses use social media. We also examined how e-business and e-commerce are changing the way that firms do business.

Summary 小结

7-1 Examine why it is important for a business to use social media.

Millions of people of all ages use social media to interact with people and share ideas, personal information, and information about products and services. The primary reason for using social media is to stay in touch with family and friends. Other reasons include sharing photos or videos and obtaining information available on the internet. Just the sheer numbers of people using social media make using social media a top priority for business. Even though companies have used social media to share information about their products and services and improve customer service, many are still uncomfortable with this new method of communicating with customers because they do not have much control over what is said about their products or services.

7-2 Discuss how businesses use social media tools.

Companies use social media to connect with customers and stakeholders, provide customer service, provide information to customers, and engage customers in product development. To share social content (information about products and services), companies can use blogs, photos, videos, and podcasts. Before creating a media sharing site, managers and employees should consider who will create the photos, videos, and podcasts, how the content will be distributed, and how much it will cost. In addition, social media also enables shoppers to access opinions, recommendations, and referrals from others within and outside their own social circle. Rating and review sites are based on the idea that people trust the opinions of others when it comes to purchasing products and services.

7-3 Explain the business objectives for using social media.

Although its popularity is a recent phenomenon, many businesses are already using social media to achieve important goals and objectives. In fact, there are many ways for businesses to use social media to take advantage of business opportunities to build connections with other businesses and consumers. For example, businesses can use social media to build a community. Social media communities are social networks based on the relationships among people. Today, there are social communities for every interest, ethnic group, and lifestyle. Different types of communities include both forums and wikis. Other reasons for using social media include crisis and reputation management, listening to stakeholders, targeting customers, social media marketing, generating new product ideas, and recruiting employees.

7-4 Describe how businesses develop a social media plan.

Before developing a plan to use social media, it is important to determine how social media can improve the organization's overall performance and how the plan "fits" with a company's objectives and other promotional activities. Once it is determined how social media links to the company's other activities, the first step is to listen to what customers like and don't like about a company's products or services. Typically, the second step is to establish social media objectives that are specific, measurable, achievable, realistic, and oriented toward the future. After listening and establishing objectives, the third step is to identify the customer or market segment a business is trying to reach with a social media promotion. The fourth step is to select the social media tools that will be used to reach customers. While it is not necessary (or even advisable) to use all of the available tools, a company can use social media communities, blogs, photos, videos, and podcasts to reach potential or existing customers. Once social media tools have been identified, a company can implement and integrate the social media plan.

Both quantitative and qualitative measurements can be used to determine the effectiveness of a social media plan. Quantitative social media measurement consists of using numerical measurements. Key performance indicators (KPIs), for example, are generally quantitative measurements. Qualitative measurement is the process of accessing the opinions and beliefs about a brand and primarily uses sentiment analysis to categorize what is being said about a company. Because social media costs both time and money, it is important to maintain, update, and measure the success of a social media plan and make adjustments and changes if needed.

7-5 Explain the meaning of e-business.

e-Business, or electronic business, can be defined as the organized effort of individuals to produce and sell, for a profit, the goods and services that satisfy society's needs *through the facilities available on the internet*. e-Commerce is a part of e-business and usually refers only to buying and selling activities conducted online. The human, material, information, and financial resources that any business requires are highly specialized for e-business. In an effort to reduce the cost of e-business resources, many firms have turned to outsourcing. It is also possible to use mobile marketing to increase sales and profits.

Using e-business activities, it is possible to satisfy new customer needs created by the internet as well as traditional ones in unique ways. Meeting customer needs is especially important when an e-business is trying to earn profits by increasing sales. Each source of revenue flowing into the firm is referred to as a revenue stream. It is also possible to reduce expenses by using e-business activities.

7-6 Define the fundamental models of e-business.

e-Business models focus attention on the identity of a firm's customers. Firms that use the internet mainly to conduct business with other businesses generally are referred to as having a business-to-business, or B2B, model. When examining B2B firms, two clear types emerge. In the first type of B2B, the focus is simply on facilitating sales transactions between businesses. A second, more complex type of the B2B model involves a company and its suppliers. In contrast to the focus of the B2B model, firms such as Macy's, Walgreens, or Dick's Sporting Goods are focused on individual buyers and are thus referred to as having a business-to-consumer, or B2C, model. In a B2C situation, understanding how consumers behave online is critical to the firm's success. Successful B2C firms often make a special effort to build long-term relationships with their customers. While B2B and B2C models are the most popular e-business models, there are other models that perform specialized e-business activities to generate revenues (refer to Table 7-2).

7-7 Identify the factors that will affect the future of the internet, social media, and e-business.

Since the beginning of commercial activity on the internet, developments in computer technology, social media, and e-business have been rapid. Today firms with a promising idea must develop a business plan to turn an idea into a reality—and a successful business. The long-term view held by the vast majority of analysts is that use of the internet will continue to expand along with related technologies. Because approximately 90 percent of Americans now have access to the internet, potential growth is limited in the United States. On the other hand, only 5.1 billion of the 7.9 billion people in the world use the internet. Clearly, the number of internet users in the world's developing countries is expected to increase dramatically.

The future of computer technology and the internet will be influenced by advances in technology, the increasing popularity of social media, and the increasing use of e-business. Other factors, including ethics, social responsibility, and internet crime, will all impact the way that businesses and consumers use the internet. Although the environmental forces at work are complex, it is useful to think of them as either internal or external forces that affect how businesses use computer technology. Internal forces are those that are closely associated with the actions and decisions taking place within a firm. In contrast, external forces are those factors affecting an e-business originating outside an organization.

Key Terms 关键术语

You should now be able to define and give an example relevant to each of the following terms:

- social media
- hashtag
- social content sites
- blog
- media sharing sites
- influencer
- podcasts
- social media communities
- forum
- wiki
- social media community manager
- social media marketing
- inbound marketing
- crowdsourcing
- crowdfunding
- quantitative social media measurement
- key performance indicators (KPIs)
- qualitative social media measurement
- sentiment analysis
- e-business (or electronic business)
- e-commerce
- mobile marketing
- outsourcing
- revenue stream
- business model
- business-to-business (or B2B) model
- business-to-consumer (or B2C) model
- cookie
- data mining
- malware
- cloud computing
- green IT

Discussion Questions 讨论题

1. Given the fast pace of everyday life, most people often feel there is not enough time to do everything that needs to be done. Yet, people do find time to post text messages and personal information, photos, etc., on Facebook, Twitter, blogs, and other social media sites. Why do you think people are so fascinated with social media?

2. How can a small cosmetics wholesaler located in Jacksonville, Florida, use social media and e-business to increase its customer base, increase revenues, and reduce expenses?

3. Is outsourcing good for an e-business firm? The firm's employees? Explain your answers.

4. What distinguishes a B2B from a B2C e-business model?

5. Experts predict that the internet, social media, and e-business will continue to expand along with related computer technologies. What effect will this expansion have on how businesses (1) market and sell merchandise, (2) get paid for merchandise, and (3) deliver merchandise to customers?

Case 7 案例 7：Target 在数字领域的大赌注

Target's Big Bet on Digital

When Target's CEO Brian Cornell announced the company would spend $7 billion for capital improvements and $1 billion more per year for operating costs to modernize operations for the digital age, investors weren't sold. "I had people shaking their heads," Cornell said. "You could see it." Target's stock price plummeted the day the announcement was made. Looking back now, Cornell knows the company made the right decision.

Target, one of the largest retailers in the United States, has spent billions on its stores and technology infrastructure.

The company reimagined its stores, built new, smaller stores in urban areas, and invested in technology and fulfillment capabilities. According to the CEO, the investment is paying off. All of these elements have worked together to drive growth, increase market share, and boost in-store and online traffic.

One of the most important initiatives was focused on remodeling existing stores and opening new small-format stores. In Target's smaller stores, the company reduced the amount of inventory and adopted a just-in-time approach to inventory management. The goal was simple: Deliver what the stores need, when they need it.

Target also invested in its supply chain in order to meet the needs of the "new" Target. For example, the company now utilizes artificial intelligence and robotics to support its warehouse teams. And, Target invested in creating backroom shipping and packaging centers in retail stores that act as distribution centers for online orders. Using its own retail stores as distribution centers gives it a significant advantage over Amazon. In-store and curbside pickup, for example, cost 90 percent less on average than fulfilling orders from a warehouse and then delivering the merchandise.

Target's $550 million acquisition of Shipt has also paid off. Shipt—a company known for offering same-day and next-day delivery—enables Target to go head-to-head against Amazon and other e-commerce retailers. It also acquired technology assets from Deliv—a same day delivery startup in California. Target is even testing the use of sort centers in areas with high delivery volume. The centers will be smaller and less expensive than Target's usual retail footprint and will be closer to customers. Target hopes that the use of sort centers will eliminate the need to sort packages at the store level and reduce its overall shipping costs.

These and other improvements have helped Target support in-store pickup, curbside delivery, and home delivery of online orders. In fact, it is now possible for "guests," as Target often calls its customers, throughout the United States and other countries to shop for all major product categories available from Target 24 hours a day, seven days a week. As an added bonus, technology has reduced the number of out-of-stock items and ultimately improved the customer's overall shopping experience.

Target's investments were well-timed. As a result of the COVID-19 pandemic and stay-at home mandates, Target's online business surged as shoppers turned to e-commerce to make purchases. In the first quarter of 2020, Target fulfilled more curbside deliveries than it did in the entire year of 2019. The company has also found that when customers shop online and use more of its delivery options, they ultimately spend more both online and in-store.

By investing in these new distribution strategies, Target is now able to compete against some big e-commerce companies. Although Target is now one of the top ten e-commerce businesses in the United States, the company has a long way to go to capture more market share. Amazon controls nearly 40 percent of U.S. retail e-commerce sales. Target, which has 1.2 percent market share, lags behind not only Amazon, but also Walmart, eBay, Apple, Home Depot, Wayfair, and Best Buy. While Target has taken some giant steps to increase sales online and in its brick-and-mortar stores, there's still room for growth as more and more customers shop online. Looking forward, Target executives will need to remember the old phrase—Where there's a will, there's a way.[33]

Questions

1. Why do you think Target's plan to spend $7 billion for capital improvements and an additional $1 billion more per year for operating costs initially worried investors? What do you believe investors think now?
2. Although many people think of Target as a big discount store that competes with Walmart, it has opened new, smaller stores that carry less inventory. What do you think is the driving force behind Target's smaller store concept?
3. Much of the information in this case describes Target's efforts to improve its supply chain. In your own words describe what the term "supply chain" means. How important is a firm's supply chain for a retailer like Target that has both in-store and online sales?

Building Skills for Career Success   为成功的职业生涯培养技能

1. Social Media Exercise

The purpose of the first part of this chapter is to introduce you to social media and its importance to business. After reading the chapter, choose a business that you either know something about, you want to start, or is the company you already work for.

Assignment

1. Develop a social media plan for that business using what you learned in this chapter.
2. What are the objectives of your social media plan?
3. What social media tools would you choose and why? How would you measure success?
4. Prepare a report that describes how this exercise has helped you understand the material in this chapter.

2. Building Team Skills

After graduating from college with a degree in marketing, your first job was working in the marketing department for a fast-food chain located in the southwestern part of the United States. After three years, you were promoted and became director of the chain's social media program. While monitoring posts about the company on Facebook and Twitter, you notice the following post from one of the firm's former employees.

> "Got fired today, but I was tired of serving low-quality food with expired expiration dates. Don't eat there or any of the chain's restaurants unless you want to get deathly ill."

To make matters worse, a couple of other employees who had recently been fired chimed in and made posts of a similar nature.

Assignment
1. Working in small teams, create a response that can be used to convince consumers that your company is committed to food freshness and quality and that these posts were made by employees who had been terminated.
2. Choose a spokesperson who will read your response to the rest of the class.
3. As a class, discuss the pros and cons of each response developed by each team.
4. Ask all members of the class to vote on the best response.
5. Finally, each team should prepare a report for the company's management that describes what happened and the response that was made to tell the company's side of this issue and restore consumer confidence in the firm's food products.

3. Researching Different Careers

Today, there are a wide assortment of career opportunities in companies that are involved in technology, social media, and e-business. In many cases, these firms want people with a fresh outlook on how technology, social media, and e-business companies can differentiate their products or services from those of other companies in the same industry. They often prefer individuals with new ideas and employees without preconceived notions about how to proceed. Website managers, designers, creative artists, and content specialists are just a few of the positions available. Many large online job sites, such as Indeed, LinkedIn, Monster.com, Glassdoor, and others, can help you to find out about employment opportunities and the special skills required for various jobs.

Assignment
1. Identify a website that provides information about careers in technology, social media, or e-business.
2. Summarize at least three positions that appear to be in high demand.
3. What are some of the special skills required to fill these jobs?
4. What salaries and benefits typically are associated with these positions?
5. Which job seems most appealing to you personally? Why?

Endnotes 注释

Chapter 1

1. Based on information in "Tesla Overtakes Toyota to Become World's Most Valuable Carmaker," BBC, July 1, 2020; James Morris, "How Did Tesla Become the Most Valuable Car Company in the World?" *Forbes*, June 14, 2020; Karen Langley, "Tesla Is Now the Most Valuable U.S. Car Maker of All Time," *The Wall Street Journal*, January 7, 2020.
2. The Horatio Alger website.
3. Ibid.
4. Greg Kumparak, "A Brief History of Oculus," the Tech Crunch website.
5. Julie Stav, "How to Invest in the Stock Market," the YouTube website.
6. The General Mills website.
7. The Bureau of Economic Analysis website.
8. The Bureau of Economic Analysis website.
9. The Bureau of Labor Statistics website.
10. The Bureau of Economic Analysis website.
11. The U.S. Debt Clock website.
12. The National Bureau of Economic Research website.
13. "Distribution of the Workforce Across Economic Sectors in the United States from 2010 to 2020," The Statista website.
14. The Environmental Protection Agency website.
15. Based on information in Company Man, "Zoom - Why They're Successful," YouTube, June 17, 2020; Alex Konrad, "Zoom, Zoom, Zoom! The Exclusive Inside Story Of The New Billionaire Behind Tech's Hottest IPO," *Forbes*, April 19, 2019; Rich Karlgaard, "Why Zoom Is Booming," *Forbes*, September 16, 2020; Samantha Murphy Kelly, "Zoom's Massive 'Overnight Success' Actually Took Nine Years," *CNN*, March 27, 2020.

Chapter 2

1. Based on information in Sara Randazzo, "Purdue Pharma Reaches $8.34 Billion Settlement Over Opioid Probes," *The Wall Street Journal*, October 21, 2020; German Lopez, "Purdue Pharma Admits to Crimes for Its OxyContin Marketing. But No One Is Going to Prison," *Vox*, October 21, 2020; Austin Frakt, "Damage From OxyContin Continues to Be Revealed," *The New York Times*, April 13, 2020; Purdue Pharma, "Purpose Statement and Values".
2. Gwen Aviles, "Kendall Jenner to Pay $90,000 Settlement for Promoting Fyre Festival," *NBCNews*, May 21, 2020; Evan Comen and Thomas C. Frohlich, "The Biggest Corporate Scandals of the Decade," *247wallst.com*, December 20, 2019.
3. Ben Popken, "Chick-fil-A Sues Chicken Producers Alleging Price Fixing on Billions of Dollars of Poultry," *NBC News*, December 7, 2020.
4. "Marketers of Pain Relief Device Settle FTC False Advertising Complaint," press release, U.S. Federal Trade Commission, March 4, 2020.
5. Chris Isadore and Matt Egan, "Robinhood Agrees to Pay a $65 Million Fine for Deceiving Clients," *CNN*, December 17, 2020.
6. Shereen Siewart, "Wausau Woman Sentenced in $700k Embezzlement Case," *Wausau Pilot & Review*, July 29, 2020.
7. Chris Prentice, "Wels Fargo to Pay $3 Billion to U.S., Admits Pressuring Workers in Fake-Account Scandal," *Reuters*, February 21, 2020.
8. Ethics Compliance Initiative, "2020 Report: Global Business Ethics Survey," p. 6.
9. Jonathan Martin, "Plagiarism Costs Degree for Senator John Walsh," *The New York Times*, October 10, 2014.
10. Rob Golum, "Electronic Arts Investors Reject Executive Pay in Rare Rebuke," *Bloomberg News*, August 7, 2020; Stan Choe, "CEO Pay: When Investors Give Thumbs-Down to Soaring Compensation Packages," *Chicago Tribune*, May 24, 2019.
11. Marshall Cohen, "Financial Disclosures Reveal Postmaster General's Business Entanglements and Likely Conflicts of Interest, Experts Say," *CNN*, August 12, 2020, (accessed December 17, 2020); Allison Durkee, "Louis DeJoy Forced to Divest from Former Company that Contracts with Postal Service," *Forbes*, October 15, 2020.
12. Procter & Gamble Company, *Our Worldwide Business Conduct Manual*, p. 51.
13. "False Advertising Consumer Class Actions Related to Coffee

Servings Continue with Suit Against Folgers," *The National Law Review*, December 4, 2020.
14. Jared Bryant, Amanda J. Beane, and Jason Howell, "$1 Million Settlement Announced in FTC's 'Made in USA' Enforcement Against Williams-Sonoma," *Consumer Protection Review*, April 24, 2020.
15. O. C. Ferrell and Larry Gresham, "A Contingency Framework for Understanding Ethical Decision Making in Marketing," *Journal of Marketing* 49 (Summer 1985), 89.
16. Starbucks, "Business Ethics and Compliance: Standards of Business Conduct".
17. "Kaiser Foundation Health Plan Will Pay $6.3 Million to Settle Medicare Advantage Fraud Allegations, Whistleblower Will Receive $1.5 Million," December 2, 2020.
18. Michael Josephson, "Can Corporate Ethics Programs Do Any Good," *Josephson Institute blog*, December 27, 2013.
19. "Google, Alphabet, Pledge $14.5 Million to Address Racial Inequity," *Philanthropy News Digest*, June 5, 2020.
20. Procter & Gamble, Tide's Loads of Hope, http://www.tide.com/en-us/about-tide/loads-of-hope/about-loads-of-hope (accessed December 18, 2020).
21. P. Terry's, https://pterrys.com/giving-back (accessed December 18, 2020).
22. Chris Kempczinski, "McDonald's CEO: How We Are Thinking Differently about Our Role in Society," *CNN*, November 25, 2020.
23. Lieff Cabraser, "11th Circuit Upholds $41 Million Individual Verdict Against RJ Reynolds and Philip Morris in Florida Tobacco Lawsuit," Lieff Cabraser Heimann & Bernstein, blog, March 24, 2020.
24. Isabella Kwai, "Consumer Groups Target Amazon Prime's Cancellation Process," *The New York Times*, January 14, 2021.
25. Larry Light, "Coca-Cola's Brand-Business Rationalization," *Forbes*, August 4, 2020; Toby Howell, "Coca-Cola Cuts 'Zombie Brands' From Its Portfolio," *Morning Brew*, October 8, 2020; "Brands," Coca-Cola Company.
26. Robert Glazer, "CVS Lost $2 Billion with 1 Decision—Here's Why They Were Right," *Forbes*, April 21, 2020.
27. Ryan Luckey, "This Pledge Day, Speak Up Against Distracted Driving," *AT&T*, press release, September 19, 2019.
28. Brittany Baumann, "Midas Hospitality and Boone Center, Inc. Create Hospitality Program," *HospitalityNet*, press release, January 31, 2020.
29. "The 2017 WBI U.S. Workplace Bullying Survey," Workplace Bullying Institute, 2017.
30. Lisa Evans, "Why the Office Bully Is Getting Promoted," *Fast Company*, October 23, 2014.
31. Robin Abcarian, "Just as We Thought: Richie Incognito Bullied Jonathan Martin," *Los Angeles Times*, February 14, 2014.
32. "Sexual Harassment," U.S. Equal Employment Opportunity Commission.
33. Sheryl Estrada, "McDonald's Hit with $500M Sexual Harassment Lawsuit," *HR Dive*, April 15, 2020.
34. "Sexual Harassment Payouts Hit All-Time High in 2019," Fisher Phillips law firm, blog, January 28, 2020.
35. Evans, "Why the Office Bully Is Getting Promoted."
36. United States Courts.
37. Food and Drug Administration, "Food Loss and Waste"; Jennifer Molidor, "Grocery Chains Need to Stop Buying into Food Waste," *Grocery Dive*, November 9, 2020; "Is 'Ugly Produce' the Key to Our Food Waste Problem?" *CBS News*, October 12, 2019.
38. "Company Fined for Ocean Pollution," *The (Kuau'i) Garden Island*, February 11, 2020.
39. Kie Relyea, "EPA Fines Company in Lynden $41,500 for Releasing Pollutants into Fishtrap Creek," *The Bellingham Herald*, June 25, 2020.
40. "Recycle Your Denim with Us," Madewell.
41. "Major Companies Using Green Energy in 2020," *SaveOnEnergy*, May 18, 2020.
42. Chipotle, "Cultivate a Better World: 2019 Sustainability Report Update," April 2020; Peter Adams, "Chipotle Lets Diners Track Environmental Impact of Burritos as Restaurants Prioritize Sustainability," *Marketing Dive*, October 26, 2020.
43. Monica J. Stover, "Environmental Marketing Claims and the FTC's 'Revised Green Guides'," *Michigan Environmental Law Journal*, 37 (Spring 2020).
44. "Environmental, Social and Governance Report, 2019," Citi, p. 114.
45. "Tae Yoo," Cisco.
46. "People Planet Play: Caesar's Entertainment 2019–2020 CSR Report," Caesar's Entertainment.
47. Whole Foods Market, "This Is Whole Trade | Whole Foods Market," *YouTube*, June 20, 2017; Whole Foods Market, "Your Guide to the Whole Trade Guarantee"; Whole Foods Market, "Whole Foods Market History"; Whole Foods Market, "Our Core Values"; Whole Foods Market, "Quality Standards"; Whole Foods Market, "Whole Benefits"; Cale Guthrie Weissman, "Whole Foods Is Becoming 'Whole Paycheck' Once Again," *Fast Company*, February 12, 2019; Andria Cheng, "Two Years After Amazon Deal, Whole Foods Is Still Working To Shed Its 'Whole Paycheck' Image," *Forbes*, August 28, 2019; Karen Weise, "Amazon Wants to Rule the Grocery Aisles, and Not Just at Whole Foods," *The New York Times*, July 28, 2019.

Chapter 3

1. Based on information in Heather Lalley, "International Starbucks Now Outnumber U.S. Units," *Restaurant Business Magazine*, January 11, 2019; Starbucks, "Starbucks Company Profile"; Starbucks, "Company Information"; Kristin

Salaky, "Starbucks Will Close 100 Additional U.S. Locations As It Continues To Adapt To Changing Consumer Habits," *Delish*, November 2, 2020; Starbucks, "Starbucks Announces New Roasting Facility in China, Extending Its Global Roasting Network," March 12, 2020.
2. "About the Coca-Cola Company," Coca-Cola Company.
3. "Company Overview," Combustion Associates, Inc.
4. "Liriope Factory," Southern United States Trade Association.
5. U.S. Census Bureau, "U.S. International Trade in Goods and Services, December 2020," February 5, 2021.
6. Ibid.
7. Jefferson Graham, "An iPhone Made in America? Why Building Apple's Smartphone in the USA Is a 'Pipe Dream'," *USA Today*, July 28, 2019.
8. "New Study: Trade Supported Over 40 Million Jobs," *Business Roundtable*, October 5, 2020.
9. "U.S. Trade in Goods and Services—Balance of Payments (BOP) Basis," U.S. Census Bureau.
10. "World Economic Outlook, January 2021," The International Monetary Fund.
11. "Canada – Country Commercial Guide," International Trade Association, August 3, 2020.
12. "Trade in Goods with European Union," U.S. Census Bureau.
13. "Trade in Goods with South and Central America," U.S. Census Bureau.
14. "Trade in Goods with Africa," U.S. Census Bureau.
15. Chuck Cartmill, "Lights and Insights: Streetlight Company Expands into New Solutions," Export Development Canada, blog, November 2, 2020.
16. Szu Ping Chan, "When Pepsi Was Swapped for Soviet Warships," BBCNews, June 13, 2019.
17. "About Us," Dunkin'.
18. Elizabeth Paton and Sapna Maheshwari, "H&M's Different Kind of Clickbait," *The New York Times*, December 18, 2019; "Supplier List," H&M Group.
19. James Bamford, Gerard Baynham, and David Ernst, "Joint Ventures and Partnerships," *Harvard Business Review*, September–October 2020, pp. 116–124.
20. "GM, Honda Announce North America Car Alliance," *Yahoo Finance*, September 3, 2020.
21. "U.S. Aluminum Industry Files Unfair Trade Cases Against Imports of Aluminum Foil from Five Countries," Globe Newswire, press release, September 29, 2020.
22. Josh Zumbrun and Bob Davis, "Tariffs on China Fail to Aid U.S. Factories," *The Wall Street Journal*, October 26, 2020, p. A1.
23. "World Outlook Database," International Monetary Fund, October 2020.
24. Scott A. Burns, "Banking the Unbanked—Lessons from the Developing World," *American Institute for Economic Research*, February 29, 2020.
25. Dylan Lyons, "Brands in Translation: 9 Cringeworthy Language Fails," *Babbel*, June 25, 2020.
26. Andrew Chatzkey, James McBride, and Mohammed Aly Sergie, "NAFTA and the USMCA: Weighing the Impact of North American Trade," Council on Foreign Relations, July 1, 2020; "Fast Facts: U.S. Trade with Canada and Mexico," USMCA Coalition.
27. Katie Lobosco, Brian Fung, and Tami Luhby, "6 Key Differences Between NAFTA and the USMCA Deal that Replaces It," *CNN*, December 17, 2019; Ana Swanson, "As New NAFTA Takes Effect, Much Remains Undone," *The New York Times*, July 1, 2020; "U.S. Relations with Canada," U.S. Department of State, July 16, 2020; and "Fast Facts: U.S. Trade with Canada and Mexico."
28. "Trade and Export," Texas Economic Development.
29. "About Citi," Citi Group.
30. "Keeping America Strong," Export-Import Bank of the United States, 2019 Annual Report.
31. The World Bank, www.worldbank.org (accessed January 20, 2021).
32. Based on information in Past To Future, "Honda History - How Soichiro Honda Started Company," *YouTube*, February 20, 2019; Honda, "History"; Honda, "Company Overview"; Michael Wayland, "GM, Honda Partner to Develop Two New All-Electric Vehicles," *CNBC*, April 2, 2020; "Honda Accelerates Its 'Electric Vision' Strategy With New 2022 Ambition," *Automotive World*, October 23, 2019; Roberto Baldwin, "Honda Kills Clarity EV, Its Only All-Electric Car in U.S.," *Car and Driver*, March 9, 2020.

Chapter 4

1. Based on information in Netflix Research, "Personalization & Search"; Jeremy Bowman, "Netflix Is Killing the Competition in This One Key Category," *The Motley Fool*, September 15, 2020; Tara Lachapelle, "Netflix Investors, We Need to Talk About Churn," *Bloomberg*, January 19, 2021.
2. "Definitions of Marketing," American Marketing Association.
3. Bryan Pearson, "12 Ways Starbucks' Loyalty Program Has Impacted the Retail Industry," *Forbes*, December 16, 2020; Bernard Marr, "Starbucks: Using Big Data, Analytics and Artificial Intelligence to Boost Performance," *Forbes*, May 28, 2018.
4. V. Kumar, *Customer Lifetime Value* (Hanover, MA: now Publishers, 2008), p. 5.
5. Rajkumar Venkatesan and V. Kumar, "A Customer Lifetime Value Framework for Customer Selection and Resource Selection and Resource Allocation Strategy," *Journal of Marketing 68* (October 2004), 106–125.
6. Walter Loeb, "Nordstrom's Management Sets a High Target for 2021," *Forbes*, February 8, 2021; Rina Raphael, "Nordstrom Local Expands Its Innovative, Inventory-Free Retail Hubs," *Fast Company*, July 9, 2018.
7. Nikki Gilliland, "30 Brand Strategies with Excellent Social

Media Strategies," *Econsultancy*, June 25, 2020; Taylen Peterson, "How Social Media Customer Success Impacts Retention," *Instapage*, January 3, 2020.
8. Hau L. Lee, "How Extreme Agility Put Zara Ahead in Fast Fashion," *Financial Times*, December 9, 2019; "The Secret of Zara's Success: A Culture of Customer Co-Creation," Martin Roll, blog, August 2018.
9. "The Story of Zipcar," Zipcar.
10. "Design Partnerships," Target.
11. Parija Kavilanz, "This Startup Is Making Glasses Kids Will Actually Want to Wear," *CNN*, January 23, 2020; Adam Blair, "Pair Eyewear Focuses on Fun and Fashion to Multiply Sales of Kids' Glasses," *Retail TouchPoints*, February 4, 2020.
12. Jefferson Graham, "Samsung Hits a New Record with the Most Expensive Smartphone: $2,000," *TechExplore*, September 1, 2020.
13. Sephora.com (accessed October 30, 2020); Parija Kavilanz, "No Testers, No Problem: Ulta and Sephora Have a New Take on 'Try Before You Buy'," *CNN*, June 18, 2020.
14. Jacob Krol, "Office 365 Is Becoming Microsoft 365 with New Features for the Same Price," *CNN*, March 30, 2020.
15. Amelia Lucas, "Powerade Is Launching 2 New Product Lines as Consumer Exercise Habits Change," *CNBC*, January 16, 2020.
16. "Social Content Ratings," Nielsen Social.
17. Ritash Pathak, "How Coca-Cola Uses Technology to Stay at the Top," *Analytic Steps*, October 24, 2020.
18. Peter Roeslier, "Consumers Find Influencers More Trustworthy Than Brands During the Pandemic," *Beauty Packaging*, May 26, 2020.
19. Evelyn Cheng, "China's Giant Middle Class Is Still Growing and Companies from Walmart to Startups Are Trying to Cash In," *CNBC*, September 30, 2019.
20. Based on information in CNBC, "How Starbucks Became an $80B Business," YouTube, January 10, 2019; Starbucks, "Starbucks Company Profile"; Starbucks, "Company Information"; Jennifer Warnick, "Five Things to Know About Starbucks (Online) Shareholders Meeting," *Starbucks Stories & News*, March 18, 2020; Kate Rogers, "Starbucks Is Speeding Up Innovation at its Seattle Research Hub," *CNBC*, May 2, 2019; Sarah Whitten and Kate Rogers, "Starbucks Cuts Long-Term Earnings per Share Forecast; Shares Fall," *CNBC*, December 13, 2018.

Chapter 5

1. Based on information in Phil Wahba, "Petco Rebrands, Bans Shock Collars in Health and Wellness Push," *Fortune*, October 7, 2020; Rhian Hunt, "Petco May Be Heading for an IPO as a $6 Billion Company," *The Motley Fool*, September 10, 2020; Petco, "Fact Sheets".
2. Matt Reynolds, "Jif, Skippy Add Flexible, Squeezable Peanut Butter Pack Formats," *Packaging World*, September 11, 2020.
3. Gillian Friedman, "Goodbye Tab: Coca-Cola Will Discontinue the Iconionc Soda," *The New York Times*, October 16, 2020.
4. Procter & Gamble, https://us.pg.com/brands/ and https://www.pg.co.uk/brands/ (accessed February 15, 2021).
5. Eric Schroeder, "Panera Debuts Flatbread Pizza," *Food Business News*, October 29, 2020.
6. Monica Watrous, "Inside Ferrara's Transformation of Keebler Cookies," *Food Business News*, July 30, 2020.
7. Eric Schroeder, "Hostess Innovates with New Snack Cake Flavors," *Food Business News*, November 12, 2020.
8. John Bowker, "Bombardier Drops Iconic Learjet to Focus on Luxury Models," *Bloomberg.com*, February 11, 2021.
9. Ashlee Vance and Brad Stone, "Air Taxi Startup Has a Working Prototype and a Fresh $100 Million," *Business Week*, February 1, 2018; Jeff Sloan, "Joby Aviation Acquires Uber Elevate," *Composites World*, December 18, 2020.
10. Mark Wilson, "Dyson's Latest Invention? A $500 Flat Iron That Won't Fry Your Hair," *Fast Company*, March 10, 2020.
11. "Brewing the American Dream," *Samuel Adams Brewing*.
12. "Only a Dyson Works Like a Dyson: The Engineering Behind Dyson Vacuums," *Dyson*.
13. Jonathan Maze, "Chick-Fil-A Is Testing a New Chicken Sandwich," *Restaurant Business*, September 18, 2020.
14. Joe Maring, "Samsung Galaxy Note 7: Everything You Need to Know!," *Android Central*, June 4, 2020.
15. Phil Wahba, "Target's Newish Athletic Line Is Now Its 10th Billion-Dollar Store Brand," *Fortune*, February 8, 2021.
16. Udo Kopka et al, "What Got Us Here Won't Get Us There: A New Model for the Consumer Goods Industry," McKinsey & Company, July 30, 2020.
17. "Mohawk Group Furthers Execution of M&A Strategy Announcing Accretive Acquisition of Mueller, Purstream, Pohl Schmitt and Spiralizer E-Commerce Brands," Globenewswire, press release, December 10, 2020.
18. Emily Price, "Why Bud Light Gave Its New Hard Seltzer the Family Name," *Fortune*, January 29, 2020.
19. Miles Socha, "Louis Vuitton Expands In Tokyo with New Tower, Café—and Chocolate Shop," *WWD*, January 27, 2021.
20. Replenish, https://myreplenish.com/ (accessed February 24, 2021); CleanPath, https://mycleanpath.com/ (accessed February 24, 2021).
21. Stefanie Valentic, "How the Coca-Cola's Recycled Bottle Redesign Is Progressing Sustainability Efforts," *Waste 360*, February 9, 2021.
22. Pamela DeLoatch, "Survey: Packaging, Labeling Determine Whether a Shopper Buys a Product," *FoodDive*, January 4, 2018.

23. Neil Patel, "How Planet Fitness Capitalizes on the Casual Gym-Goer Despite Tough Times," *The Motley Fool*, May 6, 2020; Nathaniel Meyersohn, "Planet Fitness Is Winning by Charging $10 a Month," *CNN*, January 12, 2018.
24. Amy Feldman, "Why One Entrepreneur Thinks Millions of Americans Will Spend $25 on His Personalized Shampoo," *Forbes*, August 18, 2020.
25. Bill Shaikin, "What Does the Dodgers' Dynamic Pricing Schedule Mean for Fans? A Seat That Costs $33 One Day Will Cost $80 Another Day," *Los Angeles Times*, January 26, 2018.
26. Based on information in TimesTicking, "The History of the Shinola Watch Company," *YouTube*, July 16, 2020; Jack Roskopp, "What Is Shinola and Why Did It Get a Shoutout During the Oscars?" *Click Orlando*, February 25, 2019; Shinola, "Our Story"; Randy Wimbley, "Shinola Lays off Employees, Plans to Outsource Some Operations," *Fox 2 Detroit*.

Chapter 6

1. Based on information in Sarah Nassauer, "Walmart to Combine Online and Store Product-Buying Teams," *The Wall Street Journal*, February 25, 2020; Walmart, "About Us"; Ben Unglesbee, "Walmart Cuts Corporate Jobs as It Focuses on Omnichannel Push," *Retail Dive*, July 31, 2020.
2. Pat Reynolds, "P&G Greatly Expands Eco-Box Portfolio," *Packaging World*, April 22, 2020.
3. Blake Morgan, "After a Bruising Year, Logistics and Supply Chains Are Ripe for Technology Disruption," *Tech Exec*, February 22, 2021.
4. Fareeha Ali, "US Ecommerce Grows 44.0% in 2020," *Digital Commerce 360*, January 29, 2021; Bureau of Labor Statistics, "Industries at a Glance".
5. "FTI Consulting Projects U.S. Online Retail Sales Growth to Increase 25% in 2020," FTI Consulting, press release, October 13, 2020.
6. Fareeha Ali, "Nordstrom's Ecommerce Sales Represent 61% of Revenue in Q2," *Digital Commerce 360*, August 31, 2020.
7. Caroline Jansen, "Casper Expands Physical Presence Through Tie-Up with Sam's Club," *Retail Dive*, August 10, 2020.
8. "Fact Sheets," *National Association of Convenience Stores*.
9. "About Direct Selling," *Direct Selling*.
10. *Do Not Call*, "https://www.donotcall.gov" (accessed March 4, 2021); Simon van Zuylen-Wood, "How Robocallers Outwitted the Government and Completely Wrecked the Do Not Call List," *The Washington Post*, January 11, 2018.
11. Dan Gilmore, "State of the Logistics Union 2020," *Supply Chain Digest*, June 25, 2020.
12. Ibid.
13. "Building, Executing, and Measuring an Integrated Marketing Campaign," *Marketing Dive*, April 28, 2020.
14. Jack Neff, "Marketers of the Year No. 7: E.L.F.," *AdAge*, December 7, 2020.
15. "U.S. Measured-Media Spending by Medium in 2019," *Advertising Age Marketing Fact Pack 2021*, December 21, 2020, p. 5.
16. National Association of Realtors, "NAR's 'That's Who We R' Advertising Campaign Highlights How Realtors® Open Doors to Opportunity for Their Clients and the Communities They Serve," press release, February 16, 2021.
17. Jessica Wohl, "Burger King Brings Humor to These 'Confusing Times' in Impossible Burger Radio Spots," *AdAge*, March 4, 2021.
18. Jessica Wohl, "McDonald's Launches a New Campaign to Promote Free Food for First Responders," *AdAge*, April 21, 2021.
19. "AdAge World's Largest U.S. Advertisers: 25 Biggest Spenders," *AdAge Marketing Fact Pack 2021*, December 21, 2020, p. 6.
20. "We're Disrupting the Way the World Sees Deals," RetailMeNot.
21. Mary Hanbury, "People Are Obsessed with Costco's Free Samples—But It's Actually a Brilliant Business Strategy," *Business Insider*, March 21, 2018.
22. "sandiegozoo," TikTok.
23. Sophie Cole, "How a Strong Brand Tone of Voice Can Help You Recover from Controversy," Stratton Craig, blog, July 10, 2020; Dan Tynan, "How to Survive a Public Brand Scandal and Recover Customers' Trust," Adweek, March 11, 2018.
24. Based on information in CNBC Make It, "How Casper Became A $1 Billion Mattress Start-Up," YouTube, April 9, 2019; "Casper's IPO is Officially a Disaster," *CNN*, February 5, 2020; "Casper, the Mattress Start-Up, Goes Through With Lackluster I.P.O," *The New York Times*, February 6, 2020; Clare Roth, "Mattress Unicorn Casper Accused of Misleading Investors With IPO," *Bloomberg*, June 27, 2020.

Chapter 7

1. Based on information in Netflix Research, "Personalization & Search"; Jeremy Bowman, "Netflix Is Killing the Competition in This One Key Category," *The Motley Fool*, September 15, 2020; Tara Lachapelle, "Netflix Investors, We Need to Talk About Churn," *Bloomberg*, January 19, 2021.
2. Social Media Fact Sheet," Pew Research.
3. Brent Barnhart, "Social Media Demographics to Inform Your Brand's Strategy in 2021," Sprout Social, March 9, 2021.
4. "2020 National Customer Rage Study," Customer Care Measurement and Consulting.
5. "The Top 10 Super Bowl 2020 Commercials by Digital Share

of Voice," Ad Age.
6. Rosie Murphy, "Local Consumer Review Survey 2020," BrightLocal.
7. Ibid.
8. The Wyndham Hotel website.
9. Kiva, www.kiva.org (accessed March 13, 2021).
10. "PwC Global Crisis Survey," PricewaterhouseCoopers.
11. Nina Solis, "How to Respond to a Negative Online Review," Broadly.
12. "Generation Z News," *Business Insider*.
13. Kavya Ravi, "6 Ways Nike Built a Strong Brand on Social Media," Unmetric.
14. Ibid.
15. Alexander Santo, "The Ultimate List of Marketing Spend Statistics," Brafton.
16. "More Smiles in 2020: Lay's Kicks Off Search for People Creating Joy Across the Country; Unveils Three New Flavors to Smile About," Frito-Lay.
17. "Lego Ideas," The Lego Group, March 12, 2021.
18. LinkedIn, www.linkedin.com (accessed March 3, 2021).
19. Melissa Barker, Donald Barker, Nicholas Bormann, and Krista E. Neher. *Social Media Marketing: A Strategic Approach* (Mason, OH: Cengage Publishing, 2017).
20. Emily Heaslip, "9 Wildly Successful Crowdfunded Startups," U.S. Chamber of Commerce.
21. SAP, https://www.sap.com/community.html (accessed March 5, 2021).
22. Daniela Coppola, "E-Commerce in the United States—Statistics & Facts," Statista.com.
23. Jullia Andjelic, "47 Mobile Marketing Statistics to Transform Your Business," Smallbizgenius.
24. "Quarterly Retail E-Commerce Sales," *U.S. Census Bureau News*.
25. Natalie Colarossi, "Online Black Friday Shoppers Increase Nearly 45 Percent Amid COVID-19 Pandemic," Newsweek.
26. Internet World Stats, https://www.internetworldstats.com/ (accessed March 16, 2021).
27. Ibid.
28. Brent Barnhart, "Social Media Demographics to Inform Your Brand's Strategy in 2021," Sprout Social.
29. Eugene Lee, "Can My Employer Monitor My Web Surfing or Emails at work? (2020)," California Labor and Employer Law.
30. Jacquelyn Bulao, "How Many Cyber Attacks Happen Per Day in 2020?," TechJury.
31. "Seena Gressin, " Identity Theft Awareness Week Starts Today," Federal Trade Commission.
32. Eugene Bekker, "2020 Data Breaches," IdentityForce.
33. Based on information in Melissa Repko, "Target Aims to Make Its Booming Online Business More Profitable With New Technology, Small Sort Centers," *CNBC*, May 20, 2020; Jackie Crosby, "Target CEO: $7 Billion Investment in Stores and Technology Is Paying Off," *Star Tribune*, March 2, 2019; Shelley E. Kohan, "Target's Big Investments, From Small-Format Stores To Digital, Prove Successful," *Forbes*, March 4, 2020.

Glossary 术语表

absolute advantage the ability to produce a specific product more efficiently than any other nation

accessory equipment standardized equipment used in a firm's production or office activities

advertising a paid nonpersonal message communicated to a select audience through a mass medium

advertising agency an independent firm that plans, produces, and places advertising for its clients

affirmative action program a plan designed to increase the number of employees from underrepresented groups at all levels within an organization

agent an intermediary that expedites exchanges, represents a buyer or a seller, and often is hired permanently on a commission basis

balance of payments the total flow of money into a country minus the total flow of money out of that country over a specified period of time

balance of trade the total value of a nation's exports minus the total value of its imports over a specified period of time

blog a website that allows a company to share information to increase the customer's knowledge about its products and services, and to build trust

brand a name, term, symbol, design, or any combination of these that identifies a seller's products as distinct from those of other sellers

brand equity marketing and financial value associated with a brand's strength in a market

brand extension using an existing brand to brand a new product in a different product category

brand loyalty extent to which a customer is favorable toward buying a specific brand

brand mark the part of a brand that is a symbol or distinctive design

brand name the part of a brand that can be spoken

breakeven quantity the number of units that must be sold for the total revenue (from all units sold) to equal the total cost (of all units sold)

broker an intermediary that specializes in a particular commodity, represents either a buyer or a seller, and is likely to be hired on a temporary basis

bundle pricing packaging together two or more complementary products and selling them for a single price

business the organized effort of individuals to produce and sell, for a profit, the goods and services that satisfy society's needs

business buying behavior the purchasing of products by producers, resellers, governmental units, and institutions

business cycle the recurrence of periods of growth and recession in a nation's economic activity

business ethics the application of moral standards to business situations

business model a model that represents a group of common characteristics and methods of doing business to generate sales revenues and reduce expenses

business product a product bought for resale, for making other products, or for use in a firm's operations

business service an intangible product that an organization uses in its operations

business-to-business (or B2B) model a model used by firms that conduct business with other businesses

business-to-consumer (or B2C) model a model used by firms that focus on conducting business with individual consumers

buying allowance a temporary price reduction to resellers for purchasing specified quantities of a product

buying behavior the decisions and actions of people involved in buying and using products

capitalism an economic system in which individuals own and operate the majority of businesses that provide goods and services

captioned photograph a picture accompanied by a brief explanation

captive pricing pricing the basic product in a product line low, but pricing related items at a higher level

carrier a firm that offers transportation services

catalog marketing a type of marketing in which an organization provides a catalog from which customers make selections and place orders by mail, telephone, or the internet

category killer a very large specialty store that concentrates on a single product line and competes on the basis of low prices and product availability

caveat emptor a Latin phrase meaning "let the buyer beware"

237

chain retailer a company that operates more than one retail outlet

cloud computing a type of computer usage in which services stored on the internet are provided to users on a temporary basis

code of ethics a guide to acceptable and ethical behavior as defined by the organization

command economy an economic system in which the government decides *what* goods and services will be produced, *how* they will be produced, *for whom* available goods and services will be produced, and *who* owns and controls the major factors of production

community shopping center a planned shopping center that includes one or two department stores and some specialty stores, along with convenience stores

comparative advantage the ability to produce a specific product more efficiently than any other product

comparison discounting setting a price at a specific level and comparing it with a higher price

competition rivalry among businesses for sales to potential customers

component part an item that becomes part of a physical product and is either a finished item ready for assembly or a product that needs little processing before assembly

conflict of interest when businesspeople take advantage of a situation for their own personal interest rather than for the employer's interest

consumer buying behavior the purchasing of products for personal or household use, not for business purposes

consumer price index (CPI) a monthly index that measures the changes in prices of a fixed basket of goods purchased by a typical consumer in an urban area

consumer products goods and services purchased by individuals for personal consumption

consumer sales promotion method a sales promotion method designed to attract consumers to particular retail stores and to motivate them to purchase certain new or established products

consumerism all activities undertaken to protect the rights of consumers

contract manufacturing an arrangement in which one firm contracts with another business, often in another country, to manufacture products or product components to its specifications

convenience product a relatively inexpensive, frequently purchased item for which buyers want to exert only minimal effort

convenience store a small food store that sells a limited variety of products but remains open well beyond normal business hours

cookie a small piece of software sent by a website that tracks an individual's internet use

cooperative advertising an arrangement whereby a manufacturer agrees to pay a certain amount of a retailer's media cost for advertising the manufacturer's products

corporate citizenship adopting a strategic approach to fulfilling economic, ethical, environmental, and social responsibilities

countertrade an international barter transaction

coupon reduces the retail price of a particular item by a stated amount at the time of purchase

creative selling selling products to new customers and increasing sales to current customers

crowdfunding a method of raising money to fund a project for a business, a nonprofit organization, or an individual

crowdsourcing outsourcing tasks to a group of people in order to tap into the ideas of the crowd

cultural (or workplace) diversity a system that recognizes and respects the differences among people because of their age, race, ethnicity, gender, sexual orientation, and ability

currency devaluation the reduction of the value of a nation's currency relative to the currencies of other countries

customary pricing pricing on the basis of tradition

customer lifetime value a measure of a customer's worth (sales minus costs) to a business over one's lifetime

customer relationship management (CRM) using information about customers to create marketing strategies that develop and sustain desirable customer relationships

data mining the practice of searching through data records looking for useful information

deflation a general decrease in the level of prices

demand the quantity of a product that buyers are willing to purchase at each of various prices

department store a retail store that (1) employs 25 or more persons and (2) sells at least home furnishings, appliances, family apparel, and household linens and dry goods, each in a different part of the store

depression a severe recession that lasts longer than a typical recession and has a larger decline in business activity when compared to a recession

digital distribution delivering content through the internet to a computer or other device

direct marketing the use of the telephone, internet, and nonpersonal media to introduce products to customers, who then can purchase them via mail, telephone, or the internet

direct-response marketing a type of marketing in which a retailer advertises a product and makes it available through mail, telephone, or online orders

direct selling the marketing of products to customers through face-to-face sales presentations at home or in the workplace

discount a deduction from the price of an item

discount store a self-service general-merchandise outlet that sells products at lower-than-usual prices

discretionary income disposable income less savings and expenditures on food, clothing, and housing

disposable income personal income less all personal taxes

distribution channel (or **marketing channel)** a sequence of marketing organizations that directs a product from the producer to the ultimate user

domestic system a method of manufacturing in which an entrepreneur distributes raw materials to various homes, where families process them into finished goods to be offered for sale by the entrepreneur

dumping exportation of large quantities of a product at a price lower than that of the same product in the home market

e-business (or **electronic business)** the organized effort of individuals to produce and sell, for a profit, the goods and services that satisfy society's needs through the facilities available on the internet

e-commerce a part of e-business and usually refers only to buying and selling activities conducted online

economic community an organization of nations formed to promote the free movement of resources and products among its members and to create common economic policies

economic model of social responsibility the view that society will benefit most when business is left alone to produce and market profitable products that society needs

economics the study of how wealth is created and distributed

economy the way in which people deal with the creation and distribution of wealth

embargo a complete halt to trading with a particular nation or in a particular product

entrepreneur a person who risks time, effort, and money to start and operate a business

Equal Employment Opportunity Commission (EEOC) a government agency with the power to investigate complaints of employment discrimination and the power to sue firms that practice it

ethics the study of right and wrong and of the morality of the choices individuals make

everyday low prices (EDLPs) setting a low price for products on a consistent basis

exchange control a restriction on the amount of a particular foreign currency that can be purchased or sold

exclusive distribution the use of only a single retail outlet for a product in a large geographic area

Export-Import Bank of the United States an independent agency of the U.S. government whose function is to assist in financing the exports of American firms

exporting selling and shipping raw materials or products to other nations

express warranty a written explanation of the producer's responsibilities in the event that a product is found to be defective or otherwise unsatisfactory

factors of production inputs and resources used to produce goods and services

factory system a system of manufacturing in which all the materials, machinery, and workers required to manufacture a product are assembled in one place

family branding the strategy in which a firm uses the same brand for all or most of its products

feature article a piece (of up to 3,000 words) prepared by an organization for inclusion in a particular publication

federal deficit a shortfall created when the federal government spends more in a fiscal year than it receives

fiscal policy government influence on the amount of savings and expenditures; accomplished by altering the tax structure and by changing the levels of government spending

fixed cost a cost incurred no matter how many units of a product are produced or sold

form utility utility created by people converting raw materials, finances, and information into finished products or services

forum an interactive version of a community bulletin board that focuses on threaded discussions

free enterprise the system of business in which individuals are free to decide what to produce, how to produce it, and at what price to sell it

frequent-user incentive a program developed to reward customers who engage in repeat (frequent) purchases

full-service wholesaler an intermediary that performs the entire range of wholesaler functions

General Agreement on Tariffs and Trade (GATT) an international organization of nations dedicated to reducing or eliminating tariffs and other barriers to world trade

general-merchandise wholesaler an intermediary that deals in a wide variety of products

generic product (or **generic brand)** a product with no brand at all

green IT a term used to describe all of a firm's activities to support a healthy environment and sustain the planet

green marketing the process of creating, making, delivering, and promoting products that are environmentally safe

gross domestic product (GDP) the total dollar value of all goods and services produced by all people within the boundaries of a country during a specified time period—usually a one-year period

hard-core unemployed workers with little education or vocational training and a long history of unemployment

hashtag a word or a short phrase preceded by the pound sign (#), to identify different topics

import quota a limit on the amount of a particular good that may be imported into a country during a given period of time

importing purchasing raw materials or products in other nations and bringing them into one's own country

inbound marketing a marketing term that describes new ways of gaining attention and ultimately customers by creating content on a website that pulls customers in

independent retailer a firm that operates only one retail outlet

individual branding the strategy in which a firm uses a different

Glossary

brand for each of its products

inflation a general rise in the level of prices

influencer a person known on social media who has an influence over a large number of followers

institutional advertising advertising designed to enhance a firm's image or reputation

integrated marketing communications coordination of promotion efforts to ensure maximal informational and persuasive impact on customers

intensive distribution the use of all available outlets for a product

international business all business activities that involve exchanges across national boundaries

International Monetary Fund (IMF) a 190-member international bank that makes short-term loans to developing countries experiencing balance-of-payment deficits

inventory management (control) the process of managing inventories in such a way as to minimize inventory costs, including both holding costs and potential stock-out costs

invisible hand a term created by Adam Smith to describe how an individual's personal gain benefits others and a nation's economy

key performance indicators (KPIs) measurements that define and measure the progress of an organization toward achieving its objectives

labeling the presentation of information on a product or its package

licensing a contractual agreement in which one firm permits another to produce and market its product and to use its brand name in return for a royalty or other compensation

lifestyle shopping center an open-air-environment shopping center with upscale chain specialty stores

limited-line wholesaler an intermediary that stocks only a few product lines but carries numerous product items within each line

line extension development of a new product that is closely related to one or more products in the existing product line but designed specifically to meet somewhat different customer needs

logistics all those activities concerned with the efficient flow and storage of products from the producer to the ultimate user

macroeconomics the study of the national economy and the global economy

major equipment large tools and machines used for production purposes

malware a general term that describes software designed to infiltrate a computer system without the user's consent

manufacturer (or producer) brand brand that is owned by a manufacturer

market a group of individuals or organizations, or both, that need products in a given category and that have the ability, willingness, and authority to purchase them

market economy an economic system in which businesses and individuals decide what to produce and buy, and the market determines prices and quantities sold

market price the price at which the quantity demanded is exactly equal to the quantity supplied

market segment a group of individuals or organizations within a market that shares one or more common characteristics

market segmentation the process of dividing a market into segments and directing a marketing mix at a particular segment or segments rather than at the total market

marketing the activity, set of institutions, and processes for creating, communicating, delivering, and exchanging offerings that have value for customers, clients, partners, and society at large

marketing analytics the collection, organization, and interpretation of data about marketing performance

marketing concept a business philosophy that a firm should provide goods and services that satisfy customers' needs through a coordinated set of activities that allow the firm to achieve its objectives

marketing mix a combination of product, price, distribution, and promotion developed to satisfy a particular target market

marketing plan a written document that specifies an organization's resources, objectives, strategy, and implementation and control efforts to be used in marketing a specific product or product group

marketing research the process of systematically gathering, recording, and analyzing data concerning a particular marketing problem

marketing strategy a plan that will enable an organization to make the best use of its resources and advantages to meet its objectives

markup the amount a seller adds to the cost of a product to determine its basic selling price

materials handling the actual physical handling of goods, in warehouses as well as during transportation

media sharing sites websites which allow users to upload photos, videos, and podcasts

merchant wholesaler an intermediary that purchases goods in large quantities and sells them to other wholesalers or retailers and to institutional, farm, government, professional, or industrial users

microeconomics the study of the decisions made by individuals and businesses

middleman (or marketing intermediary) a marketing organization that links a producer and user within a marketing channel

missionary salesperson a salesperson—generally employed by a manufacturer—who visits retailers to persuade them to buy the manufacturer's products

mixed economy an economy that exhibits elements of both capitalism and socialism

mobile marketing communicating with and selling to customers through mobile devices

monetary policies Federal Reserve's actions to promote maximum employment, stabilize prices, and increase or decrease interest rates

monopolistic competition a market situation in which there are many buyers along with a relatively large number of sellers who differentiate their products from the products of competitors

monopoly a market (or industry) with only one seller, and customers can only buy the product or service from that seller

multichannel (or **omnichannel) distribution** the use of a variety of marketing channels to ensure maximum distribution

multichannel retailing employing multiple types of retailing

multilateral development bank (MDB) an internationally supported bank that provides loans to developing countries to help them grow

multinational corporation a firm that operates on a worldwide scale without ties to any specific nation or region

multiple-unit pricing the strategy of setting a single price for two or more units

national debt the total of all federal deficits

negotiated pricing establishing a final price through bargaining

neighborhood shopping center a planned shopping center consisting of several small convenience and specialty stores

news release a typed page of about 300 words provided by an organization to the media as a form of publicity

non-price competition competition based on factors other than price

nonstore retailing selling that does not take place in conventional store facilities

nontariff barrier a nontax measure imposed by a government to favor domestic over foreign suppliers

odd-number pricing the strategy of setting prices using odd numbers that are slightly below whole-dollar amounts

off-price retailer a store that buys manufacturers' seconds, overruns, returns, and off-season merchandise for resale to consumers at deep discounts

oligopoly a market (or industry) in which there are few sellers

online retailing retailing that makes products available to buyers through computer or mobile connections

order getter a salesperson who is responsible for selling a firm's products to new customers and increasing sales to current customers

order processing activities involved in receiving and filling customers' purchase orders

order taker a salesperson who handles repeat sales in ways that maintain positive relationships with customers

outsourcing an arrangement in which one firm contracts manufacturing or other activities to a firm in another country that specializes in those activities and can offer them at a lower cost than domestic firms

packaging all the activities involved in developing and providing a container with graphics for a product

penetration pricing the strategy of setting a low price for a new product to build market share quickly

perfect (or **pure) competition** the market situation in which there are many buyers and sellers of a product, and no single buyer or seller is powerful enough to affect the price of that product

periodic discounting temporary reduction of prices on a patterned or systematic basis

personal income the income an individual receives from all sources

personal selling personal communication aimed at informing customers and persuading them to buy a firm's products

place utility utility created by making a product available at a location where customers wish to purchase it

plagiarism knowingly taking someone else's words, ideas, or other original material without acknowledging the source

podcasts digital audio or video files that people listen to or watch online on tablets, computers, smartphones, or other mobile devices

point-of-purchase display promotional material placed within a retail store

pollution the contamination of water, air, or land through the actions of people in an industrialized society

possession utility utility created by transferring title (or ownership) of a product to a buyer

premium a gift that a producer offers a customer in return for buying its product; the fee charged by an insurance company

premium pricing pricing the highest-quality or most-versatile products higher than other models in the product line

press conference a meeting at which invited media personnel hear important news announcements and receive supplementary textual materials and photographs

price the amount of money a seller is willing to accept in exchange for a product at a given time and under given circumstances

price competition an emphasis on setting a price equal to or lower than competitors' prices to gain sales or market share

price leaders products priced below the usual markup, near cost, or below cost

price lining the strategy of selling goods only at certain predetermined prices that reflect definite price breaks

price skimming the strategy of charging the highest possible price for a product during the introduction stage of its life cycle

primary-demand advertising advertising whose purpose is to increase the demand for all brands of a product within a specific industry

process material a material that is used directly in the production of another product but is not readily identifiable in the finished product

producer price index (PPI) a monthly index that measures prices that producers receive for their finished goods

product everything one receives in an exchange, including all tangible and intangible attributes and expected benefits; it may be a good, a service, or an idea

product deletion the elimination of one or more products from a product line

product differentiation the process of developing and promoting differences between a company's products and all competitive products

product life cycle a series of stages in which a product's sales revenue and profit increase, reach a peak, and then decline

product line a group of similar products that differ only in relatively minor characteristics

product mix all the products a firm offers for sale

product modification the process of changing one or more of a product's characteristics

productivity the average level of output per worker per hour

profit what remains after all business expenses have been deducted from sales revenue

promotion communication about an organization and its products that is intended to inform, persuade, or remind target-market members

promotion mix the particular combination of promotion methods a firm uses to reach a target market

public relations communication activities used to create and maintain favorable relationships between an organization and various public groups, both internal and external

publicity communication in news-story form about an organization, its products, or both

qualitative social media measurement the process of accessing the opinions and beliefs about a brand

quantitative social media measurement measurement using numerical measurements, such as counting the number of website visitors, number of fans and followers, number of leads generated, and the number of new customers

random discounting temporary reduction of prices on an unsystematic basis

raw material a basic material that actually becomes part of a physical product; usually comes from mines, forests, oceans, or recycled solid wastes

rebate a return of part of the purchase price of a product

recession two or more consecutive three-month periods of decline in a country's GDP

recycling converting used materials into new products or components for new products in order to prevent their unnecessary disposal

reference pricing pricing a product at a moderate level and positioning it next to a more expensive model or brand

regional shopping center a planned shopping center containing large department stores, numerous specialty stores, restaurants, movie theaters, and sometimes even hotels

relationship marketing establishing long-term, mutually satisfying buyer–seller relationships

retailer an intermediary that buys from producers or other middlemen and sells to consumers

revenue stream a source of revenue flowing into a firm

sales forecast an estimate of the amount of a product that an organization expects to sell during a certain period of time based on a specified level of marketing effort

sales promotion the use of activities or materials as direct inducements to customers or salespersons

sales support personnel employees who aid in selling but are more involved in locating prospects, educating customers, building goodwill for the firm, and providing follow-up service

sample a free product given to customers to encourage trial and purchase

Sarbanes-Oxley Act of 2002 provides sweeping legal protection for employees who report corporate misconduct

secondary-market pricing setting one price for the primary target market and a different price for another market

selective-demand (or **brand) advertising** advertising that is used to sell a particular brand of product

selective distribution the use of only a portion of the available outlets for a product in each geographic area

sentiment analysis a measurement that uses technology to detect the mood, attitudes, or emotions of people who experience a social media activity

service economy an economy in which more effort is devoted to the production of services than to the production of goods

shopping product an item for which buyers are willing to expend considerable effort on planning and making the purchase

social audit a comprehensive report of what an organization has done and is doing with regard to social issues that affect it

social content sites websites which allow companies to create and share information about their products and services

social media the online interaction that allows people and businesses to communicate and share ideas, personal information, and information about products or services

social media communities groups of people who share common interests and who want to use technology and the internet to connect with people with similar interests

social media community manager a high-level executive who is responsible for all of a company's social media activities

social responsibility the recognition that business activities have an impact on society and the consideration of that impact in business decision making

socioeconomic model of social responsibility the concept that business should emphasize not only profits but also the impact of its decisions on society

special-event pricing advertised sales or price cutting linked to a holiday, season, or event

specialization the separation of a manufacturing process into distinct tasks and the assignment of different tasks to different individuals

specialty product an item that possesses one or more unique characteristics for which a significant group of buyers is willing to expend considerable purchasing effort

specialty wholesaler an intermediary that carries a select group of products within a single line

stakeholders all the different people or groups of people who are affected by an organization's policies, decisions, and activities

standard of living a loose, subjective measure of how well off an individual or a society is, mainly in terms of want satisfaction through goods and services

store (or private) brand a brand that is owned by an individual wholesaler or retailer

strategic alliance a partnership formed to create competitive advantage on a worldwide basis

supermarket a large self-service store that sells primarily food and household products

supply the quantity of a product that producers are willing to sell at each of various prices

supply-chain management the coordination of all marketing channel activities associated with the flow and transformation of supplies, products, and information throughout the supply chain to the ultimate consumer

sustainability the ability to create and maintain conditions under which present and future generations can exist in productive harmony, and permit fulfilling the social, economic, and other requirements of future and present generations

target market a group of individuals or organizations, or both, for which a firm develops and maintains a marketing mix suitable for the specific needs and preferences of that group

tariff a tax levied on a particular foreign product entering a country

technical salesperson a salesperson who assists a company's current customers in technical matters

telemarketing the performance of marketing-related activities by telephone

television home shopping a form of selling in which products are presented to television viewers, who can buy them by calling a toll-free number and paying with a credit card

time utility utility created by making a product available when customers wish to purchase it

total cost the sum of the fixed costs and the variable costs attributed to a product

total revenue the total amount received from the sales of a product

trade deficit a negative balance of trade

trade name the complete and legal name of an organization

trade sales promotion method a sales promotion method designed to encourage wholesalers and retailers to stock and actively promote a manufacturer's product

trade salesperson a salesperson—generally employed by a food producer or processor—who assists customers in promoting products, especially in retail stores

trade show an industry-wide exhibit at which many sellers display their products

trademark a brand name or brand mark that is registered with the U.S. Patent and Trademark Office and thus is legally protected from use by anyone except its owner

trading company provides a link between buyers and sellers in different countries

traditional specialty store a store that carries a narrow product mix with deep product lines

transfer pricing prices charged in sales between an organization's units

transportation the shipment of products to customers

undifferentiated approach directing a single marketing mix at the entire market for a particular product

unemployment rate the percentage of a nation's labor force unemployed at any time

unsought product an item that people do not plan on purchasing, such as one that addresses a sudden problem or that customers are unaware of until they see it in a store or online

utility the ability of a good or service to satisfy a human need

value a customer's estimation of the worth of a product based on a comparison of its costs and benefits, including quality, relative to other products

variable cost a cost that depends on the number of units produced

vending the use of machines to dispense products

warehouse club a large-scale members-only establishment that combines features of cash-and-carry wholesaling with discount retailing

warehouse showroom a retail facility in a large, lowcost building with a large on-premises inventory and minimal service

warehousing the set of activities involved in receiving and storing goods and preparing them for reshipment

whistle-blowing informing the press or government officials about unethical practices within one's organization

wholesaler an intermediary that sells products to other firms

wiki a collaborative online working space that enables members to contribute content that can be shared with other people

World Bank a cooperative banking institution with 189 member countries

World Trade Organization (WTO) a 164-member powerful successor to GATT that facilitates world trade among member nations by mediating disputes and fostering efforts to reduce trade barriers

图书在版编目（CIP）数据

市场营销：第7版：双语教学版：英、汉 /（美）威廉·普赖德，（美）罗伯特·休斯，（美）杰克·卡普尔著；孔小磊译注. -- 北京：商务印书馆，2024.
ISBN 978-7-100-24577-7

Ⅰ. F713.50

中国国家版本馆CIP数据核字第2024YH9491号

权利保留，侵权必究。

市场营销（第7版，双语教学版）

〔美〕威廉·普赖德　罗伯特·休斯　杰克·卡普尔　著
孔小磊　译注

商 务 印 书 馆 出 版
（北京王府井大街36号　邮政编码100710）
商 务 印 书 馆 发 行
人卫印务（北京）有限公司印刷
ISBN 978-7-100-24577-7

2025年1月第1版	开本 850×1092　1/16
2025年1月北京第1次印刷	印张 16¼

定价：78.00元